I cannot in good faith take credit for the research and effort necessary to compile these research points. The heavy lifting has been done by the legal researchers and contributors to the Capital Defense Network who has graciously allowed these works to be copied from online sources. My effort here was to devise an effective delivery system of these materials to prisoners. We all know that traditional book format has been challenged by electronic formats, book readers, and the like. In the prison a paper version is still necessary.

As of this writing prisoners in the State of Florida do not have open internet access. I suspect this is true elsewhere. They cannot take advantage of the wonderful materials and opportunities available to the outside world. Therefore, to prisoners these printed materials should be like finding a fortune of buried treasure. Like a chest full of pearls and gold coinage here are legal riches beyond the belief of ordinary prisoners and indeed many lawyers.

In the volumes of the Writing Your Way Out series prisoners are almost certain to find successful claims from which they can launch their own successful research efforts. Once a useful research point is found prisoners can request that the actual pleading filed in the case be obtained. From this a model template can be created which is supported by successful case law shown here. It does not matter that these claims come from other states. Most post conviction law derives from United States Supreme Court authority. What works in Alaska is applicable in Wyoming and all states in between. Nothing succeeds like success and there is no good reason to model anything other than successful cases. To my knowledge there have never been compiled a larger fund of winners than exist in these volumes.

David M. Lamos
February 2017

Table of Contents

CAPITAL SENTENCING ERRORS[1]

I.   NUMEROUS DEFICIENCIES AND INADEQUATE MITIGATION

A.   U.S. Supreme Court Cases

2009: ***Porter v. McCollum***, 558 U.S. 30 (2009) (*Per curiam*) (sentenced in 1988). Under AEDPA, counsel ineffective in capital sentencing for failing to adequately investigate and present mitigation evidence. The defendant, after proceeding *pro se* with stand-by counsel, plead guilty to shooting his former girlfriend. His stand-by counsel was appointed to represent him in sentencing and presented only his ex-wife's testimony and an excerpt from a deposition. "The sum total of the mitigating evidence was inconsistent testimony about [the defendant's] behavior when intoxicated and testimony that [he] had a good relationship with his son." *Id.* at 33. No mental health evidence was presented and the trial court found no mitigating circumstances. Because the state court did not decide whether counsel's conduct was deficient, the Court reviewed this element of the claim *de novo*. While "counsel had an 'obligation to conduct a thorough investigation of the defendant's background,'" *id.* at 39 (quoting *Williams v. Taylor,* 529 U.S. 362, 396 (2000)), counsel "did not satisfy those norms," *id.* Counsel was appointed a month before sentencing and had only one short meeting with the defendant about the sentencing phase. "He did not obtain any of [the defendant's] school, medical, or military service records or interview any members of [the defendant's] family." Where counsel in *Wiggins* failed to "expand[] their investigation," counsel here "did not even take the first step of interviewing witnesses or requesting records." *Id.* "[H]e ignored pertinent avenues for investigation of which he should have been aware." *Id.* at 40. Even court-ordered competency evaluations revealed his limited education, his military service and combat record, and his father's "over-discipline." *Id.* While counsel asserted that the defendant was "fatalistic and uncooperative," the defendant had instructed him not to talk to his ex-wife or son, but otherwise "did not give him any other instructions limiting the witnesses he could interview." *Id.* In short, while the defendant "may have been fatalistic or uncooperative, ... that does not obviate the need for defense counsel to conduct *some* sort of mitigation investigation." *Id.* There was also prejudice. In short, the judge and jury at sentencing "heard almost nothing that would humanize [the defendant] or allow them to accurately gauge his moral culpability. They learned about [his] turbulent relationship with [the victim], his crimes, and almost nothing else." *Id.* at 41. Evidence was available that the defendant had routinely witnessed his father beat his mother. He was also routinely beaten by his father, particularly when he tried to protect his mother. His father even shot at him once. He attended classes for slow learners and left school when he was 12 or 13. He joined the Army at 17 and fought in the Korean War. His company commander testified that he fought in two major battles within a 3 month period and was wounded in both. In one of the battles his unit suffered more than 50% casualties. He was individually decorated for his actions in both battles. When he returned to the U.S., he went AWOL and was sentenced to six months' confinement, but he was honorably discharged. *Id.* at 33-34. After his discharge, he suffered from posttraumatic stress disorder (PTSD), which the Court noted is "not uncommon among veterans returning from combat," as the Secretary of Veteran Affairs testified before Congress in 2009 "that approximately 23 percent of the Iraq and Afghanistan war veterans seeking treatment at a VA medical facility had been preliminarily diagnosed with PTSD." *Id.* at 35 n.4. He also developed a serious drinking problem. An expert in neuropsychology also found that he suffered from "brain damage that could manifest in impulsive, violent behavior." *Id.* at 36. The expert testified that two statutory mitigating circumstances were

---

[1]Also look under numerous deficiencies in trial phase because some cases found IAC in both.

present: substantially impaired ability to conform conduct and extreme mental or emotional disturbance.

> Unlike the evidence presented during [the defendant's] penalty hearing, which left the jury knowing hardly anything about him other than the facts of his crimes, the new evidence described his abusive childhood, his heroic military service and the trauma he suffered because of it, his long-term substance abuse, and his impaired mental health and mental capacity.

Id. at 33. The aggravation evidence "[o]n the other side of the ledger" was not substantial. *Id.* at 41.

> Had the judge and jury been able to place [the defendant's] life history "on the mitigating side of the scale," and appropriately reduced the ballast on the aggravating side of the scale, there is clearly a reasonable probability that the advisory jury–and the sentencing judge– "would have struck a different balance," *Wiggins*, 539 U.S. at 537, and it is unreasonable to conclude otherwise.

Id. at 42. Thus, under AEDPA, the state court's finding of no prejudice was "an unreasonable application of our clearly established law." *Id.* at 44. The state court did not consider the expert testimony for purposes of nonstatutory mitigation and "unreasonably discounted the evidence of [the defendant's] childhood abuse and military service." *Id.* at 43. The evidence of childhood abuse "may have particular salience" in a case like this where the defendant killed his former girlfriend. *Id.* The military service was important as "[o]ur Nation has a long tradition of according leniency to veterans in recognition of their service, especially for those who fought on the front lines." *Id.* The military service was also relevant mitigation because of "the intense stress and mental and emotional toll that combat took." *Id.* at 44.

2005: ***Rompilla v. Beard***, 545 U.S. 374 (2005) (sentenced in November 1988). Counsel ineffective in capital sentencing for failing "to make reasonable efforts to obtain and review material that counsel [knew] the prosecution [would] probably rely on as evidence of aggravation at the sentencing phase of the trial," which would have led to significant mitigation. [For additional details, see the summary in the first section on U.S. Supreme Court cases.]

2003: ***Wiggins v. Smith***, 539 U.S. 510 (2003) (sentenced in October 1989). Counsel ineffective in capital habeas case, decided under the AEDPA, for failing to adequately prepare and present mitigation. Prior to trial, counsel had arranged for a psychologist to test Wiggins and had obtained a presentencing report and his social services records. Prior to sentencing, counsel filed a motion to bifurcate sentencing so they could present evidence in the first phase that Wiggins was not directly responsible for the murder (a finding required by state law for death eligibility) and in the second phase could present mitigation. The court denied the motion. In opening statements, counsel argued both issues and said that Wiggins had a difficult life and no prior convictions. Counsel did not present any life history evidence during mitigation though. Before closing arguments, counsel preserved the bifurcation issue and argued that, if bifurcation had been granted, counsel would have presented psychological reports and expert testimony demonstrating Wiggins' limited intellectual capacity, the absence of aggressive behavior, and his desire to function in the world. In post- conviction testimony, counsel claimed to have investigated "extensively," but counsel in making their proffer did not even mention sexual abuse. This failure is "explicable only if we assume that counsel had no knowledge of the abuse." *Id.* at 533. The Court found that this "may simply reflect a mistaken memory shaped by the passage of time. After all, the state post-conviction proceedings took place over four years after Wiggins' sentencing." *Id.* The Court described the issue in this case as "not whether counsel should have presented a mitigation case. Rather, we focus on whether the investigation supporting counsel's decision not to introduce mitigating evidence of Wiggins' background *was itself reasonable*." *Id.* at 523 (emphasis in original). In this case, the Court held that "[c]ounsel's decision not to expand their investigation beyond the PSI and the DSS records fell short of the professional standards that prevailed in Maryland in 1989," because no "social history report" was prepared even though counsel had funds available to retain a "forensic social worker." *Id.* at 524. "Counsel's conduct similarly fell short of the standards for capital defense work articulated by the American Bar Association (ABA) – standards to which we have referred as 'guides to determining what is reasonable.'" *Id.* (quoting *Strickland, supra,* at 688; *Williams v. Taylor, supra,* at 396). Applying these standards, the Court found that, "[d]espite these well-defined norms, … , counsel abandoned their investigation of petitioner's background after having acquired only rudimentary knowledge of his history from a narrow set of sources." *Id.* (citing the ABA standards again). The Court found that "[t]he scope of their investigation was also unreasonable in light of what counsel actually discovered" in the records available to them. *Id.* at 525.

> In assessing the reasonableness of an attorney's investigation, … , a court must consider not only the quantum of evidence already known to counsel, but also whether the known evidence would lead a reasonable attorney to investigate further. Even assuming [counsel] limited the scope of their investigation for strategic reasons, *Strickland* does not establish that a cursory investigation automatically justifies a tactical decision with respect to sentencing strategy. Rather, a reviewing court must consider the reasonableness of the investigation said to support the strategy.

Id. at 527. In this case, "counsel were not in a position to make a reasonable strategic choice … because the investigation supporting their choice was unreasonable." *Id.* at 536. Counsel's conduct was deficient because the trial record revealed that the "failure to investigate thoroughly resulted from inattention, not reasoned strategic judgment." *Id.* at 526. The trial record reflected that "[f]ar from focusing exclusively on petitioner's direct responsibility, … , counsel put on a halfhearted mitigation case. …" *Id.* The "strategic decision" the court's had found to be reasonable was rejected because it "resembles more a *post-hoc* rationalization of counsel's conduct than an accurate description of their deliberations prior to sentencing." *Id.* at 527-28. Prejudice was found because counsel did not discover "powerful" evidence of severe abuse from "alcoholic, absentee" parents. He also suffered "physical torment, sexual molestation, and repeated rape" in foster homes. He also spent time homeless and had "diminished mental capacities." *Id.* at 534-35. The Court found:

> Wiggins' sentencing jury heard only one significant mitigating factor – that Wiggins had no prior convictions. Had the jury been able to place petitioner's excruciating life history on the mitigating side of the scale, there is a reasonable probability that at least one juror would have struck a difference balance.

Id. at 537. In the final analysis, the Court held:

> Given both the nature and the extent of the abuse petitioner suffered, we find there to be a reasonable probability that a competent attorney, aware of this history, would have introduced it at sentencing in an admissible form. While it may well have been strategically defensible upon a reasonably thorough investigation to focus on Wiggins' direct responsibility for the murder, the two sentencing strategies are not necessarily mutually exclusive. Moreover, given the strength of the available evidence, a reasonable attorney may well have chosen to prioritize the mitigation case over the direct responsibility challenge, particularly given that Wiggins' history contained little of the double edge we have found to justify limited investigations in other cases.

Id. at 535.

2000: ***Williams v. Taylor***, 529 U.S. 362 (2000) (tried in September 1986). Counsel ineffective in capital sentencing for failure to prepare and present mitigation evidence. Counsel did not begin to prepare for the sentencing phase until a week before trial. They failed to get extensive records of Williams's childhood because they incorrectly thought that state law barred access to such records. They failed to discover a number of available mitigation witnesses due to lack of investigation and, in one instance, simply because they failed to return the phone call of a CPA, who saw Williams as a prison minister. At trial, counsel presented testimony only from Williams's mother and two neighbors (one of whom was not interviewed before but was asked to testify on the spot when noticed in the audience during the proceedings). These witnesses testified that he was "nice" and not violent. Counsel also presented a tape of a psychiatrist's testimony simply relating that Williams had removed the bullets from a gun during an earlier robbery to avoid hurting anyone. In closing, counsel argued that Williams had turned himself in and the police would not have solved the crimes otherwise, but noted that it was difficult to find a reason why the jury should spare his life. Prejudice was found because an adequate investigation would have revealed that Williams's parents had been imprisoned for criminal neglect of Williams and his siblings, that Williams had been severely and repeatedly beaten by his father, that he had been committed to the custody of social services for two years during his parents' incarceration (including time spent in an abusive foster home), and that he was returned to his parents' custody when they got out of prison. The evidence also would have revealed that Williams was "borderline mentally retarded" and only completed the 6th grade in school, that he had suffered repeated head injuries and "might have mental impairments organic in nature," that he had received commendations in prison for helping to crack a prison drug ring and for returning a guard's missing wallet, and that prison officials would have testified it was unlikely that he would be dangerous in prison. If counsel had investigated and prepared for sentencing, even the state's experts who testified to future dangerousness would have testified that Williams would not pose a future danger if kept in a structured environment, such as prison.

B.   U.S. Court of Appeals Cases

2015: **Saranchak v. Secretary, Pennsylvania Dept. of Corrections*, 802 F.3d 579 (3rd Cir. 2015) (sentenced in September 1994). Under AEDPA, counsel was ineffective in failing to adequately investigate and present mitigation evidence in sentencing. The defendant entered an open plea of guilty to murdering his grandmother and uncle, which was followed by a nonjury degree-of-guilt hearing and then jury sentencing. The defendant challenged counsel's effectiveness in the degree- of-guilt hearing, *inter alia*, for (1) failing to move to suppress the defendant's confession to police following his arrest in which the defendant "acted as if the officers questioning him were drill sergeants," and (2) failing to investigate and introduce evidence of the defendant's mental health and family history to rebut a finding of intent. No expert testimony was presented during the degree-of- guilt hearing, but counsel presented lay witnesses, including the defendant's girlfriend, to establish that the defendant was intoxicated at the time of the crimes. The girlfriend also testified concerning the defendants' strange militaristic behavior when he was intoxicated. In sentencing, the mitigation testimony, including the state's cross of the girlfriend, consisted of only 40 pages. Her testimony was similar to that during the degree-of-guilt hearing and repeated that the defendant "thinks he's a sergeant" and gives orders when intoxicated. Trial counsel also presented the testimony of Dr. Kruszewski, a court-appointed psychiatrist, who examined the defendant only for purposes of competency and capacity at the time of the offenses and the statements to the police. The psychiatrist met the defendant only once and was not provided with any background information or records other than police records and the defendant's confession, but he was aware and testified that the defendant had a prior psychiatric hospitalization following a suicide attempt. On cross, Dr. Kruszewski conceded that the defendant had no major psychiatric diagnosis or any mental disability. The jury found no mitigating circumstances, which in light of the jury's finding of two statutory aggravating circumstances, made the death penalty a mandatory sentence. In post-conviction, after having reviewed the background records denied him prior to sentencing, Dr. Kruszewski's findings "changed drastically." He testified to a "Jekyll and Hyde type syndrome" under the influence of alcohol, in which the defendant experienced delusions. He also found a history of depression with two prior suicide attempts and hospitalizations. He concluded that the defendant suffered from "a psychoactive ... alcohol induced delusional disorder and alcohol induced depressive disorder when drinking" at the time of the crimes. The defendant also presented a psychologist in post-conviction, who testified concerning the defendant's "'highly dysfunctional' family history," including an alcoholic, abusive father and depressed mother, a developmental disorder and special education classes, self-medicating with drugs and alcohol at an early age, and a failed attempt to join the military followed by a "pronounced downward spiral" into a "fantasy world about being in the military." The psychologist found a history of "atypical pervasive developmental disorder" as a child, adult attention deficit disorder, depressive disorder, and a "personality disorder ... with paranoid and anti-social features." The psychologist agreed with the "Jekyll and Hyde" type psychological problems under the influence of alcohol, which manifested as a "'full blown paranoid disorder" or 'a delusional disorder.'" He concluded that the defendant was experiencing an extreme mental or emotional disturbance at the time of the crimes. The state post-conviction court held that counsel's conduct was deficient in failing to adequately investigate and present the mitigation evidence. The Pennsylvania Supreme Court reversed finding that counsel ended his investigation at a reasonable point because the defendant, his mother, and his girlfriend failed to provide counsel with information concerning the defendant's background. This finding was rejected under AEDPA review because "the evidence before the Pennsylvania Supreme

Court clearly and convincingly demonstrates that this premise was false." Trial counsel was aware of the defendant's odd militaristic behavior at times, which was reflected in the police reports, the defendant's confession, and the girlfriend's testimony. With this knowledge, trial counsel sought a court-appointed competence evaluation and focused his theory of defense on "the mental health issue." Counsel's conduct was deficient in failing to obtain a mental health evaluation despite his belief that this was the primary issue and despite the red flags in Dr. Kruszewski's report. The state court's finding to the contrary was an unreasonable determination of the facts in light of the evidence presented in the state court proceeding. The state court's analysis was also an objectively unreasonable application of *Strickland*. Under *Strickland*, especially in light of *Wiggins* and *Rompilla* and a consideration of the ABA Guidelines for the Appointment and Performance of Counsel in Death Penalty Cases, "a defendant's failure personally to inform his counsel of possible avenues of investigation does not absolve his attorney from pursuing those avenues, particularly where counsel is aware of facts demonstrating that such an investigation may be fruitful." With respect to prejudice, the state post- conviction court found no prejudice. While the Pennsylvania Supreme Court did not reach this issue, the habeas court reviewed "through AEDPA's lens" due to the post-conviction court's adjudication. While the post-conviction court, at times, described the *Strickland* prejudice test correctly, it also, at times incorrectly described the prejudice test as outcome-determinative or a sufficiency-of-the-evidence test. "Thus, at the very least, the PCRA court's analysis constituted an unreasonable application of clearly established federal law." The state court's analysis was also unreasonable because of "[t]he PCRA court's failure to discuss the vast majority of the relevant evidence presented at the PCRA hearing." In short, "the PCRA court brushed aside Saranchak's childhood and mental health problems without analysis," even though "the portrait of Saranchak's troubled life that could have been presented to the jury and the one actually presented were stark." Prejudice was established. The state court's finding to the contrary was an unreasonable application of clearly established Supreme Court case law.

__Hardwick v. Secretary, Fla. Dept. of Corrections__, 803 F.3d 541 (11th Cir. 2015) (sentenced in March 1986). Under pre-AEDPA law, counsel was ineffective in capital sentencing for failing to adequately investigate and present mitigation evidence. Rather than present any evidence in mitigation, counsel simply relied on his closing argument: (1) attempting to undermine the statutory aggravating circumstances; and (2) appealing for mercy based on the defendant's age (25 at the time of the crime) and the sanctity of human life. Trial counsel concluded his sentencing argument with an assertion that the defendant was innocent of murder. The jury recommended death by a seven-to- five vote and the trial court imposed a death sentence. On initial review, the Eleventh Circuit rejected the state court's findings of fact and conclusions of law and remanded to the District Court for an evidentiary hearing. During the hearing "three experienced capital defense attorneys testified as to the standard among defense attorneys in the mid-1980's for investigating and presenting mitigation evidence." Counsel's conduct was deficient. Counsel believed the defendant would be convicted and that the state would seek the death penalty. Counsel was aware of "a number of red flags," that "should have highlighted the need to conduct at least some life-history investigation and at least some mitigation investigation," such as information that the defendant had been physically and sexually abused, and had lived in foster homes and been in the care of social services for a great deal of his youth. Counsel also was aware of "potential sources of mitigating evidence" from notes a public defender had taken during a preliminary interview, which listed the names of family members, schools, and contact information for a prior mental health evaluation center where the defendant had been diagnosed with schizophrenia. Counsel even had the benefit of an evaluation by a court-appointed psychiatrist. Although this evaluation was focused solely on competence and sanity and counsel failed to provide the expert with any background information or records, the report still contained "many red flags" for potential mitigation. Prejudice also established. If counsel had adequately investigated and presented the mitigation, the evidence would have supported a statutory mitigating circumstance of impaired capacity at the time of the murder. Likewise, there was "ample evidence of 'the kind of troubled history [the Supreme Court] ha[s] declared relevant to assessing a defendant's moral culpability." *Id.* at (quoting *Wiggins*, 539 U.S. at 535). The jury and the trial judge heard none of this evidence.

> All they had was a brief snapshot of the instant Hardwick's life hit rock bottom; absent was the decades-long slide of childhood neglect, abandonment, abuse, instability, mental and emotional problems, intoxication, and addiction that led to that moment.

Without this evidence, the prosecutor was free to emphasize repeatedly in closing arguments that there was no mitigation. Even without this evidence, the jury came within a single vote of recommending life. Under these circumstances, there is at least a reasonable probability that the defendant would not have received a death sentence if counsel had performed adequately.

2015: ***Pruitt v. Neal***, 788 F.3d 248 (7th Cir. 2015). Sentencing relief was granted on two issues: (1) the defendant proved intellectual disability; and (2) counsel was ineffective in failing to adequately investigate and present mitigation evidence that the defendant also suffered from schizophrenia. While trial counsel asserted that defendant was intellectually disabled, the trial court rejected this claim finding no significantly subaverage intellectual functioning and finding no significant deficits in adaptive behavior. With respect to the ineffective assistance issue, trial counsel's theory was to: (1) establish intellectual disability; (2) establish that the defendant "was suffering mental illness at or around the time of the crime"; and (3) establish that the defendant "had serious brain damage, brain injury, [or] brain dysfunction." Counsel presented one expert witness in sentencing, who testified about the defendant's intellectual disability and neuropsychological problems on the basis of one interview and his testing. This expert "had no experience in the assessment or treatment of individuals with psychotic disorders." Nonetheless, counsel also asked this expert to review the defendant's prison records and discuss his diagnoses. He testified that in 1996, while incarcerated for a different crime, doctors at the federal Bureau of Prisons had diagnosed "schizotypal personality disorder … an Axis II mental illness." With schizotypal, according to this expert, "psychotic episodes should be the exception rather than the rule." He further testified that two months after the defendant's arrest in this case, doctors at the Indiana Department of Corrections diagnosed "schizophrenia, chronic undifferentiated type compensated residual." According to the expert, this was similar to the schizotypal personality disorder diagnosis and antipsychotic medication was prescribed due to concern that the defendant "is capable of easily becoming schizophrenic at some time in the future." Based on his review, the expert concluded that the defendant's illness was "not severe enough to be called schizophrenic" so he agreed with the schizotypal personality disorder diagnosis. He then testified about the symptoms of this disorder. He opined that the defendant had been decompensating for six months prior to the crime, if not longer, but he conceded, in response to a juror's question about his firsthand knowledge of the defendant's thought processes, that they had only "talked a little bit about that" and the defendant "said to me basically what's already in the record." Counsel did not ask whether the defendant met the criteria for any statutory mitigating circumstances. Counsel's conduct was deficient in failing to investigate the evidence of mental illness and present accurate evidence on this in mitigation. Dr. Olvera, who had conducted intelligence testing prior to trial, observed possible signs of psychosis and learned that the defendant was taking antipsychotic medications. He recommended that counsel obtain an expert "in dealing with psychosis, such as schizophrenia" but counsel did not do so, despite his awareness that the defendant had been diagnosed in pretrial confinement with schizophrenia and that other examiners examining the defendant for intellectual disability had observed symptoms consistent with schizophrenia. In short, counsel acted unreasonably in ignoring these "red flags" and failing to investigate further. If counsel had done so, evidence such as that presented in post-conviction from two forensic psychiatrists and a clinical psychologist and neuropsychologist would have been available. These experts testified that the defendant suffers from paranoid schizophrenia, an Axis I mental illness, "which is characterized by delusions, hallucinations, and thought disorder." This evidence, in conjunction with the intellectual disability, supported two statutory mitigating circumstances at the time of the crime: (1) extreme mental or emotional distress; and (2) substantially impaired capacity to conform his conduct to the law. The state court denied relief on this claim finding that counsel made "a deliberate, strategic decision to concentrate on Pruitt's intellectual disability rather than his mental illness." This was an unreasonable application of *Strickland* in light of counsel's testimony that he sought to prove both intellectual disability and schizophrenia. Even assuming counsel did choose intellectual disability over schizophrenia, "that choice was made after less than thorough investigation, and as a result, the decision was not fully informed and was unreasonable." "[T]he evidence of mental illness was much weaker than the intellectual disability evidence only because counsel failed to investigate more fully Pruitt's mental health." Because the state court did not assess the prejudice prong, the Seventh Circuit's review was conducted "*de novo.*" Prejudice was established. This was not simply "a 'battle of the experts' over the severity of Pruitt's mental illness" or the correct "psychiatric terms and labels." The sentencing judge found no statutory mitigating circumstances, when at least two were established by the evidence of mental illness. Thus, there is a reasonable probability that this evidence might have affected the assessment of the defendant's "moral culpability" and the jury and the judge might have concluded that death was not warranted. It is clear from the jury's question to the defense expert that the jury waned to know the defendant's "thought processes" at the time of the crime.

Bemore v. Chappell, 788 F.3d 1151 (9th Cir. 2015) (tried and sentenced in 1989). Under AEDPA, counsel ineffective in capital sentencing for failing to adequately investigate and present mitigation evidence. Counsel's conduct was also deficient during the trial phase, but no prejudice found during trial. The trial deficiencies were considered, however, in a cumulative prejudice analysis for sentencing. In denying relief, the state court addressed the "good inmate" issue in depth, but summarily denied the other claims "without analysis or citation to authority." The federal court, therefore, applied "AEDPA deference" to the "good inmate" claim, but otherwise reviewed the issues *de novo.* The defendant was convicted of robbing and killing a clerk at a liquor store. During trial, the defendant testified asserting an alibi that he was committing a different robbery at the time of this offense. Counsel's investigation of this defense was limited to reviewing police reports of this separate robbery and the preliminary hearing testimony of eyewitnesses to that crime, who had identified the defendant as the perpetrator. Counsel's investigation and preparation of the defendant's testimony was deficient in: (1) failing to adequately prepare the defendant as a witness resulting in his inability to supply basic facts about the crime, forgetting his own direct testimony on cross, and providing details that were easily disproved, such as relying on landmarks that did not exist at the time of the crime; (2) failing to investigate the geographical layout, which would have revealed the problems with the landmark testimony and revealed that it was possible for the same perpetrator to have committed the separate robbery and the liquor store robbery based on the timing of the offenses and the distance between them; and (3) failing to interview the eyewitnesses to the separate offense, which would have revealed that one would completely recant and that the others were not certain in their identification of the defendant. Counsel's conduct was also deficient in failing to investigate a potentially viable alternative mental health defense, based on "[m]edical expert reports and statements by Bemore's family and friends, all known or readily available to" counsel at the time. If counsel had adequately investigated the mental health defense, counsel may well have "determined that a mental health defense, even if a longshot at the guilt phase, was the superior choice in view of the impending penalty phase," so as not to risk losing credibility in the sentencing phase from presentation of a weak denial defense during the trial. *Id.* at (citing *Florida v. Nixon*, 543 U.S. 175, 191-92 (2004)). With respect to sentencing, counsel's conduct was deficient in failing to adequately investigate and present the mitigating evidence. Counsel had read an article from Dr. Kenneth Fineman about his "sun children" theory – "minority children from poor homes who, because of their talents become immersed in affluent white society, but then subsequently act out and, due to the psychological stress of having to live in two different worlds, begin using drugs." Counsel hoped to use this theory for the defendant, "an African-American and former star basketball player recruited to play at several colleges." In essence, counsel's mitigation strategy was to show the defendant "as a good guy with a drug problem." She retained Dr. Fineman to conduct psychological testing and was "surprised" and "angry" when his 18 page report made no mention of "sun children." Thus, counsel did not use Dr. Fineman and instead proceeded anyway with her "good guy with a drug problem" theory. Counsel's conduct was deficient because Dr. Fineman had reported a number of psychological problems, including "'mild, diffuse organic brain impairment,' attention-deficit disorder; and poor impulse control." Based on his findings, he listed several "'diagnostic considerations,' including 'bi-polar affective disorder,' 'intermittent explosive disorder,' and 'anti-social personality disorder.'" He recommended further testing to reach a mental health diagnosis, which was not pursued. Instead, counsel called over 40 witnesses to testify about the defendant's good character. Prejudice was established, nonetheless, as "[m]any of these witnesses knew Bemore only slightly." Moreover, "a good character defense was unlikely to be persuasive to a jury that had just decided that Bemore had carried out a grizzly murder, including torturing the victim, and had lied on the stand to boot." Additionally, while some of these witnesses did mention the defendant's drug problems and tumultuous upbringing, this was "not enough" because "particularly persuasive evidence–especially evidence in the form of expert testimony–was omitted." Counsel's "good guy," including "good inmate" strategy, also opened the door to damaging rebuttal testimony about the defendant's "bad behavior in jail," including assaults and escape planning, which counsel had unreasonably failed to investigate and anticipate. Even if it were reasonable to present the "good guy" theory, this could have been presented in addition to mental health evidence. "A defense that Bemore was 'a good guy with a drug problem,' was fully consistent with a defense that he was a good guy who was plagued by a drug problem *and* mental illness." The court also considered the 25 year to life sentence imposed on the co-defendant in a separate trial by the same trial judge in the prejudice analysis. The co-defendant received this lesser sentence despite being convicted of a second robbery and murder in the same trial because his attorneys "presented evidence of impaired judgment due to drug use and organic brain damage." Finally, the findings of deficient conduct during the trial "support" the conclusion of prejudice in sentencing because "putting on a guilt phase defense both unlikely to succeed and likely adversely to affect the jury's view of Bemore for the penalty phase–must be viewed cumulatively in determining whether the *Strickland* prejudice standard was met with regard to the jury's decision to sentence Bemore to death."

Doe v. Ayers, 782 F.3d 425 (9th Cir. 2015) (tried and sentenced in 1984). Under pre-AEDPA law, counsel ineffective in capital sentencing for failing to adequately investigate and present mitigating evidence in sentencing. Because the court "discuss[ed] disturbing evidence of sexual abuse suffered by the Petitioner" and was concerned about "the possibility that publication of this information might place him at risk in a prison environment" of further details, actual names and some details were omitted from the opinion. Counsel's conduct was deficient and prejudicial in failing to adequately investigate and present evidence that "relates to sexual abuse he suffered while previously incarcerated in a notorious prison in the South, as well as to mental illness, neglect and abuse he suffered during his childhood, and substance abuse."

> "[D]eath is different[.]" *Ring v. Arizona*, 536 U.S. 584, 587, 122 S. Ct. 2428, 153 L.E.2d 556 (2002). So too are the lengths to which defense counsel must go in investigating a capital case.

Id. at 435. Counsel had only one "perfunctory" interview with his client and did not follow-up on the information learned from the "limited investigation" that was discovered and "missed clear indications ... that his client was repeatedly raped in prison." Counsel's failures "were not excused by the alleged failure of Doe (and his family) to be completely forthcoming." Counsel spoke at length only wife the defendant's mother and aunt, but when he went to the defendant's home state, he did not get out of the car. He spoke to the mother by phone, "but did not conduct any in-person interviews." He spoke to no one other than those called to testify. When the investigator "went to Doe's home state, he, at least, got out of his car," but failed to "ask obvious questions ... . about [the defendant's] upbringing or behavioral signs of mental illness." He also met "only once with each interviewee" and then only in the mother's home. "Obviously, interviewees are less likely to be forthcoming about sensitive topics in the presence of family members and friends." While counsel did retain a psychologist with "the professional expertise necessary to discover and present the compelling mitigating testimony regarding Doe's mental health that went unheard at trial, ... she was limited by the terms of her engagement," which asked her to consider only "mental state defenses" for the trial. "In addition to having a limited scope, the investigation that Dr. M.R. conducted was abbreviated." She was paid for less than 13 hours of time and provided only with police reports as background information. "This left [counsel] effectively without the assistance of any expert at all at the penalty phase," because "[h]iring an expert to evaluate possible guilt-phase mental-state defenses does not discharge defense counsel's duty to prepare for the penalty phase." The only witnesses called in sentencing "were family and friends attending the trial. Some of them were not told that they would be testifying until they arrived." The state argued that counsel's conduct was "an acceptable trial strategy," which was "both doubtful and disturbing" because "spur- of-the-moment mitigation presentations form no part of constitutionally adequate representation."

> Witness preparation is a critical function of counsel. ... A lawyer needs to know the nature of the testimony he will elicit, and a witness needs to understand the proceeding in which he is

participating. Our case law, and an elementary understanding of the function of a trial lawyer in our adversary system, make plain that although there is no requirement of rehearsal, not preparing penalty-phase witnesses *at all* is not a legitimate defense method in a capital trial.

Id. at 443. Despite the state argument, counsel conceded deficient conduct "because of a combination of inexperience and overconfidence" and "never attempted to justify his actions as based in strategy." Under these circumstances, which the court found to be "to his credit," the "presumption" of reasonable conduct fell. Counsel's conduct was also prejudicial in light of the "fairly minimal" aggravation evidence presented and the "brief … , haphazard, and thoroughly underwhelming" mitigation evidence presented. The most compelling mitigating evidence not presented was supported by multiple prison guards and inmates and consisted of the brutal and repeated rape of the defendant in prison when he was just 17-years-old and incarcerated for stealing two purses. "[T]his evidence alone would have stirred sufficient compassion or understanding in the jury to result in a life sentence." There was also "mental illness" as a result which was "obvious to those who knew him." He had symptoms of post-traumatic stress disorder, major depression, and self-medication, resulting in poly-substance dependence. This also was sufficient to establish prejudice on its own. There was also evidence of childhood abuse and neglect that "would have been powerful" and substance abuse that, while note alone prejudicial, would "have helped to sway the jury when considered cumulatively, alongside the other mitigating evidence."

2014: ***DeBruce v. Commissioner, Alabama Dept. Of Corrections***, 758 F.3d 1263 (5th Cir. 2014) (tried in February 1992). Under AEDPA, trial counsel was ineffective in failing to adequately investigate and present evidence in mitigation. Counsel's conduct was deficient and "was the result of inattention, not reasonable professional judgment." Counsel was retained only three to four weeks prior to trial and did not hire an investigator because he did not have the funds to pay for one and did not have time. Counsel interviewed only the defendant and his mother in preparation for sentencing and presented testimony only from the mother. She testified that DeBruce graduated from high school and attended college, "and that although he had an impoverished childhood, it was otherwise unremarkable." She made "passing mention to DeBruce's treatment for a mental disorder, although this statement was not accompanied by any explanation of the disorder or its effects." The state court held that counsel's conduct was not deficient in failing to investigate after a pre-trial report found the defendant competent.

[T]he Alabama Court of Criminal Appeals concluded that [counsel] did not fail to conduct a reasonable investigation because [counsel] testified during the state collateral hearing that the information he received did not lead him to question DeBruce's competence to stand trial or to consider defending DeBruce based on a lack of mental capacity. However, DeBruce's fitness to be tried and decisions about whether to present a mental health defense during the *guilt phase* are separate issues from the decision whether to investigate and present mitigating evidence during *sentencing*. … [E]ven if we accept the state court's factual determination that [counsel] made a strategic decision not to investigate mitigation evidence based on the results of the pre-trial report governing DeBruce's competency to stand trial, that decision could not have been reasonable as it would have been based on a failure to understand the law. Because no lawyer could reasonably have made a strategic decision to forego the pursuit of mitigation evidence based on the results of the pre- trial report governing competency to stand trial, the

Alabama Court of Criminal Appeals' conclusion to the contrary constitutes an unreasonable application of *Strickland's* performance prong.

Id. at (emphasis in original) (citations and footnotes omitted). Counsel's conduct "was all the more unreasonable" because the competence report, school records, and the "youthful offender investigation report" filed by a probation officer with the court contradicted the information supplied by the defendant's mother and counsel still did not investigate. "As a result, [counsel] permitted DeBruce's mother to present grossly inaccurate testimony during her son's sentencing hearing" that he had been "a successful student who had attended college." Prejudice established because the evidence through experts and the testimony of two of the defendant's sisters would have revealed that DeBruce was raised in an impoverished family of eleven child with an alcoholic father who was verbally abusive, experienced violence in his neighborhood, including being frequently attacked by gangs and witnessing stabbings and shootings, daily severe abuse at the hands of his older sister who would beat him and threaten him with a knife, as well as lock him in a closet and withhold meals, dropped out of school in the seventh grade at age 16, developed substance abuse problems during his teenage years, suffers from mental impairments, including brain damage and blackout episodes consistent with seizures), and low intellectual functional (IQ scores between 76 and 79), and has a painful intestinal disorder. The state court found no prejudice, in part, "because of its view of the mental health evidence as 'conflicting,'" but this finding "lacks support from the record." The defense experts did not present "conflicting" testimony and the state's expert, while disputing serious mental illness or defect, conceded that the defendant had low intellectual functioning.

Moreover, in applying *Strickland* in cases where counsel has failed to introduce any of the available mitigating evidence of the defendant's mental impairment and history of abuse that should have been discovered by adequate investigation, the Supreme Court has repeatedly rejected arguments that the defendant is not prejudiced by the complete omission of this type of evidence.

Id. at . Thus, the state court "unreasonably applied *Strickland*" in finding no prejudice.

Mann v. Ryan, 774 F.3d 1203 (9th Cir. 2014) (tried and sentenced in October 1994). Under AEDPA, counsel ineffective in capital sentencing for failing to adequately investigate and present mitigating evidence. The defendant was convicted and sentenced to death for the murder of two men in "another tragic tale of drugs and violence." The state primarily relied on the testimony of his ex-girlfriend who reported his involvement in the murders five years after the fact and was granted immunity. In sentencing, counsel presented very little evidence. Based on the report of the court-appointed psychologist, the trial court found that petitioner was likely a "psychopath," who was incapable of remorse, and sentenced him to death. Under AEDPA, the state court's rejection of relief for failing to prove prejudice was contrary to clearly established federal law because it applied the incorrect standard for prejudice. In finding no prejudice, the state court imported the reasoning from an earlier section of its decision denying relief on the basis of newly discovered evidence. In denying relief on this ground, the state court held petitioner "to the more-likely-than-not standard," which was expressly rejected in *Strickland*. Because the state court did not address the question of deficient conduct, this issue was addressed *de novo*. Counsel's conduct was deficient, as counsel was "not focused" on mitigation prior to conviction. He did not investigate or hire an investigator. He did not interview the former girlfriend, who was the state's star witness, despite the fact that she had lived with petitioner for 10 years and was familiar with his life history. And, counsel did not obtain petitioner's school, prison, or medical records. While counsel realized that he was unprepared following conviction and sought a continuance, counsel still did nothing to investigate. In particular, counsel did not investigate brain damage despite knowledge that petitioner had sustained a concussion in a 1985 traffic accident in which two passengers in the car he was driving died.

> In declining to pursue that lead, counsel ignored a death penalty expert at the Phoenix Capital Representation Project who advised him to seek neuropsychological testing to detect the existence of organic brain damage, and he disregarded the fact that Arizona courts at the time placed 'significant weight' on brain injuries as mitigating evidence.

Id. at 1217. There was no "reasoned strategic reason" for this failure because counsel "did not even attempt to explore that evidence." Prejudice was also established. The ex-girlfriend would have provided testimony about the petitioner's car accident, that he was deeply depressed, and extremely remorseful for the deaths of his passengers. After the accident, she noticed a dramatic and long-term impact on his personality. He began selling drugs because he was worried about the financial pressures of his medical treatment on his family and he became abusive and aggressive. A neuropsychologist, after testing, also concluded that petitioner suffers from traumatic brain injury [TBI] as a result of the accident. This expert's testimony also would have rebutted the court-appointed expert's finding of antisocial personality disorder and psychopathy because such a diagnosis "requires ruling out organic brain injury because the symptoms of the former tend to mimic the symptoms of the latter." Moreover, this expert would have pointed out that the court-appointed examiner's simply clinical interview could not have detected organic brain injury.

2013: *James v. Ryan*, 679 F.3d 780 (9th Cir. 2012) (sentenced in 1982) (reaffirmed 733 F.3d 911 (9th Cir. 2013) following Supreme Court's GVR for consideration under *Johnson v. Williams*, 133 S.Ct. 1088 (2013)). Under AEDPA, counsel ineffective in capital sentencing for failing to adequately investigate and present mitigation evidence. In a third state habeas petition, the state court held that the claim was procedurally barred. At the conclusion of the lengthy state court opinion rejecting 38 claims, the court included a paragraph holding that no hearing was warranted as no claim was "colorable." Because the state court "expressly stated" that it denied the claim "as procedurally barred," the Ninth Circuit rejected the State's argument that *Harrington v. Richter*, 131 S. Ct. 770 (2011), required a presumption that the state court's final paragraph was an alternative merits ruling. The court, thus, reviewed the claim *de novo*. Counsel's conduct was deficient because (1) counsel "failed to conduct even the most basic investigation of James's social history," despite "obvious indications that James had suffered emotional and psychological trauma during his childhood" in a pretrial competency report and a presentencing report. Counsel failed to interview James's adoptive parents, his biological family, or "others who knew him" and "failed to obtain readily available educational records." (2) Counsel failed to investigate James's mental health, despite awareness of several past suicide attempts and pretrial detention psychiatric care for "cyclothymia, a form of bipolar disorder," and medication with lithium. Counsel moved for the appointment of a forensic psychiatrist, which was denied, but then declined additional evaluation by pretrial competence examiners. (3) Counsel failed to investigate James's history of drug abuse, despite "clear cues that James had a history of polysubstance abuse and dependency" in the pretrial competence report. While counsel "argued

James's diminished capacity because of LSD intoxication at the time of the offense as a mitigating circumstance," he "failed to appreciate that chronic drug abuse itself evinces, as well as exacerbates, serious mental illness." Prejudice established because substantial mitigation was available but counsel presented only "meager mitigation evidence" in sentencing. Counsel could have presented "a detailed picture of James's troubled childhood, his mental illness, and his downward spiral of depression and drug abuse in the year before [the] murder." James had "utterly unfit parents who exposed [him] to violence, drug abuse, poverty, and sexually predatory adults." He suffered physical and sexual abuse, was a dismal student, a high school dropout, and a habitual drug user.

2012: *****Winston v. Pearson*****, 683 F.3d 489 (4th Cir. 2012) (affirming *Winston v. Kelly*, 784 F. Supp. 2d 623 (W.D. Va. 2011)) (arrested in 2002). Counsel ineffective in capital case for failing to develop and present evidence of mental retardation. In sentencing counsel presented records of the petitioner's psychological evaluations and testimony about his family history "as ordinary mitigating evidence to illuminate [the petitioner's] troubled childhood and subaverage intellectual functioning, but not to establish mental retardation." In state court, petitioner presented evidence that the petitioner's school records included a mentally retarded classification, but was unable to present any evidence concerning the basis for this diagnosis. The petitioner also had available three IQ scores in state court but all exceeded 70, which was the maximum score Virginia accepts as evidence of mental retardation. The federal district court granted an evidentiary hearing on both mental retardation and ineffective assistance. Petitioner produced for the first time a 1997 IQ test reflecting a score of 66. Counsel revealed that they obtained the school records but failed to "read the complete records" before sending them to their court-appointed mental-health expert. Thus, counsel did not notice the "mental retardation" classification or interview any teachers or counselors at the school. If they had, several school officials would have testified about the petitioner's "severe limitations in cognitive functioning." Likewise, one of these officials had the 66 IQ score saved on a computer disk in her office at the time of trial. Without this information, the court-appointed expert, who also did not recall whether he considered the mentally retarded classification in the school records, concluded that the petitioner was not mentally retarded. Without this information, counsel chose not to present the mental health expert to testify because he also concluded that the petitioner exhibited antisocial behavior and had a capacity for future dangerousness. Initially, the district court declined to consider the evidence presented in federal court and declined relief. The Fourth Circuit remanded finding that it was appropriate to consider the evidence that had not been reviewed by the state court. The District Court granted relief and this appeal followed. The Court reaffirmed its prior holding after analyzing *Pinholster* and *Richter* based on the state court's refusal to order discovery or an evidentiary hearing. Counsel's conduct was deficient in failing to review the school records and interview school officials. In relying only on the court-appointed examiner to review the school records, "counsel abdicated their responsibility" to investigate. Prejudice was also established. Although petitioner cross-appealed on the question of whether he would be allowed only a mental retardation hearing of an entirely new sentencing hearing, the state conceded that "state law likely requires" a full resentencing proceeding.

*****Stankewitz v. Wong*****, 698 F.3d 1163 (9th Cir. 2012) (affirming 659 F. Supp. 2d 1103 (E.D. Cal. 2009)) (sentenced in 1984). Under pre-AEDPA law, counsel's conduct in capital resentencing was deficient in failing "to conduct even the most basic investigation." *Id.* at 1166. Counsel did not hire an investigator or interview "teachers, foster parents, psychiatrists or anyone else who may have examined or spent time with [petitioner] during his upbringing." *Id.* Counsel did not interview anyone involved in the initial trial proceedings in 1978. Counsel did not obtain a mental health evaluation, even though he believed petitioner was incompetent. Counsel ineffective in capital case for failing to adequately investigate and present mitigating evidence. Although counsel presented six witnesses in mitigation, three provided no information specific to petitioner. The other three provided "only vague references" to petitioner's history. Counsel "also focused very little on the actual details of [petitioner's] life during his closing arguments." *Id.* Counsel's conduct was not based on strategy. In short, rather than "presenting a narrative that might have humanized [petitioner] to the jury," counsel chose "simply to ignore the state's presentation" of aggravation evidence. Prejudice found because there was substantial mitigation evidence available of: (1) a childhood of abuse/neglect; (2) a history of mental illness; and (3) substance abuse/lack of sleep prior to the murder. The jury, however, "had heard next to nothing about [petitioner's] traumatic childhood." *Id.* at 1174. Nonetheless, several jurors initially voted for life before finally reaching a unanimous verdict.

Hooks v. Workman, 689 F.3d 1148 (10th Cir. 2012). Counsel ineffective in capital sentencing for failing to adequately investigate and present mitigation, failing to mitigate aggravation evidence, and actually bolstering the aggravation case. Counsel's conduct was "woefully inadequate" in failing to investigate.

> Evidence of family and social history was sorely lacking; the mental-health evidence presented was inadequate and quite unsympathetic; and [counsel] not only failed to rebut the prosecution's case in aggravation but actually bolstered it by his own statements.

Counsel's statements and the statements of the defense expert "served to vilify [the petitioner] in the eyes of the jury." Counsel presented testimony from the petitioner's sister and mother, but neither testified for much more than one page of transcript. It "was perfunctory, to put it mildly." "Even the most minimal investigation would have uncovered a life story worth telling: a premature birth, an openly abusive father, frequent moves, educational handicaps, and personal family tragedies." Counsel also presented an expert. While the expert did say that petitioner had a "form of psychosis," he characterized the petitioner as "violent" and "crazy." Counsel "made little effort to connect [the expert's] diagnosis to the circumstance of the crime." This was deficient, because "[c]ounsel in capital cases must explain to the jury why a defendant may have acted as he did–must connect the dots between, on the one hand, a defendant's mental problems, life circumstances, and personal history and, on the other, his commission of the crime in question." To make matters worse, it was revealed on cross that the expert "knew almost nothing" about the case. He had not even read police reports or listened to the confession. In short, counsel "totally failed to prepare his witness." If counsel had adequately investigated the mental health evidence, the jury would have known that "the mental-health problems were enduring." In childhood, the petitioner struggled in school, was evaluated for mental retardation, and was placed in special education classes. While the Court rejected his mental retardation claim, "no one disputes that by the time of trial he had been clinically diagnosed with mild or borderline mental retardation." There were also "clear markers for organic brain damage due to a premature birth and head injuries from an 18-wheeler accident. This was powerful mitigation evidence because "the involuntary physical alteration of brain structures, with its attendant effects on behavior, tends to diminish moral culpability, altering the causal relationship between impulse and action." Counsel also failed to rebut evidence of a prior armed robbery conviction, which was one of the three aggravating circumstances. "Even a cursory investigation into the circumstances surrounding this crime would have revealed a much less sordid tale" than the one told by a police officer testifying for the state. The truth was that the petitioner took $35 from a cash drawer in a liquor store and returned home with that and a sack containing a handgun. He told his mother what he had done and she immediately took him to the police station. While this evidence "would not have entirely negated the violent-felony aggravator, it certainly would have softened its edge." Counsel also bolstered the prosecution's aggravation by effectively conceding the continuing threat aggravator in his opening statement. Prejudice was established.

2011: *****Blystone v. Horn**, 664 F.3d 397 (3rd Cir. 2011) (sentenced in 1984). Counsel ineffective in capital sentencing for failing to adequately investigate and present mitigation evidence. Counsel's conduct was deficient because of an "extremely limited investigation." At most, counsel interviewed the petitioner, his parents, and one sister, whom counsel "unintentionally encountered in the hallway of the courthouse during trial." Counsel sought no background records. The Court did "not delve too deeply into" this question because the Commonwealth "all but concedes" that counsel's conduct was deficient.

> [T]h[e] duty to conduct a reasonable investigation of mitigating evidence exists independently of counsel's duty to present a mitigation case to the jury. In fact, the former is a necessary predicate to the latter: if counsel had failed to conduct a reasonable investigation to *prepare* for sentencing, then he cannot possibly be said to have made a reasonable decision as to what to *present* at sentencing.

Id. at 420. Counsel's investigation of mental health evidence was limited only to reliance on a pretrial competence evaluation. As the District Court held, "[i]t is beyond cavil that the scope of an evaluation for purposes of mitigation at a capital sentencing proceeding is far broader than that for competency at trial." *Id.* at 421. Nonetheless, the competency report contained "'red flags,' which a qualified expert would have found to require follow-up prior to sentencing. But counsel never even presented the competency evaluation to an expert." *Id.* Under AEDPA, the state court conclusion that counsel's conduct was not deficient was unreasonable. Counsel's explanation that the petitioner wanted "all or nothing" was also rejected. The fact that the petitioner turned down a deal for life "in no way compels the conclusion that he wanted to die if convicted." *Id.* at 422. Regardless:

> "The investigation for preparation of the sentencing phase should be conducted regardless of any initial assertion by the client that mitigation is not to be offered." Counsel cannot avoid the consequences of his inadequate preparation simply by virtue of the serendipitous occurrence that, on the day of sentencing, his client stuck with the decision not to go forward with a mitigation case.

Id. at 422 (quoting ABA Guidelines). Here, counsel did not do that investigation. Indeed, counsel "did not even perform an investigation sufficient to provide the foundation for a reasoned strategic choice." *Id.* at 423. Instead, the failure to investigate "was merely the consequence of lackluster performance." *Id.* The Court also rejected the state court finding that the petitioner waived his right to present mitigation. The Court distinguished *Schriro v. Landrigan*, 550 U.S. 465 (2007). Trial counsel never intended to present any testimony at sentencing other than petitioner and his parents. Prior to sentencing, counsel informed the court that petitioner wished to waive mitigation. The court's colloquy "focused almost entirely" on whether petitioner wanted to take the stand or have his parents testify. The only question about whether he wanted to presented any other evidence was part of a compound question: "Do you wish to testify yourself or to have your parents testify or to *offer any other evidence in this case*?" *Id.* at 425. The petitioner "waived, at most, all lay witness testimony." *Id.* at 426. There was no indication that petitioner was even aware that "any other form" of mitigation could be presented. *Id.* Counsel still could have presented "expert mental health evidence and institutional records," *id.*, including Navy records, prior prison records, and the report of the competence evaluation. Under AEDPA, the state court's conclusion of waiver was unreasonable. Prejudice was also found. Petitioner suffers "from serious untreated brain damage and psychiatric disorders, all of which were aggravated by a history of poly-substance abuse." *Id.* at 406. The psychiatric disorders diagnosed by petitioner's experts were bipolar disorder with major depressive episodes, and borderline personality disorder. The expert testimony and records evidence would have supported mitigating circumstances of substantially impaired capacity, extreme emotional distress, and adaptability to confinement. Thus, there is a reasonable probability that the mitigation evidence "would have convinced one juror to find the mitigating factors to outweigh the single aggravating factor," *id.* at 427, of murder in the perpetration of a felony.

***Sowell v. Anderson**, 663 F.3d 783 (6th Cir. 2011) (sentenced in 1983). Under pre-AEDPA law, counsel ineffective in capital sentencing for failing to adequately investigate and present mitigation evidence. Counsel's mitigation strategy was to portray the petitioner "as a good person who lost his temper under the influence of drugs and alcohol." Counsel presented only two former probation officers, two work colleagues, petitioner's common-law wife, and an unsworn statement from the petitioner. The entire mitigation case totaled "only thirty-four pages of transcript" and included no mention of petitioner's "formative years." Counsel pursued this strategy despite having reports from court-appointed experts that "hinted at" petitioner's "difficult background" and without any investigation of petitioner's background or interviews of his family members. Because counsel failed to investigate, counsel "were not in a position to make a conscious, strategic decision about the type of mitigation case to present at sentencing." *Id.* at 790. In short:

> There is nothing wrong with a mitigation strategy that emphasizes a capital defendant's redeeming qualities. But. … [c]ounsel's failure to present evidence of [petitioner's] horrific childhood resulted from their ignorance of this evidence, not from an informed choice between mutually exclusive mitigation theories.

Id. In other words, "[a]n attorney does not make a strategic decision by choosing to ignore a body of evidence, the contents of which are unknown. This is not strategy." *Id.* at 791. Family interviews would have revealed that petitioner's "early life was abusive, impoverished, and totally chaotic." *Id.* His father was an abusive alcoholic, who was frequently absent but when present "the family lived in terror." *Id.* His mother was only 15 when she married. She "lacked basic parenting skills and vocally wished her children were dead or had never been born." *Id.* a 791-92. She often left the children "without supervision for days at a time." *Id.* at 792. The physical and psychological abuse continued into petitioner's adolescent years. His father also sexually molested petitioner's sister and threatened to kill her if she reported it. The family also lived in "extreme poverty." A younger brother died of starvation and the children often "had to beg for and steal food." *Id.* The children were also "bitten by rats, infected with worms, and lacked sufficient clothing and shoes." *Id.* Housing was also inadequate and petitioner was "living in a junkyard, on his own, in a tent" by the time he was 14. *Id.* Aside from family interviews, counsel also failed to pursue "obvious leads contained in the written reports of court-appointed experts." *Id.* These reports gave indications of the "troubled childhood." Even if counsel chose to emphasize the positive while ignoring the "horrific childhood," this "is not easily considered a reasonable mitigation strategy, particularly where the additional evidence would not have been inconsistent with–and might even have strengthened–the mitigation case counsel did present." *Id.* at 793-94. In other words, the evidence could have shown "that petitioner was capable of generosity and good acts in spite of the upbringing that he endured." *Id.* at 794. In addition, this was not "a case where counsel could have legitimately feared that digging deeper into [petitioner's] past would turn up evidence that was more damaging than favorable," because petitioner's entire criminal record and arrest history was already included in the evidence. Thus, "the panel already knew the worst." *Id.* Prejudice found. The reports of the court-appointed examiners spoke only "in generalities that lacked any details of the severe abuse and abject poverty" of petitioner's "formative years." *Id.* at 795.

> In contrast, [petitioner's] family members offered first-hand, eyewitness accounts of specific examples of extreme poverty and abuse. These specifics had far more evidentiary power than the abstractions and oblique references contained in the experts' written reports.
> What is more, the experts themselves never heard any of these details when they conducted their evaluations.

Id. At bottom:

> [Petitioner's] actions as an adult–good and bad–are merely a snapshot in time, unilluminated by the longitudinal perspective that his developmental history provides. ... It is evidence of a lifetime of privation and abuse, beginning in early childhood and continuing throughout the formative years of [petitioner's] life.

Id. at 796.

Foust v. Houk, 655 F.3d 524 (6th Cir. 2011) (sentencing in December 2001). Counsel ineffective in capital sentencing for failing to adequately investigate and present mitigation in hearing before three-judge panel. While the petitioner's parents and a psychologist testified, "their testimony pales in comparison to the horrific accounts detailed in records from Children's Services and in affidavits from [the petitioner's] siblings." Prior to trial, the court-appointed a psychologist to evaluate competence and sanity. Shortly before trial, without notice even to the psychologist, the defense sought funding to retain him as a "mitigation specialist." The psychologist informed counsel that normally a social worker is retained to prepare for capital sentencing. The psychologist recommended numerous times that counsel obtain records, including the Children's Services records, and interview witnesses, but counsel did only "minimal work" in preparation for sentencing and did not even meet with the psychologist or any of petitioner's family members, including the parents. Because the state court adjudicated the merits, "[w]e therefore afford double deference to both state-court decisions on both prongs of the *Strickland* test." Counsel's conduct was deficient in failing to obtain records and interview family members, even though the petitioner's "dire upbringing formed the crux of the mitigation strategy." The court could not "fathom why" counsel failed to obtain the Children's

Services records for the 24-year-old petitioner, especially with the psychologist pushing them to do so. "There is no question that a reasonable attorney would believe records of [the petitioner's] childhood to be relevant to a defense about the conditions of [the petitioner's] childhood." Counsel also did not interview the petitioner's siblings or even his parents, who were called to testify. Counsel had only four pages of notes and suggested questions that the psychologist prepared for them the day before sentencing began. The state court's ruling–that counsel's failure to obtain the records and interview siblings was "a tactical decision"–was "nonsensical." This was not a case like *Van Hook* where counsel failed to "dig deeper." Here, counsel "failed to interview *anyone* or seek *any*" records. Counsel's conduct was also deficient in failing to interview the psychologist about his investigation and findings. "By neither interviewing [the psychologist] about his investigation nor conducting any independent investigation, [the] attorneys in effect delegated to [the psychologist], who is not an attorney, the strategic decisionmaking about how to present [the] mitigation defense." Counsel's conduct was also deficient in failing to hire a "trained mitigation specialist," even though they had "a clinical psychologist." This is "particularly troublesome" here when counsel knew of the petitioner's "difficult background" and the psychologist informed counsel that "that most death-penalty investigations include a mitigation specialist, which he was not." Even if the psychologist was qualified as a mitigation specialist, he did not fulfill that role here as he was unable to collect the Children's Services records and did not adequately interview family members. Prejudice also found. The state court's finding to the contrary was unreasonable because "[t]he testimony at the mitigation hearing 'only scratched the surface of [the petitioner's] horrific childhood.'" The unpresented evidence "paints an altogether different picture of [the petitioner's] childhood." The petitioner grew up in squalor and chaos that was documented repeatedly by Children's Services; and suffered maternal abuse, both emotional and physical, and neglect, which was also documented by Children's Services. In sentencing, the three-judge panel heard only minimal evidence of the conditions of the home and was "misled" into believing that only the petitioner's father had been abusive. The petitioner's childhood home was also filled with incest and sexual abuse of his sisters, none of which was presented in sentencing. The petitioner's "acclimation to sexual abuse of women is particularly relevant because rape was one of the aggravating circumstances that supported the death penalty." There was also available evidence of "good acts" by the petitioner, but no "positive" evidence was presented in sentencing. The fact that the post-conviction judge that rejected relief was also the presiding judge of the three-judge sentencing panel made no difference as "Ohio law requires unanimity among a three-judge panel for a sentence of death. Thus, 'any one of the three judges alone could have prevented imposition of the death penalty.'" Moreover, the post-conviction judge's conclusion of no prejudice was not reasonable. While the aggravating circumstances were "overwhelming" and the "crime was heinous" and "gruesome," prejudice was still clear. "Powerful aggravating circumstances … do not preclude a finding of prejudice."

Goodwin v. Johnson, 632 F.3d 301 (6th Cir. 2011) (sentenced in December 1994). Counsel ineffective in capital sentencing for failing to adequately investigate and present mitigation. Counsel presented no evidence in sentencing and instead argued residual doubt. Counsel's conduct was deficient as counsel had "little contact" with petitioner and his family and did not obtain "school, medical, and family history records." Counsel claimed he did not present mitigation to avoid opening the door to evidence of five armed robberies in the petitioner's criminal history. Counsel declined a court-ordered presentence report and psychiatric evaluation because of his belief that there was "nothing psychiatrically wrong" with the petitioner. Counsel in closing even discounted youth as a mitigating factor and told the jury that it would insult their intelligence to rely on mental health evidence. Following the jury's recommendation but prior to imposition of sentence, the defendant's aunt spoke in mitigation. If counsel had obtained juvenile court records, he would have been aware that there was only two adjudications for robbery and one for criminal trespass, rather than five armed robberies. The records also revealed a serious drug problem. School records included an evaluation at age 14 that revealed an IQ of 73. A psychologist that examined the defendant at age 15 in juvenile proceedings testified that she diagnosed conduct disorder but she also found the possibility of dysthymia or depression. Family interviews revealed neglect by a drug-using mother and physical and sexual abuse by others. All of this information would have suggested the need for a mental health evaluation. Prejudice also established. Under AEDPA, the state court's determination to the contrary was unreasonable.

Cooper v. Secretary, Dept. Of Corrections, 646 F.3d 1328 (11th Cir. 2011) (sentenced in January 1984). Counsel ineffective in capital sentencing for failing to adequately investigate and present mitigation evidence. The jury recommended death for three murders with votes of 9-3 and 7-5. The only mitigation witness to testify before the jury was the petitioner's mother. A psychologist testified before the judge but was not called before the jury for strategic reasons (i.e., the defendant admitted to him firing four shots while he had admitted to police firing only two shots). Counsel's conduct was ineffective in failing to adequately investigate and to interview others, particularly the petitioner's brother and sister, his school principal, and his ex-girlfriend. Because the state did not offer any argument challenging the District Court's finding that counsel's conduct was deficient, "the State has abandoned that claim." Regardless, the court found counsel's conduct was deficient "[u]nder the prevailing standards in 1984." Counsel did not adequately investigate and unreasonably decided to end the background investigation after talking to no one other than the petitioner, his mother, and one expert. While counsel sought to argue that the petitioner was impulsive and acting under the domination of another, could "did little to follow through with this strategy." While counsel knew from the expert that the petitioner had been abused by his father, they did nothing to further develop this information once they decided not to call the expert. Under AEDPA, "fairminded jurists could not disagree about whether the state court's denial of this claim was inconsistent with earlier Supreme Court decisions." The state court's finding of no prejudice was an unreasonable determination of the facts. The petitioner's mother had testified that the petitioner's father abused her and the petitioner witnessed it. She gave no testimony about the father abusing the petitioner as the state court found. In addition, the mother's testimony "did not begin to describe the horrible abuse" described by the petitioner's brother and sister that was inflicted not just by their father but also by the older brother that testified in post-conviction proceedings. Thus, the state court's finding that the mother had presented a "substantial part" of the available mitigation was "a great exaggeration." Prejudice was, therefore, reviewed *de novo* without "AEDPA deference" and found. If counsel had adequately presented the evidence, two statutory mitigating circumstances that the trial judge had rejected would have been established: (1) age at the time of the crime; and (2) substantial domination by another. While the judge knew the petitioner was barely over 18, he did not hear the evidence that the defendant was "barely removed from being violently abused by his father and brother." Likewise, while the judge heard an expert's opinion that the petitioner was dominated by a co-defendant, the judge did not hear evidence from the lay witnesses, who described the petitioner's susceptibility to domination by older, dominant males during his childhood. In addition, the available evidence would have established multiple categories of nonstatutory mitigation including horrific abuse by his father and brother; drug and alcohol abuse by age 11; abandonment by his mother for long periods; learning deficits; an IQ of 75; and depression. The state emphasized "the dearth of evidence in mitigation" in closing arguments. Given that some jurors had voted for life even without this substantial mitigation, this evidence made it "possible" that "more jurors would have voted for life."

*__Johnson v. Secretary, DOC__, 643 F.3d 907 (11th Cir. 2011) (sentenced in 1980). Counsel ineffective in capital sentencing for failing to adequately investigate and present mitigation evidence. The jury recommended death by a 7 to 5 vote after hearing only brief testimony from family members and testimony from a psychologist who saw the defendant in a detoxication program he voluntarily entered less than five weeks before the crimes. She testified that his primary problem was "a character disorder" and that "alcoholism was secondary." While she testified that the defendant sincerely wanted to cure his problems, the program had been inadequate because "it was geared to people whose alcoholism is primary instead of secondary." Counsel's conduct was deficient. He conceded that he knew well before trial "that he had little or no chance of prevailing" on the question of guilt-or-innocence. Counsel had asked a jail psychologist to do "a personality profile," but did not interview family, "family physicians, or any school teachers," and did not obtain school records. The jail psychologist did only two personality tests, diagnosed "conduct or behavior disorder," and disclosed this information to the prosecutor and the judge, as well as defense counsel.

> The question under *Strickland* is not whether … trial counsel's overall performance at the sentence stage was exemplary or even average, but whether he conducted an adequate background investigation or reasonably decided to end the background investigation when he did. … And as the recent *Harrington* decision emphasized, because our deficiency inquiry is governed by AEDPA, the question is not just if counsel's investigative decisions were reasonable, but whether fairminded jurists could disagree about whether the state court's denial of the ineffective assistance of counsel claim was inconsistent with Supreme Court precedent or was based on an unreasonable determination of the facts. If fairminded jurists could reasonably disagree, then habeas relief is due to be denied.

Id. at 931-32 (citations omitted). Here, "[g]iven the overwhelming evidence of guilt, any reasonable attorney would have known, as [counsel] testified he actually did know, that the sentence stage was the only part of the trial in which [the defendant] had any reasonable chance of success." *Id.* at 932. Nonetheless, counsel "waited until the eleventh hour" to begin preparing for sentencing. Although counsel was aware that the defendant had a bad childhood, including an alcoholic and abusive father, counsel did not investigate or seek a continuance until after conviction on Friday with the sentencing to start on Monday. He did nothing other than speak to the defendant's father and he investigated no further when the father denied being an abusive alcoholic.

> No reasonable attorney who has every expectation that his client will be convicted and will be facing a death sentence would wait until the guilt stage ended before beginning to investigate the existence of non-statutory mitigating circumstances. No reasonable attorney, after being told by his client that he had an abusive upbringing, would fail to interview members of his client's family who were readily available and could corroborate or refute the allegations of abuse. No reasonable attorney told by his client that he had an alcoholic and abusive father would fail to pursue those non-statutory mitigating circumstances simply

> because the father denied it. …
>
> [I]t was unreasonable for him not to allocate even a few hours of time before the trial to investigating his client's claim of having been abused by an alcoholic father.
>
> This is not a case in which counsel relied on what his client told him, or failed to tell him, about his background. It is, instead, a case in which counsel failed to adequately investigate what his client did tell him.

Id. at 932-33 (citations omitted). In short, counsel's failure "was not influenced by": (1) a strong possibility of getting his client acquitted of the capital murder charge"; (2) "what his client said or failed to say," (3) "avoiding the possibility of opening the door to what could be harmful evidence"; or (4) "any difficulty in finding other family members or in getting them to talk." *Id.* at 934-35. The state court's determination was an unreasonable application of *Strickland*. "In *Harrington* terms, fairminded jurists could not disagree about whether the state court's denial of this claim was inconsistent with earlier Supreme Court decisions, including *Strickland* and *Williams v. Taylor*." *Id.* at 935. Prejudice was reviewed *de novo* as the state court had not decided the issue. "Prejudice established, as numerous family members would have testified. While the defendant's father had testified previously in sentencing, he had not been prepared and denied at that time that he was an abusive alcoholic. "The description, details, and depth of abuse … far exceeded what the jury was told." *Id.* at 936. The jury never heard even that both parents were abusive alcoholics. While the jury heard that the defendant had been placed in an orphanage and with grandparents at times, they jury was not told that it was because the father abandoned him. While the jury was given the impression that the grandparents were caring and nurturing, they inflicted horrible physical and emotional abuse on the defendant, including rubbing his face in his own urine when he wet the bed. The jury did not hear that the defendant witnessed repeated suicide attempts by his mother. Likewise, although the jury heard that the defendant blamed himself for his mother's death and his brother's death in Vietnam, the jury "did not learn that his mother killed herself the same way his brother died–with a drug overdose. And the jury was not told that [the defendant] found his mother's body, with a photograph of his dead brother clutched in her hands." *Id.* at 937.

Ferrell v. Hall, 640 F.3d 1199 (11th Cir. 2011) (sentenced in September 1988). Trial counsel ineffective in capital sentencing for failing to adequately investigate and present mitigation. Appellate counsel ineffective in failing to assert trial counsel's ineffectiveness. During sentencing, the defense presented five family witnesses, whose combined testimony and a break lasted only 26 minutes. These witnesses testified that they believed the petitioner was innocent and that he was a Christian, but they did ask for mercy. The available evidence through experts, records, and lay witnesses would have established that the petitioner suffers from organic brain damage, mental illness (probably bi-polar disorder), an epileptic or seizure disorder, and borderline mental retardation. He also had an impoverished and abused childhood, but always had a strong work ethic. His mother was schizophrenic and his family history included depression. While the Georgia Supreme Court's opinion on whether trial counsel was ineffective was viewed through the prism of AEDPA, the state court never reached the prejudice prong of the appellate counsel ineffectiveness claim and, therefore, AEDPA did not constrain federal court review. Nonetheless, the Court's "determination about prejudice would be exactly the same" whether AEDPA applied or *de novo* review. "Trial counsel conducted a profoundly incomplete investigation, and its judgment to so sharply limit its inquiry" was deficient conduct. The state court's conclusion to the contrary was an unreasonable application of

Supreme Court law. The "mental health investigation was unjustifiably and unreasonably circumscribed." While counsel did obtain a mental health evaluation pretrial, the evaluation was limited to whether the petitioner was retarded and whether he suffered from any problems that would affect the waiver of *Miranda* rights. Likewise, the expert was not asked to look for evidence of brain damage, was provided with *no* material other than school records, was *not* asked to perform a clinical interview, and was not asked to even consider mitigation despite "the many red flags" raised about the petitioner's mental health such that counsel and the retained investigator "harbored serious questions" about petitioner's mental health. In addition, the petitioner had a seizure during the charge conference, but counsel did not seek a continuance or to have a mental health evaluation. Counsel also failed to even ask the family members who testified about the petitioner's mental health. Indeed, the investigator who had actually interviewed 40-50 witnesses, "only asked statutory character evidence questions … and only followed up with them if they said anything positive" about the petitioner. The questions were basically taken from the state statute governing character evidence and sought information on reputation in the community and opinion of the petitioner's truthfulness. While counsel claimed a "residual doubt" strategy, "[t]he long and the short of it is that defense counsel had nothing else to rely on because they looked for nothing else." Thus, this "strategy" was "completely undermined" and did not "explain adequately why they unreasonably limited their mitigation investigation." Likewise, counsel's closing argument "undercut" any possible "residual doubt" strategy in that counsel said the petitioner's story of innocence was "absurd," "ludicrous," and the like. Counsel also "raised for the jury the question hovering over the entire trial, *why* [petitioner] did it—the very question that could have been answered by the powerful mitigating mental health evidence easily developed later."

> Even though counsel asked "why" … , counsel never conducted an investigation that would have begun to answer this question, and never offered the jury the slightest reason. …
> In short, the record … establishes that counsel at most pursued a half-hearted residual doubt defense, and then eviscerated that defense with his observations about the inadequacy of defendant's explanations. The real thrust of the defense at sentencing was not residual doubt, but rather, mercy.

Prejudice was also established and the state court "unreasonably determined" otherwise. First, "the 'new' mitigating evidence is consistent, unwavering, compelling, and wholly unrebutted." Second, the mental health evidence also "measurably weakens the aggravating circumstances found by the jury." The state argued that the crimes were "cold-blooded, execution-style, and planned out," such that they were "outrageously and wantonly vile." The mental health evidence would have served to reduce the volitional nature of the crimes, as well as the petitioner's ability to plan and act rationally. Third, the mental health evidence "would have easily and directly supported" the argument for mercy that "counsel offered at sentencing." It also would have answered the "repeated questions to the jury about why" the crimes were committed. Finally, the mitigation evidence presented at trial "was very sparse." Appellate counsel was also ineffective. During a motion for new trial, new counsel asserted ineffective assistance of counsel. She was provided funding to hire a mental health expert but not an investigator. While counsel asserted that trial counsel had not adequately investigated mental health, she hired a psychiatrist, but asked him to evaluate only competence and sanity. She provided him only with the trial expert's report and jail records. She did not even provide him with information known to her about the petitioner's seizure during trial, his mother's mental illness, or indications of the petitioner's mental illness. While the expert reported that the petitioner reported hearing voices, counsel did nothing with this information. The state court's determination that counsel's conduct was reasonable was an unreasonable application of *Strickland*. It was also unreasonable to conclude that the "other" mitigation investigation was not deficient. She presented three of the same family members who testified in sentencing, but did not elicit the kind of mitigating evidence that she claimed she sought to establish. She did not track down additional witnesses and did not "dig deeper with the witnesses she did have." She also "affirmatively presented harmful testimony." While the mother of petitioner's children testified that he tried to be a good father, she also provided harmful testimony. Specifically, in response to counsel's question, she could not answer whether she would have asked the jury to show mercy. Counsel also failed to even speak with the trial investigator and the limited nature of that investigation was not even referenced. Prejudice established for the same reasons as with trial counsel's ineffectiveness.

2010: ***Griffin v. Pierce***, 622 F.3d 831 (7th Cir. 2010) (Sentenced in June 1985). Counsel ineffective in capital sentencing (death sentence later commuted to life imprisonment) for failing to adequately investigate and present mitigation in sentencing. Counsel presented only the defendant and one witness, who volunteered in the courtroom, to testify briefly in mitigation. Prejudice established because the evidence would have revealed petitioner's father's alcoholism and abusiveness, his mother's absence from the home, the impact of his mother's death, his diagnosis of schizophrenic reaction, and his drug addictions. The state court held there was no reasonable probability that the sentencing judge would have found that the mitigating evidence precluded the death penalty. The Seventh Circuit held:

> The question is not whether a particular judge would have imposed a different sentence, but rather whether there was a "reasonable probability" that the sentence would have been different. In assessing that probability we conduct an objective evaluation of the evidence.

Id. at 845. The state court had also considered the seriousness of the crime and petitioner's lengthy criminal history, "but it did not properly evaluate the totality of the mitigation evidence and reweigh it against the aggravation evidence as it must." The state court's decision was also unreasonable under AEDPA because it viewed the available mitigation evidence as "cumulative and not inherently mitigating," which was wrong on both fronts. While the presentence report contained some information about petitioner's history, it was incomplete and also inaccurate as it portrayed a normal childhood with good relationships with his parents when petitioner's "childhood was anything but normal." *Id.* at 845.

2009: ***Johnson v. Mitchell***, 585 F.3d 923 (6th Cir. 2009) (retrial in 1986). Under AEDPA, counsel ineffective in capital sentencing for failing to adequately investigate and present mitigation. Counsel had represented the defendant in post-conviction arguing successfully that original counsel had failed to adequately investigate and present mitigation and then, in the retrial, counsel "himself committed the same grievous error." Counsel's sole preparation for sentencing was "reading the transcript of the … first trial" and speaking with the defendant. "Such inaction on the part of defense counsel in this case amounted to a complete abdication of the attorney's duty to investigate and present evidence in mitigation." He offered no mitigation evidence and relied only on the defendant's unsworn statement, which chastised the factfinders at length for failing to acquit him. "Thus, in effect, [counsel] merely replayed the disastrous initial trial a second time. Not surprisingly, the same result followed." When counsel did speak with the defendant, he asked only that the defendant provide him with the names of people who say anything "good" about him.

> Obviously, confining investigation in the defense of a capital case to only the "good" things that could be said about the client cannot be considered a reasonable investigation.

Id. at 942. At minimum, there were relatives willing to testify. "Without their testimony, the jury was left with no alternative but to believe that [the defendant's] own relatives were not supportive enough of him to plead for his life." *Id.* These witnesses also could have provided "a more compassionate tint to the portrait," *id.* at 943, by providing humanizing testimony about the defendant's background and life. The state court's finding that counsel's conduct was not deficient was an unreasonable application of *Strickland*. Because the state court had not reached the question of prejudice, the Sixth Circuit reviewed this issue *de novo*.

> In order to establish prejudice, the new evidence that a habeas petitioner presents must differ in a substantial way–in strength and subject matter–from the evidence actually presented at sentencing.

Id. (quoting *Hill v. Mitchell*, 400 F.3d 308, 319 (6th Cir. 2005). Here, there was evidence that the defendant had been frequently beaten by his father. He was also exposed to violence in school and in his predominantly white neighborhood where the black defendant was forced to defend himself numerous times. The defendant also had diagnoses of cocaine abuse and mixed personality disorder.

Libberton v. Ryan, 583 F.3d 1147 (9th Cir. 2009) (tried in June 1982). Under AEDPA, counsel ineffective in capital sentencing. Counsel's conduct was deficient because counsel "spent very little time preparing for sentencing." Although counsel had funds to hire an investigator, the investigator never interviewed anyone. Counsel did not interview the defendant's sister or ask the defendant's mother to testify, even though he did talk to her. Instead, counsel presented only two mitigating witnesses, "both of whom were only tenuously connected" to the defendant. Other than that, the sentencing court had a presentence report reflecting hearsay statements from the defendant's father that "his son is a liar and thief" and reflecting his opinion that his son "may have been the leader in planning the crime." Prejudice established as there was evidence available that the crimes were instigated by a co-defendant and the defendant was "merely a follower." Likewise, evidence was available to impeach a second testifying co-defendant who portrayed the defendant as an equal participant in the crimes. Finally, there was significant evidence that the defendant was seriously physically abused by his father and a step-father during his childhood. This evidence was not only mitigating but "could have seriously undercut his father's opinion" presented through the presentence report.

Hamilton v. Ayers, 583 F.3d 1100 (9th Cir. 2009) (tried and sentenced in 1982). Under AEDPA, counsel ineffective in capital sentencing for failing to adequately investigate and present mitigation evidence. Counsel's conduct was deficient in his first capital case.

> [H]e never even thought about retaining a mitigation expert or a mental health expert.

Moreover, he did not have the benefit of a more experienced attorney's advice, as he did not associate co-counsel.

The investigation consisted of five interviews conducted shortly before jury selection began. The interviews, including that of the defendant's sister, did not address the defendant's childhood at all, even though the sister "could have provided countless details about the physical and mental abuse [the defendant] suffered as a child." Counsel also failed to investigate further after his investigator learned from the defendant's uncle that the defendant's sister had been sexually abused by her father while her mother acquiesced, and the family moved from place to place in the military. This was "classic mitigating evidence" that was not pursued. The other three interviews conducted revealed nothing as "each of them lasted only one to two minutes" and related only to events around the time of the crimes. A number of available witnesses were never contacted, including a sister who was a co-defendant, and available "documentary evidence" was never pursued, even though "[m]any of these documents were in fact in defense counsel's possession, but he never reviewed them." The unreviewed records, which were collected by the investigator just prior to sentencing, included information that the defendant's father's was sexually abusive, which resulted in the defendant being placed in foster care. Counsel was aware that the defendant had attempted suicide in prison and that he was taking antidepressants at the time of trial but did not investigate and discover other records that revealed that the defendant "had suffered from serious mental illnesses throughout most of his life."

> Defense counsel thus should have retained a mental health expert and provided the expert with the information needed to form an accurate profile of [the defendant's] mental health.

While counsel testified that the defendant was uncooperative, "[a] defendant's lack of cooperation does not eliminate counsel's duty to investigate." The court found *Schriro v. Landrigan*, 550 U.S. 465 (2007), "distinguishable" because "at most [the defendant] refused to assist in his defense; he did not impede the many other avenues of mitigating evidence available to counsel." Nonetheless, during sentencing, counsel "presented almost none of the mitigating evidence he had discovered." The entire penalty phase, including counsel's "anemic presentation," covered only 39 pages of transcript. Counsel waived his opening statement. He then presented only the defendant's mother to testify, but with "scant questioning" and lack of preparation, this testimony covers only 5 pages of transcript and "left the false impression that [the defendant's] childhood, while unhappy, was not unusual." Because the mother was involved in the abuse of the defendant and his siblings and testified as a prosecution witness during the trial, she "was one of the worst witnesses that defense counsel could have presented to the jury." Counsel also did not explain "the significance of the meager mitigating evidence during closing" and mentioned the mother's testimony only once. Counsel even "validated" the prosecution's characterization of the defendant's childhood "as 'unfortunate' but neither unusual nor extreme," even though "the environment in which [the defendant] grew up was extraordinarily abusive and atypical in almost every sense." Counsel's "strategy" to beg for mercy was unreasonable under these circumstances.

> Limiting the scope of a penalty phase presentation to evidence that the defendant is a good person who has done good deeds is, in and of itself, unreasonable where there is an extreme unlikelihood that any testimony about the defendant's character would be sufficient to

humanize him.

Prejudice established. The evidence not presented would have revealed that the defendant's family moved 11 times in a 13 year period during the defendant's childhood. His father was an abusive alcoholic, who would kill the children's pets and terrorize them. He fought with his wife "wield[ing] butcher knives" in front of the children. He beat the defendant regularly, "but otherwise ignored him." The parents were sexually inappropriate in front of the children and made them watch while the mother performed oral sex on the father. The father also sexually abused the defendant's sister for four years, while the mother acquiesced and even assisted at times by holding her daughter down or participating sexually. The defendant was aware of this activity and "tried to defend his sister, but his father beat him and threatened to kill him." When the sister reported the abuse to an uncle, the parents were arrested and the children were taken into protective custody. The father was convicted and "adjudged a mentally disordered sex offender." The defendant moved "from one foster home to another" after that. He was initially placed with an uncle until he observed the uncle also molesting his sister. From the time he was twelve years old, the defendant's records revealed "serious mental health problems," including schizophrenia and depression. He had attempted suicide and was still being treated for depression at the time of trial. Mental health problems and sexual abuse "were rampant in [the defendant's] immediate and extended family as well." In denying relief, the District Court "went astray by holding counsel to a lesser standard of performance than existed in 1982," even though compliance with the ABA Standards for Criminal Justice "was as crucial in 1982 as it is today."

> [W]e need not decide whether standard practice at the time of trial included retaining a "mitigation expert"–someone specially trained in investigating and presenting mitigating evidence at the penalty phase of a capital trial–because the deficient performance here did not result from counsel's failure to hire a specialized investigator. Rather, it resulted from counsel's failure to pursue obvious leads provided by the people he did interview, to review relevant documents that were in his possession, and to present to the jury the mitigating evidence of which he was aware.

2008: *__Bond v. Beard__*, 539 F.3d 256 (3rd Cir. 2008) (sentenced in Feb. 1993). Under AEDPA, counsel ineffective in failing to adequately investigate and present mitigation. Counsel presented "seven family members and friends at the penalty phase hearing" to testify generally about "good character and willingness to help others." The post-conviction testimony "painted a very different picture than that presented at the penalty hearing." In short, the defendant "endured an extremely troubled and deprived childhood." His mother drank, gambled extensively, and physically abused the defendant. The family lived in "poverty, disrupted by periods in which the family lacked food, utilities, or adequate clothing." The defendant "ate lead paint chips at certain points in his youth." There was "pervasive drug use in the home and … heavy gang presence in their neighborhood." School records reflected substantial absences from school, which his mother testified were "caused by his unstable family circumstances." Counsel did not discover this information because "counsel did not inquire into [the defendant's] background in any meaningful fashion." Counsel did not obtain school and hospital records and had only "brief and perfunctory discussions" with the family "between the guilt and penalty phases" of trial and "did not inquire into family dynamics or background." Counsel retained a mental health expert to evaluate capacity to understand *Miranda* warnings, but did not talk to the expert after receiving his report or inquire about the tests administered or anything the expert learned about the defendant's background. Counsel's conduct was deficient.

> We do not doubt that the prospect of representing a defendant at a capital penalty phase hearing can overwhelm even experienced lawyers. Nor does it surprise us that a first-degree murder verdict would disappoint defense attorneys who have worked hard during a trial. But that does not excuse trial counsel's failure to prepare for the penalty phase prior to the handing down of the conviction. These attorneys, particularly in the face of a record so full of testimony calling for a first-degree murder verdict, should not have waited until the eve of the penalty phase to begin their preparations.

Id. at . Because counsel did not obtain "readily available" school and medical records and did not "conduct a meaningful inquiry into [the defendant's] family life," they "failed to give their consulting expert sufficient information to evaluate [the defendant] accurately."

> Trial counsel did not investigate possible mitigating circumstances or ask experts to do so. Instead, counsel conducted an *ad hoc* and perfunctory preparation for the penalty phase *the night before it began.* Their "strategy" relied on an uninformed guess as to the best available way to present [the defendant] to the jury. We will not excuse this conduct on the ground that [the defendant] and his family members did not tell counsel that his background provided fertile territory for mitigation arguments. Neither [the defendant] nor his family had a duty to instruct counsel how to perform such a basic element of competent representation as the inquiry into a defendant's background. They did not, as the Commonwealth suggests, have to volunteer "red flags" about [the defendant's] mental health when trial counsel should have discovered that information through a basic inquiry into his background.

Id. at (citing and quoting the American Bar Association's Guideline for Appointment and Performance of Counsel in Death Penalty Cases). Counsel, here, "neither began their investigation at an appropriate time nor attempted to discover reasonably available mitigation evidence. They thus failed to meet prevailing standards of timeliness and quality." Counsel compounded this error by deciding at the eleventh hour for co-counsel with no capital experience to take full responsibility for sentencing. "[N]o amount of good intentions makes up for his lack of experience and preparation." The state court "applied *Strickland* in an objectively unreasonable fashion in concluding that counsel performed adequately." The state court holding also rested "in part on the unreasonable factual determination that trial counsel began meaningful preparations for the penalty phase at a point prior to the eve of the penalty phase. The record includes no evidence to that end." The state court also "incorrectly" relied on strategy.

> It is difficult to call … counsel's decisions "strategic" when they failed to seek rudimentary background information about [the defendant]. Strategy is the result of planning informed by investigation, not guesswork.

Id. at . If counsel had performed adequately, the evidence would have established: (1) neglect, along with physical and psychological abuse, as a child; (2) severe cognitive impairments, likely from birth; (3) ingestion of lead paint chips, as well as fetal alcoholism, are consistent with a finding of organic mental deficit; and (4) Post Traumatic Stress Disorder ("PTSD"), caused by the abuse he suffered as a child, being attacked by gang members, and/or the stillborn birth of one of his children. If counsel had performed adequately, the evidence would have supported two statutory mitigating circumstances ("under the influence of extreme mental or emotional disturbance" and substantially impaired capacity "to appreciate the criminality of his conduct or to conform his conduct to the requirements of law") and the catch-all mitigating circumstance. The state court's conclusion that the state's expert had thoroughly refuted the defense experts in post-conviction, "rendering any claim based on their testimony 'meritless,' … rests on an unreasonable factual determination." "[C]ounsel could have obtained testimony from family members that would have given the jury a very different impression than that left by the other penalty phase testimony. This testimony would not contradict earlier testimony, but rather provide details not uncovered by trial counsel at the penalty phase hearing." The state court found no prejudice.

> That court apparently equated the paltry testimony at the penalty phase hearing with the vastly expanded testimony provided by friends and family members at the PCRA hearing. The two sets of testimony brook no comparison. The first left the impression that [the defendant] came from a supportive (if poor) family but went on a crime spree after the type of disappointments many people face in life. The second showed that he had grown up in an extraordinarily dysfunctional environment rife with abuse and neglect. The penalty phase testimony may have suggested some difficulties during [his] youth, but this does not prevent relief. *Strickland* permits relief where, as here, trial counsel presented some mitigation evidence but could have introduced evidence that was upgraded dramatically in quality and quantity. The PCRA court's conclusion that [the defendant] had failed to show prejudice, however construed, either reflects an unreasonable determination of fact (in the comparison of the two sets of testimony) or an objectively unreasonable application of controlling law (in denying relief on the basis that [the defendant] already had presented some mitigating evidence).

Id. at .

> A reasonable lawyer who understood [the defendant's] life history would not have proceeded on the theory that he had led a productive life before going on a crime spree as a result of a series of disappointments. Such an attorney instead would have presented evidence to the jury of [the defendant's] abusive and neglectful family life, his low intelligence, and his psychiatric and psychological problems. There is a reasonable probability that this different course, even in the face of competing expert testimony introduced by the Commonwealth, would have resulted in the imposition of a life sentence.

Id. at .

Gray v. Branker, 529 F.3d 220 (4th Cir. 2008) (sentenced in December 1993). Under AEDPA, counsel was ineffective in capital sentencing for failing to adequately prepare and present mental health evidence. The defendant, who was a dentist or "prosperous professional" (as noted by the dissenting judge) represented by retained counsel, was charged with killing his wife during ongoing, bitter divorce proceedings. Counsel's conduct was deficient because counsel was aware from the divorce proceedings, from the defendant's behavior in pretrial confinement, and from a five-week court-appointed evaluation of mental health issues, but only talked to the defendant once, pre-indictment and prior to the state's notice of intent to seek death, about the need to retain an independent mental health expert.

> Defense counsel should not have dispensed with a mental health investigation just because Gray did not want to hire an independent psychiatrist at the pre-indictment stage, well before the state announced its intention to seek the death penalty. *See* ABA Guideline 11.4.1.C ("The investigation for preparation of the sentencing phase should be conducted regardless of any initial assertion by the client that mitigation is not to be offered.").

Here, the court-appointed examiner had offered additional assistance at no charge. Additionally, counsel did not "seek court approval to hire an independent psychiatrist at state expense when [the defendant] became indigent shortly after his indictment" or even after the jury returned a guilty verdict and the defendant faced the certainty of a capital sentencing proceeding. Counsel's conduct was not excused by strategy. "There was simply no consideration of whether a defense based on psychiatric evidence might be a strategy worth exploring," before pursuing " a questionable alibi theory until days before trial" and then pursuing an accident theory. Counsel "simply missed or ignored-and failed to act on-the many signs that [the defendant] was mentally and emotionally unstable." The state court finding to the contrary was an unreasonable application of *Strickland* because the state court "failed to consider the reasonableness of counsel's actual performance under prevailing professional norms, which include the duty to make considered decisions about areas of potential investigation. The state court also erroneously found that the accident defense and the diminished mental responsibility defense were inconsistent, when "common sense dictates" to the contrary in this case. The state court also "overlooked" the mental health testimony that would have been available and unreasonably "relied heavily on [the defendant's] one-time refusal to hire an independent psychiatrist." "[A] reasonable lawyer would not rely on his client's self-assessment of his mental health, especially in a capital case. There was an independent duty to investigate." The state court held that the defendant was not indigent, but this finding was rebutted by clear and convincing evidence that he was in fact indigent at the time of trial, having placed all of his assets in an irrevocable trust for his children six months earlier." Finally, regardless of financial status, the court-appointed examiner had offered additional assistance without charge. *Schriro v. Landrigan* does not require a contrary conclusion, because '[n]othing in *Schriro* permits [the defendant's] statement to be used to relieve his counsel of their duty to investigate for mitigating mental health evidence." With respect to prejudice, the state court "required *certainty* that the jury would have reached a different result at sentencing," which is contrary to *Strickland*'s "reasonable probability" standard. The state court decision was also an unreasonable application of *Strickland* because the state court relied on determinations that the court had instructed the jury on mental health mitigating evidence and the state had presented contrary lay evidence. The state court did so without mention, as *Williams* requires, of the mitigation evidence presented at trial and by improperly discounting the evidence that could have been presented in mitigation. Independent review established prejudice. The defendant had already presented mitigation evidence establishing the defendant was a loving and dedicated father and son, who contributed to the community as a Little League baseball coach. He had no prior offenses, cooperated with law enforcement, and behaved well in confinement. The defense presented no mental health evidence, even though "[e]vidence of mental disturbance ... can be persuasive mitigating evidence for jurors considering the death penalty, and this evidence can determine the outcome." *Id.* at (citing 2003 ABA Guidelines and capital jury study article). Here, "the two mental health mitigating factors–largely ignored by defense counsel–were [the defendant's] best hope of convincing the jury that he did not deserve the death penalty." If counsel had adequately investigated, the evidence would have revealed a diagnosis of paranoid personality disorder and adjustment disorder, with the possibility of "psychotic episodes" under severe stressors, such as faced by the defendant at the time of the offense. "The jury would have known that he suffered from a severe mental illness" when he killed his wife.

*Johnson v. Bagley, 544 F.3d 592 (6th Cir. 2008) (tried and sentenced in May 1998). Under AEDPA, counsel "committed legal malpractice–or, what is worse, legal representation that amounts to constitutionally ineffective assistance–" in failing to adequately investigate and present mitigation evidence. Citing the 2003 ABA Guidelines for the Appointment and Performance of Counsel in Death Penalty Cases, the court observed that counsel had complied on a "surface level" in making the petitioner's grandmother as a positive caretaker the central theme of their sentencing strategy.

> In the abstract, this might well have been a legitimate strategic decision, one about which the Constitution would have nothing to say. But in [petitioner's] case, his counsel pursued this strategy after what can only be described as an anemic and leaderless investigation that suffered from at least three conspicuous flaws.

First, counsel never interviewed the petitioner's mother, even though counsel knew of her whereabouts. Counsel "chose" not to interview her because she had a bad background as a prostitute and drug addict and would make a bad witness.

> But [the mother's] "bad background" is precisely what should have prompted the defense team to interview her–both to see what that background entailed and to learn more fully how her prostitution and drug addiction affected [the petitioner's] childhood. That someone may make a bad witness is no explanation for not interviewing her first. And, that is particularly true with respect to this witness, who was [the petitioner's] *mother*, not a distant aunt or neighbor.

Second, counsel obtained a 12 inch thick stack of Department of Human Services (DHS) records shortly before sentencing and, without reading them, submitted them to the jury. Many of these pages were not relevant to the petitioner. Some of the records indicated concerns about the grandmother's abusive history and placing the petitioner in her care.

> A review of the records, in short, not only would have tipped them off to a different mitigation strategy but also would have avoided the pitfall of submitting records to the jury, that directly contradicted their theory that [the grandmother] was a positive force for change in his life.

Third, "these investigative blunders occurred because no one who participated in [the] penalty-phase defense made *any* deliberate decisions about the scope of the investigation, let alone the 'reasonable' ones *Strickland* requires." Counsel gave the two "alleged mitigation specialists" an initial set of names for interviews but were otherwise "not involved in the investigation" and only began thinking about "a mitigation strategy" after the petitioner was convicted. The "lead" mitigation specialist was "in the midst of a debilitating bout of depression" that ultimately resulted in suspension from the practice of law. He, "it seems clear, was almost certainly not making any significant decisions, reasonable or otherwise, regarding the scope of ... investigation." The other "alleged mitigation specialist," a graduate student with limited experience and working part-time interviewed only the witnesses on the list counsel initially gave him and gave only his notes to the defense expert. The state court's finding that counsel's conduct was not deficient was an unreasonable application of *Strickland* in finding that counsel had discovered the relevant evidence as shown by the sentencing evidence. "[T]he testimony only scratched the surface of [petitioner's] horrific childhood." While some information may have been included in the records submitted, "that does not mean defense counsel performed a reasonable investigation or for that matter reasonably used the evidence."

> [D]efense counsel was not familiar with the records; some of the records contradicted their mitigation strategy ...; and it hardly constitutes a reasonable investigation and mitigation strategy simply to obtain ... records from the State, then dump the whole file in front of the jury without organizing the files, reading them, eliminating irrelevant files or explaining to the jury how or why they are relevant.

The state court also unreasonably concluded that counsel performed adequately "without looking to the reasonableness of the investigation's scope." While counsel had presented testimony of five people about the petitioner's "troubled past" and presented an expert witness, "an unreasonably truncated mitigation investigation is not cured simply because some steps were taken prior to the penalty-phase hearing and because some evidence was placed before the jury."

> Buttressed by a reasonably adequate investigation, the defense team's ultimate presentation to the jury might have been justified as the product of strategic choice. But, that is not what happened. [Petitioner's] attorneys "were not in a position to make ... reasonable strategic choice[s] ... because the investigation supporting their choice[s] was unreasonable." *Wiggins*, 539 U.S. at 536; *Strickland*, 466 U.S. at 690-91.

Counsel's conduct was also not excused because their interviews did not yield information about the grandmother's abusive history or negative influence on the petitioner. "Uncooperative defendants and family members ... do not shield a mitigation investigation (even under AEDPA's deferential standards) if the attorneys unreasonably failed to utilize other available sources that would have undermined or contradicted information received." Because the state court did not address prejudice, the court reviewed this issue *de novo*. Counsel's errors, "particularly their lack of investigation, had a serious impact on the mitigation theory presented to the jury." First, there was "a goldmine of mitigating evidence showing that [the grandmother] was anything but a saint." She had schizoid personality disorder, had no maternal instincts, was abusive to her daughter, and allowed her daughter to be raped by a friend. While petitioner "was an indirect victim" of the neglect and abuse of his mother, "he was a direct victim as well." The grandmother was emotionally and physically abusive to him. Thus, the jury was misled to believe that she was a positive influence. Second, counsel "could have presented a detailed and horrific picture" of petitioner's mother's role in his life. She was portrayed in sentencing as "a mostly absent mother, when the truth is that her early abuse and on-again-off-again presence in his life had an irreparable and devastating impact on [him]. The evidence would have shown: (1) she was a prostitute who sold herself to buy drugs; (2) she often fed him only sugar water; (3) when he cried, she would put him in a closet and give him beer and pain killers to make him stop crying; (4) she was physically abusive, even putting a cigarette out on his eye, and threatened to kill him; (5) she was involved in many abusive relationships and tried to set fire to petitioner's father at one time; (6) she taught petitioner to cut cocaine, cook it into crack and sell it; and (7) she killed one of her abusive boyfriends and bragged to petitioner about it.

> Yet, due to counsel's bungling or sheer laziness, the jury heard none of this. "I and the public know [w]hat all schoolchildren learn," it has been said, "[t]hose to whom evil is done [d]o evil in return." W.H. Auden, "September 1, 1939." While these words may not capture a satisfactory theory of morality, they assuredly suggest a plausible theory for sparing a life at a mitigation hearing, *see* ABA Guideline 10.11(F)(1)-(2), one that on this remarkable record could well have affected a juror's vote in the case.

Third, counsel's failure to investigate led to damaging testimony from the defense expert, who diagnosed antisocial personality disorder and testified that the petitioner was not remorseful. "This unhelpful testimony could have been prevented" with a complete background picture. The defense expert "then might have been able to say, as [the PCR expert] did … , that [petitioner's] 'chaotic, abusive, neglectful' family 'play[ed] a significant role in the development of [his] personality and his addiction to alcohol and drugs and later mental illness," such that his "psychological profile is 'almost identical' to that of his mother."

> Defense attorneys, we recognize, are not obligated to shop for "the 'best' experts" who will testify in the most advantageous way possible. But it is unreasonable, after an incomplete investigation, to put an expert on the stand who will "directly contradict[] the sole defense theory" and "render worthless" other helpful testimony."

Id. (citations omitted). This is especially so when the prosecution even points out in closing that the expert testimony is harmful to the defense. In sum, "this post-conviction evidence differs from that heard by the jury not only in degree but also in kind, and forms a mitigation story that 'bears no relation' to the story the jury heard." Even though some of this information was in the documents submitted to the jury, "this jury was given no basis for construing and digesting this information" because no mitigation witness ever referred to the 12-inch thick records and counsel simply told the jury to "leaf through" them, which "likely would have discouraged the jury from reading more closely" and the references to the grandmother's "deficiencies were few."

Mason v. Mitchell, 543 F.3d 766 (6th Cir. 2008) (sentenced in June 1994). Under AEDPA (and citing the ABA Guidelines for the Appointment and Performance of Counsel in Death Penalty Cases (1989)), counsel was ineffective in failing to adequately investigate and present mitigation evidence. Counsel presented only brief testimony of adaptability to confinement, family member requests for mercy, and the defendant's unsworn denial of guilt. Counsel's decision to limit the defense presentation "to appeals for mercy and claims of residual doubt" was made after the conviction during a phone call with members of the Ohio Public Defender Office. "Therefore, the evaluation of [counsel's] performance must focus on what knowledge [counsel] then possessed regarding [the petitioner's] childhood and background and what investigation and interviews, if any, that [counsel] had performed prior to making that decision." Counsel met with the petitioner and his wife several times but did not really discuss mitigation. Counsel had been denied a mitigation investigator from the Public Defender Office and denied funding from the court. He was provided only with a brief psychiatric examination limited to "potential for rehabilitation and the likelihood of future dangerousness." He was provided voluminous records by the state concerning criminal history, involvement by Children's Services, drug treatment programs, and some educational records. From this, counsel was aware that: (1) petitioner was born into a drug-dependent family; (2) the family was involved in drug trafficking; (3) both parents had been incarcerated on trafficking charges; (4) petitioner had been exposed to a lot of violence; and (5) petitioner had prior injuries and scars he told police were due to beatings from his father. Counsel had only brief phone calls with a person at Children's Services and the petitioner's probation officer. Counsel's time records reflected only "very brief" contacts with some family members *after* that phone call. He *never* contacted some of petitioner's siblings. And, at most may have talked briefly with the petitioner's father and a brother, whose "statements appear to contradict the ample documentary evidence" already provided by the state in discovery. The failure to investigate further "is inexcusable given this apparent contrast between the facts contained in the documentary evidence and what he apparently learned" from the petitioner's father and brother.

> [Counsel's] efforts consisted of no more than reviewing documents provided by the state, arranging for a psychiatric evaluation limited to predicting [petitioner's] future dangerousness, talking to Mason himself, and very briefly talking to a small subset of [petitioner's] family members. Under the Supreme Court's governing case law regarding counsel's obligation to undertake a reasonable investigation to support strategic decisions about the presentation of mitigation evidence, we have no doubt that the performance of [petitioner's] counsel was deficient.

Prejudice established.

> [Petitioner] need only have persuaded one juror not to impose the death penalty, and [Petitioner's] jury initially reported a deadlock regarding his sentence. Even a slightly more compelling case for mitigation thus might have altered the outcome of the sentencing phase of [the petitioner's] trial.

If counsel had performed adequately, the evidence would have established: (1) petitioner's father ran a prostitution ring and a home-based drug business with 10 employees; (2) both of petitioner's parents were drug users and traffickers; (3) petitioner's mother shot his father; (4) petitioner's parents abused him and isolated him from anyone not associated with their drug dealing activities; (5) petitioner began using drugs at eight years old; (6) petitioner's father included him on drug trafficking trips when he was in junior high; and (7) petitioner has "a borderline personality disorder largely as a result of his dysfunctional home environment." This evidence would not necessarily have opened the door to damaging prosecution rebuttal evidence, which is permitted under state law only to rebut good character or rehabilitation potential evidence. The state court "unreasonably applied the *Strickland* standard" because the state court ignored the *Strickland* principle that "strategic choices made after less than complete investigation are reasonable precisely to the extent that reasonable professional judgments support the limitations on investigation." *Id.* (quoting *Strickland*, 466 U.S. at 690-91). Here, the state court "simply asserted that ... counsel had made a strategic decision regarding mitigation strategy, but that court failed to assess whether a thorough and reasonable investigation supported counsel's strategic decision." The state court's prejudice analysis was also "flawed and objectively unreasonable" because the court relied on the possibility of the state presenting rebuttal evidence to good character or rehabilitative potential evidence, which was "a mitigation strategy that [petitioner] was not advocating."

Jells v. Mitchell, 538 F.3d 478 (6th Cir. 2008) (sentenced in October 1987). Under AEDPA, counsel ineffective in failing to adequately investigate and present mitigation evidence. In so holding, the court observed: "the deference owed to counsel's strategic judgments about mitigation is directly proportional to the adequacy of the investigations supporting such judgments." Counsel's conduct was deficient in failing to timely prepare for sentencing and in failing to utilize a mitigation specialist to gather information about the defendant's background, including his educational, medical, psychological, and social history. Counsel did not contact a mental health expert until two days after conviction and 16 days prior to the mitigation hearing. Counsel did not provide the expert with "personal history records–records that would have been collected had they uses a mitigation specialist–that were necessary for the evaluation." In addition, counsel interviewed only three family members, "neglecting to speak with many other family member who had lived with [the petitioner] and were available. When speaking with the family members they did contact, their inquiry was brief and they failed to ask sufficiently probing questions; as a result they failed to discover the abuse that [the petitioner] received from his mother's live-in boyfriend and his stepfather." Counsel also failed to obtain a prior psychological report and accessible school records that revealed mental impairments. Counsel's conduct was also deficient "[i]n the context of [the petitioner's] case" in "failing to use a mitigation specialist." "While [petitioner's] counsel did not have a specific obligation to employ a mitigation specialist, they did have an obligation to fully investigate the possible mitigation evidence available." Under state law, "the range of potential mitigation evidence is quite broad." Thus, "defense counsel must conduct a reasonably thorough investigation into all possible mitigation evidence that would present a sympathetic picture of the defendant's family, social, and psychological background." Counsel conducted some investigation and made a "limited presentation of [petitioner's] unstable childhood and academic difficulties." Counsel's awareness of this limited information "should have alerted them that further investigation by a mitigation specialist might [have] proved fruitful." Counsel's failure to investigate prior to the conviction was objectively unreasonable under *Strickland* and the state court's finding to the contrary was an unreasonable application of *Strickland*. Prejudice established because "there is a reasonable probability that at least one of the [three state sentencing panel] judges may have reached a different conclusion regarding the imposition of the death penalty." Available but unpresented evidence "paints a significantly more detailed picture of [the petitioner's] troubled background." While trial counsel presented evidence of essentially a normal childhood, an IQ of 77, and no antisocial personality disorder or mental illness, petitioner had "a history of serious cognitive learning and socialization impairment" that amounted essentially to academic problems that resulted in behavioral problems with "several missed opportunities" to resolve the problems "through special education and remedial classes." These educational problems were compounded by his home. The defendant was one of seven children and his mother constantly moved in and out of relationships with abusive men making the petitioner "a witness to ... violence and cruelty" inflicted on his mother. "In short, rather than being cumulative, this evidence provides a more nuanced understanding of [petitioner's] psychological background and presents a more sympathetic picture of [him]." The state court's finding of no prejudice was unreasonable.

***Sechrest v. Ignacio**, 549 F.3d 789 (9th Cir. 2008) (sentenced in Sep. 1983). In pre-AEDPA case, counsel was ineffective in sentencing for three reasons. First, counsel permitted the prosecution to review and introduce into evidence the confidential report of a defense-retained expert counsel decided not to present as a witness. The report contained information about the defendant's "criminal history and his upbringing" revealed only to this doctor, who diagnosed a "polymorphous perversion." Counsel's conduct was deficient because the state would not have had access to this information otherwise and "defense counsel had absolutely no obligation to disclose [the] confidential report to the prosecution." Second, counsel erred in allowing the prosecution to call the defense expert as a witness.

> [C]ounsel should not have stipulated to the prosecutor calling [the same defense- retained expert] *as a witness for the prosecution*. Counsel's decision to so stipulate is indefensible. This decision put counsel in the difficult position of having to cross-examine the only mental health expert to testify during the penalty phase of ... trial, even though counsel himself had chosen [the expert] and supplied him with information about [the defendant]. Furthermore, the jury was told that [the expert] was hired by the *defense* to examine [the defendant] and report on his mental health. Given that the defense's expert not only had nothing favorable to say about [the defendant], but thought that he was beyond all hope of rehabilitation, the jurors had even less incentive to impose a sentence that they were told [improperly] by the prosecutor and the court might lead to [the defendant's] eventual release.

Id. at . Counsel's alleged strategy for not objecting was the belief that the witness would provide helpful information on the defendant's troubled background, but this was not "a sound strategic decision" because [i]f counsel truly believed that [the] testimony would be helpful, the appropriate 'strategic decision' would have been to call [the expert] to testify on behalf of the defense." In addition, counsel did not pursue or argue any mitigating factors related to troubled background. "Given these considerations, counsel cannot hide behind a later, implausible assertion that his decision was 'tactical' given that his actions show that he had no intention of presenting any mitigating evidence based on ... mental health." Finally, counsel inadequately prepared for the expert testimony. "Once counsel decided to allow the prosecution to call [the defense expert] as a witness, counsel had a duty to prepare for [the] testimony." Counsel did not speak to the expert after agreeing to let him testify for the state, which was evident in "counsel's lackluster performance at trial" eliciting on cross that the defendant could not be cured or treated. "In sum, some of the most damaging testimony presented during the penalty phase of trial was elicited by [the defendant's] own counsel, from a witness [defense] counsel had originally selected and could have prevented from testifying." Prejudice found because the expert's testimony "likely played an important role in the jury's verdict imposing the death penalty." Reversal was also required due to a due process violation in the prosecutor repeatedly making false, inflammatory statements indicating that the state board of pardon commissioners could release petitioner if the jury did not return a verdict imposing the death penalty.

Correll v. Ryan, 539 F.3d 938 (9th Cir. 2008) (tried in 1984). Under pre-AEDPA law, counsel ineffective in capital sentencing for failing to adequately investigate and present evidence of the petitioner's mental health and failing to present mitigation evidence. Counsel's conduct was deficient in numerous respects. Counsel knew the petitioner "came from a dysfunctional family, sustained a serious head injury, was committed to various psychiatric facilities, and that he was addicted to drugs; yet defense counsel did not obtain the records nor did he interview witnesses concerning these matters." Counsel only met with the petitioner possibly once and with the petitioner's father, sister, and brother once and at the same time. He did not obtain school records, police reports on prior convictions, records from the California Youth Authority, medical records, or psychiatric records. "As anemic as the defense counsel's investigation was, his presentation of mitigating evidence at the penalty phase was worse." Counsel presented no evidence, which mandated the death penalty under Arizona law because the defendant had a qualifying prior conviction and no mitigation. Defense counsel's mitigation argument did not even attempt to rebut three of the five aggravating factors urged by the State. "The entirety of his oral argument at the penalty phase consists of approximately 7 pages of transcript." "Given his virtual concession of most of the aggravating factors argued by the State, and waiver of the presentation of mitigation evidence, the outcome was obvious: imposition of the death penalty." Prejudice found because, if counsel had adequately investigated, the evidence would have established the petitioner endured an abusive childhood in which he was neglected by his mother, who spent most of her time at church. The children were physically punished if they did not understand religious doctrine. There was incest in the family. A brick wall collapsed on the petitioner's head when he was seven causing unconsciousness for some time, but no medical treatment was sought for several days. The petitioner began "self-medication" by experimenting with alcohol and drugs around age ten and was using marijuana, LSD, and amphetamines regularly by age twelve. The petitioner's parents responded by beating him and threatening to kick him out. After the petitioner was shot at age 14, his parents asked the state to terminate their parental rights and cut off all communication with him. He became a ward of the state and spent his teenage years "in various state institutions described as 'gladiator schools,' which were characterized as cruel and inhumane, even by those who worked there." Within months, he became addicted to heroin. He was committed to psychiatric institutions at least twice during his teen years and was described at age 16 as "severely psychologically impaired." He was treated with a tranquilizer/anti-psychotic drug while institutionalized, and attempted suicide on two occasions. By the time of the crimes, he was injecting a quarter gram to a gram of methamphetamine in one shot, and injecting three to four shots a day. He would go seven to ten days without sleep, followed by one to two days of continuous sleep. Expert testimony indicated that he was likely having impulse control problems and judgment impairment at the time of the crime, and may have been experiencing drug-induced paranoia. Counsel did not pursue "the classic mitigation evidence," because "he didn't think of the evidence as favorable evidence. However, it is precisely this type of evidence that the Supreme Court has termed as 'powerful.'" *Id.* (quoting *Wiggins*). While counsel also appeared to be afraid of the particular judge's reaction to the evidence, "this presumes that the judge would not follow the law–speculation that is never appropriate and that is not supported by the record here" and also ignores the fact that, under state law, the Arizona Supreme Court independently reviews the aggravating and mitigating factors and re-weighs them and conducts a proportionately review.

Williams v. Allen, 542 F.3d 1326 (11th Cir. 2008) (sentenced in April 1990). Under AEDPA, counsel ineffective in capital sentencing for failing to adequately investigate and present mitigation.

Counsel's conduct was deficient because counsel was aware of: (1) a report by a defense psychologist, who examined only competence and mental state at the time of the offenses, that the defendant had an IQ of 83 and exhibited signs of personality disorder and depression; (2) a presentencing report describing the petitioner's father as an abusive alcoholic and referring to previous psychological evaluations of the petitioner; and (3) petitioner's mother's statements. Counsel's "failure to broaden the scope of their investigation beyond these sources was unreasonable under prevailing professional norms" in the ABA Guidelines. "A reasonable investigation into the leads in this case should have included, at a minimum, interviewing other family who could corroborate the evidence of abuse and speak to the resulting impact on [the petitioner]. Counsel, however, failed to contact such witnesses."

> Counsel uncovered nothing in their limited inquiry ... to suggest that "further investigation would have been fruitless." *Wiggins*, 539 U.S. at 525, 123 S. Ct. At 2537. To the contrary, the many red flags ... would have prompted a reasonable attorney to conduct additional investigation. Moreover, acquiring additional mitigating evidence would have been consistent with the penalty phase strategy that counsel ultimately adopted. Given that counsel's sentencing case focused on establishing ... a troubled background, they had every incentive to develop the strongest mitigation case possible. *Cf. id.* at 526, 123 S. Ct. 2538. It is thus apparent that counsel's failure to expand their investigation "resulted from inattention, not reasoned strategic judgment." *Id.* at 526, 123 S. Ct. 2537.

The state court decision unreasonably applied *Strickland* by focusing "entirely on counsel's decision not to present additional mitigating evidence" without addressing "whether counsel's *investigation* into such evidence was adequate under prevailing professional norms." While other family members were available for interview, counsel relied only on the petitioner's mother, who was the sole mitigation witness, to provide "brief testimony" about the petitioner's childhood. "By choosing to rely entirely on her account, trial counsel obtained an incomplete and misleading understanding of [the petitioner's] life history." Prejudice established.

> The mitigation evidence that ... trial counsel failed to discover paints a vastly different picture of [the petitioner's] background than that created by [his mother's] abbreviated testimony. ... [T]he violence experienced by [the petitioner] as a child far exceeded–in both frequency and severity–the punishments described at sentencing. ... Moreover, contrary to the impression created by [the petitioner's mother], this violence was not of a type remotely associated with ordinary parental discipline. ... This evidence surely would have been relevant to an assessment of [the petitioner's] culpability, particularly in light of his age [nineteen] and lack of prior criminal history.

In addition, the trial court, in overriding the jury's nine to three recommendation for life, "expressly relied" upon the mother's testimony in "discounting the significance of the abuse described at sentencing." The available but unpresented mitigation evidence contradicted this finding. Prejudice was also clear because "this case is not highly aggravated." The state court's finding of no prejudice was an unreasonable application of *Strickland*" because of the "court's emphasis on the absence of a 'causal relationship' between [the] mitigating evidence and the statutory aggravator." The state court also "rested its prejudice determination on the fact that ... mitigating evidence did not undermine or rebut the evidence supporting the aggravating circumstances" without considering the "possibility that the mitigating evidence, taken as a whole, might have altered the trial judge's appraisal of ... moral culpability, notwithstanding that the evidence did not relate to his eligibility for the death penalty." The court rejected the trial court's "post-hoc statements" that additional evidence would not have impacted his decision because "the assessment should be based on an objective standard that presumes a reasonable decisionmaker."

2007: ***Morales v. Mitchell***, 507 F.3d 916 (6th Cir. 2007) (tried in December 1985). Under AEDPA, counsel was ineffective in failing to adequately investigate and present mitigation. Counsel's conduct was deficient because counsel failed to interview the petitioner's family, friends, and others who knew him; failed to obtain any background records; failed to retain a mitigation expert; and failed to adequately prepare the petitioner for his unsworn statement in sentencing. The state court's finding that counsel's conduct was not deficient was an unreasonable application of clearly established constitutional law. Because the state court did not address the issue of prejudice, the federal court's review of prejudice was *de novo*. Prejudice established because counsel presented no sworn testimony or evidence, made no opening statement, and made a closing statement that was a mere three pages long during the penalty phase. The jury was provided only with an unprepared unsworn statement by the petitioner. If counsel had adequately investigated, a number of family members and a former principal at the petitioner's school would have testified and documentary evidence was available to corroborate information about the alcohol abuse of the Petitioner's parents, his abuse by an older mentally retarded brother, his mentally disturbed sister's suicide when he was only nine, his mother's emotional problems, and the effect and role of alcohol, drugs, and Native American culture on him.

Haliym v. Mitchell, 492 F.3d 680 (6th Cir. 2007) (tried in September 1987). Under AEDPA, counsel ineffective in capital sentencing for failing to adequately prepare and present mitigation. Counsel presented three witnesses in sentencing along with an unsworn statement from the defendant. A former employer testified that the defendant was a good employee. A psychiatrist, who spent only one and a half hours with the defendant and relied on pretrial court-appointed competence and sanity reports, testified that the defendant was diagnosed with an "adjustment disorder with depressed moods" and "malingering," but that the defendant does not have a mental disease or defect. Finally, the defendant's grandmother testified that the defendant lost both his parents and a brother over a two-month period. His father died of a heroin overdose and his brother was shot. Counsel's conduct was deficient in failing to conduct "even the most basic interviews" with the defendant's family members concerning the family background, even though counsel knew the defendant's father died of a heroin overdose. "It is not the usual case where a parent copes with an addiction as serious and controlling as a heroin addiction without repercussions, often serious repercussions, being felt by the remaining family members." Even basic interviews would have revealed a family history filled with the father's physical abuse, which is "an important mitigation factor." Counsel instead presented inconsistent evidence in the defendant's statement that his parents were wonderful and in a doctor's report that the defendant denied any physical abuse. Counsel also was aware that the defendant had attempted suicide by shooting himself in the left temple, "which should have strongly suggested the need to investigate whether Petitioner had a mental defect." Instead, counsel presented evidence that the defendant had no mental disease or defect when "the limited time that [the doctor] spent with Petitioner–a mere hour and a half–sharply hindered his ability to make any independent analysis of Petitioner's mental health." The court also noted that counsel's performance fell short of the 2003

ABA Guidelines. Counsel's failure to investigate "was unlikely the result of a strategic choice. Despite the availability of funding to procure experts chosen by Petitioner at the mitigation phase, ... Petitioner's attorneys nevertheless relied upon the presentence report" of a court-appointed expert and the inadequate testimony of the expert witness presented.

> Had Petitioner's counsel taken an active role in procuring an expert to investigate Petitioner and author a report for mitigation, evidence of Petitioner's social history and brain injury would likely have come before the trial court. We can fathom no strategic reason for Petitioner's counsel's failure in this regard.

Prejudice found because adequate investigation would have revealed significant mitigation, including the defendant's father's violence against the defendant and his family, the loss of both parents and a brother when the defendant was only a teenager, which affected the defendant profoundly. Shortly afterwards, he started using heroin, leading to a drug addiction. He also became severely depressed and shot himself causing a serious brain injury and functional brain impairment, which causes problems with impulsivity, judgment, and problem solving. There is a reasonable probability that this evidence would have led to a different result before the three-judge sentencing panel, which would likely have reached a different result with evidence of a mental disease or defect.

Stevens v. McBride, 489 F.3d 883 (7th Cir. 2007) (crimes in July 1993 and affirmed on appeal in 1997). Under AEDPA, counsel ineffective in capital sentencing for failing to adequately prepare and present mental health expert and presenting the testimony of an "expert" counsel believed to be a "quack," which was very prejudicial. The defendant, described in the first sentence of the opinion as "an emotionally disturbed young man who had been abused and raped as a child," was sentenced to death for "the molestation and brutal murder" of a 10-year-old boy. He also had a prior molestation conviction for which he was on parole at the time. Prior to trial counsel retained "a defense mitigation specialist" and were aware of obvious mental health issues due to the defendant's physical, mental, and emotional abuse and his rape as a child. Medical records reflected that he had been held in a psychiatric facility following an attempted suicide and that he had been diagnosed with major depression and possible schizophrenia. The defendant also disclosed to the mitigation specialist that, at the time of the murder, he put himself in the victim's place because he had wished that the man who raped him had also killed him. Based on the mitigation specialist's recommendation, counsel retained a psychologist, who at the time was director of a child and adolescent psychiatric center. Counsel met with the doctor and asked him to evaluate the defendant but not to prepare a report. The doctor wrote a report anyway which included very prejudicial information such as no mental illness, molestation of 25-30 children, a prior murder (later recanted), lack of acceptance of responsibility, committing this murder for the purpose of avoiding a return to prison, a diagnosis of pedophilia, and future dangerousness. Counsel contacted the doctor, who said basically that he would make a good witness for them despite his report. Counsel also learned that the doctor believed that "mental illness" is a "myth" and used a "therapeutic technique described as "putting 18-year-olds on his lap and sticking a bottle in their mouth." Counsel then had "well- founded doubts" about the doctor's "fitness as a defense expert" and believed he was a "quack." Counsel's conduct was deficient though because counsel did not seek a different mental health expert and provided the state with this doctor's report prior to trial (when counsel was only required to disclose reports from expert *witnesses* who would be called to testify). During trial, rather than pursuing a mental illness defense, counsel argued a voluntary manslaughter theory, but the court refused to even charge on manslaughter. In the penalty phase before the jury, counsel presented testimony from the defendant and some family members and then called the "quack" to testify. His testimony extensively covered the doctor's beliefs and theories and some testimony about the defendant's "terrible childhood" and abuse. His testimony did not, however, provide any evaluation of the defendant's mental health at the time of the offenses. On cross, the state questioned the doctor extensively on his report, which he confirmed. The quack volunteered that the defendant had "antisocial qualities and sociopathic traits." In response to questions from the state, the doctor also confirmed that the defendant had admitted to him that he was sexually aroused by killing the child and had masturbated on the child's body. The doctor had not even disclosed this last information to defense counsel. After the jury recommended death, counsel called the doctor to testify yet again in sentencing before the judge. This time he added that the defendant posed "a great risk to society." The defendant challenged counsel's ineffectiveness for failing to present a mental health defense during trial and in mitigation. The state argued essentially that counsel was entitled to rely on their "expert" without seeking an additional expert because he was a qualified doctor. The court rejected this because "the general qualifications of an expert witness do not guarantee that the witness will provide proficient assistance in any given instance." The problem in this case arose due to the "methods" the doctor used, "his idiosyncratic view of mental disorders," and "the fact that [his] views favored the prosecution." Thus, "it would not have been reasonable for defense counsel to rely on" this doctor "based only on his credentials." While the court was "inclined to believe that their performance was ineffective" during the trial and that prejudice was established, the court, constrained by AEDPA review, did not find that the state court's contrary conclusion was an unreasonable application of *Strickland*. With respect to sentencing, however, counsel's conduct was both deficient and prejudicial because counsel presented lay testimony as essentially non-statutory mitigation, but did not present evidence of the statutory mitigating circumstances of extreme emotional disturbance and impaired capacity to appreciate the wrongfulness of his conduct at the time of the murder, which were supported by two competent experts in post-conviction. These experts diagnosed a severe dissociative disorder and found that the defendant was dissociating during the murder and killing the child because he himself wanted to be killed by the man that had raped him as a child.

> The strategic reasons that might, at a stretch, have justified this decision [not to present a mental health defense] at the guilt phase, fall apart when we consider that at the sentencing phase [the defendant] had nothing left to lose. The lawyers' decision to forego presenting this kind of mitigation evidence was made without the kind of investigation into [his] mental health that *Strickland* calls for, *after* [his] lawyers had concluded that [the doctor] was a "quack." Indeed, it is uncontested that [his] lawyers knew nothing about the content of [the doctor's] planned testimony. The lawyers confessed at the post-conviction hearing that they were utterly in the dark about what [he] would say when he took the stand. ... This is a complete failure of the duty to investigate with no professional justification. Where an expert witness's opinion is "crucial to the defense theory[,] defense counsel's failure to have questioned [the expert] ... prior to trial is inexcusable."

Id. (quoting *Combs v. Coyle,* 205 F.3d 269, 288 (6th Cir.2000)). The court also noted that counsel had the doctor's report and "we cannot imagine what they hoped to gain" by calling him to testify. In addition, if he had not been called as a witness, counsel was under no obligation to disclose his report to the prosecution. Even though counsel may not have been ineffective for not presenting mental health testimony during the trial, they were during sentencing.

> [T]here is an important difference between the statutory mitigating factors ... for capital sentencing purposes and the requirements for proving an insanity defense at the guilt phase. Furthermore, the burden on the defendant is not as heavy at sentencing as during the guilt phase. . . . As a legal matter, a mental illness mitigation defense to the imposition of a death sentence may be available even if an insanity defense to the murder charge is not.

If counsel had presented "mainstream expert psychological testimony" such as that presented in post-conviction, there is a reasonable probability of a different outcome. "Competent evidence" of "mental illness would have strengthened the general mitigation evidence presented by defense counsel ... by focusing the jury on the concrete results of years of abuse on [the defendant's] psyche." There was also "little downside" in further evidence of the defendant's "predatory pedophilia" being presented when "evidence of the most damning sort was already before the jury." Prejudice was especially clear in calling the "quack" to testify and then to do it a second time because he not only provided the only evidence of "necrophilia after the murder, he also gave the prosecution a gift by expressing his belief in ... future dangerousness–a subject that the prosecution itself is not permitted to argue as an aggravating circumstance under Indiana law." The trial court's sentencing order also was "a close reflection of [the doctor's] written report and testimony.

Lambright v. Schriro, 490 F.3d 1103 (9th Cir. 2007) (tried in 1982). Under pre-AEDPA law, counsel ineffective in failing to adequately prepare and present mitigation. Counsel's conduct was deficient because counsel "failed to do even a minimal investigation of 'classic mitigation evidence,' notwithstanding the fact that he knew such evidence potentially existed." He spent less than five hours preparing for sentencing even though counsel was aware from the pre-sentence investigation report and the court-appointed examiner's report of the defendant's long history of mental health problems, his two prior suicide attempts, his prior hospitalization in a psychiatric facility, his traumatic combat experiences in Vietnam, his serious drug problems, and his diagnosis by a court-appointed examiner of antisocial personality disorder. It was not sufficient that counsel prepared a short memorandum for the sentencing court because counsel's duty "is not discharged merely by conducting a limited investigation of these issues or by providing the sentencing court with a cursory or 'abbreviated' presentation of potentially mitigating factors." Prejudice found because counsel presented a single witness to testify about adaptability to confinement and this evidence covered less than three pages of the transcript. The court rejected the "nexus requirement" applied by the District Court.

> If evidence relating to life circumstances with no causal relationship to the crime were to be eliminated, significant aspects of a defendant's disadvantaged background, emotional and mental problems, and adverse history, as well as his positive character traits, would not be considered, even though some of these factors, both positive and negative, might cause a sentencer to determine that a life sentence, rather than death at the hands of the state, is the appropriate punishment for the particular defendant. This is simply unacceptable in any capital sentencing proceeding, given that "treating each defendant in a capital case with that degree of respect due the uniqueness of the individual," and determining whether or not he is

deserving of execution only after taking his unique life circumstances, disabilities, and traits into account, is constitutionally required. *Lockett v. Ohio*, 438 U.S. 586, 605, 98 S.Ct. 2954, 57 L.Ed.2d 973 (1978).

Prejudice established because counsel failed to even develop or argue the limited and unsubstantiated mitigating evidence that was before the court in the pre-sentence report and the state's expert report. These documents included information that the defendant's mother was "very strict" and hypochondriacal. In truth, she physically abused the defendant frequently and stayed in bed much of the time claiming to suffer from illnesses and was profoundly addicted to prescription drugs. She would even force the defendant to take Valium and sleeping pills when he acted up or had too much energy. The information before the court indicated that the defendant's family moved frequently but did not "convey" the impact on the defendant in terms of his ability to form relationships or that he never attended any school for more than a year. The information before the court indicated that the defendant was raised in a lower-middle class family, when he grew up in extreme poverty. The family moved frequently because of his father's struggle to maintain employment. The family often lived in homes with no running water or indoor plumbing and once had to live in a rat-infested house in which the walls and ceilings were lined with cardboard to block holes. The court had information about drug use but was not aware that drug and alcohol abuse were rampant in the defendant's family or that it was his mother who first exposed him to drug abuse by forcing him to take sedatives when he was a child or that he used large quantities of drugs throughout his life and would stay awake for weeks at a time on methamphetamine. The defendant also likely suffered from post-traumatic stress disorder from his combat experience and abusive background, but even the state's expert in post-conviction agreed that the defendant had a depressive disorder, which resulted in two suicide attempts, and had to be hospitalized at least once due to hallucinations. The state expert also agreed that the defendant has a personality disorder not otherwise specified with antisocial, borderline, and inadequate features, which "if properly developed and explained to the sentencer, would have had a mitigating effect under Arizona law." Even the diagnosis of antisocial personality disorder given by the court-appointed examiner at trial, "is a mitigating factor under Arizona law." Even though some mitigating evidence was before the court, prejudice was still clear.

> We do not underestimate the importance of the role of counsel in the adversarial process. The sentencing judge cannot be expected to comb the record looking for mitigating factors, particularly where the minimal evidence that exists is buried in reports that are on the whole strongly unfavorable to the defendant.

Prejudice was especially clear since there was only one aggravating factor and Arizona law at the time of sentencing "mandated the death penalty" when one aggravating factor was present and no mitigation evidence was presented.

Anderson v. Sirmons, 476 F.3d 1131 (10th Cir. 2007) (crimes in September 1996 and affirmed on appeal in 1999). Under AEDPA analysis, trial counsel ineffective in capital sentencing for failing to adequately investigate and present mitigating evidence. Although the issue was first raised in federal habeas, the court found, under unique facts not relevant here, that exhaustion was excused and the issue was not procedurally barred because the state had not established regular and consistent application of a procedural bar. Because of these rulings and the state court's failure to address the merits, the court applied *de novo* review and cited repeatedly to the 1989 and 2003 ABA Guidelines for the Appointment and Performance of Counsel in Death Penalty Cases. Counsel's conduct was deficient because counsel focused "almost exclusively on the guilt phase of his trial." *Id.* at 1143. While counsel had a mitigation investigator that investigator spent only 23 hours on the case, all of which was in the month prior to trial, did not interview the petitioner and "did not have access to life-history information, school records, or medical records." Counsel also did not have the petitioner evaluated by any mental health expert or other expert qualified to ascertain whether the petitioner "suffered from neurological or other deficits that would mitigate his moral culpability." *Id.* Although trial counsel did not provide an affidavit, the mitigation investigator's affidavit along with evidence that trial counsel's file contained no background records was sufficient to establish that the investigation of mitigation evidence was unreasonable. Prejudice established despite three "callous and brutal" murders, no residual doubt of guilt, three aggravating circumstances, and evidence the petitioner obtained drugs and a weapon and corresponded with his wife about "taking care" of witnesses while in pretrial confinement. Trial counsel had presented evidence only of petitioner's support of his family, that his mother was a "good woman," who loved him, and his daughter loved him and he could help her from prison. "Thus, rather than offering the jury a potential explanation for [the petitioner's] actions relating to the murders he participated in, trial counsel's case in mitigation was limited to a simple plea for mercy." *Id.* at 1144. This evidence "played into the prosecution's theory that the only explanation for the murders was that [the petitioner] was simply an 'evil' man." *Id.* at 1147. If counsel had adequately investigated the evidence would have established that the petitioner was raised in an environment of neglect and abuse; his mother and step-father were violent alcoholics, who battled before the children; his mother physically abused the children with anything at hand; his mother had numerous illicit affairs in the home that were known to the children; he suffered from brain damage and an IQ in the 70s, likely as a result of extensive drug and alcohol abuse begun as a child and numerous head injuries. "[T]his is just the kind of mitigation evidence trial counsel is obligated to investigate and develop as part of building an effective case in mitigation during the penalty phase of a trial." *Id.* at 1144.

2006: ***Outten v. Kearney***, 464 F.3d 401 (3rd Cir. 2006) (sentenced in March 1993). Counsel ineffective in capital sentencing for failing to adequately investigate and present mitigation evidence. The state presented evidence of the defendant's post criminal history, which was all non-violent offenses. The defense presented six people (four family members, a friend, and an ex-girlfriend, who was the mother of the defendant's children) to testify about general background and good guy evidence in mitigation. Counsel's conduct was deficient because the "investigation was cursory" in that counsel only sent the defendant a letter asking for the names of "potential penalty phase witnesses" and had only limited discussions with the defendant and his mother. Counsel's conduct was not excused by strategy to focus on the defendant being a loving, generous, and non-violent person, who did not commit the crime, and to avoid negative information.

> Simply stated, defense counsel's penalty-phase strategy was to argue to the jury-which had convicted Outten of murder unanimously and beyond a reasonable doubt-that he was a good guy and that his life should be spared because he was actually innocent.

The court found, however, that trial counsel did not "carry through this tack" because the trial court prohibited counsel from arguing actual innocence in sentencing. Trial counsel then changed tactics and stated explicitly that the defendant was guilty and had a "horrendous record." Counsel never mentioned the defendant's positive character traits. While counsel did mention the non-violent nature of the defendant's prior convictions, this was undermined byte state's cross of the mitigation witnesses about his assaults on various family members and his ex-girlfriend. Counsel's "effort fell well short of the national prevailing professional standards articulated by the American Bar Association" in the 1989 ABA Guidelines. Counsel's conduct was also unreasonable in light of "what they presumably discovered from the conversations" counsel had with the defendant and his mother. Prejudice found because, if counsel had adequately investigated, the evidence would have established that the defendant's alcoholic father was extremely physically and emotional abusive to his children all of whom ultimately suffered from alcoholism and/or drug addiction. The defendant's mother drank regularly while she was pregnant with him and was beaten by her husband. The defendant also had two serious head injuries that caused loss of consciousness as a child. He was placed in classes for the learning disabled at school. After the defendant ran away from home as a teenager to avoid his father's abuse, he was placed in foster care where he was sexually abused by his foster mother. He was ultimately placed in a facility for troubled children where counselors noted that he was depressed and hopeless. As an adult, the defendant suffered two major losses due to the death of his father from cancer (and the defendant cared for him the last 6 months of his life despite the history of abuse) and the death of his child who lived only 14 days because of the mother's drug use during pregnancy. The defendant also had a substantial history of alcohol and substance abuse beginning at age 10. Although counsel did present "some mitigating evidence" to the jury, "it does not follow that the jury was provided a comprehensive understanding" of the mitigation. "For example, while Outten's mother portrayed her husband as a 'very, very strict parent,' she did not relate to the jury the disturbing abuse. ..." The jury also heard nothing of the sexual abuse, possible neurological damage, learning disabilities, or low IQ. Prejudice was also clear due to the jury's close vote in favor of death (7 to 5). Under AEDPA, the state court's holding was an unreasonable application of *Strickland* on both prongs. With respect to sentencing it was unreasonable, in part, because the court found no prejudice because the background information also "contained some harmful information."

Williams v. Anderson, 460 F.3d 789 (6th Cir. 2006) (tried in July 1984). Under AEDPA, counsel ineffective in capital sentencing for failing to adequately prepare and present mitigation evidence. Following the defendant's conviction of hiring a person to commit the murder, counsel waived opening statement in sentencing and presented no evidence. The defendant made a brief statement and then counsel gave "a long, rambling closing, in which he arguably presented a case for residual doubt." *Id.* at 794. The remainder of the closing argument included prejudicial statements by counsel. Appellate counsel asserted counsel's ineffectiveness on direct appeal, which was denied dud to the lack of any evidence outside the trial record. Post-conviction counsel asserted the issue with supporting evidence, but the post-conviction court was prohibited from granting relief under state law because the issue had been addressed on the merits during the direct appeal. The federal court determined that its review should be based on the direct appeal opinion. While the court would normally be prohibited from considering evidence not before the court at that time, the court found cause and prejudice for the default because appellate counsel was ineffective. Counsel's conduct was deficient because "[i]t is well-established in Ohio law that where an ineffective assistance of counsel claim cannot be supported solely on the trial court record, it should not be brought on direct appeal." *Id.* at 800. Moreover, "[i]neffective assistance of counsel claims based on trial counsel's failure to investigate and present mitigation evidence can never be proven based solely on evidence in the record because the record necessarily does not contain evidence of prejudice." *Id.* Prejudice was established because the underlying claim of ineffective assistance of trial counsel had merit when supported with evidence. Trial counsel's conduct was deficient in completely failing to investigate mitigation evidence. Counsel never even discussed the possibility of a court-ordered psychiatric evaluation and pre-sentence report with the defendant until two days prior to sentencing. He did not even discuss the issue with the defendant or with his family or friend. Counsel's conduct was not excused by strategy to focus only on residual doubt "because defense counsel never conducted an investigation into mitigation before deciding to pursue residual doubt." *Id.* at 804. The state court's determination that counsel's conduct was reasonable was "contrary to federal law as articulated in *Strickland.*" *Id.* at 802. The state court did not address the question of prejudice so the federal court's review of this issue was *de novo*. Prejudice found because the available but unpresented evidence included evidence of an alcoholic, abusive mother; abandonment by his father at a young age; an uncle, who was his primary male role model, that was a career criminal; cocaine dependence and cocaine induced paranoid fears at the time of the murder; a diagnosis of Dyssocial Reaction, Mixed Personality Disorder with Anti-social and Narcissistic Features; and that the defendant had treated his wife's autistic son like his own. "In addition to presenting the jury with mitigating evidence, the testimony of Petitioner's family and friends would have humanized Petitioner." *Id.* at 805.

Poindexter v. Mitchell, 454 F.3d 564 (6th Cir. 2006) (sentenced in June 1985). Under pre-AEDPA law, counsel ineffective in failing to adequately prepare and present mitigation. In sentencing, counsel presented the testimony of three family members and a friend. This testimony included the following information: (1) the petitioner was a good student, who was involved in gymnastics in school; (2) the petitioner was peaceful and quiet and kept to himself; and (3) the petitioner read the Bible a lot, worked, and got along with everyone. The petitioner also made an unsworn statement that began with describing his relationship with his former girlfriend, whose new boyfriend was the murder victim in this case and she had also been assaulted. He described an incident when he had slapped her for wearing an "obscene" miniskirt and said her mother had instigated everything because "she disliked dreadlocks." After that point, the petitioner refused to continue reading the prepared statement and a recess was taken. Counsel convinced him to continue reading "his" statement. He read the rest, which basically said he was a good guy and believed in God. At the end, "he yelled, 'And the main thing, I didn't kill that man,' and slammed the microphone down." Counsel's conduct was deficient.

> [C]ounsel failed to conduct virtually any investigation, let alone sufficient investigation to make any strategic choices possible. They did not request medical, educational, or governmental records that would have given insight into [the petitioner's] background. They did not request funds to enlist a psychological or psychiatric expert to evaluate [the petitioner], despite the fact that he exhibited odd behavior. They did not consult with an investigator or mitigation specialist, who could have assisted in reconstructing [the petitioner's] social history. They failed to interview key family members and friends who could have described his upbringing. And they did not even begin to prepare for mitigation until [the petitioner] was convicted, which was only five days before the sentencing phase began. This was despite the fact that prevailing norms at the time of trial required counsel in a death penalty case to seek records, interview family members and friends, and obtain appropriate mental evaluations well in advance of trial.

Id. at . Counsel expressed no strategic reason. Prejudice found because, if counsel had adequately investigated, the evidence would have established the following: (1) the petitioner's father beat him, his mother, and his sister; (2) the petitioner's mother was a heavy drinker, who used marijuana almost daily; and (3) the petitioner's mother neglected her children, beat them, and once tried to kill the whole family by shutting them in the house and turning on a gas stove. An expert in forensic psychology described the family as "very dysfunctional" with "four generations of alcoholism and physical abuse and emotional abuse." In addition to his mother's problems, the petitioner was exposed to the alcohol abuse and domestic violence she endured in two of her three significant relationships. She was ultimately hospitalized and her children placed in foster homes. The petitioner functioned in the borderline range of intelligence and suffers from a paranoid personality disorder. These crimes were caused by "his paranoid personality disorder" and "a pathological jealous reaction accompanied by rage." Because of this evidence "any mitigation strategy to portray [the petitioner] as a peaceful person was unreasonable since that strategy was the product of an incomplete investigation." *Id.* at .

Dickerson v. Bagley, 453 F.3d 690 (6th Cir. 2006) (tried in November 1985). Counsel was ineffective in capital sentencing for failing to adequately investigate and present mitigation. The court quoted extensively from the ABA Guidelines for the Appointment and Performance of Defense Counsel in Death Penalty Cases in describing counsel's duties. Here, counsel failed to discover significant mitigation that included that the petitioner's biological father denied that petitioner was his son; his mother referred to him as "the moron"; he was raised in an atmosphere of pimps, prostitutes, and drug dealers; several homosexual advances were made upon him; he had a full-scale I.Q. of 77, placing him in the lower seven percent of cognitive ability; and he had a borderline personality disorder. The state court held that counsel had a strategic reason for the failure to investigate, because one of the three-judge panel had suggested to him waiver of the jury, which counsel took to mean that the judges would not impose death. This finding was an unreasonable application of Supreme Court case law because "[i]t is not reasonable to refuse to investigate when the investigator does not know the relevant facts the investigation will uncover."

> Had the investigation been conducted, reasonable lawyers surely *would not have limited* the mitigation proof in this case to simply an effort to show only that [the petitioner] was "provoked" by jealousy [in killing his former girl-friend's new lover] and could not control his impulses, and therefore suffered from "diminished capacity" at the time of the crime.

"Accordingly, the state court unreasonably applied clearly established Supreme Court precedent when it simply assumed that counsel's oversights were motivated by strategy, instead of requiring a complete and thorough mitigation investigation as mandated by *Strickland* and its progeny." Prejudice found because "[a]n argument based on reduced culpability similar to that given by the Supreme Court in *Atkins* might well have been persuasive in [this] case too."

Frierson v. Woodford, 463 F.3d 982 (9th Cir. 2006) (crimes in 1978 and third trial in 1986). Under pre-AEDPA law, counsel ineffective in third capital sentencing for failing to adequately prepare and present mitigation and for failing to challenge a significant mitigation witness' invocation of his Fifth Amendment right against self-incrimination. Counsel's conduct was deficient because counsel failed to adequately investigate, even though "[t]he imperative to cast a wide net for all relevant mitigating evidence is heightened at a capital sentencing hearing." *Id.* at 989. "[T]he reasonableness of counsel's investigatory and preparatory work at the penalty phase should be examined in a different, more exacting, manner than other parts of the trial." *Id.* at 993. Here, counsel did not review the prior sentencing transcripts, which would have revealed a thorough drug history by an expert, along with a series of psychiatric evaluations while the defendant was in the custody of the California Youth Authority (CYA). These records revealed symptoms of organic brain dysfunction. Counsel also did not obtain readily available school, hospital, prison, and juvenile records. These records revealed significant head injuries as a child that required hospitalization, an IQ score of 71, and a documented learning disability. Although counsel knew of the head injuries, he "ignored the red flag of possible brain damage caused by multiple childhood head injuries by failing to consult a neurologist, and instead relied on the lay opinion of [the defendant's] parents" who saw no change in behavior following the injuries. *Id.* at 991. Counsel also claimed to have relied on the prior testimony of a forensic psychiatrist that there was no evidence of brain damage, but the "failure to consult with a neurologist–the only expert qualified to evaluate organic *brain dysfunction* caused by multiple childhood head trauma–[was] not ameliorated" on this basis, in part, because it was clear that counsel had not been aware of the prior testimony. Counsel's conduct was not excused by "strategy" because "strategy presupposes investigation." *Id.* at 992. Prejudice found because the omitted evidence, taken as a whole, might well have influenced the jury's appraisal of the defendant's moral culpability. Counsel's conduct was also deficient in adequately preparing and responding to the state's evidence that the defendant had a juvenile adjudication for murder for which he was committed to CYA. Counsel presented several witnesses who testified that the defendant was not the shooter, but these witnesses lacked much credibility. Counsel then sought to present the testimony of the juvenile co-defendant that counsel believed to be the shooter but basically encouraged this witness to invoke his Fifth Amendment rights even though this witness had confessed to counsel and his investigator that he was, in fact, the shooter. Counsel's conduct was deficient because, much like counsel in *Rompilla*, counsel failed to review the prior juvenile records, which would have disclosed that this witness had been tried and acquitted on this charge and thus could not assert the Fifth Amendment privilege because double jeopardy barred trying him again for this murder. Prejudice was also established for this error because this prior homicide was "the central focus of the penalty hearing" and the prosecution's closing argument. Had the jury heard testimony that the co-defendant confessed to the murder rather than a simple invocation of his Fifth Amendment rights there is a reasonable probability that at least one juror would have struck a different balance in the outcome.

Hovey v. Ayers, 458 F.3d 892 (9th Cir. 2006) (tried in 1982). Under pre-AEDPA law, counsel ineffective in capital sentencing for failing to adequately prepare and present mental health evidence during the trial, where a finding of premeditation was required before the petitioner was eligible for the death penalty, and sentencing. In exchange for the exclusion of other unrelated charges, the petitioner stipulated his guilt with the exception of the intent element. Early in the trial, the court convened a two-day hearing because of the court's concerns about primary *counsel's competence.* The court found him competent, but no one even informed the petitioner about this hearing. Following his conviction with a finding of premeditation, the defense presented eighteen witnesses, including twelve friends and three family members, who described him as a well-meaning and introspective young man from an unexceptional middle-class family. He attended college and had been living at home and working sporadically at the time of the murder. Witnesses described his behavior in the months leading up to his crimes as increasingly eccentric. The primary defense witness, a psychiatrist, testified (primarily just on his interviews with the petitioner) that the petitioner suffers from schizophrenia, which caused him to lose control and kill the victim. Counsel's conduct was deficient.

> A defense attorney in the sentencing phase of a capital trial has "a professional responsibility to investigate and bring to the attention of mental health experts who are examining his client[ ] facts that the experts do not request." Regardless of whether a defense expert requests specific information relevant to a defendant's background, it is defense counsel's "duty to seek out such evidence and bring it to the attention of the experts."

Id. at . While the petitioner's mental health was the "heart" of the mitigation case, this evidence came almost exclusively through the testimony of the psychiatrist. Counsel had not provided the psychiatrist with relevant background information, including records from the petitioner's hospitalization a year before these crimes due to what doctors initially believed was an acute "catatonic" schizophrenic episode. These records "would have strengthened" and "confirmed" the psychiatrist's diagnosis and "corroborated [his] testimony and bolstered the credibility of his response to the prosecution, whose primary strategy in attacking [the psychiatrist] was to suggest that [the petitioner] had never suffered from mental illness." *Id. at* . Without these records, the psychiatrist testified in cross-examination that he was not aware of the petitioner receiving any treatment or diagnosis prior to his arrest. The prosecution focused on the lack of support for the doctor's testimony in closing arguments in sentencing. "The prosecutor's closing argument, in combination with [the psychiatrist's] ignorance of [petitioner's] experience [in his prior hospitalization], strongly suggested that the defense had concocted the mitigating mental illness evidence." *Id. at* . Prejudice found because "[t]his evidence, coming as it did from doctors who had no connection to the defense or incentive to invent a diagnosis and thus who were invulnerable to charges of fabrication, could very well have made the difference in a life as opposed to death verdict." *Id. at* . Moreover, even though the prior doctors ultimately concluded that the petitioner suffered from "drug-induced psychosis," this was based on his own statements that were not confirmed by blood tests. Regardless of the diagnosis, he "displayed symptoms consistent with" the defense expert's diagnosis and the initial diagnosis of the prior doctors of an "acute schizophrenic episode." "[A]ll potentially mitigating evidence is relevant at the sentencing phase of a death case, so ... mental problems may help even if they don't rise to a specific, technically-defined level." *Id.* at . Finally, during deliberations, the jury specifically asked that the defense expert's "testimony be re-read, suggesting that the jury placed importance on it." *Id.* at . Counsel also failed to provide the psychiatrist "with important information about the circumstances surrounding" a kidnapping that occurred after these crimes.

> This information would have prevented the prosecutor from portraying [the psychiatrist] as ill-prepared and foolish and thereby impugning his medical conclusions. Because [the psychiatrist] was not adequately prepared, the prosecution was able to demonstrate that [he] was completely ignorant of several important facts, including that [the petitioner] was regularly and successfully attending a training school at the time of [this] murder, that [the petitioner] altered his appearance after [this] murder and before the [separate] kidnapping, and that [the petitioner] released [the kidnapping victim] only after being discovered and pursued by two witnesses to his crime.

Id. at . The prosecution also focused on the doctor's ignorance of these facts in closing arguments. Prejudice found because "there is a reasonable probability that [the psychiatrist's] ignorance of basic background facts related to the [separate] kidnapping affected the jury's sentencing decision."

> The clear implication of the prosecution's argument was that [the psychiatrist] was uninformed about the subject of his diagnosis and that his conclusions stemmed from a general misunderstanding of the facts. Even if the background information did not change [his] diagnosis, he at least would have been able to testify more knowledgeably about the case and better weather the prosecution's attempts to discredit him. He would have been able to anticipate the prosecution's questions during cross-examination and explain how [the petitioner's] activities around the time of the offense could be consistent with a diagnosis of schizophrenia. Instead, [the psychiatrist] was caught by surprise, in an embarrassed and vulnerable situation. He was entirely discredited by his lack of critical information, information that lay in the hands of [petitioner's] counsel.

Id. at . In a footnote, the court addressed additional prejudice due to counsel's failure to provide the psychiatrist with a probation report after he plead guilty to the separate kidnapping and with hospital records from post-arrest hospitalizations. While these documents reflected diagnoses of schizoid personality rather than schizophrenia, they also contained observations by medical professions, "including descriptions of his delusions and grandiose ideas, that are consistent with [the psychiatrist's] observations and diagnosis." In short, whatever the precise diagnosis, medical professionals repeatedly had concluded that [the petitioner] was seriously mentally disturbed."

2005: ***Marshall v. Cathel***, 428 F.3d 452 (3rd Cir. 2005) (affirming 313 F. Supp. 2d 423 (D.N.J. 2004)) (tried in March 1986). Counsel ineffective in capital sentencing for failing to adequately investigate and present mitigation evidence, failing to seek a continuance to do so, failing to adequately consult with the defendant concerning his options and the procedure in the sentencing proceeding, and did not even make a plea for his client's life. Following conviction for hiring someone to murder his wife, the defendant proceeded immediately to sentencing after being checked at the hospital after fainting following his conviction. Counsel had not prepared at all for the penalty phase and had not investigated at all on this front or retained any experts. Nonetheless, counsel did not request a continuance to prepare. Instead, counsel "agreed" with the prosecutor that both sides would waive opening and would not present evidence in sentencing and would only do a short closing argument. The state also dismissed two of the three aggravating factors charged and stipulated a single mitigating factor–that the defendant did not have a prior criminal record. Analyzing the case under AEDPA, the court found that counsel's conduct was deficient because "the lack of preparation is striking and inexplicable," *id.* at 466, "in light of his knowledge from the inception that the case would be a capital one and that his client faced powerful State's evidence," *id.* at 472. While the defendant was a "difficult client to control" and the community, and perhaps his family, had turned against him, "neither circumstance excuses counsel's failure to conduct any investigation into possibly mitigating factors or prepare a case for life." *Id.* at 467. Counsel also failed to adequately consult with the defendant and did not even explain to him that he "had the right to allocute at the penalty phase." The defendant's failure to cooperate with the preparation of mitigation does nothing to relieve counsel "of his constitutional duty as an attorney." As the District Court put it:

> Even when clients strongly assert their innocence and refuse to discuss the possibility of being found guilty, an attorney must find a way to prepare for and investigate a mitigation case. … No matter how difficult, [counsel] had an obligation either to convince [the defendant] to cooperate with him in preparing a case for life, or to find a way to conduct an investigation without [the defendant's] assistance. *Marshall v. Hendricks*, 313 F. Supp. 2d 423, 451 (D.N.J. 2004).

"Widely accepted national guidelines, state specific standards, and [counsel's] own testimony regarding his previous capital experience–all of which aid in our evaluation of the reasonableness of [counsel's] preparation–make clear that [counsel] understood but abdicated his responsibility as counsel to a client facing a possible death sentence." *Id.* at 467 (citing the ABA Standards for Criminal Justice).

> Regardless of counsel's trial strategy of denying guilt, "[w]ith the outright rejection of [the] defense, which is the only way the guilty verdict can be interpreted, [counsel] knew that the jury also had rejected the character evidence submitted in support of that defense. Indeed, it would only be fair to assume that they had found [the defendant] to be a liar and a despicable person for paying someone to have his wife killed. [Counsel's] clear duty at that point was to shift his focus away from absolving [the defendant] of involvement in his wife's murder–certainly, the evidence for the guilt phase had not worked for that purpose–to saving his life.

Id. at 469. Counsel's most glaring omission was failing to interview the defendant's sons even though he believed they would be hostile to the defendant. "[C]ounsel's 'beliefs' are not a substitute for informed strategy." *Id.* at 471. The court also viewed counsel's "agreement" with the state as an "abdication of his role." *Id.* at 472. Counsel "was not merely agreeing to hold back on the production of evidence–he had no evidence to introduce. … Far from a strategic, bargained-for exchange, the agreement appears to have been the only option." *Id.* While counsel argued that the defendant was a law abiding citizen with no significant history of prior criminal activity, these are "relatively insignificant aspects–essentially applicable to any and every first time offender of a brutal crime–that are anything but 'humanizing.'" *Id.* at 473. Counsel's presentation was only a "bland emotionless argument." Prejudice was found because the general character testimony presented during the trial was only general, "cursory" information. Counsel's conduct was not excused by strategy. "Rather, it is a situation where [counsel] inadequately prepared for the penalty phase and put in no mitigating evidence because he had none to present." Likewise, counsel only gave a "verbal shrug of the shoulders" in arguments and did not even make a plea for mercy. Prejudice was found because an adequate investigation would have revealed numerous family members and friends willing to ask for mercy and to testify about the harmful impact of execution on the defendant's family, particularly his son. The state court's finding of no prejudice was an unreasonable application of *Strickland*.

Harries v. Bell, 417 F.3d 631 (6th Cir. 2005) (tried in 1981). Counsel was ineffective in capital sentencing for failing to prepare and present evidence in mitigation in case analyzed under pre-AEDPA standards. Despite the requirements of the ABA Guidelines to investigate "to discover all reasonably available mitigating evidence," *id.* 638 (quoting ABA Guidelines for the Appointment and Performance of Counsel in Death Penalty Cases § 11.4.1©, p. 93 (1989), counsel limited their investigation to a few phone calls with family members, sending requests for information to some of the institutions in which the petitioner had been confined, and interviewing the defendant, his co-defendant, and two state witnesses. While the petitioner had requested that counsel not pursue mental illness as a defense and counsel believed that background evidence "would not persuade the jury," counsel's conduct was unreasonable because "defendant resistance to disclosure of information does not excuse counsel's duty to independently investigate." *Id.* at 639 (quoting *Coleman v. Mitchell*, 268 F.3d 417, 449-50 (6th Cir. 2001)). Counsel's conduct was also deficient because counsel was aware of the defendant's poor mental health and troubled family background, which left "no 'room for debate'" that their truncated investigation was deficient. *Id.* at 639 (quoting *Rompilla v. Beard*, 545 U.S. 374, (2005)). Prejudice was found because adequate investigation would have revealed a traumatic childhood, involving physical abuse by petitioner's mother, stepfather, and grandmother. He had been hit on the head with a frying pan and choked so severely, at age 11, that his eyes hemorrhaged. A year later, staff at a detention home noted multiple traumatic scars on his head. He was also exposed to his father and stepfather beating his mother and both his father and stepfather had ultimately been murdered themselves. Since age 11, he spent all of his life, except a combined total of 36 months, combined in institutions, many of which were violent or unsanitary. He had also had numerous heard injuries and had attempted suicide and suffered carbon monoxide poisoning at age 20. He had frontal lobe damage, even according to the state's experts, which "can result from head injuries and can interfere with a person's judgment and decrease a person's ability to control impulses." *Id.* at 640. He also suffered from a mental disorder although the exact diagnoses ranged from bipolar mood disorder, trauma-induced anxiety, anxiety disorder, post-traumatic stress disorder, and antisocial personality disorder. "This evidence adds up to a mitigation case that bears no relation to the few naked pleas for mercy actually put before the jury." *Id.* (quoting *Rompilla*, 125 S. Ct. at 2469). While the State argued that admission of this evidence would have opened the door to evidence of numerous prior criminal acts, Tennessee law prohibited this evidence. Even if it was admissible, however, prejudice was still found because the petitioner in *Williams v. Taylor*, 529 U.S. 362, 396 (2000), "had a criminal history … at least as serious" as the petitioner's and the Court still found prejudice. *Id.* at 641. Tennessee law also supported a finding of prejudice because counsel's failure to present mitigation evidence left the jury with no choice but to impose the death penalty.

Summerlin v. Schriro, 427 F.3d 623 (9th Cir. 2005) (sentencing in July 1982). Counsel ineffective in capital case for failing to prepare and present mitigation evidence. Analyzing the case under pre-AEDPA law, the court held that counsel "utterly failed" to investigate the defendant's family and social history or to develop a mental health defense. Counsel instead relied "on the limited information developed in [the defendant's] pre-trial competency examination, which was prepared for an entirely different purpose" than mitigation. *Id.* at 631. Counsel did so even though he was aware of the "preliminary mental health information" from the defendant's prior counsel. He even failed to interview the state's experts even though counsel knew the state intended to call these experts in sentencing. During the month between the trial and sentencing hearing, counsel did not meet with his client. In sentencing, counsel sought only to present testimony of consulting psychiatrist retained by the defendant's prior counsel. Before this witness was sworn, the defendant interrupted and apparently requested that the witness not be called so the defense presented no testimony.

> Even if [the defendant] had instructed counsel not to present a mitigation defense, that fact would have no effect on the deficient conduct prong of *Strickland* because counsel had already demonstrated ineffectiveness by failing to thoroughly investigate the existence of

mitigating factors. Although the allocation of control between attorney and client typically dictate that 'the client decides the 'ends' of the lawsuit while the attorney controls the 'means,'" it does not relieve an attorney of the duty to investigate potential defenses, consult with the client, and provide advice as to the risks and potential consequences of any fundamental trial decision within the client's control.

Id. at 638 (citation omitted). The court stated that "[t]his is especially true in capital cases." *Id.* (citing the ABA Standards for Criminal Justice and ABA Guidelines for the Appointment and Performance of Counsel in Death Penalty Cases). Prejudice found even in the "context of judge- sentencing." If counsel had adequately investigated, the evidence would have shown a "tortured family history" in which the defendant's father deserted him and was later killed in a police shootout and the defendant's alcoholic mother beat him frequently and punished him by locking him in a room with ammonia fumes. He had electric shock treatments, at his mother's behest, to control his temper. He had a learning disability that left "him functionally mentally retarded." He had also been diagnosed as a paranoid schizophrenic and had been treated with anti-psychotic medications. He also had a temporal lobe seizure disorder and there were indications of organic brain syndrome and impaired impulse control. Instead of developing and presenting this evidence, counsel presented no evidence in sentencing and only asked the court to consider a report attached to the presentencing report. Counsel's argument covered only three pages of transcript. In addition to failing to present mitigation evidence, counsel also failed to present evidence mitigating one of the statutory aggravating circumstances (a prior violent felony conviction). The defendant's prior aggravated assault conviction was a result of the defendant showing a pocket knife to the driver of a car that veered off the road, jumped the curb, and struck the defendant's wife causing serious injuries that required hospitalization. The knife was pulled at the scene, but the driver was not physically injured. Counsel knew of this information because he had represented the defendant on this prior assault but still did not present this information. Finally, counsel also failed to object to the presentence report prepared by a probation officer that contained numerous sentencing recommendations from the probation officer, the victim's family and friends, police officers, and others. All of this material was hearsay and inadmissible and almost all was damaging to the defendant. Instead of objecting, counsel made it worse by requesting that the court review a report attached to it. Counsel's failure to present mitigation "all but assured the imposition of a death sentence" under state law that mandated death if there was a qualifying prior conviction and no mitigation. The court also found that this "was not by any means a clear-cut death penalty case" because the initial very experienced prosecutor did not believe he could get a death sentence and offered to allow the defendant to plead to second-degree murder for a 21 year sentence that would have allowed the defendant's release in 14 years. (This offer was withdrawn when the initial prosecutor and defense counsel were replaced.)

2004: *Smith v. Mullin*, 379 F.3d 919 (10th Cir. 2004) (trial in October 1994). Counsel was ineffective in capital sentencing for failing to adequately prepare and present mitigation. Counsel's conduct during the trial was "troubling" but the court found no prejudice in light of the overwhelming evidence of guilt and disposed of these claims on that basis. In addressing the right to effective assistance in sentencing–"the most critical phase of a death penalty case," *id.* at –the court declared:

> [W]e are particularly vigilant in guarding this right when the defendant faces a sentence of death. Our heightened attention parallels the heightened demands on counsel in a capital case.

> *See* ABA Standards for Criminal Justice 4-1.2© (3d ed. 1993) ("Since the death penalty differs from other criminal penalties in its finality, defense counsel in a capital case should respond to this difference by making extraordinary efforts on behalf of the accused.").

Id. at (other internal citations omitted). Here, counsel had no experience or training in capital cases and inadequate funding from the defendant's family. In addition, while counsel presented some mental health evidence during the trial, it was done in an "incoherent and haphazard" way. *Id. at* . Counsel did not present any additional mental health evidence during sentencing because counsel was unaware that he could do so. Counsel presented only on a few witnesses to testify that the defendant was kind and considerate but "made no attempt to explain how this kind and considerate person could commit such a horrendous crime, although mental health evidence providing such an explanation was at his fingertips." *Id. at* . The evidence in mitigation was "pitifully incomplete, and in some respects, bordered on the absurd." *Id. at* . Counsel's arguments concerning the trial mental health evidence in sentencing also "were at best belittling of the evidence and at worst damning" of the defendant. If counsel had performed adequately, the evidence would have established that the defendant was completely illiterate, mentally retarded or borderline mentally retarded, and had significant brain damage due to a near drowning and lack of oxygen to the brain when the defendant was quite young. The defendant had been taunted, tormented, and then beaten in school to the extent that the defendant's mother kept him home for an entire year. He also had an unstable home and had been abused by an aunt charged with his care.

> The Supreme Court has, time and again, cited "the standards for capital defense work articulated by the American Bar Association (ABA) … as 'guides to determining what is reasonable'" performance. Those standards repeatedly reference mental health evidence, describing it as "of vital importance to the jury's decision at the punishment phase." *See* ABA Guidelines for the Appointment and Performance of Defense Counsel in Death Penalty Cases 1.1, 4.1, 10.4, 10.7, 10.11. It was patently unreasonable for [counsel] to omit this evidence from his case for mitigation."

Id. at (other internal citations omitted). Prejudice found because the mitigating evidence omitted in this case "is exactly the sort of evidence that garners the most sympathy from jurors," according to "available empirical evidence as to juror attitudes." *Id.* at . This evidence could have provided the *"explanation"* of how a "kind-hearted person" could commit these crimes because the "organic brain damage caused these outbursts of violence." *Id.* at .

2003: *Lewis v. Dretke*, 355 F.3d. 364 (5th Cir. 2003) (sentencing in May 1987). Counsel was ineffective in capital sentencing for failing to adequately investigate and present evidence of the petitioner's abusive childhood. Applying pre-AEDPA law, the court gave no deference to the state court's resolution of the claims because the state court did not make any factual findings. Under *Wiggins*, "[a] limited investigation into mitigating evidence may be reasonable only if counsel has a basis for believing that further investigation would be counterproductive or fruitless." *Id.* at 367. Here, counsel's performance was deficient. While the record was limited by counsel's hazy memories and the fact that neither counsel had their file from the trial conducted 14 years before, the petitioner's sisters testified credibly that counsel had never interviewed any of them. Nothing in counsel's testimony indicated a tactical decision for failure to do so. Although the district court found the sisters' testimony was not credible, the Fifth Circuit rejected this finding because the testimony of the sisters was remarkably consistent in that each testified that their father beat them all with extension cords, switches, sticks, or anything else within his reach and that he regularly made them undress and whipped them in their genital areas. The court also found that there was corroborating evidence in the records, which revealed that the defendant's father was a violent drug abuser who shot the defendant's mother, almost killing her; and that he beat the defendant's mother on numerous occasions in front of the children. Medical records also establish that the children made numerous trips to the hospital emergency room for treatment of injuries consistent with the described beatings. The defendant had been hospitalized for cuts on his penis and his sister had been hospitalized for severe burns on her back. The defendant's mother had been hospitalized for a gunshot wound. There was also evidence of numerous domestic disturbance calls to the home. Prejudice was found even though the defendant's grandmother testified that the defendant had been abused. "[H]er conclusional testimony contained none of the details provided by Lewis' siblings at the habeas hearing, which could have been truly beneficial. [Her] skeletal testimony concerning the abuse of her grandson was wholly inadequate to present to the jury a true picture of the tortured childhood experienced by Lewis." *Id.* at 368. "[H]ad this evidence [of Petitioner's abuse] been presented, it is quite likely that it would have affected the sentencing decision of at least one juror." *Id.* at 369. The district court found that the testimony would have been inadmissible or given little weight due to the elapsed time between the child abuse and the crimes and the fact that the defendant had intervening criminal convictions, but this finding was erroneous. Mitigating evidence was considered in both *Williams v. Taylor* and *Wiggins* despite the elapsed time in both cases and the defendant in *Williams* had many intervening criminal convictions. "The district court's conclusion regarding the temporal nexus requirement was therefore erroneous." *Id.*

*Hamblin v. Mitchell, 354 F.3d 482 (6th Cir. 2003) (sentenced in April 1983). Counsel was ineffective in capital sentencing for failing to adequately prepare and present mitigation. Counsel did not attempt to obtain any family history or any facts concerning the defendant's psychological background and mental illness and counsel did not seek any advice or expert consultation. Despite a large body of mitigating evidence, counsel did nothing to discover what was available or introduce it in evidence. Analyzing the case under pre-AEDPA standards, the court held:

> the *Wiggins* case now stands for the proposition that the ABA standards for counsel in death penalty cases provide the guiding rules and standards to be used in defining the "prevailing professional norms" in ineffective assistance cases. This principle adds clarity, detail, and content to the more generalized and indefinite 20-year-old language of *Strickland*.

Id. at 486. Even though Hamblin was tried before the 1989 ABA standards were published, the Court held:

> The standards merely represent the codification of long-standing, common-sense principles of representation understood by diligent, competent counsel in death penalty cases. The ABA standards are not aspirational in the sense that they represent norms newly discovered after *Strickland*. They are the same type of longstanding norms referred to in *Strickland* in 1984 as "prevailing professional norms" as "guided" by "American Bar Association standards and the like."

Id. at 487. The court also held:

> New ABA Guidelines adopted in 2003 simply explain in greater detail than the 1989 Guidelines the obligations of counsel to investigate mitigating evidence. The 2003 ABA Guidelines do not depart in principle or concept from *Strickland*, *Wiggins*, or our court's previous cases concerning counsel's obligation to investigate mitigation circumstances.

Id. While the court recognized that it was required to measure counsel's performance against the prevailing standards at the time of trial,

> We cite the 1989 and 2003 ABA guidelines simply because they are the clearest exposition of counsel's duties at the penalty phase of a capital case, duties that were recognized by this court as applicable to the 1982 trial of the defendant in *Glenn v. Tate*. ...

Id. at 488. The district court held that counsel had a strategic reason for the failure to investigate and to rely instead on a residual doubt theory in sentencing (which has since been rejected by the Ohio Supreme Court as an improper mitigating factor). Counsel's conduct was deficient because counsel did not prepare in any way until after the guilty verdict. Counsel only interviewed the mother of Hamblin's daughter. Counsel did not gather any medical information, including psychological information, in part, because counsel believed that the only mental condition relevant was the defendant's competence to stand trial. In sentencing, the mother of the defendant's daughter testified only that the defendant had a good relationship with his child. She had nothing else positive to say and did not want to testify. The only other mitigation was a relatively short rambling, almost incoherent, unsworn statement by the defendant explaining his background. Counsel did nothing to prepare the defendant in giving this statement. The only explanation for the failure to prepare was that counsel believed the case would plead out and not go to trial. While the district court found a strategy because counsel would have uncovered harmful evidence and because the defendant expressed that he did not want to present evidence in mitigation; the Sixth Circuit rejected these findings

> because counsel does not know what an investigation will reveal is no reason not to conduct the investigation. Counsel was obligated to find out the facts not to guess or assume or suppose some facts may be adverse.

Id. at 492. Likewise, the court observed that

> ABA and judicial standards do not permit the court to excuse counsel's failure to investigate or prepare because the defendant so requested. ... The Guidelines state that "the investigation regarding penalty should be conducted regardless of any statement by the client that evidence bearing upon penalty is not to be collected or presented," because
>
> > [c]ounsel cannot responsibly advise a client about the merits of different courses of action, the client cannot make informed decisions, and counsel cannot be sure of the clients competency to make such decisions, unless counsel has first conducted a thorough investigation. ...

Id. (citing the 2003 ABA guidelines). Prejudice found because, if counsel had adequately investigated and presented mitigation, the evidence would have shown Hamblin's unstable and deprived childhood in which he grew up in extreme poverty and neglect surrounded by family violence and instability. He had a poor education and likely suffered from a mental disability or disorder. Hamblin's father was violent and beat his wife regularly. He ran a still and was arrested for public intoxication, manufacture of moonshine, and child neglect. Hamblin's mother often abandoned her children, leaving them to fend for themselves, and she at times resorted to prostitution. Hamblin tried to provide for himself and his younger sister by stealing food as a very young child. He started getting in trouble with the law as a teenager and left home at 13 the first time and left permanently at 16. He started showing signs of mental disorder when he was a teenager, probably resulting from his poor family situation and possibly from a severe blow to the head at age 8 inflicted by his father with a dog chain. His mother also had a severe infection while pregnant with him as a result of being stabbed by the defendant's father. In light of the "substantial evidence of a childhood in which abuse, neglect, violence and hunger were common," *id.* at 493, the court was convinced that had the available evidence been presented "at least one juror would have voted against the death penalty," *id.*

Frazier v. Huffman, 343 F.3d 780, *supplemented on denial of rehearing*, 348 F.3d 174 (6th Cir. 2003) (tried in August 1991). Counsel was ineffective in capital sentencing for failing to prepare and present mitigation evidence concerning a brain injury and a lack of impulse control that reasonably was a result of that injury. The defendant had been charged with killing his stepdaughter after she filed sexual assault charges against him in state court. During trial, the defense theory was one of innocence and the defense presented no evidence. In sentencing, the state had already proven the aggravating circumstances and state law required the jury to weigh aggravating and mitigating circumstances, but the defense presented no evidence, relying instead only on the defendant's brief statement to the jury in which he denied guilt, but asked for mercy. The court found that defense counsel was aware from a review of records about the brain injury and that there could be no reasonable trial strategy that would justify failing to investigate and present evidence of the brain impairment and instead rely exclusively on the hope that the jury would spare the defendant's life due to doubt about guilt. The court also noted that residual doubt is not a mitigating factor under Ohio law. The defendant "had everything to gain and nothing to lose by introducing evidence of his brain injury in the penalty phase of the case. Yet they sat on their hands." In analyzing the case under the AEDPA, the court found that the state court's determination that counsel had performed in a competent manner was not simply erroneous but unreasonable. The court also found prejudice because evidence of the brain injury could easily have been used by counsel to argue a scenario where the defendant did not intend to kill the victim and did so only due to the impulsively and stress. The state court's conclusion that counsel was effective was found to be an unreasonable application of clearly established Supreme Court precedent.

Powell v. Collins, 332 F.3d 376 (6th Cir. 2003) (tried in January 1987). Counsel ineffective in capital sentencing for failing to prepare and present mitigation evidence. Prior to trial, counsel repeatedly sought appointment of a psychiatrist or psychologist to assist the defense during the trial. The court denied the motions and instead ordered an evaluation by a court-appointed, neutral examiner, who found that the defendant suffered from antisocial personality disorder. During the trial the defense called the court-appointed examiner as a defense witness. In addition to the personality disorder information, she testified that the defendant did not enjoy a nurturing environment as a child and had been medicated with anti-psychotic medications for anxiety and behavior problems. She also testified that his IQ scores "fluctuated between the mild and borderline ranges of mental retardation." *Id.* at 383. Following conviction, counsel again requested expert assistance and the court granted it and ordered the court appointed examiner to address mitigation but refused to allow a continuance. The court-appointed examiner was the only witness called by the defense in sentencing. She repeated her trial testimony and stated that she did not have sufficient time to conduct a sufficient investigation and stated that she was not qualified to conduct the neuropsychological testing the defense wanted, although she believed that the defendant might have organic brain dysfunction. Because the habeas petition was filed in 1994, the court applied the standards applicable prior to the AEDPA. Relying heavily on the ABA Guidelines, the court found counsel's conduct to be deficient because counsel did not investigate mitigation and, in recalling the court-appointed expert, they presented harmful information that the defendant was not mentally ill and is dangerous. The court rejected a strategic reason for not presenting mitigation because counsel could not have a valid strategic reason when counsel had failed to investigate. Prejudice was found because numerous family members and other individuals that knew the defendant were available and willing to testify. Even though their testimony would have duplicated some of the testimony by the court-appointed expert, prejudice was established because the "jurors would have heard first-hand accounts from those who knew Petitioner best." *Id.* at 400. This "personal testimony" would have been more powerful than the expert, who had not even interviewed the family and friends. Prejudice was also clear where the prosecutor cited the "mitigation testimony" in support of the state's closing and the jury almost deadlocked even without any mitigation. In addition to this ineffective assistance of counsel finding, the court also found that relief was required due to the court's failure to appoint an independent defense expert and the court's denial of a continuance prior to sentencing.

Douglas v. Woodford, 316 F.3d 1079 (9th Cir. 2003) (tried in 1984). Counsel ineffective in failing to adequately prepare and present mitigation evidence. Petitioner, claiming an alibi, was convicted of killing two teenage girls in the desert, primarily based on the immunized testimony of an accomplice. During sentencing, the state presented testimony concerning similar bad acts involving forcing women to pose nude and engage in sex acts with other women for photographs. He also planned to make movies involving torture and killing of young women and had previously pled *nolo contendre* to charges arising from this planning. In mitigation, the defense presented only the defendant's wife and son and a neighbor to testify to good character, nonviolent nature, generosity, and a difficult background as an orphan. In "very general terms," they described a difficult childhood, running away at fifteen to join the Marines, and being very poor and hungry as a child. Prior to trial, counsel retained mental health experts because the defendant was experiencing severe claustrophobia in his cell, which was related to having been locked in closets by abusive parents as a child. Because of the focus on claustrophobia, petitioner was unable to focus on his defense. The experts did brief testing and interviewing and found no mental disorders, but did recommend additional mental health testing. After the defendant was moved to a private cell and the claustrophobia issue addressed, he refused to cooperate with any further mental health testing and insisted on an alibi defense during trial. He was also "less than helpful" in providing background information and reported that "his parents were dead and that his past was a 'blank.'" *Id.* at 1087. He also refused to provide names of relatives or friends to provide information on his childhood abuse. Analyzing the case under pre-AEDPA standards, the court found counsel's conduct deficient for failing to discover and present significant mitigation evidence. Even though petitioner "was not forthcoming with useful information, … this does not excuse counsel's obligation to obtain mitigating evidence from other sources." *Id.* at 1088. Counsel had enough information to put him "on notice" that petitioner had "a particularly difficult childhood," but did not attempt to contact persons who could provide the details or even to interview and prepare the witnesses that did testify so their testimony "was less than compelling." *Id.* Counsel did not even present some of the information he was aware of such as the claustrophobia due to being locked in closets as a child. Likewise, counsel had obtained the file pertaining to the defendant's prior conviction and that file contained an order for a psychological examination. If counsel had obtained that testing and interviewed that expert, he would have discovered a conclusion of serious and outstanding mental illness and possible organic impairment. That expert noted severe paranoia, chronic alcoholism, constant exposure to toxic solvents in the furniture refinishing business, and a serious head injury in a car accident, which the expert believed led to diminished capacity. If counsel had investigated the social background further, counsel would have discovered significant evidence that the petitioner was abandoned as a child and placed in foster homes, where an abusive alcoholic foster father would lock him in closets for long periods of time. He was extremely poor and often had to scavenge for food in garbage cans and eat just lard or ketchup sandwiches. He ran away at fifteen to join the Marines, but was arrested and put in a Florida jail where he was beaten and gang-raped by other inmates. When he did join the Marines, he received a number of medals and commendations. Counsel's failure to prepare and present mitigation counsel not be attributed to his client's lack of cooperation, because counsel had already "disregarded his client's wishes and did put on what mitigating evidence he had unearthed." *Id.* at 1089. Moreover, the jury had already convicted the defendant and rejected his alibi evidence, so "'lingering doubt' was not a viable option." *Id.* at 1090. Thus "there was nothing to lose" by presenting social history and mental health evidence. *Id.* at 1091. Prejudice was found, despite "the gruesome nature" of the offenses, *id.*, because the available "social background and mental health" evidence was "critical for a jury to consider when deciding whether to impose a death sentence," *id.* at 1090. This evidence could have "invoked sympathy" from at least one juror. *Id.*

2002: ***Simmons v. Luebbers***, 299 F.3d 929 (8th Cir. 2002) (direct appeals in 1997). Under AEDPA, counsel ineffective in failing to prepare and present mitigating evidence in two separate capital trials. Counsel presented only the defendant's mother to testify that she loved her son and wanted a continued relationship with him. Counsel's conduct was deficient. Four mental health professionals examined the defendant on the issue of competence and "the evaluations uncovered character and background issues that his attorneys could have presented to the jury as mitigating evidence during the penalty phase." Prejudiced established because the evidence could have shown: he was raised in poverty in a "neighborhood frequented bystreet violence"; his mother was extremely religious and very strict; he was beaten with rulers, straps, and belts and often had welts and bruises until age 17; he was so afraid of being beaten that he would urinate on himself prior to the beatings; his father had a drinking problem and would frequently beat his mother with the defendant trying to intervene to protect his mother; he ran away from home at 12 and was robbed, beaten, and possibly raped (he would not discuss it) at a bus terminal in Chicago; and he had an IQ of 83. The state court's decision of reasonable strategy was an unreasonable determination of the facts in light of the evidence presented in the State court proceeding. The state court held that the evidence had been presented and rejected in the initial trial and sentencing, but the record did not support this finding and reflected instead that counsel presented evidence that the defendant's mother was "an upstanding person." Counsel's conduct was unreasonable in failing to present the evidence of the "childhood experiences." By the time the defense case in sentencing began, "the jury had yet to hear any evidence that was sympathetic to [him]. Instead, the jury had only heard evidence of his ruthless character." In addition, counsel "should have been aware that they could not rely on pleas from [the defendant's] mother in an effort to spare [his] life" because this evidence had been presented unsuccessfully twice before. Counsel also did not make a reasonable strategic decision not to present this evidence in order to avoid comparisons to the defendant's successful brother. There was no evidence the brother "was beaten as consistently or severely" or had "sexually assaulted during his childhood."

> Moreover, considering the overwhelming amount of aggravating evidence that had been proffered by the state, ... comparisons to a successful brother would [not] have made the jury's perception ... any worse. ... Mitigating evidence was essential to provide some sort of explanation for [the defendant's] abhorrent behavior."

Id. at 938-39. Prejudice found because the state portrayed the defendant as violent to women that rejected him. The defense could have countered this with evidence "that his compulsive, violent reactions were the result of an abusive and traumatic childhood. In addition, "a vivid description of [the defendant's] poverty stricken childhood, particularly the physical abuse, and the assault in Chicago, may have influenced the jury's assessment of his moral culpability."

Karis v. Calderon, 283 F.3d 1117 (9th Cir. 2002) (tried in 1982). Counsel ineffective for failing to prepare and present mitigating evidence of the defendant's troubled childhood, during which he suffered repeated abuse and watched his mother being regularly and violently abused by men. "[T]he failure to present important mitigating evidence in the penalty phase can be as devastating as a failure to present proof of innocence in the guilt phase." *Id.* at 1135. Counsel's conduct was deficient because counsel failed to investigate and offered no reasonable explanation for the failure. Counsel had intended to present this evidence through a mental health expert but then chose not to do so because there was also damaging evidence in the expert's report. While counsel was not ineffective for not calling the expert, counsel was ineffective for failing to prepare and present the evidence through family members and other witnesses. The duty to investigate is not excused because the family did not readily offer the information because counsel knew the information was there and "should have explained ... the gravity" of the situation to the family members. *Id.* at 1136. Prejudice found because counsel presented only 48 minutes of mitigation, which included only that the defendant had artistic and academic talent, that his mother was divorced, and that he had saved his brother from drowning as a child. This evidence allowed the prosecutor to argue that the defendant was "intelligent" and "cunning" and to argue the absence of any mitigation when there was substantial mitigation available. Even with the weak mitigation presented, the sentencing jury took three days to render a verdict.

Caro v. Woodford, 280 F.3d 1247 (9th Cir. 2002) (tried in 1981). Counsel ineffective in capital sentencing for failing to prepare and present evidence of the defendant's brain damage due to a long history of exposure to toxic pesticides and chemicals, history of severe head injuries, and significant abuse as a child. Counsel's conduct was deficient because counsel knew of the long history of exposure to toxic pesticides, but did not inform the experts that examined the defendant and did not seek out an expert to assess the damage done to the defendant's brain. Counsel conceded no strategy explained the failure. The defendant was prejudiced because, as the court said at the very beginning of the opinion, "A little explanation can go a long way. In this case, it might have made the difference between life and death." "Prejudice found because rather than premeditation this evidence revealed the effects of "*physiological defects* ... on his behavior, such as causing him to have impulse discontrol and irrational aggressiveness. By explaining that his behavior was physically compelled, not premeditated, or even due to a lack of emotional control, his moral culpability would have been reduced." *Id.* at 1258. The prejudice was heightened where the state's evidence of premeditation was not particularly strong and where, "[m]ore than any other singular factor, mental defects have been respected as a reason for leniency in our criminal justice system." Also of significance, the court rejected the state's arguments that high grades, satisfactory military performance, negative blood results for pesticides, a reasonably high IQ, rationality of actions following the murders, and normal psychiatric and neurological evaluations was inconsistent with the finding of brain damage. As one expert (Jonathan Pincus) explained, damage to a person's frontal lobes may not affect other brain functions controlled by other parts of the brain.

Silva v. Woodford, 279 F.3d 825 (9th Cir. 2002) (tried in January 1982). In pre-AEDPA case, counsel ineffective in capital sentencing for failing to prepare and present mitigation. Deficient conduct found despite the assertion that the defendant instructed counsel that he did not want his family called as witnesses. Such an instruction does not alleviate the need to investigate or at least to adequately inform the defendant of the potential consequences of the decision and to assure that the defendant has made an informed and knowing judgment. Moreover, there was significant mitigation evidence available outside of contacting the defendant's family, including prior psychiatric reports and presentencing report in a pending drug case. Court notes that the ABA guidelines, cited favorably in *Williams v. Taylor*, "suggest that a lawyer's duty to investigate is virtually absolute, regardless of a client's expressed wishes." *Id.* at 840. "Indeed, if a client forecloses certain avenues of investigation, it arguably becomes even more incumbent upon trial counsel to seek out and find alternative sources of information and evidence, especially in the context of a capital murder trial." *Id.* at 847. Counsel "could not make a reasoned tactical decision about the trial precisely because counsel did not even know what evidence was available." *Id.* at 847 (quotation omitted). Prejudice found due to the prosecution's "emphasis on the utter lack of mitigating evidence, "*id.* at 847, and "in spite of the undeniably horrific circumstances" of the murders, "this is not a case in which a death sentence was inevitable," *id.* at 849 (quotation omitted). Indeed, the court noted that a co-defendant was sentenced to life and that defendant's jury sought an explanation of "life without parole." *Id.* at 849. "These questions suggest that a death sentence ... was not a foregone conclusion ..." *Id.* at 849-50. The available and unpresented mitigation included evidence of abuse and neglect by alcoholic parents, the possibility of brain damage from Fetal Alcohol Syndrome, the possibility of Post-Traumatic Stress Disorder, Attention Deficit Disorder that caused failures in school, self-medication through drug use, and amphetamine-induced organic mental disorders and withdrawal symptoms of the time of the offenses.

Hooper v. Mullin, 314 F.3d 1162 (10th Cir. 2002) (tried in June 1995). Under AEDPA, counsel ineffective in failing to adequately prepare and present mitigation. Eight months prior to the crimes, the defendant received anger management counseling and was given several neuropsychological tests. The doctor reported that his testing showed a possible learning disability, some emotional and psychological problems, and that he had difficulty controlling his anger and coping with everyday problems. Prior to trial counsel retained another psychologist to review this report. This doctor issued a one-page summary stating that there was evidence of "mild but probable brain damage" that could increase the likelihood of violence, especially if the defendant was under the influence of alcohol or other substances, and the possibility of a "serious psychiatric thought disorder." The doctor qualified his "impressions" by noting that "further diagnostic investigation" was needed "to confirm." Six months later (and the day the defendant was convicted), counsel called the expert asking him to testify the following day. Despite the expert's objection that he ethically could not testify because he had not personally examined the defendant and that his testimony "likely would be aggravating rather than mitigating," counsel subpoenaed him to testify and sought permission to treat him as a hostile witness, "in light of the extreme hostility [the doctor] directed toward defense counsel and court personnel." His report and the previous doctor's report were admitted through his testimony in which he asserted the prior doctor would be in the best position to address whether there was brain damage. The State called the prior doctor in rebuttal and he testified that there was no brain damage or psychological problem that would cause the defendant to lose touch with reality or make him incapable of controlling himself or his anger. As the state court found, prejudice was established because neither doctor "offered any mitigating evidence and their combined testimony was disastrous" for the defense. The state court's finding that counsel's conduct was not deficient was an objectively unreasonable application of *Strickland.* While counsel did have a strategy to suggest the defendant "might have brain damage which could have produced violent conduct," this was not reasonable because "counsel deliberately pursued this strategy without conducting a thorough investigation." Counsel asserted additional testing was not done because counsel feared further investigation might negate the argument that there might be brain damage. Counsel also failed to speak to either of these experts "and had no idea what these experts would say on the witness stand."

> In addition, although the defense did not intend to call [the first doctor] as a mitigation witness, defense counsel should have foreseen that the State might use him in rebuttal after the defense specifically relied on his report as mitigating evidence. Had counsel not offered this testimony, [this] report would have remained privileged and inadmissible.

__Brownlee v. Haley__, 306 F.3d 1043 (11th Cir. 2002) (tried in January 1987). Counsel ineffective in pre-AEDPA case for failing to prepare and present mitigation in capital sentencing. Defendant was convicted of murder and armed robbery in a bar. Nine eyewitnesses testified during the trial, but none was able to identify the defendant. No forensic evidence linked defendant to the crime. A codefendant, who was identified by four eyewitnesses and had plead guilty in exchange for a life sentence, testified that he participated in the crime along with defendant and another codefendant, but even this witness was unable to state whether defendant shot the victim. Several other witnesses provided incriminating testimony about defendant's actions and statements before and after the crimes, but their testimony contradicted the codefendant in some respects. Following conviction, in the jury phase of sentencing where an Alabama jury renders an advisory verdict, counsel presented no evidence in mitigation and offered only a brief closing argument. The jury deliberated for 38 minutes and recommended a sentence of death by an 11-1 vote. Prior to the second phase of sentencing where the trial court must "consider" the jury's recommendation and can consider additional evidence in aggravation and mitigation, the trial court suggested that counsel should have the defendant examined by a clinical psychologist. In the hearing before the trial court, counsel presented the psychologist to testify that defendant has a mixed substance abuse disorder, a mixed personality disorder, and

borderline intellectual functioning, with an IQ of 70 (in the mildly retarded range) but adaptive skills at a higher level. Two sisters also testified that defendant had been previously taken to a psychiatric hospital after jumping out a second floor window of the family apartment, a history of mood changes, complaints of severe headaches, and seizures for a couple of years, including one incident where he slashed himself across the chest with a knife. After hearing this evidence and considering a presentence report, the trial court found no mitigating factors and sentenced defendant to death. Counsel's conduct was deficient because counsel conducted no pretrial discovery and conducted virtually no investigation. Counsel spoke only with one sister and that was after the jury's recommendation of death and just prior to the sentencing hearing before the judge. Counsel did not have the defendant examined by a psychologist until the court suggested it because counsel observed no mental problems and believed the defendant had above average intelligence. Counsel did not pursue evidence of drug problems because they did not believe the jury would be sympathetic. If counsel had adequately investigated the evidence would have shown that the defendant grew up in a high crime area. On separate occasions, he had been stabbed in the chest and shot multiple times, including in the head. The psychologist, based on the additional information, would have testified that the defendant was either mildly mentally retarded or borderline intelligence and suffered from mental disorders, including schizotypal and antisocial personality disorders, multiple drug dependencies, and a seizure disorder (due to seizures for several years following the shot to the head). The psychologist would have testified that the defendant's capacity at the time of the crimes was possibly diminished due to the combination of mental disorders, limited intelligence, and drugs. The psychologist and a correctional officer that had previously supervised defendant in prison also both testified that the defendant was a model inmate and was unlikely to engage in violent behavior in prison. Prejudice found because presentation of this evidence would have provided compelling evidence supporting two statutory mitigating circumstances ((1) influence of extreme mental or emotional disturbance and (2) substantially impaired capacity at the time of the crimes) and several significant non-statutory mitigating factors, including the defendant's "severe intellectual limitations." *Id.* at (citing *Atkins v. Virginia*, 122 S. Ct. 2242 (2002)). The prejudice was also clear because of the weaknesses in the state's evidence linking the defendant to the murder. Due to counsel's failure to present, "anything at all about the defendant … [a]n individualized sentence, as required by law, was … impossible."
Id. at . The court found a reasonable probability that the jury would have recommended a life sentence if counsel had adequately presented the mitigation. The prejudice was not cured by the trial court's ultimate review because, under state law, the trial court was required to "consider" the jury's recommendation. "[T]he use of the term 'shall consider' indicates that a court is required to reflect actively and carefully on the jury's recommendation, as consideration clearly involves more than a passing thought." *Id.* at .

2001: ***Jermyn v. Horn***, 266 F.3d 257 (3d Cir. 2001) (tried in August 1985). Counsel ineffective, under AEDPA, in capital sentencing for failing to prepare and present mitigating evidence. During the trial for murder of the defendant's mother, counsel presented two alternative arguments: either the defendant's mother accidentally set the fire that killed her and the defendant was innocent or the defendant committed the crimes and was insane at the time. This evidence included testimony from an expert that the defendant was a chronic paranoid schizophrenic. During sentencing, counsel only presented brief testimony that the defendant should not be sentenced to death because he was adaptable to confinement. He also argued that the defendant was mentally ill and argued about the defendant's deprived childhood, although no evidence about this had been presented. Counsel was only out of law school for "less than two years, this was his first capital case, and the first case he had tried which involved mental health issues." *Id.* at 275. He also did not hire an investigator and admitted that his time prior to trial was largely consumed with other cases. Counsel's conduct was deficient because the trial expert had informed him of the physical abuse suffered by the defendant and the significance of this in explaining the defendant's behavior. Nonetheless, counsel did not present this evidence and offered no strategic reason for the failure to do so. Indeed, counsel did not do anything in preparation for sentencing until after the guilty verdict. Counsel also testified that he did not realize the importance of the childhood until the end of sentencing, which is why he argued – on the basis of no evidence – about the childhood. Prejudice found because, if counsel had adequately investigated, the evidence would have revealed that the defendant's father was physically abusive, showed no affection, and virtually banished the defendant from his presence. At times, he was even chained to a dog leash and made to eat out of a dog bowl. Eventually, his mother placed him in a residential school for "orphans" or "unwanted children," to get him out of the home. Experts, including the defense expert at trial, observed that the defendant's childhood experiences were severe and "contributed significantly to his mental illness which they diagnosed as paranoid schizophrenia." *Id.* at 274. The state court decision was unreasonable, under 28 U.S.C. § 2254(d)(1), because the Pennsylvania Supreme Court unreasonably applied *Strickland*'s prejudice inquiry in light of the totality of mitigating evidence adduced at trial and in the habeas proceedings.

Coleman v. Mitchell, 268 F.3d 417 (6th Cir. 2001) (tried in June 1985). Counsel ineffective in pre-AEDPA capital sentencing for failing to prepare and present mitigating evidence. The mitigation evidence presented at trial was limited to the defendant's unsworn statement. Counsel's argument in sentencing was limited to two issues: the circumstantial nature of the murder evidence and the evils of execution by the electric chair. Counsel's conduct was deficient because counsel failed to investigate and present the mitigation evidence. This conduct was not excused by strategy because residual doubt is not a permissible argument in sentencing in Ohio. Likewise, any decision to make "a generalized, mercy-based critique of the electric chair over a particularized account of Petitioner's social and mental history," *id.* at 447, without any investigation, was unreasonable. Moreover, despite the District Court's finding to the contrary, the record did not support the finding that the defendant had waived the presentation of mitigation evidence. Instead, the defendant had waived his right to a pre-sentence investigation and mental examination under state law, which is distinguishable from any mitigation. Furthermore, even assuming that the defendant had instructed counsel not to present mitigation, because of counsel's failure to investigate counsel could not adequately advise the defendant of what he was waiving and the record did not support a finding "that Petitioner had any understanding of competing mitigation strategies." *Id.* The court found in this case "involving a defendant with low intelligence, limited education and an unsettling past, whose strongest demand for self-representation [or controlling the presentation of mitigation evidence] consisted of 'No, I don't' responses when asked if he wanted a pre-sentence investigation and mental evaluation," that a finding that the defendant had knowingly and intelligently waived the presentation of mitigation evidence "hollows the Sixth Amendment." *Id.* at 449. "Further, defendant resistance to disclosure of information does not excuse counsel's duty to independently investigate." *Id.* at 449-50. If counsel had adequately investigated and presented the evidence, they jury would have heard that the defendant's mother abandoned him as an infant in a garbage can and she spent lengthy periods of time in psychiatric hospitals. His grandmother, who was his primary caretaker, abused him both physically and psychologically, as well as neglecting him while running her home as a brothel and gambling house. She also told him that their home was surrounded by enemies that wanted to poison them and involved him in her voodoo practice by having him kill animals and collect their body parts for use in her magic potions. He was exposed to group sex, sometimes including his mother or grandmother, as well as bestiality and pedophilia. The defendant was also admitted to the hospital on two occasions for head injuries. Petitioner had also been examined previously for competence to stand trial on a federal kidnapping charge. Those examiners, even though only examining competence, had found that the defendant had elevated test results "under the psychopathic--deviant and paranoia categories, as well as a full-scale I.Q. score of 82, falling in the low-normal range, and a verbal I.Q. score of 79, falling at the upper limits of the borderline retarded range." They also found that he "had probable mixed personality disorder with antisocial, narcissistic and obsessive features." An earlier examination had also revealed borderline personality. In addition, experts in the post-conviction proceedings found "borderline personality disorder, a likelihood of organic brain dysfunction, [and] … probable manic- depressive psychosis." *Id.* at 450-52 (footnotes omitted in quotes).

__Mayfield v. Woodford__, 270 F.3d 915 (9th Cir. 2001) (en banc) (murder and counsel appointed in 1983). The majority in a split decision found counsel ineffective in the capital sentencing hearing (in pre-AEDPA case) for failing to prepare and present mitigation evidence. Counsel's investigation was deficient where counsel billed only 40 hours in preparation for both the trial and the penalty phases of trial and had only one substantive meeting with his client – the morning trial began – and even then did not discuss with him possible witnesses or trial strategies. Counsel also failed to associate co-counsel to assist in the defense, even though state law entitled the defendant to a second attorney. Counsel also spent less than half the defense investigation budget authorized by the county and did not obtain all of the defendant's medical records or consult with experts in endocrinology or toxicology, even though his investigator's limited efforts revealed evidence of diabetes and substance abuse. During sentence, counsel waived the opening statement and called only one witness – an expert – that had interviewed the defendant twice and testified "regarding Mayfield's family and childhood background, his health history including his diabetes, his work history, his psychiatric profile, and his substance abuse." *Id.* at 928. The expert also related a story that informed the jury that the defendant "could be a kind, generous human being" and informed the jury that the defendant "had indicated considerable remorse for what he had done." *Id.* Outside of this one witness, counsel presented no evidence and even stipulated – erroneously – that the defendant's urine tested negative for PCP the day after the crime, "indicating to the jury both that [the defendant] did not have a substance abuse problem and that [he] had lied about it" in his statement to police. *Id.* Counsel did not call the defendant's mother and uncle to testify for specific reasons but he did not even attempt to interview or present the testimony of other family members or friends. He also made no effort in his closing argument "to explain to the jury the significance of the mitigating evidence presented" by the one expert witness. "In short, [counsel] did not, as *Williams v. Taylor* requires, adequately investigate and prepare for the penalty phase or present and explain to the jury the significance of all the available mitigating evidence." *Id.* Prejudice found even though the state's aggravation evidence was "strong" and the mitigation evidence presented at trial was "substantial." *Id.* at 929. The evidence counsel presented included evidence that the defendant was diagnosed with diabetes at age nine and was hospitalized 20 to 30 times because his diabetes was never under very good control. The trial expert also testified that the defendant had low average intelligence and had been diagnosed with a child behavioral disorder caused by depression. He began using PCP two or three times a week in his late teens and by the time of the murder was using it on a daily basis. The expert erroneously informed the jury, however, that the defendant was not under the influence of drugs or alcohol the night of the crimes. The defense expert then testified that the defendant's score was moderately elevated on a "psychopathic deviance" test and that he was "lacking in emotion," but that he had demonstrated remorse and "had good rapport with the prison guards." *Id.* at 930. The defense expert also read for the jury the conclusion of a neurologist that the crime "could be explained only on the basis of definite cerebral impairment due to alcohol and drug abuse." *Id.* On the basis of this evidence, the jury deliberated for a day and a half (and had even sent out a note asking if the jury had to be unanimous in order to sentence the defendant to life without parole) before sentencing the defendant to death. In addition to other evidence, if counsel had adequately prepared and presented the evidence, the jury would have also heard that the defendant suffered abdominal and chest pain, dehydration, fatigue, dizziness, nausea, loss of consciousness, and comas due to his diabetes. He sometimes had to be hospitalized as much as five times a month. Prior to the diabetes, he was essentially a normal child, but the physical and psychological traumas caused drastic changes in him and precipitated his drug use. During the months prior to the crime, he was hospitalized again for high blood sugar levels and using increasing amounts of drugs due to stressors, including his pregnant girlfriend leaving him. In addition, the jury could have heard substantial lay witness testimony that the defendant was a good person, that he was non-violent, and that his family loved him and wanted the jury to spare his life. Prejudice found "[i]n light of the quantity and quality of the mitigating evidence [counsel] failed to present at trial, the duration of the jury's deliberations, and the jury's communication to the trial judge." *Id.* at 932.

__Ainsworth v. Woodford__, 268 F.3d 868 (9th Cir. 2001) (trial in January 1982). Counsel ineffective in pre-AEDPA capital sentencing for failing to prepare and present mitigating evidence. Counsel waived the opening statement in sentencing and then called only four witnesses in mitigation that covered "just under nine transcript pages." These witnesses revealed that the defendant's father had committed suicide; that the defendant had attended some college and held down a full-time job at which he was a good worker; that he had a three-month old son; and that he was kind, non-violent, and a talented artist. One of these witnesses also testified, however, that the defendant had planned to rob bank before but stopped because there were too many police around. *Id.* at 872. As the court found, "While it is true that the testimony touched upon general areas of mitigation, counsel's cursory examination of the witnesses failed to adduce any substantive evidence in mitigation. In fact, counsel's ill-preparation resulted in the testimony of one defense witness ... contributing to the evidence in aggravation." *Id.* at 874-75. Counsel's conduct was deficient because counsel "sought no assistance from a law clerk, paralegal, or another attorney in his preparation for the penalty phase, nor did he seek advice or aid from investigators or experts. In addition, he did not seek any state funds to prepare for the penalty phase although funding for the use of investigators and experts in capital cases was available" under state law. *Id.* at 876. He interviewed only one defense witness and that was on the morning she was scheduled to testify. He also failed to obtain "employment records, medical records, prison records, past probation reports, and military records," although he did get school records. Counsel even admitted in a deposition "that he abdicated the investigation of Ainsworth's psychosocial history to one of Ainsworth's female relatives." *Id.* at 874. Counsel's closing argument did not reference even the evidence counsel did present or refute the aggravation. Instead counsel only argued that the defendant was a "nice person" and argued "against the death penalty in general to a jury that had at *voir dire* already indicated no opposition to the death penalty." *Id.* at 875. If counsel had adequately prepared and presented the evidence, the jury would have heard evidence of the defendant's troubled childhood, his history of substance abuse, and his mental and emotional problems. Both of his parents were volatile alcoholics, who argued daily. His father was physically, verbally, and emotionally abusive and attempted to kill the defendant at least twice. His father ultimately committed suicide after four previous unsuccessful attempts. The defendant blamed himself for this and felt an overwhelming sense of guilt following his father's death. The defendant began ingesting alcohol at age five. By age 16, the defendant had attempted suicide and was admitted to a psychiatric ward for treatment for alcoholism. He joined the military at age 17, but was discharged because of his addiction to alcohol and morphine. He was then again admitted to a hospital and diagnosed with acute alcoholic intoxication, psychoneurotic disorder, and depressive reaction. Throughout his adult life, the defendant "regularly abused alcohol and drugs, including heroin, amphetamines, LSD, marijuana, and peyote. He resorted to gasoline when he was unable to access other drugs. He attempted suicide six or seven times by slashing his wrists." *Id.* at 875. Post-conviction experts supplied all of this information and testified that the substance abuse was a form of self-medication. Prejudice found because the jury heard no evidence of the defendant's "troubled background and his emotional stability and what led to the development of the person who committed the crime." *Id.* at 878. Defense counsel also failed to present evidence of the defendant's "favorable prison record which could be important in deciding whether, if given a life sentence without parole, he would be a danger to other prisoners or prison personnel." *Id.*

Battenfield v. Gibson, 236 F.3d 1215 (10th Cir. 2001) (tried in February 1985). Counsel ineffective in capital sentencing for failing to adequately investigate and present mitigating evidence, despite the purported waiver of mitigation by the defendant and the limited review necessitated by the AEDPA. Counsel's conduct was deficient because he spent very little time investigating mitigation and planned only to present the defendant's parents to beg for sympathy and mercy. Counsel never interviewed the parents, the defendant, or anyone else, however, concerning the defendant's background. Court cites approvingly "Stephen B. Bright, *Advocate in Residence: The Death Penalty As the Answer to Crime: Costly, Counterproductive and Corrupting*, 36 Santa Clara Rev. 1069, 1085-86 (1996) ('The responsibility of the lawyer is to walk a mile in the shoes of the client, to see who he is, to get to know his family and the people who care about him, and then to present that information to the jury in a way that can be taken into account in deciding whether the client is so beyond redemption that he should be eliminated from the human community.')." 236 F.3d at 1229. No strategy excused counsel's choice to only beg for sympathy and mercy. "[T]here was no strategic decision at all because [counsel] was ignorant of various other mitigation strategies he could have employed." *Id.* at 1229. Moreover, counsel knew the state planned to rely on evidence of the defendant's prior conviction for assault and battery with a dangerous weapon but never investigated to determine the underlying facts of that conviction. The state court did not address the lack of investigative efforts at all so the federal court exercised its independent judgment on this issue. Alternatively, the court concluded that the state court unreasonably applied *Strickland* in finding counsel's conduct to be reasonable. The court also found that counsel's failure was not excused by the defendant's waiver of the right to present mitigation because counsel's "failure to investigate clearly affected his ability to competently advise Battenfield regarding the meaning of mitigation evidence and the availability of possible mitigation strategies." *Id.* Counsel could not have discussed the available mitigation with the defendant because he was unaware of the evidence. Thus, counsel informed the defendant only of the intent to have his parents beg for mercy. The defendant thus waived mitigation because he did not want his parents to testify. The state court found the waiver to be knowing and intelligent, but the federal court rejected this finding as both factually and legally unreasonable because neither counsel nor the state court provided sufficient information for the defendant to make a knowing and intelligent choice. The federal court also rejected the state court's finding that counsel was reasonable for relying on the defendant's waiver because the court failed "to see how [the defendant] can be held responsible for [counsel's] failure to present mitigating evidence unknown to [the defendant]." *Id.* at 1233. The court found this to be "a patently unreasonable application of *Strickland.*" Prejudice found because the only valid aggravating circumstance found by the jury was a continuing threat based in substantial part on the state's evidence of a prior violent conviction. If counsel had adequately investigated, however, this evidence could have been rebutted with evidence that the prior assault may have been an act of self defense committed while under the influence of alcohol and drugs. If counsel had adequately investigated, the evidence available in mitigation would have also included (a) the defendant's involvement in a serious car accident at age 18, during which he sustained a serious head injury and after which he heavily used alcohol and drugs, (b) a family history of alcoholism and possible drug addiction, (c) evidence from family members and friends indicating that the defendant was known for his compassion, gentleness, and lack of violence, even when provoked, and (d) testimony of prison personnel describing the security and drug and alcohol treatment programs where the defendant would be incarcerated if given a life sentence. The federal court's finding of prejudice was not constrained by the AEDPA standards because the state court never addressed this issue.

2000: ***Lockett v. Anderson***, 230 F.3d 695 (5th Cir. 2000) (tried in 1986). Counsel ineffective in murder case for murdering husband and wife for failing to prepare and present adequate mitigation evidence with respect to the wife. Defendant was tried and sentenced separately for these offenses, although they were combined in federal habeas. District Court had already granted new trial on husband's murder case. Counsel ineffective because counsel failed to adequately prepare due to illness of counsel's mother, these two murder cases one month apart, and two other capital trials. Counsel lacked basic "familiarity" with "psychological tests" performed on his client, but he knew client had a history of seizure problems and head injuries. Counsel did not investigate, however, even after defendant's mother retained a psychiatrist who recommended additional testing, including neuropsychological testing. Counsel was aware of recommendations. Counsel was also aware of "black-outs, delusional stories, references to self as another name, family troubles, drug and/or alcohol addiction," which should have "put him on notice that pursuit of the basic leads that were before him may have led to medical evidence that Lockett had mental and psychological abnormalities that seriously affected his ability to control his behavior. Counsel thus may have had a strong predicate from which to argue to the jury that Lockett was rendered less morally culpable for the ruthless, cruel, and senseless murders he had committed." *Id. at* . Strategic decision does not excuse counsel's conduct because counsel did not even follow the recommendation for additional testing recommended by defense psychiatrist. Court also rejected argument of strategic decision to avoid devastating cross-examination because trial defense counsel never considered the strategy. Prejudice found even though crimes were particularly aggravated and some of this evidence could have been aggravating because it could support future dangerousness because additional testing and investigation would have revealed temporal lobe lesion or epilepsy and/or schizophrenia and a troubled childhood with trauma. Without this evidence, counsel just asked jury for mercy and presented no real evidence or argument in mitigation.

Carter v. Bell, 218 F.3d 581 (6th Cir. 2000) (indicted March 1984 and affirmed on appeal in 1986). Counsel ineffective in capital sentencing where counsel neither investigated nor introduced any evidence of mitigating factors. The defense only argued residual doubt when the state's evidence consisted of an eyewitness who saw the defendant with the victim and the testimony of a co-defendant who had already plead guilty and defense evidence was one alibi witness. Counsel spoke to only a few family members and they could not say whether they had even discussed mitigation. Counsel did not even obtain a release from client so they could view his personal or prison records and they did not seek any available records on defendant or his family. Counsel had prepared motion for expert but did not pursue it after defendant said he did not want to pursue insanity defense. Available mitigation evidence included evidence of "illegitimacy, extreme childhood poverty and neglect, family violence and instability during childhood, poor education, mental disability and disorder, military history, and positive relationships with step-children, adult family, and friends." Family history included one sibling dying in fire set by mom's boyfriend, two siblings dying of birth defects as infants, and all six remaining siblings having criminal records. Defendant's mother and sister were both hospitalized in mental health institutions and his grandfather, father, mother, step-father, and brother all suffered from alcoholism. Defendant's childhood home was also violent and unstable in that the family never lived in one place more than two years. Mother drank and would often drink up her welfare check and let the children go hungry. At the age of three, defendant and his then five year old sister were abandoned by their mother for more than a week, subsisting on milk stolen from the neighbors' porches. The welfare department placed the two in a children's home for several weeks. They subsequently lived with their aunt until their mother regained custody a year later. The defendant also suffered seriously from childhood rheumatic fever. He was whipped and beaten as an infant for crying from the illness. He also suffered frequent serious breathing problems as a child that led to numerous trips to the emergency room. The records show both childhood and adult head injuries from accidents and fights. He was also diagnosed with diabetes in 1977, when he apparently was brought to the hospital in a coma. Defendant had limited schooling and an IQ of only 79. Just prior to trial, a corrections doctor recommended "psychiatric hospitalization" because defendant's "nerves seemed stretched to the breaking point." Defendant was ultimately diagnosed after trial with schizophrenia and a history of partial seizures. Counsel's deficient conduct was not excused because defendant did not tell them of history. "The sole source of mitigating factors cannot properly be that information which defendant may volunteer; counsel must make some effort at independent investigation in order to make a reasoned, informed decision as to their utility." *Id.* at 596. Defendant's reluctance to present mental health evidence or testify also does not excuse failure to investigate. Conduct also not excused by argument that state would have rebutted with other crimes and bad character evidence because Tennessee law would permit rebuttal of the mitigating evidence submitted only and not general bad character evidence.

Jackson v. Calderon, 211 F.3d 1148 (9th Cir. 2000) (tried in early 1984). Counsel ineffective for failing to prepare and present mitigation evidence. Defendant was smoking PCP and engaging in bizarre behaviors, such as diving head first into pavement and pulling and slapping his hair. A police officer responding to the call to investigate told the defendant to sit and ultimately hit him in the back of the legs with the baton when the defendant attempted to walk away. They struggled and the defendant was maced in the face a number of times. When officer ran to driver's side of patrol car possibly to call for backup, the defendant reached in passenger side and the two struggled for a shotgun. The defendant got it. Evidence conflicting, but it appeared that both put their weapons on the roof of the car at some point and then defendant grabbed shotgun up and fired. One pellet entered officer's eye and killed him. When other officers arrived, the defendant would not surrender and threatened to kill. A police dog caused the defendant to drop the weapon and the defendant was subdued after a struggle in which he tried to get another weapon. Shortly after the arrest, the defendant's blood pressure dropped drastically and he has hospitalized due to incoherence, shock, and semiconsciousness. Prior to trial, the defense had the defendant examined by two psychiatrists but did not call either because they could not establish affirmative defense and would reveal potentially damaging information. The defense did call one psychiatrist, who had not examined the defendant, to testify generically about the effects of PCP. During sentencing, the defense presented testimony only from the defendant's estranged wife and mother. The wife testified that the defendant was a good provider, good father, and good husband, except for drug use, which was the reason she left him. She related an instance when he thought the house was charged with electricity due to drug use. The mother testified that the defendant's father was a hustler, who was never around, and that the defendant's troubles started at age 14 when he started sniffing glue. Both witnesses were cross-examined about the defendant's prior offenses. Counsel's conduct was deficient because counsel conducted only two hours of investigation related to sentencing weeks before the trial because of the belief that they would not reach sentencing. Thus, counsel, who had no prior capital case experience, only interviewed the wife and mother and reviewed juvenile and military records. If counsel had adequately investigated, the evidence would have revealed that the defendant suffered repeated beatings in childhood, his mother would choke him when she was angry, his childhood was characterized by neglect and instability, and he showed signs of mental illness as a child and had been diagnosed with schizophrenia at one time. In addition, if counsel had presented the testimony of one of the examining psychiatrists during sentencing, the jury would have heard that the defendant was grossly impaired by PCP at the time of the offenses. Finally, counsel also failed to investigate and object to the testimony of an alleged victim of a prior sodomy because it was questionable that the sodomy was committed by force or threat of force, which was a prerequisite for admissibility in sentencing.

1999: *Smith v. Stewart*, 189 F.3d 1004 (9th Cir. 1999) (tried in 1987 and affirmed on appeal in 1989). Counsel ineffective in sentencing phase for failing to prepare and present mitigation and failing to challenge the state's aggravation evidence related to prior convictions. Defendant was tried for two different rape-murders. After first conviction by jury, defendant plead guilty to the second one, even though the prosecutor argued that defendant was emotionally unstable and his plea may not be voluntary. During first sentencing under statute that allowed only consideration of statutory mitigating circumstances, counsel presented testimony from two experts, who testified that defendant had internal conflicts bordering on psychosis that caused tensions leading to a compulsion to commit sexually sadistic murders. These experts had minimal information about the defendant's history and had conducted only short interviews, but testified in an effort to establish impaired ability to conform conduct to law. Defendant was granted a new sentencing trial after the statute was held to be unconstitutional. Although counsel could now present non-statutory mitigating evidence, he did no investigation, called no witnesses, and only reargued that the court should consider the testimony of the previous experts as mitigation. Complete failure to investigate, when the prosecutor even questioned the defendant's emotional stability, was deficient. Court found prejudice because, if counsel had adequately investigated and presented mitigation, the evidence would have at least established that the defense investigator and a pastor had observed multiple personalities in the defendant. His girlfriend would have testified that he treated her well but had wild mood swings. He had attempted suicide in prison. He had developed serious psychosexual problems stemming from his childhood with deeply religious parents, one of whom beat him severely and the other emotionally neglected and abandoned him. This evidence, at a minimum, would have supported the testimony of the previous experts which had been rejected by the courts for lack of foundation and credibility. "A lawyer who should have known but does not inform his expert witnesses about essential information going to the heart of the defendant's case for mitigation does not function as 'counsel' under the Sixth Amendment." *Id.* at . Court also found that counsel was ineffective for failing to challenge the state's aggravation evidence of two prior rape convictions as a prior violent offense. Both of the convictions occurred when Arizona law did not include violence as an element of rape. Likewise, one of the convictions was obtained when it appeared that the defendant's counsel had a conflict of interest. The failure to challenge the aggravating circumstances and present mitigation evidence was prejudicial despite the "horrific nature of the crimes" in this case, especially because the Arizona statute requires a death sentence in the absence of mitigating evidence.

Collier v. Turpin, 177 F.3d 1184 (11th Cir. 1999) (tried in September 1978). Counsel ineffective in capital sentencing for failing to adequately prepare and present mitigation evidence. The defendant, who lived in Tennessee, drove to Georgia and committed three armed robberies. During his drive back to Tennessee, he was stopped by several officers. He grabbed one of the officers' weapons and shot both officers killing one. Because of eyewitnesses and a full confession, a conviction was essentially a foregone conclusion. During the sentencing phase, which lasted only an hour and a half, trial counsel presented 10 defense witnesses, including the defendant's wife but essentially elicited only one or two word answers from them that established that the defendant was a good worker, supported his family, and a good reputation for truth and veracity (which was irrelevant since he did not testify). The claim of ineffective assistance was not raised in the first state habeas petition. Ultimately after navigating the procedural quagmire of bouncing back and forth between federal and state habeas petitions, the Court found counsel to be ineffective in this fourth habeas petition. The Court found cause for the default of not raising the issue in the first state and federal habeas petitions because the trial attorneys had represented the defendant in those proceedings. Counsel were ineffective because they failed to develop the mitigation evidence that they were aware of. The witnesses who testified could have presented substantial evidence that the defendant was a good family man and an upstanding public citizen, who had a background of poverty but who had worked hard as a child and as an adult to support his family and close relatives. Instead of the "hollow shell" of mitigation, *Id.* at , trial counsel could have established the defendant had a gentle disposition, his record of helping his family in times of need, specific instances of heroism and compassion, and evidence of his circumstances at the time of the crimes, including his recent loss of his job, his poverty, and his diabetic condition. Counsel was also ineffective for failing to seek and present an expert on diabetes when they were aware of the diabetes and that the defendant's crimes were totally out of character for him. If counsel had performed adequately, the evidence would have established that the defendant had trouble controlling his behavior when he was not properly medicated, which would have mitigated the crime itself. An expert could have testified that the defendant's behavior was possibly caused by an episode of hypoglycemia brought on by the defendant's failure to eat that day in combination with an excessive insulin dose. Prejudice found because a juror who had known of the "stark contrast between [the defendant's] acts on the day of the crimes and his history" may not have voted for death. The Court concludes, "The jury was called upon to determine whether a man whom they did not know would live or die; they were not presented with the particularized circumstances of his past and of his actions on the day of the crime that would have allowed them fairly to balance the seriousness of his transgressions with the conditions of his life. Had they been able to do so, we believe that it is at least reasonably probable that the jury would have returned a sentence other than death." *Id.* at .

1998: ***Bean v. Calderon***, 163 F.3d 1073 (9th Cir. 1998) (crimes in 1980 and affirmed on appeal in 1988). Counsel ineffective in sentencing phase of double murder trial for failing to prepare and present mitigation evidence. First counsel was appointed to represent defendant and investigated competency defense. A second counsel was appointed a month and a half before the penalty hearing. The penalty phase counsel relied solely on the evidence prepared by the guilt-or-innocence phase counsel. The first counsel believed that he was prohibited from participating in the sentencing phase so he did nothing either. Prior to trial, the first counsel had contacted two mental health experts, who strongly recommended neuropsychological testing for brain damage, but this testing was not completed until ten months later during the weekend before the penalty hearing. Counsel were unaware of the results when the penalty phase started. Counsel also failed to furnish other necessary information to the experts who testified during the penalty phase and failed to adequately prepare these experts for their testimony. The only expert who had reviewed any documents did not testify. One expert who did testify had requested social, medical, and educational information, which had not been provided, and met with counsel to prepare for testimony only a day or two before testimony. He could testify only that Bean had an organic personality disorder and was moderately defective in intelligence, but could not definitively state whether Bean had brain damage or whether he was able to appreciate criminality. The other expert to testify also did not have any information other than her last-minute testing. She testified that Bean has brain damage and his ability to appreciate criminality was impaired, but she had not studied the relevant California legal standards. Subsequent review of the evidence by these experts and others resulted in testimony that Bean was functionally mentally retarded, suffered from post-traumatic stress disorder, was brain damaged, was using drugs during the time of the offenses, and was incompetent at the time of trial. The Court stated: "When experts request necessary information and are denied it, when testing requested by expert witnesses is not performed, and when experts are placed on the stand with virtually no preparation or foundation, a capital defendant has not received effective penalty phase assistance of counsel." *Id.* at 1079. The Court also found prejudice because the two experts who did testify lacked preparation and foundational information for their conclusions which severely undercut their credibility. In addition, counsel presented only an "unfocused snapshot" of Bean's life in sentencing so the jury had no knowledge of the "indisputably sadistic treatment Bean received as a child, including repeated beatings which left a permanent indentation in his head." *Id.* at 1081. Counsel also failed to discover and present evidence of Bean's developmental delays, including placement in classes for the "educable mentally retarded." Prejudice was found because this was not a case in which the death sentence was inevitable due to the enormity of the aggravating circumstances. In fact, the state presented little aggravating evidence and the jury initially divided over the appropriateness of the death penalty, deadlocking on both murders. Ultimately, the jury returned with one death verdict and life verdict.

Smith v. Stewart, 140 F.3d 1263 (9th Cir. 1998) (tried in 1984). Counsel ineffective in capital sentencing phase for failing to prepare and present mitigation and for failing to make any argument on defendant's behalf. Counsel stated only that defendant still denied his guilt and that he was only 30-years-old. Counsel spoke with defendant and his mother but asked only a few generalized questions which revealed nothing of significance. While the court recognized that counsel's task is difficult without the client's assistance, the court could not "find any reason, tactical or otherwise for the failure of counsel to develop any mitigation at all for the purpose of defending [the defendant] against the death penalty." 140 F.3d at 1269. Likewise, counsel's failure to even request leniency amounted to no representation at all. 140 F.3d at 1270. Available evidence included evidence of antisocial personality disorder, extensive drug history, change in personality after a PCP overdose, and good family relationships, including his love and support of his children. In assessing prejudice, the court stated, "we are not asked to imagine what the effect of certain testimony would have been upon us personally," 140 F.3d at 1271, but what the effect would have been on the sentencer, which under Arizona law is the judge. Prejudice found in this case because facts were "bad" but not "overwhelmingly horrifying" such that is was "highly improbable that mitigating factors of any ordinary stripe would help." 140 F.3d at 1270. Likewise, under the Arizona sentencing scheme, the judge is required to sentence the defendant to death if there are aggravating circumstances and "no mitigating circumstances sufficiently substantial to call for leniency." 140 F.3d at 1270. Counsel's failure to present mitigation or argue for leniency thus amounted to "a virtual admission that the death penalty should be imposed." 140 F.3d at 1270.

Dobbs v. Turpin, 142 F.3d 1383 (11th Cir. 1998) (tried in May 1974). Counsel ineffective in capital sentencing phase because counsel failed to investigate and present any mitigating evidence and made an inadequate closing argument. Counsel spoke to very few potential mitigation witnesses, including the defendant's mother. Available but unpresented mitigation included witnesses to testify that defendant had an unfortunate childhood, his mother often would not let him stay in the house with her, and when she did allow him to stay, she ran a brothel where she exposed him to sexual promiscuity, alcohol, and violence. Counsels' reasons for failure were insufficient. Counsel believed erroneously that evidence of defendant's childhood was inadmissible and that mitigating evidence could only be admitted to mitigate the crime, as opposed to the sentence. The court held, "'[S]trategic decisions based on a misunderstanding of the law are entitled to less deference." 142 F.3d at 1388. Counsel also stated that the defendant did not want him to present mitigation evidence. The court held "that lawyers may not 'blindly follow' such commands. Although the decision whether to use mitigating evidence is for the client, this court has stated, 'the lawyer first must evaluate potential avenues and advise the client of those offering possible merit.'" 142 F.3d at 1388 (quoting *Thompson v. Wainwright*, 787 F.2d 1447, 1451 (11th Cir. 1986)). Counsel's argument in sentencing consisted of reading Justice Brennan's concurring opinion in *Furman* and arguing that the current death penalty statute would also be found unconstitutional. Counsel's argument was ineffective because it minimized the jury's responsibility for determining the appropriateness of the death penalty and failed to focus on the character and record of the defendant and the circumstances of the offense. In addition, counsel's argument was deficient because he never asked the jury for mercy or for a life sentence. He merely asked the jury to impose a sentence with which the jurors could live. Counsel offered no reason for the inadequate argument.

1997: *Austin v. Bell*, 126 F.3d 843 (6th Cir. 1997) (crimes in 1977 and affirmed on appeal in 1981). District court found IAC in both guilt and sentencing, but the court of appeals found only IAC in sentencing.

Counsel were ineffective for failing to prepare and present mitigation evidence because they didn't think it would do any good. Relatives, friends, death penalty experts, and a minister were available and willing to testify.

> *Hall v. Washington*, 106 F.3d 742 (7th Cir. 1997) (sentenced in April 1984). Trial counsel ineffective (even under AEDPA standards) in sentencing for failing to adequately advise the defendant of the consequences of waiving a jury in a sentencing, for failing to investigate and discover readily available mitigation evidence which included good character and adaptability testimony from a correctional officer when the victim was also a correctional officer and good character evidence from other witnesses. Investigation is required. "This does not mean that only a scorch-the-earth strategy will suffice, … but it does mean that the attorney must look into readily available sources of evidence. Where it is apparent from evidence concerning the crime itself, from conversation with the defendant, or from other readily available sources of information, that the defendant has some mental or other condition that would likely qualify as a mitigating factor, the failure to investigate will be ineffective assistance." *Id.* at 749-50. Here, counsel did not contact the defendant in the six weeks after conviction and prior to sentencing to even inquire about possible mitigating evidence or witnesses who might be available to testify on his behalf. They did not even return telephone calls or write back to individuals who were volunteering to offer mitigating testimony. Prejudice found even though judge alone trial because if not for IAC might not have been judge alone and even if it had, trial court found no mitigation evidence at the time of sentencing. Trial counsel also ineffective for sentencing phase closing which did not even focus on defendant, but rather focused on life sentence because the death penalty is barbaric.

1996: *Emerson v. Gramley*, 91 F.3d 898 (7th Cir. 1996) (affirming 883 F. Supp. 225 (N.D. Ill. 1995)) (second trial in March 1985). Trial counsel ineffective for failing to prepare and present mitigation evidence and making no sentencing argument at all where the state presented aggravation evidence of seven prior convictions of robbery. Counsel had failed to conduct *any* investigation, however brief, into the possible existence of evidence of mitigating circumstances. Available mitigation would have shown that at age 8 the defendant was shot when he was an innocent bystander during robbery, he lacked emotional and educational support from his parents, he lost a young child, and had a diminished IQ.

1995: *Glenn v. Tate*, 71 F.3d 1204 (6th Cir. 1995) (sentenced in September 1982). Trial counsel ineffective for failing to adequately prepare and present mitigation evidence in case where defendant killed police officer while helping older brother escape from jail. Counsel requested court-appointed examination and examiners reported no organic brain damage although no testing was done. Counsel made virtually no attempt to prepare for the sentencing phase of the trial until after the jury returned its verdict of guilty even though "[i]t was obvious, or should have been, that the sentencing phase was likely" to be reached. Counsel only arranged for the preparation of a videotape, even though the admissibility "was obviously questionable" (and the tape was not admitted), that showed the neighborhood where the defendant grew up, along with commentary by a narrator, the defendant's mother, and a former employer. Only a teacher with limited knowledge and a minister, who had never met the defendant and testified only to religious principles against the death penalty, testified. Available but unpresented evidence included mental retardation (school records), physical abuse, hyperactivity as a child. Neurological examination showed global brain damage probably caused by general anesthesia given mother early in pregnancy. "[W]hile juries tend to distrust claims of insanity, they are more likely to react sympathetically when their attention is drawn to organic brain problems such as mental retardation." *Id.* at 1211. Probation officer if interviewed and called would have testified that defendant was a follower and was particularly susceptible to the influence of his older brother.

Antwine v. Delo, 54 F.3d 1357 (8th Cir. 1995) (sentenced in August 1985). Counsel ineffective for failing to investigate and present available mitigation. Counsel was aware that defendant was acting oddly for months before offense and that a cursory 20 minute exam by state experts found abnormal behavior consistent with PCP intoxication but that defendant denied using PCP at the time of the offense and the state examiner's had conducted no psychological testing. Counsel failed to follow up on this inconsistency by requesting an independent examination. Adequate examination and testing revealed bipolar disorder. Counsel presented only an emotional plea for mercy in sentencing. The proffered "strategic" reason was that counsel believed the jury had already determined that death was appropriate with the guilty verdict and that counsel would have lost credibility since mental health evidence of a manic state at the time of the crime would have contradicted the chosen self-defense theory. The court rejected any strategic explanation because "[c]ounsel's failure to request a second mental examination is more like inadequate trial preparation than a strategic choice."

Hendricks v. Calderon, 70 F.3d 1032 (9th Cir. 1995) (tried in 1981). Trial counsel ineffective for failing to adequately prepare and present mitigation evidence even though a defense expert was called. *See also Hendricks v. Calderon*, 864 F. Supp. 929 (N.D. Cal. 1994). Neither trial counsel nor his investigators conducted any investigation directed at developing mitigating evidence and decided simply to beg for mercy as had been done in the only other capital case counsel had participated in. This was rejected as strategy because "[t]he choice that must be defended as strategic is not a decision about how best to present mitigating evidence, but one about whether to investigate mitigating evidence at all." If counsel had adequately prepared and presented the mitigation, the evidence would have shown that defendant: was blamed by his family for his mother's death giving birth; lived in a two-room house with grandmother and 15 relatives; was beaten with a frying pan and switch by grandmother; had to drink kerosene and sugar as medicine; was sexually abused by prostitutes who worked for father; was raped by a stranger and attempted suicide shortly afterwards; had a son who died from rare skin disease; and had a history of drug and alcohol use and male prostitution. A mental health expert would have testified that defendant is genetically predisposed to serious mental illness which was exacerbated by background. Expert testimony would have also shown that defendant suffered from schizoaffective disorder, PTSD, and polysubstance abuse. Expert would have even testified that defendant was insane at the time of the offenses. All of this evidence would have supported at least three statutory mitigating circumstances that were not presented to the jury. Although the jury was given some lay evidence in mitigation, the jury was given no guidance of how to connect the facts and expert testimony about background to the mitigating factors.

Clabourne v. Lewis, 64 F.3d 1373 (9th Cir. 1995) (crimes in 1980). Counsel ineffective for failing to prepare and present mitigation evidence. Counsel sought a defense expert evaluation five days prior to sentencing, but took no other action when that was denied. Trial counsel did not call any witnesses in sentencing even though a detective would have testified that it was the co-defendant who was responsible for the depraved manner in which the crime was committed and depravity was the only aggravating circumstance found. Trial counsel also did not prepare and present expert testimony. The defense expert who testified at trial had seen the defendant six years earlier and was not provided with any subsequent records, including records concerning offense. If additional information had been provided, defense expert would have diagnosed schizophrenia instead of anti-social personality. Likewise, state experts testified at trial that defendant was sane, but were never provided with information about defendant's history or offenses or asked about mitigation. If defense counsel had provided the information and talked to them, state experts would also have diagnosed schizophrenia and agreed that co-defendant had manipulated defendant.

*__Baxter v. Thomas__, 45 F.3d 1501 (11th Cir. 1995) (sentenced in September 1983). Trial counsel ineffective during penalty phase of capital trial for failing to adequately investigate and present mitigation evidence. Counsel talked to the defendant's mother and brother and visited a boys home he had been committed to. They did not, however, request State Hospital records, school records, or social service records, and did not interview defendant's sister, neighbor, or social worker, even though counsel was aware of defendant's odd behavior and even requested a mental health evaluation. Because of these failures, trial counsel did not discover or present evidence that the defendant spent approximately three years of his teenage life in a psychiatric hospital and that he was mentally retarded.

*__Jackson v. Herring__, 42 F.3d 1350 (11th Cir. 1995) (*affirming Jackson v. Thigpen*, 752 F. Supp. 1551 (N.D. Ala. 1990)) (sentenced in December 1981). Trial counsel ineffective during penalty phase of capital trial for failing to adequately investigate and present mitigation evidence. Neither counsel conducted any investigation or preparation for sentencing - partly, because they did not believe the defendant would be convicted of murder, and partly because each counsel thought the other was responsible for sentencing. Available but unpresented mitigation evidence included: substantial personal hardships, including having to quit school in 8th grade because defendant was pregnant; brutal and abusive childhood at the hands of an alcoholic mother; devotion to her mother, sister, and daughter; borderline mental retardation; good work history; and abuse by her boyfriend, who was the murder victim, both for a long time preceding his death and immediately prior to his death.

1994: *__Hill v. Lockhart__, 28 F.3d 832 (8th Cir. 1994) (*affirming* 824 F. Supp. 1327 (E.D. Ark. 1993)) (tried in July 1980). Trial counsel ineffective at penalty phase for failing to prepare and present evidence of defendant's mental state at the time of the offenses, and that defendant had a long history of schizophrenia but he was taking antipsychotic medication at the time of offenses. The defendant told counsel of his past psychiatric hospitalizations in Oklahoma and Arkansas and counsel obtained the Arkansas records but made no attempt to obtain the Oklahoma records until just before trial and never obtained some of them.

*__Wade v. Calderon__, 29 F.3d 1312 (9th Cir. 1994) (tried in May 1982). Trial counsel ineffective during penalty phase of capital trial for failing to call defendant's family to corroborate abusive background; calling forth alternate personality that committed crimes (defendant had multiple personality disorder) during defendant's testimony and eliciting damaging statements and essentially a challenge to the jury to execute defendant; and by arguing during closing argument that 1) defendant's life should be spared so doctors could examine him as human "guinea pig"; 2) that jurors had already decided on death; and 3) that executing defendant may "free him from this horror." While evidence of abuse had been mentioned by experts during trial, the jury was instructed not to consider that for the truth and no evidence was presented in sentencing on this other than the defendant's testimony.

1992: *Loyd v. Whitley*, 977 F.2d 149 (5th Cir. 1992) (sentencing in 1985). Trial counsel ineffective in sentencing phase for failing to obtain independent mental health evaluation when funds were available and sanity was a critical issue, but counsel assumed funds were not available and did not pursue issue. Proper investigation would have revealed: evidence that defendant was unable at time of offense to distinguish between right and wrong or appreciate the significance or consequences of his acts because of psychotic delusions; child abuse; substance abuse; psychosis (not anti-social as the state contended at trial); and brain damage (frontal lobe dysfunction).

Mak v. Blodgett, 970 F.2d 614 (9th Cir. 1992) (*affirming* 754 F. Supp. 1490 (W.D. Wash. 1991)) (sentenced in October 1983). Trial counsel ineffective for failing to prepare and present mitigating evidence regarding defendant's background, family relationships, and the effects of assimilation problems and cultural conflict on young Chinese immigrants. Counsel spent substantial hours preparing to present evidence that another person actually committed the crimes, which they assumed incorrectly would be admitted in sentencing, even though improper during trial but they prepared no social history information.

Cave v. Singletary, 971 F.2d 1513 (11th Cir. 1992) (notice of appeal filed in January 1983). Petitioner given death sentence for robbery and murder. At trial, counsel emphasized the fact that petitioner admitted he was guilty of robbery. Court found that although this demonstrated that counsel did not understand the felony murder rule, petitioner was not prejudiced because the jury would have made the same decision based on the evidence of guilt of the robbery. Counsel was found ineffective at sentencing phase, however, because she was under the "grandiose, perhaps even delusional belief" that she would win an acquittal for her client and, therefore, failed to prepare and present available character evidence and the fact that defendant had no prior criminal record in mitigation. State argued lack of character evidence in closing argument. Counsel had even met with some of the defendant's family members prior to trial but told them their testimony would not be needed. The court characterized the representation in this case as "an embarrassment to the legal profession." *Id.* at 1519.

1991: *Kenley v. Armontrout*, 937 F.2d 1298 (8th Cir. 1991) (tried in 1984). Counsel ineffective for failing to investigate and present mitigation evidence. Counsel received a letter from a social worker that had previously seen the defendant, who also informed counsel of another prior mental health expert. Counsel requested and received the social worker's records but never spoke to her and never contacted the other prior mental health expert. Counsel also requested no other records that were referenced in these files or interviewed family members. Instead, counsel requested a court-appointed evaluation, which was conducted, and then consulted a different non-examining expert and decided not to pursue this line because counsel erroneously believed that the evidence was too old and insubstantial, which was based, in part, on the court-appointed psychiatrist's report which was itself incomplete because based on limited information. Adequate investigation would have revealed a history of "an extreme personality or emotional disorder or disturbance, suicidal tendencies, and alcohol abuse and intoxication."

Blanco v. Singletary, 943 F.2d 1477 (11th Cir. 1991) (*affirming Blanco v. Dugger*, 691 F. Supp. 308 (S.D. Fla. 1988)) (tried in June 1982). At sentencing, counsel failed to present any mitigating evidence. Counsel failed to investigate for sentencing prior to trial even though counsel knew the court intended to proceed straight to sentencing after conviction. Even after the court granted a four-day continuance, counsel still only spoke to the defendant's brother. He never spoke to other potential witnesses and thus failed to prepare and present the available evidence of childhood poverty, seizures, family history of psychosis, organic brain damage, borderline retardation, epileptic disorders and paranoid and depressive behaviors. Counsel also asked for continuance to procure psychiatric exam and then never had one conducted. Counsel told trial court that no mental health mitigation existed. Counsel also revealed damaging information, violating client confidences, to trial judge.

Horton v. Zant, 941 F.2d 1449 (11th Cir. 1991) (sentenced in February 1981). Counsel conducted no sentencing investigation prior to trial and only called the defendant's mother the night before sentencing to ask if she would attend trial. She declined because of the flu and counsel asked no further questions. The court rejected the proffered "strategic reason" not to present mitigation as unreasonable since counsel erroneously believed that mitigation was appropriate only in gruesome cases involving torture. Available mitigation would have shown that defendant was a hard worker, a good youth, able to provide for his common law wife and their daughter, and had successfully adjusted to previous stays in prison. Counsel also ineffective for arguing that they were local lawyers, not "bleeding heart, anti-death penalty lawyers" and calling the defendant a "worthless man" that defense counsel hates and conceding that maybe the defendant "ought to die" during closing argument.

1990: *Brewer v. Aiken*, 935 F.2d 850 (7th Cir. 1990) (sentenced in March 1978). Defense counsel ineffective in death penalty phase of trial for failing to fully investigate defendant's family and mental history and present evidence in mitigation. This was the first capital case tried under Indiana's statute passed post-*Furman* and counsel was unaware that the sentencing hearing would begin immediately after conviction. Counsel requested a continuance of a week to prepare because he had just received information of an extensive psychiatric history and problems in childhood. The continuance was denied an no mitigation evidence was presented other than the defendant's testimony, which was damaging because it opened the door to another armed robbery the same day as these crimes since the defendant claimed a co-defendant was the actual killer. Counsel did not even ask the defendant about his psychiatric history or background. An investigation would have revealed shock therapy, brain damage, mental retardation, susceptibility to the influence of others, and disadvantaged family life.

Cunningham v. Zant, 928 F.2d 1006 (11th Cir. 1990) (tried in October 1979). Counsel ineffective during the penalty phase of a capital murder case. Counsel spoke briefly with the defendant's mother, his employer, and his supervisor on the eve of trial or during trial and presented very limited background information from them in sentencing, but counsel did not thoroughly interview these witnesses or conduct any other background investigation which would have revealed substantial evidence of mental retardation, head injury that resulted in a metal plate in the defendant's head and substantial headaches and affects, socioeconomic background and reputation as good father and worker in mitigation.

1989: *Kubat v. Thieret*, 867 F.2d 351 (7th Cir. 1989) (*affirming* 679 F. Supp. 788 (N.D. Ill. 1988)) (tried in June 1980). Trial counsel ineffective during sentencing for failing to investigate and present available character evidence in mitigation, making a bizarre and prejudicial closing argument which conceded that counsel "was not going to convince" jury and invited the jury to "decide" between the defendant and victim, and failing to object to improper sentencing instructions which misstated the law by calling for unanimous agreement on a decision not to impose the death sentence. If counsel had adequately investigated "fifteen character witnesses," of which "most were neighbors and coworkers; all were well-respected citizens in their community; [and] one was a deputy sheriff," would have testified. Only two of these witnesses had even been contacted prior to trial and not even their testimony was presented. In the district court, the state argued that Kubat's attorneys made a rational strategic decision to forego character testimony and to rely instead upon a plea for mercy during closing argument. The court rejected this as a reasonable strategy in this case, in part, because the argument could not "even charitably, be called a plea for mercy" and was, instead, an aggravating, "rambling, incoherent discourse" that even invited the jury to choose between the defendant and the victim, which was "utter lunacy for defense counsel" to do. *Id.* at 368. In finding prejudice, the court was particularly impressed

> that at least one of the fifteen available character witnesses was a deputy sheriff. The introduction of testimony by a law enforcement officer that the defendant had a salvageable character might not have gone totally unnoticed by the jury. Indeed, . ..if just *one* juror had been sufficiently influenced by the character testimony, the death penalty could not have been imposed.

Id. at 639.

Deutscher v. Whitley, 884 F.2d 1152 (9th Cir. 1989) (decision vacated and remanded by Supreme Court several times; last opinion which again finds IAC is *Deutscher v. Angelone*, 16 F.3d 981 (9th Cir. 1994) (tried in 1977). Trial counsel ineffective in penalty phase of capital trial for not investigating and presenting mitigating evidence despite knowledge of some history and argument in sentencing that the defendant must have had some mental problems. Counsel did not have a strategy to avoid presentation of this evidence, but simply failed to investigate. Adequate investigation would have revealed diagnoses of schizophrenia, pathological intoxication, and organic brain damage; commitments to mental institutions; and a history of good behavior in institutional settings.

Harris v. Dugger, 874 F.2d 756 (11th Cir. 1989) (sentenced in September 1981). Attorneys rendered IAC in a capital murder case where they failed to prepare or present mitigation evidence because each lawyer believed that the other was responsible for preparing penalty phase of case. Because neither lawyer had investigated they were ignorant of the types of evidence available and could not make a strategic decision on whether to introduce the available mitigation evidence that the defendant was a devoted father, husband, and brother, and a "decent, loving man."

1988: *Evans v. Lewis*, 855 F.2d 631 (9th Cir. 1988) (sentenced in March 1979). Trial counsel ineffective for failing to investigate and present evidence in mitigation in resentencing. Counsel was aware the defendant had a history of mental problems from his records of incarceration in state mental facility for inmates and prior suicide attempts. Nonetheless, counsel conducted no investigation to determine the extent of the mental problems. Evidence would have shown that defendant is schizophrenic and possibly insane at time of offenses. Instead of this evidence which would have supported at least one statutory mitigating circumstance, counsel presented no evidence in mitigation, even though Arizona death penalty statute required death penalty if no mitigating factor is established, & at least one aggravating factor is found (at least one aggravating factor, prior conviction, was obviously present).

Middleton v. Dugger, 849 F.2d 491 (11th Cir. 1988) (tried in 1980). Counsel ineffective for failure to conduct investigation into petitioner's background even though counsel discussed the existence of mitigating evidence with the defendant. Investigation and collection of records would have revealed a history of schizophrenia since age 12; childhood neglect, physical, sexual, and drug abuse; and low IQ. In addition, expert testimony would have established that the defendant was under extreme emotional duress at the time of the homicide and had very little capacity to conform his conduct to the law at the time.

Stephens v. Kemp, 846 F.2d 642 (11th Cir. 1988) (tried in 1980). Counsel ineffective for failing to investigate mental health issues, even though counsel learned from the defendant's sister that the defendant had spent five days in a mental hospital four to six months before the shooting occurred. Counsel sought a court-appointed competence and sanity evaluation but pursued his investigation no further after receiving the examiner's report. While this was sufficient for trial issues, the court held that it was inadequate for sentencing purposes.

> [W]hen a capital sentencing proceeding is contemplated by counsel aware of the facts of which appellant's trial counsel was aware, professionally reasonable representation requires more of an investigation into the possibility of introducing evidence of the defendant's mental history and mental capacity in the sentencing phase than was conducted by trial counsel in this case. Although trial counsel was aware well in advance of trial that appellant had spent at least a brief period of time in a mental hospital shortly before the shooting, and that for some reason a psychiatric evaluation had already been ordered, he completely ignored the possible ramifications of those facts as regards the sentencing proceeding.

Id. at 653. As a result, the jury was not provided with the available evidence of the defendant's mental history and bizarre behaviors.

1987: *Lewis v. Lane*, 832 F.2d 1446 (7th Cir. 1987) (tried in 1979). Counsel ineffective for stipulating to prior felony convictions the defendant did not have. He failed to ask the State's Attorney whether he had actual proof of those convictions in the form of certified copies and instead relied on petitioner's uninformed representation that he thought the information contained in the "FBI rap sheet" was accurate, without explaining to petitioner the importance of that information and the critical distinctions between arrest and conviction and between felony and misdemeanor. Prejudice found because one charge had been dismissed and a second pled as a misdemeanor when these had been presented to the jury as violent assault with weapons convictions.

Armstrong v. Dugger, 833 F.2d 1430 (11th Cir. 1987) (tried in September 1975). Trial counsel ineffective during sentencing phase for failing to prepare and present mitigation evidence. Counsel spoke with the defendant's parole officer and arranged for her to testify at the sentencing trial, but conducted no other investigation other than a single conversation with the petitioner, his mother and stepfather after the conviction. Available evidence would have shown impoverished childhood, good worker, nonviolent, religious, mental retardation, and organic brain damage.

Magill v. Dugger, 824 F.2d 879 (11th Cir. 1987) (tried in March 1977). Trial counsel ineffective in sentencing. Counsel began representation on the first day of jury selection, met with defendant for 15 minutes prior to defendant's testimony, failed to discuss with defendant the possibility that the state would seek to prove premeditation during his testimony on cross-examination, failed to object when the prosecutor asked the defendant to concede his guilt to capital murder, and did not develop or present to the jury the defense theory that defendant committed the killing without premeditation. No prejudice on findings, but in combination with errors of counsel in sentencing, prejudice found in sentencing phase. Sentencing errors included counsel's failure to argue defendant's emotional problems which would discount defendant's guilt phase testimony admitting that the killing was intentional and premeditated. In addition, counsel failed to prepare and present available mitigating evidence of a history of serious emotional problems. Specifically, counsel was aware of a mental health expert that had previously treated the defendant and would have testified that he exhibited signs of serious emotional problems at the age of thirteen. He described the defendant as "explosive," and "a time bomb." Finally, counsel called a court-appointed psychiatrist, who had never been asked to examine the defendant regarding the applicability of statutory mitigating circumstances, as a *defense* witness and this witness' testimony virtually precluded finding a statutory mitigating circumstance.

1986: *Jones v. Thigpen*, 788 F.2d 1101 (5th Cir. 1986) (tried in December 1977). Trial counsel ineffective during sentencing phase for failing to prepare and present evidence in mitigation when evidence was available to prove that defendant is mentally retarded, 17 at the time of the offense, and did not have any intent to kill victim killed by accomplice during robbery.

Thomas v. Kemp, 796 F.2d 1322 (11th Cir. 1986) (direct appeal in 1980). Counsel ineffective in capital sentencing for failing to adequately prepare and present mitigation.

> Thomas' lawyer made little effort to investigate possible sources of mitigation evidence. Although Thomas' mother, who was to be the main witness at the penalty phase, was interviewed, she was not present, for reasons not apparent from the record. No attempt was made to obtain possible mitigation testimony from other family members or individuals who knew Thomas from school, work, or the neighborhood. The lawyer testified that he made little effort to produce mitigating evidence because Thomas had stated that he did not want to take the stand and did not "want anyone to cry for him."

Id. at 1324. The record supports the District Court's finding of deficient conduct and prejudice. The evidence would have established that the defendant was mentally and physically abuse, his mother had a drinking problem, and, although he was a slow learner, he worked to improve his grades. In addition, he was an excellent worker when given simple work assignments, was always punctual, and was a loving son who cared deeply for his mother. A psychiatrist could have presented testimony showing him "as a pathetically sick youngster who had struggled to succeed in life, both in school and on the job, despite a chaotic home environment and a major mental illness." *Id.* at 1325.

Johnson v. Kemp, 781 F.2d 1482 (11th Cir. 1986) (*affirming* 615 F. Supp. 355 (D.C. Ga. 1985)) (tried in July 1975). Trial counsel ineffective in sentencing phase for failing to investigate and present available mitigation. Counsel only talked to defendant and defendant's parents without even asking them about possible sentencing witnesses or explaining the need for mitigation and did nothing more. Available mitigation included 19 good character witnesses and no criminal history, neither of which was presented to jury.

1985: *Blake v. Kemp*, 758 F.2d 523 (11th Cir. 1985) (tried in February 1976). Trial counsel ineffective for making no preparations whatsoever for sentencing phase because of his belief that defendant would be found not guilty by reason of insanity. (State psychiatrist found "reactive- depressive" condition, but did not give opinion on sanity question because of insufficient information from defendant.) Counsel met with the defendant's parents but never asked about character witnesses. If trial counsel had adequately investigated he could have presented character evidence that the defendant was "a man who was respectful toward others, who generally got along well with people and who gladly offered to help whenever anyone needed something."

Tyler v. Kemp, 755 F.2d 741 (11th Cir. 1985) (tried in 1980). Counsel ineffective in sentencing phase for failing to prepare and present mitigating evidence. Counsel had interviewed members of the family, including the defendant's grandmother, aunt, and brother, concerning the defendant's background prior to trial. When counsel asked them to testify, they declined because "they knew nothing of the murder and had nothing to tell." *Id.* at 744. In essence, counsel never told them that their testimony was needed on any subject other than guilt or innocence and did not explain the sentencing phase of the trial or that evidence of a mitigating nature was needed. If counsel had explained this evidence was available that the defendant had no prior criminal record, had a good work record, had an alcoholic abusive husband (who was the victim in the case), and was a good mother.

1984: *King v. Strickland*, 748 F.2d 1462 (11th Cir. 1984) (tried in July 1977). Counsel ineffective for failing to prepare mitigation. Following the conviction, counsel sought a continuance of one day because he had not even discussed sentencing with the defendant. The continuance was denied. Counsel presented a minister and former employer to testimony. If counsel had adequately investigated there were available character witnesses. Counsel also heightened the prejudice by emphasizing during closing argument the reprehensible nature of the crime and the fact that he had reluctantly represented the defendant. "In effect, counsel separated himself from his client, conveying to the jury that he had reluctantly represented a defendant who had committed a reprehensible crime. ... Rather than attempting to humanize King, counsel in his closing argument stressed the inhumanity of the crime." *King v. Strickland*, 714 F.2d 1481, 1491 (11th Cir. 1983).

*Capital Case

C.   U.S. District Court Cases

2016: **McNish v. Westbrooks*,   F. Supp. 3d   , 2016 WL 755634 (E.D. Tenn. Feb. 25, 2016) (trial and sentencing in 1984). Counsel ineffective in capital sentencing for failing to adequately investigate and present mitigating evidence. This issue was first raised on appeal of the denial of state post-conviction. The District Court held the issue was procedurally defaulted but the Sixth Circuit remanded following the decisions in *Martinez v. Ryan* and *Trevino v. Thaler*. On remand, the District Court held that post-conviction counsel's conduct was deficient in failing to assert trial counsel's ineffectiveness and the issue was "substantial." Therefore, the procedural default was excused. Trial counsel's conduct was deficient because trial counsel "failed to explore a wealth of evidence that was available" concerning the defendant's social, mental, and family history. While counsel had available records that indicated "a history of attempted suicides, depression, blackouts, and drug abuse," as well as indications of the defendant's traumatic childhood, counsel "chose not to investigate petitioner's family history any further because of their decision to pursue a reasonable doubt defense." This decision was not a valid strategic decision "because counsel did not fulfill their obligation to independently investigate this evidence in order to make an informed decision." Moreover, the decision to "limit their investigation" was not reasonable, "particularly considering that counsel had a general knowledge of the difficulties of Petitioner's family history." Prejudice was established. "The sum of the testimony portrayed Petitioner as a good-hearted, tender, and compassionate person who was not violent and loved his family and friends," which was "undermined by the nature of the crime for which Petitioner had been convicted." If counsel had adequately investigated and presented the evidence, the jury would have heard evidence of the "degenerative environment Petitioner grew up in" with parents that ran a bootleg business in a dry county. The petitioner was physically and sexually abused by his parents, their customers, and his older siblings. He became addicted to prescription medications after back and head injuries. He attempted suicide and was admitted to a mental health center where he was diagnosed with "hysterical personality and drug dependence."

2015: **Apelt v. Ryan*,   F. Supp. 3d   , 2015 WL 7732670 (D. Ariz. Dec. 1, 2015) (sentenced in 1990). Counsel ineffective in capital sentencing in failing to adequately investigate and present mitigating evidence. The district court previously held that the state court's rejection of the claim was unreasonable and invited briefing on whether an evidentiary hearing was necessary. As both parties argued that no hearing was necessary, the court proceeded to the merits. Likewise, because the state did not argue that counsel performed competently, the court focused only on the issue of prejudice. The state argued in sentencing that the defendant had a "normal" childhood and no evidence was presented to the contrary despite substantial available evidence of "extreme poverty, physical abuse, developmental delays, … mental health problems," and evidence that the defendant, as a child, had been sexually assaulted twice by older men, once at knife point. "As a result, the court was given a picture of Apelt's background that bore 'no relation' to the picture that could have been presented if sentencing counsel had performed competently." *Id.* at (quoting *Rompilla v. Beard*, 545 U.S. 374, 392-93 (2005)). Prejudice established.

2014: **Hall v. Beard*, 55 F. Supp. 3d 618 (E.D. Pa. 2014) (sentenced in October 1994). Under AEDPA (with the court citing the ABA Guidelines numerous times), counsel was ineffective in capital sentencing for failing to adequately investigate, development, and present mitigating evidence. During sentencing, counsel called only two witnesses, the defendant's mother and the mother of one of his two children, "who testified generally to [his] good character and willingness to help others." Trial counsel testified that he did not investigate further because "he was trying to 'speed this up as quickly as possible and give [the jury] the nuts and bolts and … [not] all the little flowers and trimmings." Counsel's conduct was deficient in failing to "reasonably investigate his life, medical, educational, and employment history, and performed no expert mental health evaluation." While the Commonwealth argued that the defendant and his family failed to inform counsel of the defendant's background, despite conversations with counsel, the court rejected this argument because a defendant "does not have 'a duty to instruct counsel how to perform such a basic element of competent representation as the inquiry into a defendant's background.'" *Id.* at (quoting *Bond v. Beard*, 539 F.3d 256, 288 (3rd Cir. 2008)). Because the state court decision that counsel was not ineffective based, primarily on this argument, the state court's decision was "contrary to United States Supreme Court precedent because it fails to address the question of whether trial counsel's investigation for potentially mitigating evidence is reasonable under prevailing professional norms." Because the state court did not address the prejudice prong, the court reviewed this issue *de novo*. Prejudice established as the records and testimony established that the defendant suffered an abusive and neglectful childhood, a history of seizures and several severe head traumas, but his school records established his ability to adjust to a structured environment during his years in a court- ordered placement in "disciplinary school." The evidence supported two statutory mitigating circumstances that had not been presented to the jury: (1) the defendant was under the influence of extreme mental and emotional disturbance and (2) his capacity to conform his conduct to the requirements of the law was substantially impaired. Additionally, the evidence would have given additional weight to "the catch-all factor" that the jury did consider.

2013: ***Bridges v. Beard***, 941 F. Supp. 2d 584 (E.D. Pa. 2013) (tried in 1998). Under AEDPA, counsel was ineffective in capital sentencing for failing to adequately investigate, development, and present mitigating evidence. Counsel did not investigate the petitioner's "life history" and did not obtain a mental health evaluation, even though funding was approved for an expert to assist with the penalty phase. Counsel did not express a strategic reason for this and instead admitted that he simply did not see evidence of "psychological disturbance." Instead, counsel presented "thirteen witnesses, nearly all of them family or acquaintances," to testify to the petitioner's good character. Even with this limited presentation, the jury deliberated for more than six hours and reported being deadlocked before reaching a death verdict. Counsel's conduct was deficient. The state court's finding to the contrary was an unreasonable application of federal law. The state court essentially found that counsel made valid strategic decisions based on his discussions with petitioner and that counsel simply had no further information that should have led to investigation.

> First, it is simply not the case that the lawyer's duty to investigate begins and ends with discussions with his client. Even a "fatalistic and uncooperative" client does not absolve a lawyer from independent investigation. … [I]t is not the duty of the defendant to provide information on mitigation to the lawyer; rather, it is the lawyer's duty to uncover it.

Id. at (quoting *Porter v. McCollum*, 130 S. Ct. 447, 453 (2009)). Second:

> The state court is incorrect in suggesting that, under *Wiggins* [*v. Smith*, 539 U.S. 510 (2003)]

> a lawyer is only obligated to investigate areas of mitigation of which he has knowledge already. The Supreme Court has specifically rebuked lawyers for "ignor[ing] pertinent avenues for investigation of which he *should* have been aware."

Id. at (quoting *Porter*, 130 S. Ct. at 453 (emphasis added)).

> Moreover, even if the state court's characterization of the *Wiggins* rule were accurate, there was plenty of evidence of which [counsel] was already aware that should have triggered a wider investigation.

Counsel knew of petitioner's health problems and that petitioner had often been left in his grandmother's case. Prejudice was also established. The state courts one-sentence assessment was simply that petitioner "failed to prove the factors counsel was unaware of would have changed the outcome of the penalty phase proceeding." "This is the wrong standard," which is explicit in the examples given by the Court in *Williams v. Taylor*, 529 U.S. 362, 405-06 (2000). Thus, the state court's decision is "contrary to" clearly established federal law and is entitled to no deference. Prejudice was clear as "compelling mitigation" was available "that would have helped the jury to 'see the client as someone they do not want to kill.'" *Id.* at (quoting American Bar Association Guidelines for the Appointment and Performance of Counsel in Death Penalty Cases Commentary, Guideline 11.8.6 (1989). In short, the petitioner was raised in an unstable home by a single mother who was addicted to crack and he moved frequently between this chaotic life and the relative structure of his father's home. Petitioner had to move frequently as a child and attended three different schools in his first three school years. His mother's crack addiction was "debilitating." Medical records showed that she tested positive for cocaine while pregnant with petitioner's sibling. She gave up another sibling for adoption. She and the children were on food stamps and welfare through most of petitioner's childhood. She would often disappear for two to three weeks at a time leaving petitioner with his grandmother or aunt. Petitioner's father suspected that she was engaging in prostitution to support her drug habit. Many of her boyfriends were violent and beat her in front of petitioner. She made frequent visits to hospitals with physical injuries that were most likely caused by abuse. Petitioner also "suffered debilitating illness and hospitalizations as a child." Specifically, while he was in the fifth grade, he was hospitalized for severe groin and leg pain. He was diagnosed with acute rheumatic fever and anemia. A year later, he was readmitted for rheumatic fever. Doctors recommended chronic care hospitalization, bed rest, and a wheelchair, but the family, who never visited while he was hospitalized, took petitioner home.

> Rheumatic fever is associated with untreated strep throat, and thus can be a sign of neglect. If left untreated, it can damage the heart valves–precisely what happened to [petitioner], who was forced at age 17 to undergo open-heart surgery. His mother never visited him in the hospital during his surgery or recovery.

"This evidence would not excuse [petitioner's] crimes, but it would have provided context for it."

> A proper life history … would have helped the jury see that [petitioner's] witnessing of the abuse of his mother could have spurred a strong sense of over-protectiveness of his girlfriend that could have explained his violent reaction to the robbery that preceded the murders. …

> This evidence could well have convinced the jury that [petitioner] was less culpable for his criminal behavior.

In finding prejudice, the court also considered the "relative weakness of the aggravation." Even without the available mitigation, the jury struggled through roughly six hours, additional requested instructions on mitigation and weighing aggravation and mitigation, and a deadlock, before reaching a death verdict. Additionally, "the jury rejected the prosecution's theory of the case–that it was related to drug trafficking–when it rejected the aggravating factor relating to the drug trade." Under these circumstances, "it is reasonably probable than an effective presentation of the available mitigating evidence would have convinced at least one juror to find that the mitigation outweighed the aggravation." Convictions and death sentence also vacated due to the prosecution's *Brady* violation.

2012: *Johnson v. United States*, 860 F. Supp. 2d 663 (N.D. Iowa 2012) (sentenced in June 2005). Counsel was ineffective in capital sentencing for failing to adequately investigate and challenge the government's aggravation evidence and arguments and failing to adequately investigate and present mitigation evidence. The defendant was convicted of five murders in furtherance of a continuing criminal enterprise. Even though she was tried as an "aider and abettor," she received four death sentences and one life sentence, while her boyfriend/the principal received only two death sentences in his separate trial. One of the persons killed was a drug dealer, who worked for the defendant's boyfriend. He was killed after the defendant's boyfriend was indicted on drug charges, due to fear that he might cooperate with law enforcement. His girlfriend, and her two children "simply had the misfortune to be at home" and they were also killed. The fifth victim was also a drug dealer for the defendant's boyfriend and was the defendant's "ex-boyfriend in what had been a stormy and physically abusive relationship." The defendant was sentenced to death for all but the first drug dealer's murder while her boyfriend/the principal was sentenced to death only for the murder of the two children. First, counsel was ineffective in failing to challenge the prosecution's theory that the ex-boyfriend was killed due to the defendant's motive for "revenge for the beatings that he had inflicted upon her." Counsel did not present evidence that the defendant suffered from battered woman's syndrome, which made the "revenge" theory untenable. This evidence would have addressed the defendant's "mental state at the time of the offense." Prejudice was established with respect to the ex-boyfriend's murder. Counsel was also ineffective in failing to provide the defense psychiatric pharmacologist with data regarding the defendant's drug history. The expert testified about methamphetamine generally "from an informational perspective." He knew nothing at all and did not testify about the defendant. This expert could have testified that the defendant was a methamphetamine addict and about the effect of her chronic addiction on her at the time of the crime, even if she was not using at the time (which she claimed as she was pregnant at the time of the offenses). Even without this connection, four jurors found her methamphetamine addiction to be mitigating. While the trial expert did not testify in these proceedings, the court found that the assertions about what his testimony could have been was "not based on mere speculation."

> It is not speculation to find that … he would have been able to cast his testimony about the effects of methamphetamine use in terms of the effects of methamphetamine *on Johnson* in light of her drug use history, rather than simply in terms of the effects of methamphetamine *on people* who use some amounts of methamphetamine in certain ways.

Finally, counsel also failed to adequately investigate, prepare, and present mitigation evidence from experts and lay witnesses about the defendant's mental state at the time of the offenses. During the trial, counsel relied on a "mental state" defense in arguing that the defendant was present for the first four crimes but "did not have the requisite intent." Likewise, counsel argued that, while she lured her ex-boyfriend to a meeting where he was killed, she was not present and did not have the intent to kill him. Counsel's conduct was deficient in failing to pursue mental state at the time of the crimes in mitigation. Counsel retained an expert to explore her mental state at the time of the offenses but "pulled the plug" after his initial evaluation, which revealed "red flags" suggesting "brain impairments." Likewise, a second expert identified possible brain impairments and recommended further testing. "Thus, the hired experts' own advice called for further development of mental health evidence to support their opinions, suggesting that the limited bases for and scope of their opinions developed so far rendered those opinions inadequate."

> The lack of a reasonable investigation of mental health mitigation evidence here deprives the decision not to pursue a mitigation case based on mental state at the time of the offenses of any presumption of reasonableness.

Moreover, counsel's explanation that he decided to pull the plug "based on a bad experience that he had had with disclosure of mental health evidence in a capital case many years earlier" was inadequate "in the context of this case." As the Court stated:

> If [the] decision to reject such a mitigation defense was in some sense strategic, it was the worst strategic decision by any defense counsel that I have ever seen in my entire career: It effectively doomed [the] mitigation case from the start.

If counsel had adequately investigated, numerous experts could have testified about the defendant's impaired capacity at the time of the crimes based on a borderline personality disorder, and her brain dysfunction, including possibly temporal lobe disease, bipolar disorder, chronic methamphetamine abuse, dependent personality disorder, and post-traumatic stress disorder.

2009: *Turner v. Wong*, 641 F. Supp. 2d 1010 (E.D. Cal. 2009) (Sentencing in November 1984). In pre-AEDPA case, counsel ineffective in capital sentencing for failing adequately investigate and present mitigation evidence. Prior to sentencing, counsel informed the court that he was not prepared for the penalty phase. During sentencing, counsel presented brief, superficial testimony from the defendant's mother, half-sister, cousin, neighbor, and "job developer." Counsel argued "lingering doubt," despite the defendant's confession that he killed the victim after a homosexual advance and took his car and items from the home. Counsel also "referred to the Bible passage about not judging others" and summed up the defendant's life: "He's lived, the drug thing is wrong, the prior robbery is wrong, the prior receiving charge is wrong, this Defendant was wrong. Four item [sic] wrongness." Evidence that was available but not presented included: "early childhood abuse, his borderline intellectual capabilities, his drug abuse history, as well as [the victim's] predatory sexual practices." When the defendant was only five or six years old, his father would get drunk and abuse him by "thumping" him on the head, "whooping" him with a razor strap, and giving him karate punches in the stomach. The father also was verbally abusive berating the defendant as "stupid" and "dumb." The defendant's parents also fought frequently in front of the children, including physical fights that would leave the mother with knots on her head and black eyes. When the father moved out, he moved in with a woman and her four children just down the street. The defendant had an extensive history of drug and alcohol abuse that began in early adolescence. He used marijuana and smoked cigarettes dipped in PCP ("sherms") pretty much daily. He frequently engaged in bizarre behavior, such as running down the street and attempting to fly. On the day of the crimes, he was using marijuana, PCP, methamphetamine ("speed"), and drinking alcohol. PCP was confirmed in blood samples taken two days after the crimes. Trial defense counsel did not have his file and could not remember a lot of details about the counsel but recalled that he chose not to rely on the PCP evidence because he believed it was inconsistent with the focus on the homosexual advances. He was also aware of information from family members that the defendant was violent on PCP. He recalled only one group contact with family members, but did not recall much of what was discussed. He did not recall learning about beatings, physical abuse, or the father's alcoholism. Counsel's conduct was deficient. The background investigation "was minimal and superficial." Counsel focused only on the defendant's mother and did not interview his sister's even though one was present during a group interview. Counsel also failed to interview the numerous family members and acquaintances interviewed by detectives or numerous people that had previously provided statements in support of a prior probation. "The problem with the investigation was not a lack of quantity of witnesses interviewed, but the quality of the interviews." At the very least, the defendant's mother, sisters, and others "were aware of serious family dysfunction in the [] household during [the defendant's] childhood and early adolescence." These witnesses "were not asked the questions which would have elicited the information. Without the questions having been asked, there is no indication that the subject matter would have been obviously important to the family members, and thus volunteered." "Conducting an adequate investigation to inform strategic decisions is exactly what is required, and is exactly what wasn't accomplished." The "very limited penalty phase evidence and argument of Turner's good character, paternal abandonment, and occupational responsibility," during summation "was not a reasonable strategy for casting [the defendant] in a positive light. It was disjointed, confusing and lacking in real mitigation value." The requirements for competent counsel were not lower in the 1980's.

> The notion that the standard for death penalty cases was merely good character and good deeds also is refuted by the May 1983 article authored by Gary Goodpaster about how defense attorneys should try a capital case. The Goodpaster article is cited by the Supreme Court in *Strickland,* 466 U.S. at 689-90, itself decided May 14, 1984.

Id. at (quoting Gary Goodpaster, "The Trial for Life: Effective Assistance of Counsel in Death Penalty Cases," 58 N.Y.U.L.Rev. 299, 335-36 (1983)).

> Even earlier, in 1982, the Supreme Court held that evidence about a defendant's upbringing and turbulent family history is relevant to the individualized sentencing process in a death penalty trial. *See Eddings v. Oklahoma,* 455 U.S. 104, 115, 102 S.Ct. 869, 71 L.Ed.2d 1 (1982).

Here, counsel "either didn't even think of developing background evidence, or, if he did, ... he inexplicably chose not to pursue it. Neither course is reasonable, especially since there was no downside to the admission of evidence about [the defendant's] childhood victimization." "[A]t best," counsel gave "a distorted view of normalcy and non-violence in [the] family." Likewise, "there was no down side to presenting the jury with evidence of [the defendant's] depressed intelligence beyond the testimony of his paid defense expert." "There was no reasonable investigation or strategy supporting the decision to 'minimize the whole PCP episode.'"

> The PCP use may well have explained to the jury why the defense theory of the case was consistent with the [defendant's] actions in committing the crime (the excessive number of wounds) and immediately afterwards (stealing the television yet leaving the jewelry). Contrary to [counsel's] fears, [the defendant's] chronic drug use and the reasons therefor, were valid mitigating factors that could and should have been presented at the penalty phase.

Nonetheless, counsel continued his "indefensible adherence to [the] sexual advance resistance defense strategy when he could not or would not substantiate it. A reasonable attorney would have adjusted the trial strategy to theories that could be substantiated, like childhood abuse, borderline mental retardation, and PCP intoxication." Prejudice was also established. "[T]he background information presented at the penalty phase trial was general and superficial." In short, it was "a sanitized version of [the defendant's] life with no explanation of his turbulent childhood, severe intellectual limitations, or dependence on PCP."

McNeill v. Branker, 601 F. Supp. 2d 694 (E.D.N.C. 2009) (tried in April 1996). Under AEDPA, counsel ineffective in failing to adequately investigate and present mitigation evidence. During sentencing, the defense presented family members to testify about the defendant's positive traits and deeds, lack of criminal history, honorable military service, and how he was easily influenced by his brother, who was also a co-defendant. Although counsel had retained a mental health expert to examine the defendant, counsel did not present any evidence of the defendant's depression, troubled family background, or suicide attempt. Relying on the 1989 ABA Guidelines for the Appointment and Performance of Counsel in Death Penalty Cases, the court found deficient conduct in the investigation because "counsel focused their attention on the guilt phase of trial and made only minimal effort to investigate potential mitigating evidence," which consisted only of asking the defendant and his parents "their impression on the subject." Counsel did not request funding for a "mitigation expert," even though "funds for mitigation experts were granted in capital cases during that time period." In addition, the defense psychiatric expert was given very little background information and was asked only to focus on the defendant's competence and criminal responsibility rather than sentencing issues. Counsel never contacted the defendant's sister, family members, former girlfriend, friends, and neighbors. The state court unreasonably "placed the responsibility on [the defendant] and his family for failing to inform counsel of petitioner's suicide attempt, depression, alcohol abuse, and troubled background."

> Rather than investigating the accuracy of the impression they received from [the defendant] and his parents in discussion or seeking other potential mitigating evidence, counsel did little more than work to confirm the opinion that petitioner had a good or "normal" childhood.

"The few people whom counsel did call at sentencing were not interviewed by counsel or the defense investigator to learn what type of evidence or information they could provide." Counsel also "failed to inform themselves of and develop information in their possession," including failure to review the defendant's "diary or autobiography, 84 pages long, with information about his life and upbringing," which was prepared at counsel's request. "It included references to ... depression, regular abuse of alcohol, dysfunction in family relationships, and his suicide attempt." If counsel had adequately investigated the evidence would have established that: numerous family members suffered from depression and/or mental illness; the defendant's father sexually abused one of the defendant's sisters and, physically abuse, and ruled by threatening severe beatings; the defendant "exhibited symptoms of mental health problems as young as seven years-old when he began self-mutilating himself by pulling out all of his eyelashes and developed a nervous habit of clearing his throat"; and as a teenager he experienced serious depression, struggled with substance abuse, and eventually attempted suicide. Counsel's conduct was not excused by strategy, due to the failure to investigate. In addition, the available but unpresented evidence would not have conflicted with the evidence counsel presented in sentencing because the defendant's "helpful and reliable nature, military service, and positive character traits would have been more admirable in light of his personal struggle with mental health issues and substance abuse." Prejudice established because "[t]here is a 'belief, long held by this society, that defendants who commit criminal acts that are attributable to a disadvantaged background, or to emotional and mental problems, may be less culpable than defendants who have no such excuse.'" *Id.* at (quoting *Boyde v. California*, 494 U.S. 370, 382 (1990)).

2008: ***Ben-Sholom v. Ayers***, 566 F. Supp. 2d 1053 (E.D. Cal. 2008), *aff'd on other grounds*, 674 F.3d 1095 (9th Cir. 2012) (sentenced in Feb. 1986). Under pre-AEDPA law, counsel ineffective in failing to adequately investigate and present mitigation. The 18-year-old defendant's confessions suggested that he wanted to be a "mercenary," planned to "fight communists in Burma," and the crimes were a "mission." Although counsel "consulted with five mental health experts during trial preparation [concerning a possible diminished capacity defense], he presented no expert testimony at penalty proceedings" and did not provide his mental health experts with records or social history information. He presented only a few family members, associates, and the defendant to testify. Counsel's conduct was deficient.

> It is manifest that to counter the effect of the aggravating circumstances of the crime [counsel] was obligated to show something mitigating about [the defendant's] mental state during his homicidal actions. ... What was missing was evidence explaining why [he] committed this awful crime and an effort on [counsel's] part to develop that evidence.

Id. at .

> In this case, however, it was not the quantity of sources consulted but the quality of the investigation and the assimilation of that information into a coherent mitigation case. Because [counsel] hung onto a "strategy" of not providing experts with pertinent background information and the belief that a clinical interview was unnecessary for psychological testing, the expert consultations he arranged were worse than worthless because not only were they based on insufficient information, but on fabricated information [the defendant] supplied. Digging deeper in this case meant that [counsel] needed to ascertain the true facts about [the defendant].

Id. at . Counsel's "opinion about mental defenses being a 'hard sell' and that the jury would have been disgusted" with such evidence was not borne out by other attorney testimony in the case, including a "*Strickland* expert." [The court also considered CLE publications prior to trial in determining the applicable standards.] Counsel's "conscious decision to provide no documents to most of his experts and only a few document[s] to" one was also unreasonable. The "idea that any psychologist could offer evidence of empirical test results without a clinical interview was totally wrong." "[N]ot giving his experts all relevant information, good and bad, totally defeated the purpose of a mental health examination." "Because [counsel] failed to verify [the defendant's] background information, he did not (and could not) provide what he didn't know to his experts." Counsel's actions (in not providing sufficient information to the one mental health expert he wanted to testify) were not justified by concerns that the four bad reports he had already received would be disclosed. Rather than providing these negative reports, counsel could have supplied the expert with the "*actual* background" information through witness interviews.

> The problem with [counsel's] approach was that since he provided his experts with no substantiated background information, they could not be sure how much of what [the defendant] told them during clinical interviews was embellished, exaggerated, or true. The resulting opinions were uninformed, incomplete, and unfounded. ... The lack of verifiable, true information about [the actual] background disabled the experts from giving the assistance for which they had been retained.

Id. . Counsel's failure to present mental health evidence in sentencing was not justified by "clearly anti-social behavior in [the defendant's] past," which could be presented in rebuttal by the state's expert.

> [T]he cause for that behavior, including the merciless abuse inflicted by his father, the sense of abandonment by his mother, the depression over losing his life-long dream of being in the Army, and his lack of identity, were mitigating and could have been developed to explain why and how [the defendant] became involved in the unrealistic, military mission that tragically ended [the victim's] life. [Counsel's] failure to expose the [false] foundation for [the state expert's] potential testimony was constitutionally ineffective.

Id. at . The court "accept[ed]" the opinion of the "*Strickland* expert, knowledgeable about the standard of professional performance at the time" that "the entire trial presentation was confused and at cross purposes." Since counsel "viewed a penalty phase a certainty, the guilt phase opening statement should have raised penalty phase mitigation concepts."

> While [counsel] did explain the idea that [the defendant] and his companions perceived the entire crime as a military mission with the ultimate purpose of going to Burma, he didn't argue that the mission was fantasy, but instead told the jurors they would have to determine for themselves whether the military purpose of the crime was reality or fantasy.

Counsel then "negated" the military mission notion in trial closing. Counsel referenced some potential mitigation in the sentencing opening, "but failed to explain how those facts were mitigating and failed to mention these subjects again on summation." Counsel also failed to mention other significant aspects of mitigation, including the defendant's testimony "of his remorse and substantial domination (following the order to kill [the victim] 'explicitly')," in closing. Prejudice was established because the evidence would have shown: (1) abuse as a toddler "during the critically important time of toilet training"; (2) his father's "sadistic abuse" from the time he was seven years old; (3) 13 different schools; (4) a history of nightmares, depression, and preoccupation with suicide; (5) "extreme emotional and mental disturbances at the time of the crime, including PTSD, borderline personality disorder, identity fragmentation, and major depression; (5) hypertension for which he received a prescription of "Inderal, which can exacerbate depression"; and (6) humiliation and demeaning "by his anti-Semitic father because he was Jewish." Yet, the defendant sought and "responded well to therapy, revealing his hurt and consistent efforts to escape an untenable home life (by running away) and seeking help from therapists." While counsel presented some of the background facts through lay witnesses in sentencing, "the depth and breadth of the evidence paled in comparison with the understanding the mental health experts added."

> [A]t least one member of … [the] penalty phase jury would have voted for life without the possibility of parole had [counsel] presented mental state evidence through the testimony of mental health experts. This conclusion is strengthened by the fact that the penalty verdict following the paltry mitigation evidence presented was not an instant victory for the prosecution. The deliberations began with a vote favoring life by eight to four and deliberations were protracted, lasting nearly 17 hours in contrast to the two and one half hours from beginning to end of the actual penalty phase case. The state of these deliberations suggest a close case.

Id. at (citations omitted).

> [The defendant] was sentenced to death by a jury that had no understanding of the "indisputably sadistic treatment" inflicted upon him as a child. Nor was the jury aware of well-established psychological criteria for [his] mental state at the time of the crime.

Id. at (citation omitted).

Sowell v. Collins, 557 F. Supp. 2d 843 (S.D. Ohio 2008) (sentenced in November 1983). Counsel, in pre-AEDPA case, ineffective in capital sentencing for failing to adequately investigate and present mitigation evidence. Counsel's mitigation strategy was to emphasize petitioner's good deeds during his adult life. Counsel presented lay witnesses (probation officers and acquaintances) on this, an unsworn statement by the petitioner, mental health reports of court-appointed examinations requested by counsel, and a presentencing (PSI) report. Citing the ABA Guidelines for the Appointment and Performance of Counsel in Death Penalty Cases (1989), the court found deficient conduct.

> [P]etitioner's case closely resembles that of *Wiggins*. [Petitioner's] trial counsel did not request or obtain a mitigation specialist or investigator, and instead relied on the investigations of others who were not trained to conduct the type of investigation required in a capital case. Counsel failed to investigate highly relevant mitigating evidence of petitioner's family background. Counsel relied on the information contained in the PSI and the brief mitigation reports prepared by [court- appointed examiners], and did not "dig deeper" and investigate several leads contained in those reports. Counsel did not call one family member

to testify, and there is no evidence that counsel conducted even the most basic interviews with petitioner's siblings and other family members for the purpose of investigating petitioner's background. Like *Wiggins,* counsel abandoned their duty to investigate after "having acquired only rudimentary knowledge of his history from a narrow set of sources." 539 U.S. at 524, 123 S. Ct. 2527.

The court-appointed examiner reports "contained hints of petitioner's violent and deprived background," and "morsels of evidence," but "counsel did not investigate further."

[C]ounsel's investigation into petitioner's background did not reflect reasonable professional judgment. Counsel's failure to interview members of petitioner's family was neither consistent with the professional standards that prevailed in 1983, nor reasonable in light of the evidence contained in the PSI and the psychological reports that would have led a reasonable attorney to investigate further. ...

This is not a case where counsel presented absolutely no evidence in mitigation. Counsel did present a case emphasizing the good in petitioner. The Court cannot conclude, however, that counsel's decision to emphasize the good rather than the bad was reasonable trial strategy, not because there was insufficient evidence to support that theory, but because there simply is no evidence that counsel were even aware of petitioner's troubled past because they did not sufficiently investigate petitioner's background. ... In this case, counsel were not in a position to elect to pursue one strategy over another because they had not reasonably investigated petitioner's background. Pursuing the leads regarding petitioner's background was necessary to making an informed choice regarding available mitigation strategies. Furthermore, ... a reasonable investigation would have revealed that the information concerning petitioner's background was not inconsistent with, and might actually have bolstered, counsel's mitigation theory.

Prejudice established because the available evidence "paint[s] a more complete picture of petitioner" and "is qualitatively different than the information that was presented during the mitigation hearing." The evidence was "powerful" and established: (1) severe deprivation, neglect, and physical and emotional abuse as a child; (2) extreme poverty, including malnourishment, a younger brother dying of starvation, inadequate clothing, and being bitten by rats; (3) beatings and head injuries as a child; and (4) living in a tent in a junkyard at age 14 to escape his father's home. This evidence "was significant, and qualitatively different" and "would have painted an entirely different portrait of petitioner." This evidence also "would have bolstered their mitigation case by demonstrating that petitioner was capable of generosity and good acts in spite of the upbringing that he endured."

"he testimony regarding his childhood could not have possibly made petitioner appear more culpable. Rather, the evidence, if discovered and presented, is of the type that might well have affected the [three-judge] panel's appraisal of his moral culpability. ... The evidence would have helped illustrate the manner in which [petitioner's] violent background contributed to his conduct and violent reaction to the theft that he perceived.

This is also not a case where counsel could have reasonably feared opening the door to negative information that the panel would not have otherwise learned about petitioner. The door was already opened by the information [presented in sentencing] ... . Yet, the panel did not hear any evidence of how violence was so very prevalent during the formative years of petitioner's life-evidence which may have explained why petitioner grew into the kind of adult who found himself frequently reacting in a violent manner. Evidence of petitioner's background would have helped explain petitioner's significant repressed rage, and had the panel been able to place petitioner's "excruciating life history on the mitigating side of the scale," there is a reasonable probability that at least one member of the panel "would have struck a different balance." *Wiggins*, 539 U.S. at 537, 123 S. Ct. 2527.

Richie v. Sirmons, 563 F. Supp. 2d 1250 (N.D. Okla. 2008), *aff'd on other grounds sub nom. Richie v. Workman*, 599 F.3d 1131 (10th Cir. 2010) (sentenced in October 1993). Under AEDPA, counsel ineffective in capital sentencing for failing to develop and present neuropsychological evidence. Counsel presented family member testimony of alcoholism in the family, verbal and physical abuse of petitioner, petitioner's prior hospitalization for stab wounds, and petitioner's drug problems and prior problems with the law.

> Consisting solely of testimony from family members, the thrust of Petitioner's mitigation defense focused on Petitioner's family history. Some of the family members touched briefly upon Petitioner's social and educational background. However, other than the mention of one hospitalization, there was no testimony regarding Petitioner's medical history, religious and cultural influences, or employment history. Notably, there was no testimony from a medical expert concerning Petitioner's mental state and mental abilities. ... Omission of mental health evidence from Petitioner's case for mitigation was unreasonable, and resulted in prejudice to Petitioner.

Petitioner had a series of head injuries as a teenager and a long history of severe headaches.

> Nothing in the record indicates that trial counsel's failure to investigate and obtain a neurological expert was a strategic decision. Counsel simply did not take any action to determine whether such evidence was available.

While counsel did retain a psychologist prior to trial, his "evaluation was based on personality tests, rather than neuropsychological tests which are designed to detect brain damage." If counsel had performed adequately, the evidence would have included evidence of brain dysfunction, a history of significant alcohol and marijuana dependency, and limited intellectual capacity. Reversal was also required because petitioner was denied an instruction on second degree depraved mind murder, which was supported by the record.

King v. Bell, 392 F. Supp. 2d 964 (M.D. Tenn. 2005) (trial in November 1982). Counsel ineffective in capital sentencing for failing to adequately prepare and present mitigation and failing to object to the prosecutor's argument expressing his personal opinion. Counsel's conduct was deficient under *Strickland* and the ABA Standards for Criminal Justice. Counsel "focused their limited sentencing efforts on researching the statutory aggravating and mitigating factors and consulting with each other about the content of closing argument" after the guilty verdict. *Id.* at 975. Counsel did not interview family members or otherwise investigate. Counsel also failed to even discuss sentencing with the defendant or prepare him for his testimony. Even if counsel were not aware of any of the defendant's history before, counsel knew the basics about the defendant's background from his testimony during the trial. Nonetheless, counsel did not seek to delay sentencing to allow more time for investigation and preparation for sentencing. In short, "it appears trial counsel failed to conduct *any investigation whatsoever*." *Id.* at 986. Prejudice found based on the failure to present mitigation and the failure to object to the prosecutor's improper arguments expressing his personal opinion that the defendant deserved the death penalty without objection. If counsel had adequately investigated the evidence would have established that the defendant's biological parents separated when he was nine months old. His father moved to New York. His alcoholic mother gave him over to his aunt and uncle to raise. She died when he was 14 for cirrhosis of the liver. The defendant was raised in a good loving home with discipline even though they lived in "the projects." As a teenager, the defendant started getting into trouble running around with a biological brother raised in a different home nearby. After he was disciplined, he asked to move to New York with his father, which was allowed. His father did not maintain discipline and the defendant started skipping school and getting into trouble. Thus, the defendant "spent his formative years in New York with little supervision." *Id.* at 979. He became addicted to heroin before returning to Tennessee as a young adult. The turning point in his life though came when his aunt and uncle were murdered in 1975 by Black Moslems in retaliation for a mentally retarded, schizophrenic shooting one of their own. They were abducted and their bodies were later found shot in a burned out vehicle. Four other homes, including those of the defendant's brother and cousin who were raised in the same home with him, were firebombed. The murders "overwhelmed" him and he began seeing and hearing his "Mama" (the aunt) and using drugs to "an even greater extent than before." *Id.* at 980. He would often call out to her in his sleep and wake up sweating with nightmares. He had "anxiety attacks" and passed out a few times at work. He was also hospitalized for three gunshot wounds and a heroin overdose. His records showed "episodes of depression, heavy alcohol abuse, and IV drug abuse" and a referral for psychiatric treatment. Mental health experts could have testified that the defendant had Post Traumatic Stress Disorder and an organic brain syndrome, along with panic attacks associated with an anxiety disorder. The state court decision was an objectively unreasonable application of *Strickland*. The court withheld a final ruling, however, in order to conduct an evidentiary hearing to obtain counsel's testimony and "to resolve any factual disputes that may remain."

2002: ***United States ex rel. Madej v. Schomig***, 223 F. Supp. 2d 968 (N.D. Ill. 2002) (affirmed on appeal in 1985). Even under AEDPA, counsel ineffective in capital sentencing for failing to prepare and present mitigation evidence. The sentencing hearing was held one day after conviction. Defense counsel had not prepared because he mistakenly believed that he would have time to do so after conviction. The only mitigation presented was the defendant's testimony. Court finds that prejudice should be presumed under *Cronic* because "counsel failed to conduct any investigation that would submit the question of Madej's eligibility for the death penalty to 'meaningful adversarial testing,'" (quoting *Cronic*, 466 U.S. at 659), and even conceded eligibility for the death penalty. Court further finds that, even if *Cronic* does not apply, prejudice was shown under *Strickland*. Available but unpresented evidence included: evidence that the defendant protected her from physical abuse for years; a plea for mercy from the victim's husband; evidence that petitioner was a good person; evidence of a troubled childhood; and expert testimony about petitioner's history of substance abuse and its impact on his "psychological and neurological health." The Illinois Supreme Court's finding of no prejudice was "clear error" because the state court "looked at each category of mitigating evidence in isolation" rather than considering whether "there is a reasonable probability the outcome would have been different based on all of the mitigating evidence." Court held: "There can be no confidence in the outcome of a capital sentencing hearing where the defendant was represented by an attorney who failed to present any evidence to counsel against imposition of the death penalty." Although not considered individually prejudicial, the court included in the cumulative prejudice analysis, counsel's failure to advise his client that state law required a unanimous jury and only one juror had to hold out in order to avoid death, which resulted in the petitioner waiving his right to jury and being sentenced by judge alone.

Pursell v. Horn, 187 F. Supp. 2d 260 (W.D. Pa. 2002) (tried in January 1982). Counsel ineffective in capital sentencing for failing to prepare and present mitigation evidence. Although the case was reviewed under AEDPA, this issue was reviewed *de novo* because the state court did not address the merits of the claim. The district court also held that no evidentiary hearing was required because the state presented no contrary evidence. Thus, the court expanded the record to include Purcell's affidavits and held that the AEDPA was not violated because Purcell was denied a hearing on this issue in state court. Counsel's conduct was deficient because "[t]rial counsel has an 'obligation to conduct a thorough investigation of the defendant's background' in capital cases." (quoting *Williams v. Taylor*, 529 U.S. at 396). Here, counsel had no basis for failing to investigate, because counsel focused only on defeating the one aggravating circumstance of torture. Counsel presented no mitigating evidence and his discussion of it in closing covered only one page. This decision could not reasonably "foreclose any investigation into mitigating evidence" though. If counsel had investigated, he would have discovered that the defendant was the son of a prostitute, who lived in squalor in his first four years. After he was abandoned by his mother to another family, he was physically and sexually abused by an alcoholic father. He began self-medicating with drugs at an early age and was a drug addict by the time he was a teenager. These problems caused neurological damage that affected impulse control and ability to understand right from wrong. Despite all of this, the defendant was a loving father, caring brother, a dear friend, and a man to be trusted. Before the jury, the defendant, "the man was a mere skeleton: a young killer with a prior criminal record and a girlfriend, nothing more and nothing less. Had [his] lawyer tapped into the mitigating evidence available to him, however, he would have added flesh, bones, a mind, and a heart" to the defendant. Ultimately, the jury "may have believed that his life, though shattered beyond repair, was still worth saving." The jury also may have found that the murder was not "preplanned or premeditated," due to the impulse control problems caused by his brain damage. This would also have impacted the consideration of the torture aggravator. In short, this jury "did not have the chance to see [the defendant], the man. It did not have the opportunity to feel sympathy or pity. ... While this evidence may not have swayed every juror, [the defendant] need only show a reasonable probability that one juror would have found death an inappropriate punishment." Here, while "[a] jury in a capital case may not be barred from hearing any mitigation evidence offered by the defendant concerning his character or background[,] [i]n the present case, the jury was prevented from hearing such evidence, not because the court precluded its admission, but merely because [defense] counsel made an objectively unreasonable decision not to look for it."

2001: *Horn v. Holloway*, 161 F. Supp. 2d 452 (E.D. Pa. 2001), *rev'd on other grounds*, 355 F.3d 707 (3d Cir. 2004) (tried in May 1986).[2] Counsel ineffective in capital sentencing, under AEDPA, for failing

---

[2]The IAC finding was not addressed on appeal. The Court of Appeals granted a new trial on other grounds.

to request appointment of a mental health expert to assist the defense. Although the defendant waived his right to present testimony of family and friends, he did not waive his right to have a mental health expert testify on his behalf. "[E]ven when a defendant is uncooperative, counsel still has a duty to interview friends and relatives and otherwise investigate to discover whether mitigating evidence exists." *Id.* at 567.

> Because the post-trial evaluations show that mental health evidence existed prior to trial, both a complete failure to investigate and a partial investigation that failed to uncover such evidence must be considered unreasonable because counsel probably would have discovered such evidence had his investigation been reasonable. Likewise, because such evidence probably would have been discovered, counsel's decision not to make such an investigation, if indeed he made such a decision, must be considered unreasonable. Further, whether or not an investigation was conducted and whether or not evidence as to mental health issues was uncovered, such evidence must have existed, and therefore counsel acted unreasonably in failing to request that a defense mental health expert be appointed. Trial counsel demonstrated a lack of either preparation or knowledge, or both, in failing to request that the trial court appoint a defense expert to assist in the preparation of Petitioner's mitigation defense at the penalty phase.

Id. at 567-68 (citations and footnotes omitted). Prejudice found because, with the assistance of a mental health expert, the available evidence included cognitive defects; the effects of emotional, physical and sexual abuse; and the effects of chronic drug and alcohol abuse. Thus, there is a reasonable probability that a juror would have weighed the aggravating and mitigating factors differently. "Counsel's deficient performance prejudiced Petitioner by depriving him of any informed presentation of mental infirmities." *Id.* at 573. There can be no strategic or tactical reason for counsel's failure to request that a mental health expert be appointed to assist the defense when mental health issues could be a significant factor at either the trial or penalty phases, because such an expert is necessary to effectively develop and present such evidence, as well as to assist counsel and his client in deciding whether such evidence should be presented at trial. With respect to the state court decision, the court held that the state court had not adjudicated this claim on the merits even though it was properly presented. Thus, the court was applying *de novo* review rather than the standard of 2254(d). The court also held that even if 2254(d) applied, the state court decision was unreasonable because the state court purported to deny post-conviction relief because of the denial of relief on direct appeal when this claim was factually and legally different than the claim raised on direct appeal. "A decision based on an analysis of one set of facts and legal theories cannot reasonably be applied to another set of facts and legal theories only tangentially related to the former set." *Id.* at 565 n. 130.

Laird v. Horn, 159 F. Supp. 2d 58 (E.D. Pa. 2001), *aff'd on other grounds*, 414 F.3d 419 (3d Cir. 2005) (sentenced in May 1988). Under AEDPA, counsel ineffective in capital sentencing for failing to adequately prepare and present mitigation. Counsel presented an innocence defense during the trial. "There is no evidence that trial counsel conducted any inquiry into petitioner's background and medical history in connection with the penalty phase." Counsel presented only the defendant's fiancé (and the mother of one of his children) to plead for mercy and did not prepare her or explain mitigation to her. If counsel had adequately investigated the jury would have heard evidence of the defendant's traumatic childhood, severe childhood physical and sexual abuse, a significant history of mental and emotional disturbance, including Attention Deficit Hyperactivity Disorder, a history of significant head traumas including a skull fracture; the effects of his history of alcohol and drug addiction, and that he suffers from Post-Traumatic Stress Disorder. In short, there was "an overwhelming amount of highly compelling evidence." The state court's decision was based on an unreasonable determination of the facts in light of the evidence presented in the State court. In addition, the state court's conclusion that "[c]ounsel will not be deemed ineffective for pursuing a particular strategy, as long as the course chosen was reasonable," ... does not comport with *Strickland* 's holding that counsel has a duty to "make reasonable investigations or to make a reasonable decision that makes particular investigations unnecessary." Likewise, "the fact trial counsel presented some mitigating evidence does not warrant the conclusion that his failure to investigate other potential sources of mitigating evidence was thus reasonable."

> Finally, the state supreme court's post-hoc speculation regarding possible reasons for trial counsel's actions does not somehow render trial counsel's performance constitutionally adequate. As explained by the Fourth Circuit, "courts should not conjure up tactical decisions an attorney could have made, but plainly did not.... Tolerance of tactical miscalculations is one thing; fabrication of tactical excuses is quite another."

Id. at (quoting *Griffin v. Warden*, 970 F.2d 1355, 1358-59 (4th Cir.1992)). Reversal also required for other reasons.

Jacobs v. Horn, 129 F. Supp. 2d 390 (M.D. Pa. 2001), *rev'd on other grounds*, 395 F.3d 92 (3d Cir. 2005) (tried in 1992).[3] Counsel ineffective in failing to adequately prepare and present mitigation evidence. Counsel made no effort to perform an investigation into the defendant's past other than speaking with a few relatives who attended the trial. Counsel consulted with a psychiatrist, but did not tell him it was a death penalty case and did not ask him to consider mitigation. He was asked only to examine competence and sanity. Counsel also failed to provide the expert with any background information concerning the crimes or the defendant's history. The only mitigation presented was testimony from the defendant and testimony from his mother that he loved his daughter (one of the victims) and that he was sorry. If counsel had adequately performed, the evidence would have established that the defendant has mild mental retardation, organic brain damage, and schizoid personality disorder. He was also a witness and victim of abuse and suffered from drug and alcohol addictions. The state court held that counsel was not ineffective because counsel had retained a psychiatrist. "At issue, currently, however, is whether an evaluation was performed with regard to *mitigating* evidence not whether the petitioner suffered a mental impairment that would have affected his criminal responsibility or competency to stand trial." In addition, the expert retained explained that "an evaluation for mitigating evidence is different from an evaluation for criminal responsibility/competency to stand trial," but he was asked only to perform the latter and was not informed that the prosecution was seeking the death penalty. The state court also found that counsel did not have the additional background information that the trial expert required. The state court's finding was an unreasonable application of Supreme Court precedent because

> The important point is not that counsel did not have the information, but rather, we must examine *why* counsel did not have the information. Here, counsel did not have the

---

[3]The Court of Appeals held that counsel's ineffectiveness also prejudiced the defendant during the trial.

information because he failed to investigate and obtain the relevant information. The fact that trial counsel did not have such information merely supports the conclusion that he did not fully investigate–it does not justify the failure to investigate and present evidence. ...

"[T]he great weight of federal law requires defense counsel in a capital case to investigate a defendant's background, cognitive status and mental health for mitigating evidence." Because counsel did not do so here, counsel's conduct was deficient. Prejudice was also found.

Pirtle v. Lambert, 150 F. Supp. 2d 1078 (E.D. Wash. 2001), *aff'd on other grounds*, 313 F.3d 1160 (9th Cir. 2002) (sentenced in July 1993). Trial and appellate counsel ineffective in capital sentencing for failing to interview officers prior to trial and failing to object to admission of statement taken in violation of Miranda. While the defendant was on the ground, handcuffed, with an officer's knee in his back, and officers threatening to "blow his head off" if he was not cooperative, an officer, without prior Miranda warnings, asked the defendant if he knew why he was under arrest and the defendant said, "Of course I do, you might as well shoot me now." The officers did not include this statement in their reports and the state did not disclose the statement prior to trial. During the trial, the state offered the statement in evidence without objection and argued on the basis of the statement in both the trial and sentencing. With respect to the lack of Miranda warnings, the court found that "the Washington Supreme Court unreasonably determined that Deputy Walker was not interrogating [the defendant], but rather was just asking background booking questions." The district court found this to be unreasonable because this clearly was not a booking situation or question. With respect to the state's failure to disclose the statement and hold a hearing on voluntariness, the state court held that no disclosure or hearing was required because the prosecutor did not know of the statement until the officer's testimony. The District Court found this to be an unreasonable application of Supreme Court law since "the United States Supreme Court has clearly held that knowledge of police officers is imputed to the prosecution." With respect to the ineffective assistance claim, the court was "firmly convinced that the Washington Supreme Court erred and failed to reasonably apply the holding of *Strickland* to the facts of this case." The court found no prejudice during the trial due to "extremely strong" evidence, including the defendant's testimony admitting guilt. Prejudice found in sentencing though, but the court analyzed the "prejudice" in conjunction with the analysis of whether "'actual prejudice' resulted because a constitutional violation had substantial and injurious effect or influence in determining the jury's verdict. *Brecht v. Abrahamson*, 507 U.S. 619, 623 (1993)."[4] In any event, the court could not "find that no juror was influenced or persuaded by the fact that [the defendant] had acknowledged he should die for what he had done which then became a part of that juror or jurors' s moral judgment analysis."

1998: *Christy v. Horn*, 28 F. Supp. 2d 307 (W.D. Pa. 1998) (tried in December 1993). Counsel ineffective in capital sentencing phase for failing to adequately prepare and present mental health mitigation evidence, presenting damaging character evidence, failing to object to state's improper arguments in sentencing, and misstating the law in closing argument. From 1973-79, the defendant, while incarcerated for other crimes had been involuntarily committed to a number of mental health institutions due to mental illness. The medical records established that he suffered from paranoid

[4]Note that under the Court's analysis in *Kyles v. Whitley*, 514 U.S. 419 (1995), the Court stated that no additional harmless error review is necessary after materiality is found. Because the "materiality" standard of *Kyles* is the same as the "reasonable probability" standard of *Strickland*, *United States v. Bagley*, 473 U.S. 667, 682, 685 (1985), it was unnecessary for the court to address *Brecht* at all with respect to the ineffective assistance of counsel claim.

schizophrenia, organic brain syndrome, depression, personality disorder, psychosis, delusions, and long-term drug and alcohol addiction. Within months of his release from confinement, the defendant broke into a business and ran into the night watchman. The guard shot the defendant in the wrist, but was apparently unaware that the wound was superficial and put down his gun and walked away. The defendant grabbed the gun and shot the watchman as the watchman rushed him. He then shot him in the head while the watchman was crouched on the floor. During a trial on unrelated charges, the defendant confessed to this murder. Prior to trial, the defense requested appointment of a defense psychiatrist, but the trial court denied the motion and appointed a court psychiatrist instead. The court psychiatrist testified during a competence hearing that the defendant was competent and sane and suffered only from antisocial personality disorder. The defense did not cross-examine the psychiatrist concerning diminished capacity or mitigation and sought only to introduce the defendant's medical records. The trial court held that the records would not be admitted without testimony from persons who prepared them. Counsel presented a diminished capacity defense and self defense arguments and had the defendant testify, but did not contact any of the defendant's previous doctors or present any psychiatric evidence at all. The state, despite the fact that the prosecutor had previously presided over a number of the defendant's commitment hearings as a county mental health officer, argued without objection that the defendant was faking mental illness and that if any evidence were available it would have been presented. Counsel also elicited testimony of the defendant's prior incarcerations and failed to object to state's argument that the defendant just cycled back and forth between prison, mental health facilities, and the streets. During sentencing the defense presented only two witnesses– the defendant's mother and a prosecution witness who had previously been incarcerated with the defendant. He testified to the defendant's good character, but also testified that the defendant was not "crazy" and had told him that he would kill people, especially any witnesses to a murder that he might commit. During arguments, the state argued without objection and contrary to Pennsylvania law, that the defendant posed a future danger, that the jurors should sentence him to death to avoid becoming another victim, and even if the jury found one aggravating circumstance, the sentence must be death. Defense counsel then argued, contrary to Pennsylvania law, that all 12 jurors had to agree on whatever the verdict was. The Court held that trial counsels' conduct was deficient because they failed to "investigate the mountain of mitigating evidence readily available to them." Slip Op. at *15. Trial counsels' statements that they were hard pressed to find mitigation only proved that they failed to prepare for sentencing. Failure to present the mental health evidence was not a tactical decision, especially in light of the state's arguments that the defendant was only faking mental illness. Counsel simply stated that they did not present psychiatric evidence because of the court psychiatrist's testimony that the defendant was sane and competent. Counsel simply failed to comprehend that this finding did not preclude a finding of mitigating circumstances as defined under state law. This "failure to comprehend the law of mitigating circumstances is objectively unreasonable." Slip Op. at *15-16. Counsel was also unreasonable for failing to object to the state's arguments on the revolving door and the return of the defendant to the community, because under state law, the defendant would not have been eligible for parole. Likewise, counsel failed to object to the state's argument that if one aggravator was found, state law required death, when state law actually required that aggravating and mitigating factors be weighed. Counsel's only offered reason was that they did not want to appear to be a jack-in-the-box. This reason clearly is insufficient. Counsel were also ineffective for presenting evidence of the defendant's good character, because they knew that would open the door to cross-examination and knew that the witness would state that the defendant had told him that he would kill any witnesses. Counsel stated that they called the witness to impeach his testimony for the state by showing that he had been incarcerated previously. Counsel could have done that without presenting him as a character witness and presenting evidence that the defendant had previously been incarcerated. Finally, counsel was ineffective for arguing that all jurors had to agree when, under state law, a less than unanimous agreement for death would result in a life sentence. Making the legally incorrect argument was unreasonable. Prejudice was found based solely on the failure to present the mental health evidence which would have established that the defendant was not "the totally evil person," Slip Op. at *16, the jury found him to be, and would have undermined the state's argument that he was faking. It would have given the jury a reason to be lenient after weighing the aggs and the mits. As it was, the jury found two aggs (one of which was set aside on direct appeal) and no mits. Thus, the jury could not properly fulfill its sentencing function. [In addition to IAC, the Court also held that reversal of the convictions and sentence was required under *Ake v. Oklahoma*, 470 U.S. 68 (1985), due to the court's refusal to appoint a defense psychiatrist, and that reversal of the sentence was required due to the state's improper arguments.]

1994: *Ford v. Lockhart*, 861 F. Supp. 1447 (E.D. Ark. 1994), *aff'd on other grounds*, 67 F.3d 162 (8th Cir. 1995) (tried in June 1981). Trial counsel ineffective for failing to prepare and present mitigation evidence. Counsel admitted that he never investigated the defendant's background or talked to family members about his background. Investigation would have revealed that: defendant suffered severe physical and psychological abuse from father, including being hung from the rafters in a cotton sack or by his wrists all day long and being beaten periodically with extension cord; and defendant witnessed father beating mother and siblings. In addition, counsel failed to investigate and present evidence of intoxication at time of the offense despite the fact that hospital records after capture showed that he was "vomiting and drunk."

1989: *Eutzy v. Dugger*, 746 F. Supp. 1492 (N.D. Fla. 1989) (tried in 1983). Trial counsel ineffective for failing to prepare and present mitigation evidence. Counsel conducted virtually no investigation at all. He never asked the defendant himself about his family background, his marriages, his children, or his employment history, never asked the defendant about possible sources of mitigating evidence, never initiated contact with anyone to determine whether there were facts about the defendant which could be helpful at sentencing, and never sought copies of any of the defendant's school, medical or prison records. Even assuming that the defendant did not want his family involved, counsel's failure to investigate was not excused. Available mitigation would have shown: defendant was a non-violent, caring person, with good character and an outstanding work history; a turbulent family history marked by poverty, chaotic home, alcoholic mother; defendant began drinking at age 12 and had a long history of alcoholism and amphetamine abuse; defendant had been hospitalized twice for psychiatric reasons; and prior prison records reflected adaptability.

***Mathis v. Zant*,** 704 F. Supp. 1062 (N.D. Ga. 1989) (tried in May 1981). Trial counsel ineffective in sentencing phase for failing to investigate and present evidence in mitigation. Even though counsel had limited knowledge of the defendant's "troubled background," he "made inquiries that amounted to an investigation in name only." Specifically, he only interviewed one family member, consulted a three page psychiatric report based on a single visit with petitioner, neglected to contact petitioner's employer, and failed to obtain copies of any of petitioner's school or prison records. Investigation would have shown: impoverished childhood marked by emotional and physical abuse of alcoholic father; borderline mental retardation and low intellectual functioning; history of alcohol and drug abuse marked by blackouts; and evidence of good behavior in prison. In addition to the lack of mitigation evidence, counsel was ineffective for failing to ask for mercy, but rather essentially apologizing to the jury in sentencing argument for representing defendant.

1988: *Newlon v. Armontrout*, 693 F. Supp. 799 (W.D. Mo. 1988), *aff'd on other grounds*, 885 F.2d 1328 (8th Cir. 1989) (tried in August 1979). Trial counsel ineffective for completely failing to prepare and present mitigation evidence. Counsel failed to even explain the importance of mitigation or discuss a sentencing defense strategy with the defendant. Investigation would have shown that defendant had a low IQ, a turbulent family history, a non-violent history, and a reputation as a follower. In addition, trial counsel was ineffective for failing to object to prosecutor's improper closing argument or rebutting in his own argument. Prosecutor improperly argued his personal belief that death was appropriate based on his position of authority; compared defendant to Charles Manson and Son of Sam; personalized decision by asking jurors to consider that it had been their own children killed; told jury (incorrectly) that the trial judge would review their decision; argued that life sentence was only temporary confinement because parole laws could be changed or sentence commuted; argued courage; and argued that all murders should be punished by death.

1987: *Gaines v. Thieret*, 665 F. Supp. 1342 (N.D. Ill. 1987), *rev'd on other grounds*, 846 F.2d 402 (7th Cir. 1988) (tried in October 1979). Trial counsel ineffective in sentencing phase for failing to investigate and present evidence in mitigation. Counsel talked with the defendant, some family members, "a girlfriend," and an employer, but could not remember specifically asking about the existence of mitigating evidence. If counsel had adequately investigated, the evidence would have shown that defendant: was repeatedly and severely beaten by father, sometimes while naked and tied up; had a good work history during six months prior to murder; was kind to his live-in girlfriend and her son and helped to support them; had a good character; and was placed in an adult prison when he was 15 and spent time in isolation ward and psychiatric ward and witnesses would have testified that this confinement had a seriously disturbing effect on defendant. In addition to failing to present evidence, counsel's entire closing argument was simply to ask for a life sentence without offering any reason why it should be given.

1980: *Voyles v. Watkins*, 489 F. Supp. 901 (N.D. Miss. 1980) (tried in June 1977). Counsel ineffective in trial and sentencing for failing to adequately investigate and present a defense and mitigation. The defendant was initially arrested with a codefendant and each of them implicated the other in the murder. Ultimately, after the defendant's trial, the codefendant was allowed to plead guilty to accessory. Although counsel learned shortly before trial that the codefendant would testify for the state, he made no inquiry "as to what arrangements, if any, had been made" with him and made no effort to obtain witnesses concerning the codefendant's bad reputation for veracity or the defendant's good character, despite being given the names of several possible witnesses by the defendant. Counsel made no effort to interview them because of counsel's belief that they had a poor reputation in the community when in fact "[t]hey had an established automobile business, were persons without criminal convictions and were regular churchgoers in a family having three ministers" and would have given "impressive, unimpeached testimony." Other witnesses were also available as character witnesses but never interviewed. During trial, counsel cross-examined the codefendant about his prior criminal convictions, but failed to produce the records when the codefendant denied the prior convictions. Counsel also failed to elicit the codefendant's testimony, which would have been given, that he expected to receive favorable consideration from the state if the defendant was convicted. Counsel also failed to elicit testimony about the codefendant's prior inconsistent statements or that he had initially been charged with the murder and defendant only as an accessory until he agreed to testify against the defendant. Counsel then failed to request that the court issue the standard jury instruction that uncorroborated testimony of an accomplice should be viewed by the jury with care and caution. Following conviction, counsel offered no evidence in mitigation. Counsel did not have the defendant to even testify because counsel believed he had not been a good witness in the trial and that the jury had reacted unfavorably to his testimony. "The wisdom of this course, in a death case, is debatable." In any event, a number of witnesses could have testified that the defendant had a stable employment record, was a hardworking, dependable person, and had a "mild and nonviolent disposition." He also had two children and "made personal sacrifices to aid destitute members of his family." All of the available witnesses could have been located with a single phone call to the two witnesses (who were brothers) initially named by the defendant.

D.   State Cases

2016: ***State v. Bright***, So. 3d   , 2016 WL 3348432 (Fla. Jun. 16, 2016) (sentencing in 2009). Counsel ineffective in capital sentencing for failing to adequately investigate and present mitigating evidence. The defendant was sentenced to death by an eight to four vote. The defendant, who was a former Marine, killed his two roommates with a hammer. His ex-wife testified that he had had problems with the roommates, who had essentially taken over the house for the purpose of selling drugs. They had made multiple calls to the police but did not pursue charges out of fear of retaliation. After his arrest, the defendant made statements to multiple people consistent with this testimony. He also said that on the night of the killing, one of the two victim's was waving a gun around and the defendant "lost it." The defendant struggled with him and the gun went off. The gun then jammed and the defendant grabbed a hammer and killed both men. In sentencing, counsel presented testimony that the defendant had been a good Marine for over nine years but was discharged due to abuse of alcohol. Friends, family, and co-workers described him as a good man, who struggled with alcohol and drug abuse. Before the judge, a psychologist (Miller) testified about the defendant's dependency problems. While he had attempted rehabilitation, the treatment never addressed the underlying emotional issues. Relying on this testimony, the court found one statutory mitigating circumstance – extreme mental or emotional disturbance – but still imposed death. Counsel's conduct was deficient in failing to adequately investigate and present other available mitigation evidence. Lead counsel designated his co-counsel as "penalty phase counsel." Co- counsel retained a psychologist (Krop) to evaluate competence to stand trial and potentially to evaluate mitigation. In an initial letter, Krop informed counsel that the defendant was competent, "but asked whether he should conduct a more comprehensive mitigation evaluation and requested additional background information and records, particularly his VA psychiatric records," as well as family interviews. In a subsequent letter ten days later, Krop provided a detailed history report based on the defendant's statements, "alerting counsel to a history of family mental health problems, bipolar disorder, as well as a prior involuntary commitment." Following that letter, co-counsel obtained information that the most of the defendant's prior arrests were drug-related and obtained some VA medical records, but "the investigation ended there." A year later, Krop, who had been provided no additional information, wrote to co-counsel requesting the same documents and interviews earlier requested. With still no response, Krop wrote two months later noting that counsel had not arranged the family interviews requested. Krop was never contacted again until post- conviction counsel contacted him. "[L]ead counsel was predominantly out of the loop" and knew nothing about Krop. He scrambled only after the conviction to prepare and present the limited sentencing evidence that was presented. If counsel had investigated and provided the available records and information to the experts, Dr. Miller's suspicions of "deeper emotional and mental health struggles" would have been confirmed. Between 1983 and 1997, the defendant had been treated for mental health problems on multiple occasions. In 1997, he was involuntarily committed because he was suicidal and behaving erratically. He was diagnosed with depressive disorders. Correctional records indicated diagnoses of depression, anxiety, and bipolar disorder. These records also reflected a family history of mental health problems. School records reflected low academic performance related to the "effect of a horrific childhood." While the defendant's sister had testified in sentencing, her testimony in post-conviction provided far more information about how the defendant "grew up in a situation that could have easily been referred to as child labor and slave labor." The sister described "destitute" living; forced labor in their father's junkyard; physical, verbal, and emotional abuse of the defendant, his siblings, and their mother by their alcoholic father; and physical and sexual abuse of the defendant by his older brother. Expert testimony "explained for the first time" in post-conviction how this abuse caused severe trauma leading to severe mental disorders, including major depression, obsessive compulsive disorder (OCD), social phobia, substance abuse, and post-traumatic stress disorder (PTSD). Prejudice established. At minimum, this additional evidence would have supported the additional mitigating factor of lack of capacity to conform conduct to the law. Moreover, even without this additional information, the sentencing court "expressed notable hesitation" in imposing a death sentence.

*Salazar v. State, So. 3d , 2016 WL 636103 (Fla. Feb. 18, 2016) (trial and sentencing in 2006). Counsel ineffective in capital sentencing for failing to adequately investigate and present mitigating evidence. The state conceded that counsel's conduct was deficient, as counsel failed to conduct any investigation. Counsel also failed to followup on the recommendations of the one expert who conducted a preliminary evaluation of the defendant one week before trial. The expert noted the possibility of mental health impairments and possible organic brain damage that should be investigated. Instead, counsel presented only the testimony of the defendant's two sisters about the love and support the defendant provided to his family. Prejudice was established as there was significant available evidence of the defendant's low IQ, borderline intellectual functioning, and deficits in adaptive behavior. There was also significant mitigating evidence about the defendant's family history and traumatic childhood.

2015: *Commonwealth v. Solano*, A.3d, 2015 WL 9283031 (Pa. Dec. 21, 2015). Counsel ineffective in capital sentencing for failing to adequately investigate and present mitigating evidence "of the cognitive and psychological impact of Solano's traumatic and abusive childhood." Counsel, who had only graduated from law school two years earlier and had no experience in homicide or capital cases, did not use available investigators in the public defender office and instead conducted her own mitigation investigation. Counsel met with the defendant only about five times and found him to be "guarded," but "she did nothing to foster a rapport with him in an effort to enable him to be more open with her." Counsel contacted only the defendant's mother and brother, despite having the names and locations of extended family members. Counsel did not interview the defendant's Children and Youth Services (CYS) caseworker. While she obtained a mental health evaluation, she did not discuss the evaluation with the examiner before deciding not to call him as a witness because of his anti-social personality diagnosis. In sentencing, counsel presented testimony only from the CYS caseworker, who had not been interviewed or provided a copy of the CYS records, the defendant's mother, and former foster parents. If counsel had adequately investigated, a number of the defendant's school teachers and aunts and uncles would have testified. The presentencing mental health expert, who had not been provided with information from these witnesses or the records of the defendant's parents, also would have provided substantial mitigating testimony. The CYS caseworker would have provided much stronger mitigating testimony, if he had been interviewed and provided the prior records. Neuropsychological testing would have established a cognitive disorder. Prejudice established. Even though the jury found the "catch-all mitigator," if counsel had adequately investigated and presented the evidence, "the jury may have given this mitigator more weight had counsel presented additional life-history mitigating evidence." The available but unpresented evidence "was not merely cumulative – it provided significant details concerning Solano's background that were not mentioned at the penalty phase."

Chatman v. Walker, 773 S.E.2d 192 (Ga. 2015). Counsel ineffective in capital sentencing for failing to adequately investigate and present mitigation. Counsel obtained funded for a mitigation specialist and hired William Scott, based on the recommendation of someone counsel had worked with on a prior capital case. According to counsel, Scott claimed to be a "Ph.D." with experience in capital cases, but his curriculum vitae did not support these claims. Counsel hired him without investigating further and delegated responsibility for developing mitigation to him. Scott, on the other hand, testified that he disclosed his limited experience to counsel and was relying to counsel to guide him and obtain records. Over a six month period prior to trial, Scott billed for 82 hours, less than 20 of which was devoted to interviews. Then three months before trial, counsel retained a psychiatric expert, who provided a report detailing five areas of potential mitigation, which were not pursued. Counsel asked Scott for a report and received only a half-page summary of his work and conclusions, along with four pages of sparse handwritten notes. Scott also provided a "script" for his proposed testimony. Although counsel were concerned about Scott's level of preparation, counsel was focused on obtaining an "acquittal" and believed it was too late to obtain a different mitigation specialist. During sentencing, counsel presented testimony only from the defendant's aunt, Scott, and the psychiatrist. Scott essentially testified that life was good for the defendant until his father died when the defendant was fifteen years old, which contradicted the testimony of the defense psychiatrist and "eventually devolved into opinions about Walker's characterological problems and the alignment of the planets." Counsel's conduct was deficient in hiring Scott "without any investigation into his qualifications and then delegat[ing] to him responsibility for the mitigation investigation without sufficient supervision." Prejudice established. While the psychiatrist made some effort, "his account of Walker's life provided, at best, an overview and was cause for further investigation" into the extensive domestic violence in the defendant's childhood home between his parents, as well as the extreme physical abuse by his caretakers. In light of the "inaccurate, impersonal" sentencing presentation, the state was able to argue that the defendant's "childhood wasn't that bad" and his siblings were "doing quite well." If counsel had performed adequately, the jury would have had substantial evidence of the defendant's "exposure to pervasive violence in the forms of domestic violence, physical abuse, and abusive corporal punishment, which came from nearly every adult in [his] life who acted in a parental role." The witnesses that could have provided this testimony could also have "explained how and why Walker differed from his siblings."

2014: ***State v. Herring***, 28 N.E.3d 1217 (Ohio 2014) (tried and sentenced in 1997). Counsel ineffective in failing to adequately investigate and present mitigation evidence, instead presenting only positive-mitigation evidence. The defendant and five other individuals robbed a bar and shot five people, three of whom died. The defendant was the "ringleader." If counsel had adequately investigated and conducted psychological testing, the evidence would have established that the defendant suffers from alcohol and substance abuse/dependence; depressive disorder; personality disorder with narcissistic and antisocial features; and learning disabilities. Other available evidence would have established the defendant's deeply troubled childhood, such that most of the adults around him were drug addicts, a complete lack of any positive role models, membership in gangs, as well as the possibility of organic brain impairment. While the mitigation specialist hired performed inadequately, it was counsel's responsibility to ensure an adequate investigation. While the state argued that counsel made a strategic decision to present only positive evidence, this argument was rejected because "counsel's decision to pursue a positive-mitigation theory was not justified because it was made before an adequate investigation had been conducted into Herring's background." Likewise, Herring's failure to be "forthcoming" about negative information about his family did not excuse counsel's failures.

Prejudice established.

Commonwealth v. Daniels, 104 A.3d 267 (Pa. 2014) (sentenced in November 1989). Counsel for defendant Pelzer, who was jointly tried with his co-defendant Daniels, was ineffective in capital sentencing for failing to adequately investigate and present mental health evidence in mitigation. Both were convicted of kidnapping for ransom and murder after holding the victim bound and gagged in the trunk of a car for more than 24 hours and then shooting him four times in the back of the neck to make sure he was dead. Pelzer's mitigation in sentencing consisted only of his own testimony and four pages of testimony from his aunt, with whom he lived as a teenager. Counsel's conduct was deficient in failing to adequately investigate and present additional mitigation from the aunt, who testified for 46 pages in post-conviction in a "more pointed" fashion. Additionally, another aunt and uncle were available to testify. This testimony would have established that Pelzer's mother was a compulsive gambler who permitted her home to be taken over by drug dealers. There were frequent changes of homes and schools and violently abusive men in the home. Pelzer was using drugs and alcohol by age 15. Counsel also failed to obtain school records despite his knowledge that the defendant was a "slow learner." The records indicated a learning disability, depression, feelings of inadequacy, and anxiety and should have led to counsel to investigate mental health evidence. A pre-sentencing report prepared for the court indicated a mixed personality disorder. Defense experts in post-conviction testified that he met the standards for two mitigating circumstances: (1) the defendant was under the influence of extreme mental and emotional disturbance and (2) his capacity to conform his conduct to the requirements of the law was substantially impaired. Both of these were statutory mitigating circumstances that the jury had not been instructed to consider. Prejudice was established, despite the Commonwealth's presentation of contradictory expert testimony in post- conviction and the despite the presence of four aggravating circumstances, one of which was torture. Despite "the relative paucity of the mitigation presented by counsel at trial," the court found it significant that "the jurors were still receptive enough to find two mitigators, one unanimously." Specifically, the jury unanimously found the lack of a significant prior criminal history and a single juror found "the catchall mitigator."

> When analyzing Strickland prejudice in the context of the penalty phase of a capital trial, we must also keep in mind how tailored death penalty proceedings are toward life sentences, largely under the command of the U.S. Supreme Court, not only in the channeling of aggravators and the differing burdens of proof governing aggravators and mitigators, but also in the fact that a single juror can effectively negate the prospect of a death sentence.

Here, the evidence arguably would have supported two additional statutory mitigating factors and would have strengthened and added weight to "the catchall mitigator." "There is a reasonable probability that at least one juror would view both the mitigation case differently, and the overall penalty judgment differently, and would have decided against the imposition of the death penalty."

Commonwealth v. Tharp, 101 A.3d 736 (Pa. 2014) (tried in November 2000). Counsel ineffective in capital sentencing for failing to adequately investigate and present mental health evidence in mitigation. The defendant was convicted of deliberately starving her seven-year-old daughter to death. The defendant had three other children and did not mistreat or neglect them. The victim in this case, however, the second born, was born prematurely and spent the first year of her life hospitalized.

At age 7, she died from malnutrition due to starvation. She weighed less than 12 pounds and was only 31 inches tall. The defendant testified during the trial and denied guilt. She further testified about her background asserting that she had been the victim of physical and emotional abuse at the hands of her parents, step-parents, and previous boyfriends, including the fathers of her children. In sentencing, counsel presented no additional evidence, with the exception of a stipulation that the defendant had no prior criminal history. Counsel's conduct was deficient in failing to investigate and present evidence of the defendant's brain damage, mental health disorders, and low I.Q. Counsel conceded that they had interviewed two family members "for purposes of the guilt phase" but did not even inquire about mitigation. They interviewed no other family members and did not obtain any school, medical, or prison records. Additionally, despite a pretrial competence report indicating borderline intellectual functioning, schizoaffective disorder, adjustment disorder with anxiety, depressive personality disorder, and passive-aggressive personality disorder, counsel did not investigate further or call the competence examiner to testify in sentencing. Counsel also failed to obtain prior medical records indicating that the defendant was suffering from depression, even prior to the birth of the deceased child, and pretrial confinement records indicating that the defendant was being treated for major depression. Counsel conceded that there was strategic reason for these failures. Post-conviction examiners diagnosed brain damage, cognitive disorder, post-traumatic stress disorder (based on her prior abuse as a child), major depressive disorder, borderline intellectual functioning, borderline independent personality disorders, polysubstance abuse, dissociative disorder, adjustment disorder, and encephalopathy (altered brain function). The pretrial competence examiner agreed with these experts that at the time of the crimes, (1) the defendant was under the influence of extreme mental and emotional disturbance and (2) her capacity to conform her conduct to the requirements of the law was substantially impaired. Both of these were statutory mitigating circumstances that the jury had not been instructed to consider. Prejudice established where the sole aggravating circumstance was the age of the victim.

Weik v. State, 409 S.C. 214, 761 S.E.2d 757 (2014) (tried in June 1999). Trial counsel were ineffective in capital sentencing for failing to develop and present social history mitigation evidence. The defendant killed his girlfriend following an argument over the couple's child. He confessed to the shooting and cooperated with law enforcement. "There was never any dispute regarding guilt." The aggravating factors asserted by the state were burglary and torture because the shooting occurred on the victim's property and there were multiple shots. The defense presented three mental health experts in sentencing who testified that Weik suffers from "paranoid schizophrenia, including auditory and visual hallucinations, suicidal ideations, and paranoid delusions." Weik's confession indicated that he was hearing voices just before the shooting and he quietly chanted Bible verses throughout his trial so the voices would not bother him. The only social history mitigation presented was through Weik's sister, who testified very briefly (three pages of transcript "out of a multi- thousand page record") about Weik's childhood. She described his childhood as "rough" and said that all the children suffered from "abuse." She made "cursory and nonspecific" references to her father's "military flashbacks" and described him as "paranoid, abusive." The state countered with two mental health experts who testified that Weik did not have schizophrenia and suffered only schizotypal personality disorder. The state's psychologist also testified that Weik essentially had a "normal" childhood. Counsel's conduct was deficit in failing to investigate and present the true nature of Weik's social history. Weik's family had initially retained counsel, but after the state served notice of intent to seek the death penalty, the retained counsel and the public defender were appointed in July 1998. Lead counsel was an experienced criminal defense lawyer but had never tried a capital case or even "attended any seminars or continuing legal education courses dedicated to capital defense." The public defender "is currently suspended from the practice of law" due to a number of ethical violations including competence, diligence, and misconduct involving dishonesty. In March 1999, "a mere eleven weeks prior to trial" an experienced mitigation investigator was hired. Counsel met with the investigator only once and did not provide the investigator with assistance in providing information or obtaining records despite the investigator's repeated requests. Nonetheless, the investigator provided counsel with a potential witness list for sentencing, including Weik's family members and their contact information, a list of records that should be obtained, and "detailed investigative interviews with Weik's family members that revealed pervasive mental health issues throughout the Weik family and that Weik endured severe emotional, psychological, and physical abuse during his childhood." After six to seven weeks, the investigator resigned because of counsel's failure to assist her or respond to requests. A week later, a different mitigation investigator was hired and he requested a two month continuance. Instead, counsel sought a continuance of only two weeks so that some medical records could be obtained – records which the initial investigator had pushed counsel to obtain months earlier. Counsel told the trial judge only that the initial investigator had resigned due to "communication problems" without revealing the true reason for the departure or the investigator's detailed resignation letter. The continuance was denied. The new investigator interviewed the family members and provided reports to counsel but counsel never followed up on the information or reviewed it. Lead counsel testified that he focused on the trial phase and the public defender was responsible for the sentencing phase but during the trial she "was present, occupying space, but did not contribute anything useful or of substance during the entire case." The public defender testified that she had "limited" involvement and was just a "paper person" and "silent party" not involved in strategy or trial preparation at all. The court found this "especially troubling, for she simply washed her hands of the case, leaving the entire representation" to lead counsel. Counsel's conduct was clearly deficient due to "counsel's failure to review the investigators' reports they possessed in their own case files to become aware of the wealth of information that had been uncovered." This failure was not "the product of a strategic decision" so counsel's decision to present only the testimony of Weik's sister, Amy, "resulted from counsel's inattention, not reasoned strategic judgment."

> Indeed, counsel did not undertake a strategic decision to omit … [social history mitigation]; counsel simply did not read the investigators' reports and therefore did not know such evidence was available. Decisions made in ignorance of relevant, available information cannot be characterized as strategic.

The court declared:

> "The sentencing stage is the most critical phase of a death penalty case." *Romano v. Gibson*, 239 F.3d 1156, 1180 (10th Cir. 2001). … Important sentencing phase considerations include a defendant's "medical history, educational history, employment and training history, *family and social history*, prior adult and juvenile correctional experience, and religious and cultural influences. *Wiggins*, 539 U.S. at 524.

Id. at (emphasis in original). Here, the post-conviction judge erred in finding that counsel's conduct was not deficient.

> Though counsel introduced *psychological* testimony regarding Petitioner's mental illness, counsel failed to present even a skeletal version of Petitioner's *social history*, even though there was abundant social history evidence available to them.

Here, the available evidence revealed that Weik had an "extremely dysfunctional, unstable, and abusive childhood." Weik's house was "filthy" and had no "running water for a period of several years." His father, Russell, "compulsively hoarded things (particularly military-related items such as guns, knives, swords, and other weapons and munitions) such that the inside and outside of the house were piled high with junk and debris." Weik and his siblings were constantly teased by other children because they were "so poor." Weik was also teased because of his "large head" and for being "slow." He had a learning disability and attended special education classes. He ultimately was expelled from school after he fought another student who teased him for being "slow." Russell "experienced daily Vietnam flashbacks" and told his children that he had executed over two thousand people in Vietnam. He taught his children "how to kill people by 'crushing the windpipe' and 'snatching the heart.'" He also tormented his sons in order to "toughen them up" by making them do things like "stand at attention outside at all hours of the night in their underwear." Russell had served in the military from 1961 to 1965 when he was honorably discharged after being hospitalized for chronic schizophrenia. He had not, however, served in Vietnam or ever had any combat experience. Russell was also physically abusive and had beaten Weik with "rubber hoses, rose bush switches, a car antenna, a coax cable, and a machete." He would also punish the children by locking them in a "sweltering hot attic" for hours at a time. Russell was also verbally abusive and "consistently berated all of the children," but especially Weik who he called "'worthless' and 'stupid.'" He told Weik "he would never be good for anything." The children "always had to walk on eggshells" to avoid triggering "a fit of rage" from Russell. Their mother did not protect them from the abuse at all except on one occasion when she knocked Russell unconscious with a frying pan to stop him from choking his eight year old daughter during a "flashback" because he mistook her for "Charlie." Weik had "odd behaviors as a child, including that he 'would laugh at things that weren't really funny.'" He was also "slow learning to talk" but when he did learn he would speak "veryquickly" and ramble from "thought to thought." He also had developmental delays in walking, being "potty trained," and "he didn't seem to grasp things as quickly as other children did." As a teenager, he was a loner and "experienced dramatic personality swings and became unpredictably irritable." Weik's father and paternal grandfather were hospitalized for "psychiatric illness." Weik's mother and all of his siblings "suffered from some form of mental health issue, such as depression, or alcohol or drug abuse problems." Prejudice was established. Weik's sister's testimony in sentencing "was general, vague, and offered no detail or insight into the degree of abuse Weik suffered as a child. Thus, the jury remained unaware of the severity and pervasiveness of the physical and psychological abuse Weik faced and the full extent of his father's mental illness." Additionally, the available but unpresented evidence "would have demonstrated Petitioner's genetic predisposition to schizophrenia and helped explain his auditory and visual hallucinations at the time of the shooting."

__Davidson v. State__, 453 S.W.3d 386 (Tenn. 2014) (trial and sentencing in August 1997). Counsel was ineffective in capital sentencing for failing to adequately investigate and present evidence of the defendant's brain damage and cognitive disorders. Counsel possessed evidence that the defendant suffered from severe lifelong cognitive impairments and personality disorders and was predisposed to sexual violence. While counsel retained a neuropsychologist shortly before trial, counsel did not provide the expert with most of the evidence available. Likewise, counsel retained a mitigation specialist shortly before trial but did not seek a continuance as this expert advised. During sentencing, defense counsel presented only cursory social history evidence. Counsel's conduct was deficient and prejudicial. "Counsel held in their hands compelling evidence that Mr. Davidson has a broken brain and a tragic past," but failed to present this persuasive evidence. The court was not persuaded by the state's argument about a "two-edged sword" because the jury was already exposed to aggravation evidence of "a long history of sexual violence against women. The evidence from Mr. Davidson's mental health records held little potential to demean him further in the jury's eyes. However, it had great potential to help explain the invisible mental machinations that made him behave this way."

2013: ***Shellito v. State***, 121 So. 3d 445 (Fla. 2013). Counsel ineffective in capital sentencing for failing to adequately investigate and present significant mental health evidence and social history evidence. Following the conviction, but in the month prior to sentencing, could requested a psychiatric evaluation and prior records, which indicated prior diagnoses of organic brain disorder and mental health issues. Counsel did not present expert testimony primarily because counsel's only conversation with an expert focused only the issue of insanity and not mitigation and counsel was concerned about opening the door to significant negative information. Thus, "there was no true follow-up" after receiving the prior records. "Yet counsel made a marginal attempt to present organic brain damage and other impairment as mitigation" through family member testimony. Counsel's conduct was deficient in failing to follow up on the mental health evidence and in failing to have the "mental health issues presented by an expert at trial to explain their significance and impact on his behavior at the time of the murder." Prejudice was established because the trial court found "no mental health mitigation, statutory or otherwise" when the prior records and additional expert evaluation, including a PET scan, revealed bipolar disorder and organic brain damage, which would have supported both statutory and nonstatutory mitigating factors. In evidence, while the lay witnesses had presented a picture in sentence that the defendant had been raised in a stable home, the post-conviction evidence revealed that he was raised in an abusive home. He was physically and sexually abused by his mother, and was neglected, such that there was no structure in the home and the defendant was left without food or supervision for days at a time, such that he would sometimes have to scavenge for food in neighbors' garbage cans.

2012: ***Simmons v. State***, 105 So. 3d 405 (Fla. 2012) (sentenced December 2003). Counsel ineffective in capital sentencing for failing to adequately investigate or present mitigation evidence concerning the defendant's childhood and mental health. During the jury hearing, counsel presented testimony from once jailer and the defendant's sister. The jury unanimously recommended a death sentence. Before the judge, counsel also presented an expert who testified that the defendant had a moderate to severe learning disability and no significant history of violence. Counsel's conduct was deficient in failing to consult with a mental health expert or to otherwise investigate "mental mitigation." The expert presented before the judge had been retained by initial counsel and had not ordered a PET scan, despite knowledge that the defendant had "experienced a partial suffocation incident as a toddler that required medical intervention." If counsel had obtained the available records and a neuropsychological evaluation confirmed by a PET scan, the evidence would have established an IQ of 79, a history of special education and emotional handicap classes, a history of untreated attention deficit hyperactivity disorder (ADHD), brain damage that resulted in "impulsivity and behavioral problems," and borderline personality disorder. This evidence would have supported two statutory mitigating circumstances: (1) extreme mental or emotional disturbance; and (2) impaired capacity to appreciate the criminality of conduct. Counsel also failed to "have any significant conversations with" the defendant's family and did not even "consider hiring a mitigation specialist to do an investigation." Adequate investigation also would have revealed that the defendant's father abused alcohol and marijuana and the defendant "modeled" this behavior beginning at age nine and continuing into adulthood. Counsel's conduct was not excused by any alleged strategy to present only good character mitigation. Counsel conducted no investigation and presented "almost nothing" on good character either. The defendant also was not "told what mitigation he was waiving – or the effect of such a waiver – in following this strategy." Prejudice established even though the state presented an expert to assert that, based on the PET scan, the defendant's brain was not abnormal. "Even without convincing proof of the brain abnormality, [the defendant] established the existence of substantial mental mitigation that was not presented to the jury or the judge."

*__Robinson v. State__, 95 So. 3d 171 (Fla. 2012). Counsel ineffective in capital sentencing for failing to adequately investigate and present mitigation evidence that would have legally precluded the trial court from overriding the jury's life recommendation. Before the jury, counsel presented only the defendant's mother and a psychologist that had interviewed the defendant twice. The jury recommended life. In the hearing before the judge, counsel added only "character letters" even though counsel was aware that the Florida Supreme Court "had a history of affirming life overrides in the absence of substantial factual mitigation." The only mitigation the judge found, before overriding the jury vote and imposing death, was that the defendant "maintained close family ties and had been supportive of his mother." Counsel's conduct was deficient in failing to adequately investigate. Counsel did not obtain the court files of priors, obtain a mitigation expert, or provide sufficient information to the defense expert, even after the expert indicated that the defendant "was not an adequate historian." As a result, the sentencing testimony "pales in comparison to the postconviction testimony." The defendant's father was a violent, abusive drug abuser and dealer, who introduced the defendant to drugs at an early age. The defendant was also exposed to illegal activities by an older brother and attended an alternative school known for ongoing physical and sexual abuse (Okeechobee Boys' Home). The trial judge found that there was no prejudice because he was aware at the time of sentencing that the defendant "was a perpetual witness to violence, that he grew up impoverished and in a crime-ridden neighborhood, and that he spent his childhood in a chaotic environment." This finding was rejected, however, because, as one example: "testimony that [the defendant] grew up in a crime-ridden neighborhood does not reveal that he witnessed a murder at the age of five years old."

*__Walker v. State__, 88 So. 3d 128 (Fla. 2012) (offenses in 2003 and appeal in 2007). Counsel ineffective in capital sentencing for failing to adequately investigate and present mitigation evidence. In sentencing, counsel presented testimony from two mental health experts, who diagnosed bipolar disorder based primarily only on the defendant's self-reporting. The jury recommended death by a 7 to 5 vote. Before the judge, counsel presented only letters from the defendant's sister and a friend asking for mercy. Another friend testified that the defendant was addicted to drugs and that the drugs made him violent. The trial court in post-conviction proceedings found counsel ineffective. Counsel's investigation consisted only of five phone calls with the defendant's mother and sister and "unidentified 'local people.'" Counsel "never sought medical, educational, criminal, drug treatment, or social service records." Counsel also failed even to interview the defendant's cousin, despite the fact that the defendant had been using his name and identification at the time of the crimes. Counsel also failed to attempt to speak to "any other immediate or extended family members" of "former neighbors, correctional officers, or teachers." If counsel had investigated, he could have presented extensive testimony from family and friends and two mental health experts with "specific" knowledge of the defendant's "drug addiction and lifelong emotional and educational problems." The defendant's parents often hosted chaotic parties that involved violence, drugs, and alcohol during which the children were neglected and allowed to sample drugs. The children often had to find their own meals. The defendant ended up addicted to drugs, including methamphetamine, which resulted in paranoia and violence. He was referred to therapy by a juvenile court at age 15. A psychopharmacologist testified about the drug abuse, which "typically results in drug-induced delirium, pronounced paranoia, and psychosis." This information "'gave considerable insight into [the defendant's] childhood and young adulthood,' serving to humanize him to the jury."

*__Davis v. State__, 87 So. 3d 465 (Miss. 2012). Counsel ineffective in capital sentencing for failing to adequately investigate and present mitigation evidence. The defendant killed his friend, but immediately turned himself over to police, waived *Miranda* rights, and cooperated fully with the police. After learning that the State would seek death, counsel met with the defendant only twice, the second of which took place on the day before trial.

> Almost all of [counsel's] interviews of mitigation witnesses and preparation for the penalty phase of [the] trial took place the day before trial. [Counsel] made no attempt to obtain medical, school, or military records; he never interviewed any of the prison personnel where [the defendant] was incarcerated prior to trial; and he did not produce any evidence that described the alleged abuse [the defendant] had suffered as a child, at the hands of his father.

Id. at 467. In sentencing, counsel "made no opening statement. The total, combined testimony of mitigation witnesses consumed less than fifteen pages of transcript." The defendant's mother had met counsel only twice. The first time, she characterized as "a lot of nothing." The second time, which was the day before sentencing, counsel told her to "beg for [your] son's life." The defendant's sister also testified. She had met with counsel for only 10 minutes the day before sentencing. The defendant's landlord testified, at the defendant's suggestion, with "no preparation whatsoever." Finally, a highway patrolman testified about the defendant's criminal record. Counsel's conduct was deficient.

> [N]o trial strategy was involved here. It takes no deep legal analysis to conclude that an attorney who never seeks out or interviews important witnesses and who fails to request vital information was not engaging in trial strategy.
> [Counsel] had a duty to conduct a reasonable, independent investigation to seek out mitigation witnesses, facts, and evidence for the sentencing phase of [the] trial. Instead, he conducted *no* investigation, relying on witnesses whom [the defendant] suggested, and whom [counsel] failed to properly prepare.

Id. at 469 (footnote omitted) (emphasis in original). Likewise, counsel's explanation that he was not aware that the defendant was from the local community did not excuse counsel's failures. Except for his time in the military, the defendant "had lived in the local community his entire life." *Id.* at 470. Prejudice was also clear. Evidence was available from a lifelong friend of the defendant's family that he basically was a good guy, who helped everyone in the neighborhood, including a crippled, elderly woman. Evidence was also available from "the office deputy" of the Sheriff's Department that the defendant was a "trusty" in pretrial confinement. He ran errands within and even outside the jail. He was even allowed to drive patrol cars, unescorted, and in civilian clothes to a facility where he changed the oil in the cars. He never caused trouble and was "a very nice and polite fellow," who "had adjusted well to the prison environment." The defendant's sister, if prepared and asked, could have testified that the defendant's father was an abusive alcoholic. On one occasion, when the defendant was 12, he tried to save his mother who was being strangled by his father. He was unsuccessful and ran to a neighbor's house for help. When he returned home, his father threatened to kill him and forced him to sleep outside. The sister testified that this type of event happened "at least every weekend." Seven other witnesses--a church deacon, the husband of defendant's Sunday School teacher, three past employers, an ex-brother-in-law, and a long-time neighbor--would have testified if asked. All testified that the defendant (1) volunteered around the community and in church, (2) was not violent, and (3) had a "good work ethic."

Commonwealth v. Keaton, 45 A.3d 1050 (Pa. 2012) (tried and sentenced in 1994). Counsel was ineffective in capital sentencing for failing to adequately prepare and present mitigation evidence. Counsel retained a mental health expert to evaluate the defendant, but did not call him to testify or follow-up on the expert's request for records or recommendation of additional testing. Despite the expert's request, counsel did not obtain basic records, such as school, dependency, hospital, and pre-sentence reports that revealed substantial mitigation. During sentencing, counsel presented two younger sisters, an aunt, a family friend, and a minister to testify. In general, the testimony was that the defendant was helpful, respectful, and kind when he was not on drugs, but he was addicted drugs. The defendant also testified against the advice of counsel and admitted his drug addiction while claiming innocence. Counsel argued in closing that the jury should consider as mitigation: (1) age (31) because the defendant was young enough to have time to be rehabilitated if sentenced to life; (2) mental or emotional disturbance due to drug use; and (3) the defendant was worth saving. The jury found no mitigation. Counsel's conduct was deficient. Counsel did not prepare the sisters or inquire about the defendant's childhood. He spoke to them only outside the courtroom immediately prior to the sentencing hearing. They could have testified that the defendant was physically abused in childhood and witnessed his mother and siblings being beaten by the defendant's father and the mother's boyfriends. The family lived in extreme poverty. A psychologist, who treated the defendant in group therapy at age 13 because of his academic difficulties, confirmed the domestic violence in the home and that the defendant was ostracized by other children because of his extreme poverty. The psychologist retained by the defense conducted screening tests that revealed "a strong possibility of underlying organic or brain dysfunction." He reported these findings to counsel, recommended additional testing, and requested records. All he was provided, however, "was part of the police discovery materials." In post-conviction, he was provided with records from school, adolescent counseling, juvenile dependency, and drug treatment. These records, among other things, showed a "'squalid' background of neglect and poverty, treatment for depression and suicidal ideation, drug dependence, auditory and visual hallucinations when he was on drugs, which suggested "brain involvement." A neuropsychologist, who evaluated the defendant in post-conviction, found borderline intelligence and neurocognitive deficits in executive functioning. The brain damage could have been caused by chronic poly-substance abuse, serial beatings to the head, or a gunshot wound to the head. Another expert confirmed the neurological problems and testified, based on examination and the records available, that the defendant had untreated attention deficit hyperactive disorder and bipolar disorder characterized by episodes of grandiosity and mania. This evidence would have supported at least three statutory mitigating factors. Thus, there was "a reasonable probability at least one juror may have struck a different balance, had such evidence been presented."

2011: ***Coleman v. State***, 64 So.3d 1210 (Fla. 2011) (crime in 1988 and direct appeal in 1992). Counsel ineffective in capital sentencing for failing to adequately investigate and present available mitigation evidence that would have legally precluded the trial judge's override of the jury's life recommendation. The jury recommended life by a vote of six to six. Despite knowing the defendant grew up in Liberty City in horrendous conditions, counsel did not retain an investigator or seek a mental health evaluation because he claimed he believed the defendant's alibi defense. Counsel also stated that he did not believe mitigation would have made a difference to the court. Under state law, the focus is on "the reasonableness of the jury recommendation, not on the judge's determinations or personal inclinations." Likewise, state law provides that residual doubt is not an appropriate mitigating circumstance. Substantial mitigating evidence, including an impoverished, chaotic childhood, special education, substance abuse from a young age, sexual molestation, head injuries, and "mental health illness and deficiencies." Under state law, a trial court could not override a recommendation of life, unless "the facts suggesting a sentence of death should be so clear and convincing that virtually no reasonable person could differ." Here, if the true mitigation evidence had been presented, the trial judge would have had to view it in the light most favorable to the defense and would have been precluded from overriding the jury. Thus, the defendant was prejudiced not just in the trial proceedings, but also in direct appeal. Remanded for imposition of a life sentence.

Perkins v. Hall, 708 S.E.2d 335 (Ga. 2011) (sentenced in 1997). Counsel ineffective in capital sentencing for failing to investigate brain injuries and unduly limiting interviews of family and friends of the defendant. Counsel's conduct was deficient. "There is some tension, if not outright contradiction, between lead counsel's and co-counsel's accounts of who was responsible for preparing for the sentencing phase." Each claimed that the other was responsible, which helped "explain, at least in part," why the investigation was inadequate. Original counsel had discovered records of a head injury that left an "identifiable hole in his skull." The defendant insisted he did not want to pursue this mental health evidence and demanded her removal as counsel. Thereafter, the defendant refused to cooperate with a mental health evaluation. Counsel contacted only a few family members taking the word of the defendant's mother that others were "unavailable," even though numerous witnesses would have cooperated and testified. Citing the 1989 ABA Guidelines, the court found counsel's conduct deficient. Prejudice also established. While the mother testified about the defendant's traumatic childhood in sentencing, the available evidence of "his abusive background is admittedly somewhat cumulative, but overall it is far more compelling." Even more powerful was the evidence of the defendant's "change in behavior and apparent mental distress following two head injuries." While the defendant "resisted investigation of this sort of evidence and refused expert mental health evaluations, he did not preclude his trial counsel from presenting a mitigation defense that included details about his personal history."

2010: ***State v. Gamble***, 63 So.3d 707 (Ala. Crim. App. 2010) (sentenced in November 1997). Counsel was ineffective in capital sentencing for failing to adequately investigate and present mitigating evidence. Counsel spoke to the 18-year-old defendant one time and initially attempted contact with his family by simply sending them letters several months before trial. Later, eleven days before trial, he went to the defendant's neighborhood and simply stopped people at random to ask if they knew the defendant and what their opinion of him was. Counsel made no other efforts to investigate mitigate despite knowledge that the defendant had "cognitive limitation" and that his father had served in Vietnam and subsequently exhibited violence, erratic behavior, and alcoholism. Counsel initially filed a motion seeking funds for a mitigation investigator but abandoned this request. While counsel did speak to some family members right before trial in a group discussion lasting approximately 10 minutes, counsel did not call any of them to testify because he "had no idea what he wanted the family members to testify about." It was also clear based on counsel's closing argument in sentencing and his post-conviction testimony that counsel believed that the only mitigating evidence that was admissible in sentencing was evidence that fit within one of the statutory mitigating circumstances. The court considered the case in light of the 1989 ABA Guidelines for the Appointment and Performance of Counsel in Death Penalty Cases. The court held that could sought none of the information set forth in Guideline 11.4.1, except that counsel requested that the defendant, "who presented obvious cognitive deficits, compose a journal that would include his biography." On this evidence alone, counsel's conduct was deficient. Prejudice established because family members and friends would have testified that the defendant's father was an abusive, alcoholic. His mother was also an alcoholic, who had been in special education and was "slow." The defendant was raised in a small "run down shack" occupied by 14-20 people. His mother had taken him to Atlanta when he was just a child and had abandoned him. The defendant was in a special needs remedial program in school. Aside from these witnesses, available records documented that the defendant's mother was mentally retarded. His father's IQ was only 72 in school and later testing documented an organic mental disorder because of "heavy alcohol consumption" and possible schizophrenia. The defendant was hospitalized at 3 months when he was "dirty and emaciated." He was in the custody of the Department of Human Resources for seven months due to parental neglect, but then returned to his mother. Until he was seven he lived in his paternal grandmother's "run down shack" with 23 relatives in 4 rooms. When he was 7, his mother took him to Atlanta where he attended four schools in two years. After returning to Alabama at age 9, the defendant and his sister were passed from relative to relative for a year. He and his mother then lived with his mother's friend for 9 years. The friend sold drugs out of the house and frequently had the defendant to assist her. School records showed frequent absences, repeating the fourth grade three times, a social promotion in the fifth grade, and dropping out in the 7th grade at age 15. School records showed an 82 IQ, but the state's expert found a 77 IQ in pretrial testing. Prejudice established as the trial judge, who presided over the defendant's trial and sentenced him to death following a 10-2 jury recommendation of the death verdict, found prejudice. This finding was entitled to "considerable weight," especially in light of the "plethora of evidence that could have been presented" rather than presenting no mitigation evidence at all.

Ferrell v. State, 29 So.3d 959 (Fla. 2010). The trial court's finding of ineffective assistance in capital sentencing for failing to adequately investigate and present mitigation was upheld. The defendant did not make a knowing and voluntary waiver of the right to present mitigation. "Each of the witnesses who testified for [the defendant] stated that they made repeated unsuccessful attempts to contact trial counsel and were never contacted by him. There is simply no indication that trial counsel performed any investigation into the penalty phase." Counsel also failed to retain or consult with a mental health expert concerning mitigation, although court-appointed examiners did examine competence and sanity issues. The trial court's finding of prejudice was also supported by the evidence. In addition to failing to present mitigation, counsel failed to object to improper sentencing arguments by the prosecutor. The prosecutor invited the jury to disregard the law, argued improperly the age mitigator could not apply to the defendant, argued improperly that the case deserved the death penalty, and improperly vouched for the credibility of several witnesses. Cumulative prejudice was clear in that the jury vote for death was only seven to five and the defendant was not the triggerman in the murder.

Commonwealth v. Martin, 5 A.3d 177 (Pa. 2010) (crimes in 1993 and direct appeal in 1998). Counsel was ineffective in capital sentencing for failing to adequately investigate and present mitigation evidence, especially evidence of chronic post-traumatic stress disorder and depression as a result of sexual abuse he suffered as a child at the hands of his uncle. Counsel did not contact any of the defendant's prior doctors or obtain records from his prior substance abuse and mental health treatments, even though the defendant's mother gave them names and addresses, along with the dates of treatment. The day prior to sentencing, the mother, due to concern that counsel had not obtained the prior records, delivered some of the defendant's mental health records to counsel. Nonetheless, the only mitigation evidence presented was the mother's testimony that mentioned prior drug and mental health treatments following sexual abuse by his uncle, who was later convicted for the molestations. Counsel's conduct was deficient and not the result of reasonable strategy. While the state asserted that the defendant directed counsel not to investigate or not to present evidence regarding his mental health history, the record did not support such a finding. Likewise, counsel testified that he had a strategic decision to rely solely on the defendant's mother because, in his view, jurors in the county "view psychiatry as 'one step above witchcraft.'" The trial court rejected this, however, because counsel did not receive the defendant's mental health records until the day before the penalty hearing. He did not contact the defendant's prior documents. Thus, the court held that "the scope of his investigation was the result of lack of attention rather than reasoned strategic judgment." *Id.* at 202. In addition, the record did not support an alleged strategic decision not to present this evidence, due to concerns about "open[ing] the door" to evidence of another murder committed after this one. Counsel did not testify that he had such strategy and the defendant had not been convicted of the subsequent murder in Nevada at the time of this trial. Prejudice established. The mental health records and the testimony of two prior treating physicians, who were never contacted but would have been willing to testify in sentencing, documented Chronic PTSD and depression due to past sexual abuse as early as age 15 and continuing until after the murder at issue, committed when the defendant was 21. This evidence was particularly significant in this case where the victim was a 74 year old homosexual man, who had offered the defendant money for sex, which resulted in his murder by the defendant. Two statutory mitigating circumstances were present, yet never presented to the jury: (1) extreme mental or emotional disturbance; and (2) substantially impaired capacity to appreciate criminality or to conform his conduct. The record supported the PCRA court's finding "that it was probable that at least one juror would have accepted at least one mitigating circumstance, and found that it outweighed the aggravating circumstances found." Aside from deference to the PCRA court's findings, the Court agreed with the assessment of prejudice.

Commonwealth v. Smith, 995 A.2d 1143 (Pa. 2010) (sentenced in May 1995). Counsel ineffective in capital sentencing in failing to adequately develop and present mitigation. During trial, in a challenge to the degree of murder, the defense presented one expert to testify that the defendant was suffering a cocaine-induced psychotic disorder. The testimony of a second expert was excluded as cumulative. The state presented a rebuttal expert. The defense again sought to present its second expert, but this testimony was again precluded. In sentencing, the defense presented testimony from the defendant's mother and a case manager from a job training program the defendant had attended. A videotape of the second expert's testimony was also played. Lead counsel conceded that he "was primarily concerned with the guilt phase defense, and turned over preparation for the penalty phase to [co-counsel] one month before trial, but gave her no direction." Indeed, it was doubtful counsel "had any meaningful conversations concerning what mitigation evidence might be helpful." Lead counsel was aware of the defendant's abusive childhood, drug abuse, and past treatment for addiction but did not delve into the details, including during the defendant's mother's testimony. Counsel had not previously "mentioned or explained" to the mother "mitigation evidence." Counsel had had only a few brief calls with family members prior to trial and had obtained only the defendant's parole and military records. Counsel had an expert to examine the defendant for trial issues of diminished capacity, but did not ask the expert to evaluate him for sentencing mitigation purposes even after the expert and co-counsel suggested that he do so. In short, lead counsel "ignored the possibility that mental health mitigating evidence existed which would be helpful in the penalty phase; instead, he myopically focused only on the guilt phase defense of cocaine-induced psychosis, offering only generalized character evidence at the penalty phase." Counsel's conduct was deficient and not based on reasonable strategy.

> This is the type of case described by *Bobby [v. Van Hook*, 130 S. Ct. 13, 19 (2009)] as one where "potentially powerful mitigating evidence ... would have been apparent from documents any reasonable attorney would have obtained."

Prejudice was established. If counsel had performed adequately, the testimony of family members and other lay witnesses would have established that the defendant had meningitis and head injuries as a baby. He suffered neglect and physical abuse from his father and also witnessed his father beating his mother and siblings. The defendant abused drugs and his personality would change when he was on drugs. After serving in the military, the defendant's attitude towards white people became almost paranoid. A neuropsychologist testified that the defendant's "poor school performance, impoverished and abusive childhood, and drug use suggested the possibility of cognitive impairments." In testing, the defendant had a full scale IQ of 76 and had moderate to severe impairments on neuropsychological testing "designed to test for brain damage." These cognitive impairments would affect the defendant's "ability to reason, use judgment, and see the consequences of his actions; these abilities would become even more impaired by drug use, particularly cocaine." This expert's testimony would have supported several statutory mitigating factors. Another expert testified that the defendant's juvenile and hospital records included a number of "red flags" for potential mental disorders. The juvenile records, which were admitted in post-conviction "documented the dysfunctional environment in which he was raised, his psychological and mental impairments, and his cognitive deficits." The medical records, which were also admitted, revealed "treatment for drug and alcohol addiction." While the Commonwealth's expert testified and raised the issue of malingering, he conceded that the defendant had brain damage.

2009: ***Hurst v. State***, 18 So. 3d 975 (Fla. 2009) (affirmed on direct appeal in 2002). Counsel ineffective in capital sentencing for failing to present expert mental health evidence in mitigation to establish the defendant's low IQ, borderline intellectual functioning, and possible organic brain damage caused by fetal alcohol syndrome. Counsel's conduct was deficient in failing to have the defendant examined by a mental health expert, even though prior counsel had filed a motion for an evaluation. Counsel also did not obtain school records that revealed a low IQ and the defendant had been in special education classes and dropped out of school after repeating the tenth grade. Counsel had sufficient information, however, to "place him on notice that further investigation of mental mitigation was necessary." Information from the family indicated he probably had borderline intelligence and was emotionally immature. Counsel also knew the defendant's mother drank heavily during her pregnancy, which could lead to fetal alcohol syndrome. Counsel also could have easily obtained the school records. Counsel's conduct was not excused by reasonable strategy as counsel simply believed that the defendant did not have a "mental problem," the defendant would be acquitted due to his claim of innocence, and that presentation of mental mitigation would have been inconsistent with evidence that the defendant was a good person.

> [B]ecause counsel never had [the defendant] examined and could not know what a mental health expert might discover, he could not make an informed tactical decision that the mental mitigation would be inconsistent with the defense or with other mitigation. Moreover, presentation of the mental mitigation discovered in this case... would not have been an admission that he committed the murder but would have been *consistent* with and supportive of the other mitigation that [the defendant] was slow, emotionally immature, and a follower.

In addition, even if counsel was concerned about inconsistency of the evidence before the jury, there was no explanation for not presenting the evidence before the judge. Prejudice established as both the prosecutor and the trial judge criticized the lack of any mental health expert testimony and the available evidence would have had an impact of the process of weighing the aggravation and mitigation in this case.

Parker v. State, 3 So. 3d 974 (Fla. 2009) (trial in 1990). Counsel ineffective for failing to fully investigate and present mitigating evidence regarding defendant's chaotic and dysfunctional childhood and mental health. If counsel had adequately investigated, the evidence would have shown: (1) defendant was abandoned by father as baby; (2) defendant's mother was frequently hospitalized with mental health issues; (3) defendant spent his childhood in a series of foster homes and attended 17 different schools; (4) defendant was physically and sexually abused; and (5) defendant had a long history of alcohol abuse and violent and "crazy" behavior. Counsel did not request any records and did not interview anyone other than the defendant, his mother, and his ex- wife. "The only investigator employed ... was asked to investigate the victim's background and guilt phase issues."

> While trial counsel presented a 'bare bones' rendition of some of ... [the defendant's background], it was not enough to establish mitigation even though there was a wealth of witnesses who were never interviewed and documents that were never sought that could have fleshed out and established the mitigating circumstances. ... In addition to this failure to conduct an adequate investigation, ... counsel presented the information about his childhood and background through the hearsay testimony of the public defender investigators and not from first-hand sources.

Counsel also gave the defense mental health expert, "quite sparse materials" and "no background records," such that the expert had to rely only on the defendant's self-report and a brief phone call with his mother. Counsel erroneously believed "it was the doctor's responsibility to seek out this information." If the expert had seen the records and been given background information, including the mother's mental health history and school records indicating significant behavioral and intellectual functioning problems, he would have supported additional nonstatutory mitigating factors and recommended additional evaluation and further testing that would have revealed "some type of neuropsychological impairment that affects his executive brain functions."

Doss v. State, 19 So. 3d 690 (Miss. 2009). On rehearing, counsel found ineffective in capital sentencing for failing to adequately investigate and present mitigation. Counsel had only a "cursory telephone interview" with the defendant's mother, who was the sole mitigation witness in sentencing. Counsel's conduct was deficient in failing to investigate despite awareness of prior head injuries and possession of some of the prior records, which were provided by the defendant's counsel in a separate case. Counsel also failed to interview possible witnesses and "failed to ask a single question" about possible abuse, the environment the defendant had grown up in, how he did in school, "or anything else that could have been mitigating." Prejudice established as there was significant evidence that the defendant's mother drank and was taking Valium during her pregnancy and was beaten and infected by gonorrhea by her husband during her pregnancy. The defendant had lead poisoning as a child and witnessed the man he thought was his father (but he was not) beating his mother and abusing drugs. The family also "lived in a very poor, bad, drug-infested neighborhood where gangs were prevalent in Chicago." The defendant began drinking and using drugs by age 11. He had a low IQ and was placed in special education classes.

Rosemond v. Catoe, 383 S.C. 320, 680 S.E.2d 5 (2009). Counsel ineffective in capital sentencing for failing to present evidence of the defendant's mental illness. There was no need to "speculate about the mitigation evidence known by trial counsel as the evidence was presented during pretrial competency hearings." Specifically, two defense experts testified that the defendant was "clearly paranoid" and suffered either from a delusional disorder or schizophrenia but a diagnosis could not be made because the defendant was evasive and guarded even with the experts. A court-appointed examiner was also willing to testify that the defendant might be in the early stages of schizophrenia. Trial counsel did not present this evidence in sentencing because he "mistakenly believed" that the trial court's finding of competence to stand trial "precluded him from presenting ... mental health mitigation evidence in the sentencing phase." "Counsel's erroneous belief clearly constituted deficient representation." Prejudice was also established because counsel only presented a few family members and friends to portray the defendant as a good boy and a mental health expert gave "conclusory" testimony that the defendant "could adjust to prison." The expert conceded on cross, however, that he had not diagnosed a mental illness. In short, "the theme of the evidence was the absence of any mental health concerns." Even with only this evidence, the jury deliberated for more than 11 hours of two days and received an *Allen* charge before reaching its death verdict. "Given the jury's struggle during the sentencing phase and the want of any mental health mitigation evidence," prejudice found.

2008: *State v. Pearce*, 994 So. 2d 1094 (Fla. 2008) (arrest in 1999, direct appeal in 2004). Counsel ineffective for failing to adequately investigate mitigation in order to advise client prior to his waiver of presentation of mitigation and argument in sentencing. Counsel "did not conduct any preparation for the penalty phase of the trial." Counsel did not obtain any background records, never contacted any of defendant's family members, and never investigated mental health issues. If counsel had investigated, the following information would have been able: (1) defendant received "whoopings" with a belt or switch as a child; (2) he had "temper tantrums and mood swings" as a child; (3) there was a family history of bipolar disorder; (4) defendant fell down stairs as a baby and fell out of a truck, resulting in head injuries; (5) he was a drug user; (6) his ex-wife physically abused him; (7) he suffers from brain damage and (8) has bipolar disorder and "is predominantly manic and goes for long periods of time in manic states." Although the defendant "did not want any form of mitigation presented during the penalty phase. ..., an attorney's obligation to investigate and prepare for the penalty portion of a capital case cannot be overstated because this is an integral part of a capital case."

> Although a defendant may waive mitigation, he should not do so blindly. Counsel must first investigate and advise the defendant so that the defendant reasonably understands what is being waived and reasonably understands the ramifications of a waiver. The defendant must be able to make an informed, intelligent decision.

Id. at 1102. The "waiver of the presentation of mitigating evidence was not knowingly, voluntarily, and intelligently made." Prejudice established "because there was substantial mitigating evidence which was available but undiscovered."

Lowe v. State, 2 So. 3d 21 (Fla. 2008). Counsel ineffective in sentencing for failing to investigate and present two witnesses, who would have testified that a state witness, who denied involvement at trial, had previously admitted participation in the robbery and to killing the victim. Counsel's conduct was deficient. The state's theory was that the defendant acted alone and specifically excluding the state witness. Defense counsel believed the state witness was involved. Counsel's conduct was deficient because he failed to investigate even though one of the potential witnesses was mentioned in a police report and an officer's deposition as having information about the crime. This witness was aware of the other witness and could have provided that information. No prejudice during trial because his statements did not exclude the defendant and there was substantial evidence of the defendant's involvement in the crimes. Prejudice was found in sentencing even though there were "some inconsistencies ... as to the specific details." In addition, these witnesses supported two mitigating factors raised by the defense but rejected by the trial judge: the disproportionate punishment mitigator and the relatively minor participation mitigator. Finally, while the evidence at trial proved the defendant was involved, including his confession also implicating the state witness, there was no evidence presented that conclusively showed that he was the actual killer.

Williams v. State, 987 So. 2d 1 (Fla. 2008) (crimes in 1988 and direct appeal in 1993). Counsel ineffective in capital sentencing for failing to present a detailed report from a mental health expert in the override hearing before the trial court. The defendant was convicted of ordering the murders of three people and other charges stemming from the victims' alleged theft of drugs and money from the defendant in a drug trafficking ring. Counsel was aware that three co-defendants had already proceeded separately to trial. Each received a life verdict from the jury, but the same judge as defendant had overrode the verdict and imposed death. Counsel possessed an expert report that revealed that the defendant had: 1) an IQ of 75 and functioned mentally at the age level of a thirteen or fourteen-year-old; 2) abusive, alcoholic parents and an impoverished childhood; and 3) a lengthy drug abuse history. Counsel did not present this evidence before the jury or the trial court and instead presented only brief evidence that the defendant was a loving son and father. The jury recommended life by a vote of eleven to one, but the trial court overrode the verdict and imposed death. Counsel's conduct was deficient, especially since counsel was aware of the overrides for the co-defendants. Counsel's conduct was not based on strategy.

> It appears counsel's decision to withhold [the mental health expert's] evidence was based upon counsel's overconfidence that a life sentence would be imposed and his erroneous belief that it was not necessary since his research seemed to show that this Court generally did not approve of overrides. However, counsel clearly missed the mark in overlooking our extensive case law that consistently requires some reasonable evidentiary basis for a life sentence in order to bar an override. Under Florida law, a trial judge is prohibited from rejecting a jury's recommendation of life imprisonment if there is competent evidence of mitigation supporting a life recommendation at the time of sentencing.

The court also noted that counsel had "nothing to lose in presenting this evidence" to the court. Prejudice was clear even though the trial court held that it would have made no difference to his override ruling. The evidence would have "provided an objective and reasonable basis for the jury's recommendation and a sentence of life" and, thus, would "preclude a trial judge's override of the jury's decision."

State v. Larzelere, 979 So. 2d 195 (Fla. 2008) (convicted in February 1992). Counsel was ineffective in capital sentencing for failing to adequately investigate and present mitigation evidence. Even though the defendant waived presentation of mitigation evidence, the jury recommended death only by a vote of seven to five. The defendant was convicted of planning and directly the murder of her husband for assets and insurance money. Counsel did not conduct any investigation concerning the defendant's background or interview her family members about mitigation. They even discounted reports from a prior investigator of her father's alcoholism, possible child abuse, and possible spousal abuse. They did not hire a mental health expert until after the jury's recommendation and then did not provide him with the investigator's report or other relevant information and did not even attend the state's deposition of the defense expert. Counsel even told the expert that "no family members were available to assist in his evaluation." The defendant's waiver was "not made knowingly and intelligently" because counsel "did not investigate possible mitigation sufficiently before [she] waived her right to present penalty-phase evidence." Counsel's conduct was deficient in failing to investigate, despite the investigative report, and in failing to obtain "an informed mental health evaluation … in advance of the penalty phase." Prejudice was established because the evidence would have revealed that the defendant was: 1) sexually abused as a child by her father and uncle; 2) physically abused as an adult; and 3) suffered from narcissistic and histrionic personality disorders. She also may have suffered from post-traumatic stress disorder and obsessive compulsive disorder. Although the state could have presented rebuttal evidence in sentencing, the prejudice was still clear, especially in light of the bare majority of jurors voting for death even in the absence of any mitigation evidence.

Hall v. McPherson, 663 S.E.2d 659 (Ga. 2008) (sentenced in September 2000). Counsel ineffective in capital sentencing for failing to adequately investigate and present mitigation evidence and rebuttal to aggravation evidence. Initially, the court rejected the state's argument that the "habeas court erred as a matter of law by relying upon the American Bar Association Guidelines for the Appointment and Performance of Counsel in Death Penalty Cases and the Southern Center for Human Rights Defense Manual in evaluating counsel's performance." Counsel's conduct was deficient. Counsel did not hire a mitigation investigator and instead arranged with the defendant's mother to bring anyone "she wished to bring with her" to his office during one evening a week. Counsel did so despite having a court-appointed examiner's report that reflected that the mother was alcoholic and had physically and verbally abused the defendant and his brother and neglected them during their childhood. Counsel also did not interview the defendant's brother or a foster mother and did not obtain records from youth detention centers, group homes, or foster homes that the defendant informed him about. Counsel also did not adequately investigate and present evidence of the defendant's drug history and the "psychiatric mitigating evidence" related to that, despite the "thrust" of state's case at both phases being the defendant's drug addiction and intoxication when he left detoxification treatment against medical advice and killed his live-in girlfriend shortly afterwards. Trial counsel were on notice of this and had been provided with some records of prior detox treatments reflecting discharge prior to completion. Counsel failed, however, to obtain the complete records or to interview prior doctors, although eliciting testimony about these treatments from the defendant's mother and sister. While counsel proceeded on a theory of "residual doubt," counsel also "propounded a broad mitigation theory" that encompassed "lack of parental supervision, his early introduction to drugs and alcohol, and the absence of a positive male role model in his life." "Trial counsel's [investigation and] presentation was not strategic, as the testimony presented in the habeas evidentiary hearing would have supported counsel's arguments at the sentencing phase of trial." Counsel argued about the defendant's rough life and use of drugs at an early age, but did not present any evidence of juvenile drug use. He also presented evidence of abandonment by the defendant's father but "the witnesses only hinted at the extent and scope of the neglect that [the defendant] suffered from his mother, and there was no testimony regarding his childhood history of abuse or his placement in foster homes and group homes as a youth." Prejudice found based primarily on the testimony of the defendant's foster mother and brother concerning the mother's extreme physical and verbal abuse and neglect, such that the defendant would sleep in abandoned cars and get food from dumpsters when she chased him from the home and he was on his own for days at a time. The older brother also testified that he introduced the defendant to marijuana, LSD, and other drugs when the defendant was 12. The jury did not hear this evidence and, in fact, heard evidence portraying the defendant as a child simply unsupervised because his mother was working two jobs, but doing "everything she possibly could to help her son, including trying to keep him away from drugs." The jury also did not hear testimony from a prior doctor that diagnosed a major depressive disorder and drug dependence following a suicide attempt. This doctor would have also testified about the defendant's genetic predisposition to substance dependence, such that he "never had a choice in the matter of whether to develop drug and alcohol addiction problems in his life." He also would have testified that the defendant did not complete detox on that occasion because his insurance would not cover it and no other funds were available. This doctor "would have willingly testified at ... trial without charging a fee for his time." Information in the records also rebutted the state's claim that the defendant "chose his life of addiction" by establishing the defendant's struggles and intense desire for help.

Taylor v. State, 262 S.W.3d 231 (Mo. 2008) (tried in January 2003). Counsel ineffective in capital sentencing for failing to adequately prepare and present mitigation evidence. The case involved a killing in prison. The defense presented substantial expert testimony concerning mental health history and issues in the trial in pursuing a not guilty by reason of mental disease or defect verdict, but otherwise presented only videotaped deposition testimony from the superintendent of the correctional facility, who testified that the defendant would present minimal risk to correctional officers and other inmates under his conditions of confinement. "Because of the unique nature of capital sentencing–both the stakes and the character of the evidence to be presented–capital defense counsel have a heightened duty to present mitigation evidence to the jury." Counsel's conduct was deficient. Where there is strong mitigation evidence available, "and the jury has recently convicted a defendant of first-degree murder while in a maximum security prison, it is not reasonable for defense counsel to only present mitigation evidence that the defendant is unlikely to commit crimes in prison." Here, four of five experts that testified in the trial were limited and the fifth focused on the affirmative defense. These experts could have been recalled in sentencing "for their own merit, as evidence of ... [the] history of mental illness" without limitations "at a time when their instructions would have permitted them to give mitigating effect to their conclusions about ... [the] history of mental illness-testimony that in itself provided no defense in the guilt phase." Likewise, while one of the experts testified about the defendant's "abusive upbringing and other difficulties in childhood," this testimony was "provided primarily to support his conclusion at the guilt phase" on the affirmative defense. "Reasonable trial counsel would have recognized the need to put on additional mitigation evidence regarding the defendant's character and background at the penalty phase, particularly after the jury had rejected the expert's ultimate conclusion." Counsel also failed to introduce any of the records supporting the conclusions regarding the "abusive background, history of mental illness, and eventual diagnosis," which the jury asked for during the trial.

> Despite the jury's specific desire to see these available records, which were replete with statements showing [the defendant] had suffered from mental illness since long before the murder, counsel made no attempt to fill this evidentiary void by introducing them in the penalty phase.

Counsel did not present the records because of potentially harmful information.

> While not all of the evidence in the records was favorable ... , such records seldom are. Where the only basis of defense is that one's client has long had a mental illness that reduces his responsibility, the failure to introduce records that present not only support for his history of mental health evaluations and treatment beginning at the extremely young age of 7, but also a treasure trove of mitigation regarding [his] abusive childhood, simply is not a reasonable trial strategy.

Counsel could also have presented record and family member testimony of the defendant's father's abuse of him and his mother, living in an abuse shelter, struggling in school, the early onset of mental illness hearing voices at 11 or 12, belief in "demons" so badly that "they attempted a church exorcism when he was in early adolescence," running away from home, command hallucinations, and suicide threats and behavior. Prejudice found. "A vivid description of [the defendant's] poverty-stricken childhood, particularly the physical abuse, and the assault ... , may have influenced the jury's assessment of his moral culpability." *Id.* at 253 (quoting *Simmons v. Luebbers,* 299 F.3d 929, 939 (8th Cir.2002)). In addition the "contemporaneous records documenting ... mental health problems, more than any testimony the defense offered at the guilt phase, could have persuaded the jury that the mental health evidence had value as mitigation of punishment, and that, perhaps, [the defendant] deserved a punishment other than death for his crime." "If competent counsel had presented and explained the significance of all the available mitigation evidence, there is a 'reasonable probability that the result of the sentencing proceeding would have been different.'" Reversal was also required due to *Brady* error because the state failed to disclose impeachment evidence related to jailhouse snitch, which was material in sentencing.

Littlejohn v. State, 181 P.3d 736 (Okla. Crim. App. 2008) (crimes in 2002). Counsel found ineffective, as conceded by the state, in capital sentencing for failing to adequately investigate and present mitigation. The defendant was charged with three co-defendants for felony murder arising from a car-jacking. Throughout the trial and sentencing, the defendant admitted participation but denied only that he was the triggerman. Counsel did not conduct any investigation and presented only the unprepared testimony of the defendant and his mother to testify in sentencing. Prejudice found because there was available evidence the defendant had: (1) a low IQ and attended special education classes; (2) suffered domestic abuse from his mother and step-father, who were drug dealers and users; (3) the defendant did not learn his step-father was not his father until he was a teenager; and (4) expressed remorse and suicidal ideation shortly after the crimes.

Commonwealth v. Sattazahn, 952 A.2d 640 (Pa. 2008) (retrial in 1999). Counsel ineffective in retrial for failing to adequately investigate and present mitigation evidence. Counsel obtained school and prison records and spoke to the defendant' mother, a prison employee, and perhaps a school teacher and then offered "brief testimony" only from the defendant's mother and a former employer. Counsel's conduct was deficient because counsel failed to review the file of defendant's prior murder conviction, including the prison records, which "contained red flags concerning potential mental-health and/or cognitive impairment." Counsel also failed to investigate potential mental, cognitive, emotional and/or social difficulties despite awareness the defendant had failed several grades and was placed in special classes during early childhood development. Counsel's conduct was not justified by strategy. Prejudice found because "[t]he difference in the very nature and quality of the evidence adduced at trial versus that put forward at the post-conviction stage after a fuller investigation is substantial" and the additional evidence would have supported several statutory mitigating factors that "bore upon the degree of [the defendant's] culpability in terms of selecting between capital punishment and a life sentence." In addition to the actual evidence of difficulties in school, the available evidence included mental health experts to testify about the defendant's long history of learning disabilities, attention deficit hyperactivity disorder, chronic brain dysfunction, Aspergers syndrome, and pervasive developmental and schizotypal personality disorders.

Commonwealth v. Williams, 950 A.2d 294 (Pa. 2008) (sentenced in June 1990). Counsel was ineffective in capital sentencing for failing to adequately investigate and present mental health mitigation evidence. Previous counsel had filed a notice of intent to assert an insanity defense, which referenced two prior psychiatric hospitalizations (one involuntary) in the seven months prior to these offenses. The defendant, who was a Vietnam veteran, had been diagnosed with adjustment disorder, depression and dysthymic disorder. Counsel's conduct was deficient in failing to obtain these records or a mental health evaluation and failure to investigate information about the defendant's bizarre behaviors, etc. Prejudice found because the jury heard only good character evidence in mitigation rather than evidence that the defendant's mental-health condition impacted on his conduct in a way that was relevant to the assessment of the degree of his moral culpability.

Council v. State, 380 S.C. 159, 670 S.E.2d 356 (2008) (sentenced in October 1996). Counsel ineffective in capital sentencing for failing to adequately investigate and present mitigation. Defense counsel asserted during trial and sentencing that the defendant was "merely present at the time" of the crimes, which were committed by another man. The only mitigation evidence presented was "extremely limited testimony" of the defendant's mother. Counsel's conduct was deficient, as follows:

> Initially, trial counsel was deficient in not beginning his investigation into [the defendant's] background once the State served its notice of intent to seek the death penalty, counsel discovered that [the defendant's] DNA was found at the scene of the crime, and counsel learned of Respondent's inculpatory statements to police indicating that he sexually assaulted the victim. Clearly counsel should have been aware that the defense accomplice theory was not that strong and that mitigation evidence was the only means of influencing the jury to recommend a life sentence.

Nonetheless, counsel sought only limited records prior to trial, did not request other records until the day jury selection began, did not have the defendant examined by a defense psychiatrist "until one month before trial," and provided the defense psychiatrist "with only limited records." "As in *Wiggins*, counsel's conduct fell below the standards set by the ABA." *Id.* at (citing 1989 ABA Guidelines for the Appointment and Performance of Counsel in Death Penalty Cases). "Even the limited information obtained should have put counsel on notice that [the defendant's] background, with additional investigation, could potentially yield powerful mitigating evidence. "[N]ot only did counsel delay in investigating [the defendant's] background, he failed to conduct an adequate investigation." "Significantly," counsel "failed to provide his only expert witness ... with sufficient records and only directed him to evaluate ... competency to stand trial and criminal responsibility." The expert, "at the direction of counsel" also "only met with [the defendant] "on two occasions, the first being shortly before trial."

> Furthermore, even though the funding was available, trial counsel chose not to hire a social history investigator. Instead, he relied on his law partner and private investigator to collect potentially relevant information. However, neither of these individuals was qualified in terms of social work experience, to evaluate the information to assess [the defendant's] background.

> Finally, we believe it was unreasonable for trial counsel not to obtain ... family records. First it is inexplicable that trial counsel deemed these records unimportant because they did not directly involve [the defendant].

Id. at (citing 1989 Guidelines). Second, counsel's "brief interviews" with family and DJJ records "should have alerted him to the fact that the family was dysfunctional, [the defendant] had been raised in a violent home environment, and experienced learning disabilities. All of these factors constituted mitigating evidence and warranted further investigation." "Even if trial counsel's investigation could be deemed sufficient or adequate, we believe trial counsel also failed to present any significant mitigating evidence." Counsel's conduct was not excused by strategy because:

> [S]trategic choices made by counsel after an incomplete investigation are reasonable only to the extent that reasonable professional judgment supports the limitations on the investigation. Secondly, counsel was already aware the jury had rejected the defense theory that [the defendant] was not the actual perpetrator but was merely present. Thirdly, it would not have been inconsistent for trial counsel to present the accomplice theory during the guilt phase but mitigation evidence in the penalty phase. Finally, given the State had already presented damaging character evidence, we do not believe [the defendant's] character could have been damaged any further by the presentation of additional mitigating evidence. Trial counsel essentially would have had "nothing to lose" and "everything to gain" by presenting this evidence.

Id. at (citations omitted). Prejudice found despite "overwhelming" evidence of guilt and the jury's finding of six aggravating factors because the jury did not hear "very strong mitigating evidence," including: (1) "medical evidence or other testimony describing mental health issues or that several of his immediate family members suffered from mental illness," such as "schizophrenia, bipolar disorder, depression, and borderline personality disorder"; (2) alcoholic father and parents' divorce on the basis of physical cruelty; (3) "bad neighborhoods" and extreme poverty; (4) a significant drop in I.Q. between the ages of seven and ten "which may have been the result of a head injury or the onset of mental illness; (5) "began getting into trouble at the age of ten years most likely as the result of his violent family environment and negative influence of his siblings"; (6) alcohol and drug use beginning at age sixteen; (7) attempted suicide in his twenties; (8) "a borderline I.Q. and frontal lobe brain dysfunction"; and (9) "the onset of ... schizophrenia [which is undisputed now and has rendered the defendant incompetent since at least 2001] may have begun in early adolescence or childhood." The court concluded: "We cannot say beyond a reasonable doubt that the undiscovered mitigating evidence, taken as a whole, would not have influenced at least one juror to recommend a life sentence."

2007: *In re Hardy*, 163 P.3d 853 (Cal. 2007) (trial in 1983). Counsel was ineffective in capital sentencing for failing to adequately investigate and present evidence of a third party's culpability that would have undermined the state's theory that the defendant was the actual killer. The case involved a conspiracy headed by a man who sought to kill his wife and son for life insurance money and solicited the defendant and several others to assist him. Counsel's conduct was deficient and not explained by strategy because counsel sought to convince the jury that Calvin Boyd was involved rather than the defendant. This was counsel's primary strategy that he pursued in cross-examining the state's and codefendants' witnesses. Counsel's conduct was deficient because adequate investigation would have revealed that Boyd made incriminating statements to a number of people, strongly suggesting he had participated in the murders. He habitually carried a knife similar to the murder weapon and did around the time of the crimes. He had previously committed several assaults and threatened people with a knife. He had cuts on his hands after the murders and made up a false story to explain them. He made up a false alibi and pressured his wife and others to support that alibi. He had a motive to commit the murder because he was a habitual drug and alcohol user, who was unemployed at the time of the murders. He testified falsely during petitioner's preliminary hearing and trial. There was no prejudice during trial because the state argued primarily that the defendant was the actual killer but also argued conspiracy and aiding and abetting, which also allowed for the murder conviction. Prejudice established in sentencing though because, in addition, to the evidence of Boyd's guilt, this evidence would have undermined his credibility in testifying that the husband admitted to him that the defendant was one of the conspirators and that he saw the husband and the defendant together shortly before the crimes. Without this testimony, the evidence that the defendant was the actual killer was "weak and circumstantial." He was young and had only a minor criminal record. He had descended into despair and drug abuse following his brother's suicide. Given these circumstances it would have made a difference if the jury heard substantial evidence that he "was likely not the actual killer, but merely participated in the conspiracy to kill for insurance proceeds." While the state argued that he personally stabbed the victims in a "brutal and horrific manner" solely for money, this evidence would have made a difference.

> "[I]f he did not kill anyone, if he merely conspired … , if he did not show up at the appointed hour, if he was lying passed out from drink and drugs that fateful night instead of stabbing a defenseless woman and child in the dark of night, the nature of his moral culpability is quite different. More to the point, the jury's weighing of the relevant aggravating and mitigating factors would have been entirely different.

Id. at 895.

Ross v. State, 954 So. 2d 968 (Miss. 2007) (sentencing in October 1987). Counsel ineffective in capital sentencing for failing to adequately investigate and present mitigation evidence. "[C]ounsel may be deemed ineffective for relying almost exclusively on material furnished by the State during discovery and conducting no independent investigation." Id. at 1005. Likewise, "[i]t is not reasonable to refuse to investigate when the investigator does not know the relevant facts the investigation will uncover." Id. at 1006 (quoting Dickerson v. Bagley, 453 F.3d 690, 696097 (6th Cir. 2006)). Counsel's conduct was deficient in failing to investigate even though a court-appointed evaluation disclosed a "a number of potential mitigating factors, including accounts of physical and sexual abuse, possible alcoholism, accounts of visual and auditory hallucinations, and the deaths of his ex-wife and four young children in a car accident in 1985 and the brutal murder of his sister in 1982." He was also taking anti-psychotic and anti-depressant medications at the time of the evaluation. Although counsel was aware of this information, they did not pursue mental health issues simply because the defendant informed counsel that "he wasn't 'crazy.'" Id. at 1006. The failure to investigate was unreasonable "given the serious mitigating issues evident." Id. Likewise, while lay witnesses, including the defendant, testified about some of this background information "defense counsel provided no expert evidence about how these events had affected [the defendant] psychologically." Id. Even more problematic, however, was counsel's failure to properly investigate the defendant's record as an inmate prior to making his adaptability to confinement a central argument in sentencing, which opened the door to rebuttal evidence that the defendant had been moved from the local jail to a more secure facility prior to trial because he possessed a hacksaw blade and planned an escape and that he had been disciplined for making alcoholic beverages during a prior confinement. "This failure falls below an objective standard of reasonableness and was undoubtedly highly prejudicial, as it tended to cast Ross as unrepentant, a habitual criminal, and a danger to society." Id. The court also found that the defendant was entitled to a new trial due to "cumulative error," which included counsel's failure to object to a tainted venire panel after a venireperson stated that she had testified against the defendant in federal court that she had been the victim of a crime when counsel was aware that she was the victim in the defendant's prior armed bank robbery. Counsel did not object to her statements, move to remove her after her initial statements, request a curative instruction, or query the remaining venire members about the possible prejudice from her statements.

Glass v. State, 227 S.W.3d 463 (Mo. 2007) (crimes in July 2001 and affirmed on appeal in 2004). Counsel ineffective in capital sentencing for failing to adequately prepare and present mitigation. Counsel presented the testimony of family members, friends, and former employers in sentencing, but did not investigate and present evidence from "school officials and prior professionals" who were "more 'disinterested' witnesses." Prejudice found because available witnesses included a doctor that admitted the defendant to the hospital for bacterial meningitis when the defendant was less than two years old. While an aunt testified about the meningitis, she could not explain "the long-term effects of meningitis" and the impact on the defendant's "impaired mental functioning." Former teachers were also available to testify concerning the defendant's impaired intellectual functioning. Former probation officers were available to testify that for about 18 months prior to the offenses the defendant had no probation violations and was cooperative. Counsel argued in closing that the crimes were "out of character" for the defendant and this testimony would have supported that argument. Counsel also failed to present the testimony of a neuropsychologist concerning the defendant's deficits even though "neuropsychologicial deficits have 'powerful, inherent mitigating value,'" especially in a case like this where the "jury heard from no experts." Counsel also failed to present the testimony of "a speech and language pathologist" concerning the defendant's impaired intellectual functioning, which is "valid mitigating evidence in the penalty phase of capital case, regardless of whether defendant has established a nexus between his mental capacity and crime." Finally, counsel failed to present the testimony of "a toxicologist and pharmacologist" concerning the influence of alcohol at the time of the offenses, which would have supported two statutory mitigating circumstances (substantially impaired capacity to appreciate the criminality of his conduct and conform to the requirements of law and extreme mental and emotional disturbance).

Marquez-Burrola v. State, 157 P.3d 749 (Okla Crim. App. 2007) (tried in February 2003). Counsel ineffective in capital sentencing for failing to conduct a meaningful mitigation investigation. The defendant, a Mexican foreign national, was convicted of killing his wife of 17 years. Retained counsel had participated in one capital case, but hired an associate counsel with no capital experience to prepare for sentencing. The first associate left one month before trial and a second associate who had only been an intern on one capital case was hired to prepare for sentencing. Well before trial counsel had been provided with sample funding motions for experts and other services to prepare mitigation by the Mexican Legal Assistance Program (MCLAP), counsel for Mexico. Counsel did obtain funding for a psychiatrist and an investigator but these people focused only on a "heat of passion" defense for the guilt-or-innocence stage of trial. Just days before trial, counsel for Mexico expressed concern to the trial court about the lack of preparation for sentencing because no investigation had been conducted other than speaking to a few family members one week prior to trial about testifying. The trial court told defense counsel it would be accommodating to additional request for funding but none was made. Counsel, who spoke no Spanish, also did not obtain the services of an interpreter to communication with the defendant, who spoke very little English when an interpreter had to be used even during his interrogation. Counsel used the brother of the victim and the defendant's 12-year-old nephew to interpret even during matters of legal significance. Counsel also did not attempt to overcome the "logistical challenges" involved because almost everyone who could offer insight into the defendant's past and his school, medical, and other records were in Mexico. Counsel's conduct was deficient because "[d]efense counsel has a duty to take all necessary steps to ensure that available mitigating evidence is presented, *id.* at 765, including "seeking funds from the court and specifying why they were necessary." Counsel's conduct was also not explained by strategy because, even with testimony from all three defense counsel, "the actual strategy with regard to mitigation remains elusive." *Id.* The defendant was prejudiced because "mitigation evidence can, quite literally, make the difference between life and death in a capital case." *Id.* at 764. "One important purpose of mitigation evidence is to humanize the defendant in the eyes of the jury and, if possible, to explain what might have driven him to commit the crime." *Id.* at 766. Here, the mitigation consisted of less than fifteen pages of testimony from the defendant's father, mother, and sister that the defendant had been a good man and asking the jury to spare his life. If counsel had adequately investigated, a number of witnesses, some of whom made "substantial sacrifices" to come from Mexico to testify, would have "offered unique and moving vignettes about [the defendant's] good character." This evidence could have made the difference because there is a

> *qualitative* difference between having a family member generally ask the jury to spare the life of the defendant, and having third parties offer the jury *more objective and specific* examples of *why* the defendant's life should be spared. … Jurors may well understand that a defendant's mother will almost always extol the virtues of her son; but they may give different treatment, and perhaps greater weight, to the testimony of less biased witnesses which illuminates the man whose life is in their hands. … [T]he stories of Appellant growing up and doing good things in his rural Mexican community might well have resonated with citizens of a rural Oklahoma county.

Id. at 766-67 (emphasis in original). Preparation for sentencing was especially important because "[t]his case may fairly be called a 'second stage' case," where "[t]he only real question appeared to be what punishment was appropriate." *Id.* at 767. With adequate investigation, the defense could also have countered the state's argument that the defendant was "an abusive monster who was unreasonably jealous and controlling over his wife. *Id.* The evidence would have established that his "jealousy in the months leading up to the homicide might not have been unfounded, and that [his] marital problems may have had a marked effect on his mental health." *Id.* Prejudice was also established because the jury, at some point during deliberations, which evenly split on whether life or death should be imposed. This "strongly suggest[s] how outcome-determinative a real mitigation investigation might have been." *Id.* Finally, while there was argument in the case about whether a "mitigation specialist" is necessary in a capital case, the court held that "the real issue is whether defense counsel understands what kind of mitigation evidence can make a difference, what kind of mitigation evidence is available, and whether counsel makes reasonable efforts to obtain it." *Id.* at 768. The court also rejected the "suggestion that it was the responsibility of [the defendant] and his family to understand the nature of mitigation on their own, and to bring relevant evidence to defense counsel's doorstep." *Id.* Although the usual remedy would be to grant a new sentencing trial, the court modified the defendant's death sentence to life without parole because "[a]ll of the mitigating evidence, viewed together, clearly outweighed the evidence supporting the aggravating circumstances." *Id.*

2006: ***Blackwood v. State***, 946 So. 2d 960 (Fla. 2006) (sentencing in early 1993). Counsel ineffective in capital sentencing for murder of former girlfriend for failing to adequately prepare and present mitigation. During sentencing before the jury, counsel presented eleven witnesses consisting of friends and family, as well as a detention officer who testified that the defendant demonstrated good behavior while incarcerated and had become an inmate trustee. Counsel's conduct was deficient because counsel never even met with the retained defense expert, who had previously found the defendant incompetent, or even attempted to schedule an evaluation of the defendant for sentencing purposes until two weeks prior to sentencing. That expert notified counsel that he could not testify concerning statutory mitigating circumstances, but counsel never asked about non-statutory mitigation. Rather than ask for a continuance or contact the court-appointed doctors, who had also examined competence, counsel did nothing and presented no mental health evidence. Prejudice found because even one of the court-appointed examiners would have testified that the defendant was depressed and emotionally disturbed at the time of the offense. She would also have testified that his verbal IQ was 70, placing him in the borderline mentally retarded range of intelligence. Her testing also indicated some neurological impairment and she would have recommended a neurological evaluation had counsel asked. She also would have testified that the defendant had no prior criminal history and was a good candidate for rehabilitation. Additional available testimony, if counsel had adequately prepared and presented the evidence reflected that the defendant suffered from major depression and avoidant personality traits with masochistic features and was experiencing extreme emotional disturbance at the time of the crime. While the court-appointed examiner testified before the trial court, the court was required to give great weight to the jury recommendation, which was 9 to 3 in favor of death.

Commonwealth v. Gorby, 909 A.2d 775 (Pa. 2006) (crimes in December 1985 and affirmed on appeal in 1991). Trial counsel ineffective in capital sentencing for failing to adequately investigate and present mitigation evidence. Trial counsel's conduct was deficient because counsel knew the defendant behaved irrationally around the time of the offenses, had a history of drug abuse and a "rough childhood," and had been hospitalized previously for head injuries. Nonetheless, counsel did not investigate further than discussions with his client, his mother, and his step-father because he did not believe that any of this was potentially mitigating. In sentencing, counsel called only the step-father to testify that the defendant sometimes assisted him in work around the home. Prejudice found because if counsel had adequately investigated and presented the evidence the jury would have been aware that the defendant was raised in an impoverished, dysfunctional household. He endured substantial verbal and physical abuse and sexual molestation. He witnessed violent and life-threatening altercations between his mother and several husbands, in which he attempted to defend her. He would rock back and forth and bang his head against walls at times. He was also homeless during a substantial portion of his teenage years after his step-father kicked him out of the home. Mental health experts would have testified that the defendant suffered from "cognitive disorder (brain injury affecting thought process), major depression, post-traumatic stress syndrome, borderline personality disorder, and poly-substance abuse." Prejudice found.

Commonwealth v. Sneed, 899 A.2d 1067 (Pa. 2006) (sentencing in March 1985). Counsel ineffective in failing to adequately prepare and present mitigation evidence. Counsel failed to conduct any investigation or to even interview family members, with the sole exception being one of the defendant's sisters, even though the defendant informed counsel that he had a "hard childhood," had abused drugs and alcohol, and had previously been incarcerated. Counsel presented no mitigation in sentencing. Counsel's conduct was deficient.

> "The onus is not upon a criminal defendant to identify what types of evidence may be relevant and require development and pursuit. Counsel's duty is to discover such evidence through his own efforts, including pointed questioning of his client." Therefore, although it is true that appellee never volunteered to counsel all of the alarming details of his childhood, it was not necessarily his responsibility to do so. Counsel is charged with the duty of asking probing questions of his client, and with the duty of discovering and developing mitigation evidence ... .

Id. at (quoting *Commonwealth v. Malloy*, 856 A.2d 767 (Pa. 2004)). Prejudice found because an adequate investigation would have revealed that the defendant grew up in extreme poverty with an alcoholic mother, who drank during pregnancy and while breast-feeding the defendant. He was often abandoned as a child while his mother was on drinking binges. He was exposed to his mother's prostitution and his alcoholic grandmother's making and selling of illegal liquor. He was physically abused by his mother and grandparents and malnourished such that he was often forced to steal in order to have any food.

Ex parte Gonzales, 204 S.W.3d 391 (Tex. Crim. App. 2006) (sentencing in February 1997). Counsel ineffective in capital sentencing for failing to adequately prepare and present mitigation. Specifically, counsel failed to ask the defendant, his mother, or his sister whether the defendant had been abused as a child. Counsel's conduct was deficient because he spoke to the mother only once before trial and the sister once during the trial but did not ask about the issue of abuse. "[A]n objective standard of reasonable performance for defense counsel in a capital case would have required counsel to inquire whether the defendant had been abused as a child." *Id.* at 397. The only evidence counsel presented was general background testimony from the defendant's sister. Prejudice found because, if counsel had performed adequately, the evidence would have established the defendant's childhood abuse by his father, which included forced oral and anal sex. He was physically abusive if the defendant resisted and would threaten to kill him and his mother if he told anyone about the abuse. A psychiatrist could also have testified that the defendant suffers from Post-Traumatic Stress Disorder due to the repeated physical and sexual abuse he suffered. This expert would also have testified that, if treated, the defendant could perhaps become a productive, law abiding member of society.

2005: ***Orme v. State***, 896 So. 2d 725 (Fla. 2005) (arrest in 1992 and direct appeal in 1996). Counsel ineffective in capital sentencing for failing to adequately investigate and present evidence of the defendant's mental state, including a diagnosis of bipolar disorder. Counsel were concerned the defendant was suicidal and sought treatment for him aware. He was diagnosed with bipolar disorder and medicated, but the doctor that diagnosed him died prior to trial and the initial defense counsel withdrew from the case. New counsel saw the doctor's letter and diagnosis but did not present any evidence on this issue "because he had no other information to corroborate it. As he put it, he did not want his expert to stick his neck out and get his head cut off." Counsel's conduct was deficient because counsel failed to investigate with family and friends to establish that the defendant "had exhibited behavior in accord with a bipolar diagnosis." Counsel also failed to inform his trial experts of the diagnosis or to give them the prison medical records showing the medications he had been prescribed to treat the disorder. One of the trial defense experts saw the defendant once prior to trial and was informed by the defendant of the diagnosis and medications, but he had no corroboration. He diagnosed only "mixed personality disorder with chronic intermittent depression and addiction to cocaine." In post-conviction, he was provided the prison records, the prior doctor's letter with the diagnosis, and "affidavits prepared by … friends and family which provide anecdotal information about … past behavior indicative of someone with bipolar disorder." With this information, he diagnosed "probable bipolar in a depressed phase," which as a "major mental illness [linked] to his drug addiction because statistically bipolars are significantly more likely to abuse drugs." The other trial defense expert, also without the relevant information, was asked to testify about symptoms without a diagnosis and testified that the defendant was "a depressed cocaine addict," who was "anxious about his situation." If he had been asked a diagnosis, he would have diagnosed bipolar disorder. Prejudice established. In sentencing, evidence was presented of intoxication from cocaine, pills, and alcohol without any evidence of mental illness. The prosecution argued that the jury should not allow the defendant to "stand behind his crack pipe," which would have been undermined by "testimony linking his drug use to his bipolar disorder." This evidence " would explain to the jury that he was ill and that the mental illness made his addiction even greater." Prejudice was also clear because, even without this evidence, the jury voted to recommend death only in a vote of seven to five.

Commonwealth v. Collins, 888 A.2d 564 (Pa. 2005) (sentencing in October 1991). Counsel ineffective in failing to adequately investigate and presentation mitigation evidence. Counsel presented evidence of the defendant's "good character" and also presented expert testimony demonstrating that the defendant had low intelligence, a history of drug and alcohol abuse, a lack of self esteem, and that he lacked a male role model in his life because his father left the family when the defendant was young. Counsel's conduct was deficient though because counsel did not obtain a "social history" and met only briefly with the defendant's family just prior to sentencing and told them to say "good things" about the defendant. Counsel failed to secure relevant school and mental health records, which would have demonstrated that the defendant was diagnosed with serious emotional problems from an early age and that such problems were compounded by a head injury he sustained in 1990. While the defendant had denied any head injuries, counsel had not asked anyone other than the defendant and could easily have obtained this information from family members. Prejudice found because if counsel had obtained these records and provided them to the defense psychologist at trial, he would have recommended neurological and neuropsychological testing. The evidence would have established that the defendant was abused by his father and other men as a child. He had cognitive defects and emotional problems, which supported two statutory mitigating circumstances: (1) the defendant was under the influence of extreme mental or emotional disturbance; and (2) the defendant's capacity to appreciate the criminality of his conduct or conform his conduct to the requirements of law was substantially impaired.

Commonwealth v. Zook, 887 A.2d 1218 (Pa. 2005) (trial in January 1990). Counsel ineffective in capital resentencing trial for failing to adequately prepare and present mitigation evidence. Counsel believed that they had no significant evidence in mitigation even though counsel were aware that the defendant had suffered a head injury prior to the murders. Counsel also were provided with the defendant's prison records, which revealed the opinion of a consulting psychiatrist that the defendant had a change in behavior consistent with post-concussion syndrome and recommending a neuropsychiatric evaluation. Counsel failed to provide these records to their experts. One of these experts was aware of the head injury from hospital records and testified that it was his general practice to recommend additional evaluation by a neurologist. If counsel had adequately investigated, the evidence would have established that the defendant has organic brain damage, which would have exacerbated his underlying antisocial personality disorder. The defendant was unconscious for 45 minutes due to the head injury and developed seizures and post-traumatic amnesia as a result. In addition, the defendant had a "dramatic behavior change" with respect to violent tendencies which "was well-documented" in the prison records. This evidence would have supported two statutory mitigating circumstances: (1) extreme mental and emotional disturbance; and (2) substantially impaired capacity to appreciate the criminality of his conduct or conform his conduct to the requirements of the law. "Had the jury heard this relevant evidence, there is a reasonable probability that at least one juror would have found an additional mitigating circumstance and struck a different balance in weighing the aggravating and mitigating circumstances."

2004: ***In re Lucas***, 94 P.3d 477 (Cal. 2004) (crimes in October 1986 and affirmed on appeal in 1995). Counsel ineffective in capital sentencing for failing to adequately investigate and present mitigation. Counsel's conduct was deficient under the "norms prevailing in California" and the ABA standards because counsel waited until just before sentencing and then conducted only a few brief interviews of family members and did not follow up on the information they provided to conduct additional investigation and gather records. Counsel's stated reason for failing to follow up on the information concerning the defendant's childhood abuse and confinement and other information was that the information was too remote and trivial and would make the defendant look like a career criminal. Counsel "did not regard evidence of child abuse or alcoholism in the family as particularly mitigating–an apparently idiosyncratic view not commonly shared by contemporary capital defense attorneys." Counsel intended only to present testimony from the defendant and his wife, but the wife refused to testify and then the defendant also refused. Thus, no mitigation evidence was presented. Counsel's conduct was not excused by the defendant's refusal to testify or alleged failure to provide information about his background because "the accused would not necessarily understand the significance of the information that would be uncovered by such an investigation." There was also no evidence that counsel actually pressed the defendant for the information. Prejudice established because adequate investigation would have revealed severe emotional and physical abuse as a young child, institutionalization from age seven in a home staffed by abusive, violent adults, and then juvenile confinement in facilities known for crowding, neglect, and abuse. This evidence would have provided some "explanation for petitioner's criminal propensities and some basis for the exercise of mercy."

State v. Duncan, 894 So. 2d 817 (Fla. 2004) (crimes in 1990 and direct appeal in 1993). Counsel ineffective in capital sentencing for failing to adequately investigate and present mental health evidence in mitigation. Counsel's conduct was deficient because there was a pretrial expert available, who had concluded that the defendant "suffered from a mental illness, specifically a chronic, long-lasting psychotic disturbance, and that there was evidence of delusional paranoid thinking." The expert also found that psychological testing "suggested brain injury" and lay witnesses he interviewed "corroborated symptoms of a psychotic disturbance and significant drug abuse." Having found deficient conduct, "[i]t was then the State's obligation to demonstrate, either through the trial record or the testimony of ... trial counsel, a reasonable, objective justification for counsel's failure to present the available evidence of mental health mitigation." Here, counsel offered no explanation and there was a "complete absence in the record ... of any reason to support why the doctor was not called to testify). Prejudice established because there would have been substantial evidence to support two statutory mitigating circumstances considered by the trial court but rejected by the appellate court on appeal ((1) extreme mental or emotional disturbance; and (2) mental disturbance that interfered with knowledge of right and wrong).

Hutchison v. State, 150 S.W.3d 292 (Mo. 2004) (crimes in late 1995 and affirmed on appeal in 1997). Counsel ineffective for failing to adequately prepare and present mitigation evidence. Counsel's conduct was deficient because "[t]hey spent nearly the entire time before trial preparing for the guilt phase and virtually no time preparing for the penalty phase." *Id.* at 297. They hired only one expert because the family lacked additional money and did not investigate the defendant's "life history or obtain any records documenting his troubled background and his mental and emotional deficits." In short, they "were overwhelmed, under-prepared and under-funded by the time they arrived at the penalty phase. ... Counsel knew that they needed to prepare for the penalty phase, but they left no time to prepare adequately and to present such evidence" after they were denied a continuance which left them with only eight months to prepare for trial. *Id.* at 302. Counsel argued that the defendant was a "follower" influenced by his co-defendants but "failed to investigate and present testimony in support of this theory." *Id.* at 303.

> Readily available records that trial counsel admitted they did not attempt to obtain would have documented [the defendant's] troubled childhood, mental health problems, drug and alcohol addiction, history of sex abuse, attention deficit hyperactivity disorder, learning disabilities, memory problems and social and emotional problems.

Id. at 304. The one expert counsel retained provided information about the defendant's "severe psychiatric problems," that he had been hospitalized, that he had an IQ of 76 and trouble in school, and that the defendant had suffered emotional and sexual abuse. Prejudice found because counsel presented only brief testimony from the defendant's parents about his learning disability and placement in special education classes. The court rejected any requirement of "a nexus between his mental capacity and the crime to admit such mitigating evidence." *Id.* at 305. The court also rejected piecemeal consideration of prejudice from "each family member's testimony," because "[t]he question is whether, when all the mitigation evidence is added together, is there a reasonable probability that the outcome would have been different?" *Id.* at 306. The testimony of the defense expert was not sufficient because of his "reliance solely on the background information" provided by the defendant, which left him "open to impeachment at trial." He also spent less than three hours with the defendant and "his report was very short" and "did not address the effect" the defendant's deficits had on him at the time of the crimes. *Id.* This was caused, in part, because trial counsel had instructed him to consider only where the defendant "was competent and whether he suffered from a mental disease or defect." *Id.* This expert did not address any statutory mitigating factors and "gave no interpretations and provided no testimony to assist the jurors in making an educated determination about [the defendant's] mental condition and whether it mitigated the offense." *Id.* at 306-07. The court noted that there was no allegation that counsel should have "shop[ped] for a more favorable expert," but alleged "only that the expert they hired should have conducted a more thorough investigation and evaluation." *Id.* at 307.

> Although [the defendant's] family could not afford these experts, failure to do *any* follow-up cannot, under these circumstances, satisfy *Wiggins'* mandate to discover all "reasonably available mitigating evidence." The evidence, readily obtained and presented by postconviction counsel established that with adequate mental health evaluations, the jury would have heard significant evidence for mitigation.

Id.

State v. Chew, 844 A.2d 487 (N.J. 2004) (trial in June 1995). Counsel ineffective in capital sentencing for failing to adequately prepare and present mitigation. In preparation for sentencing, counsel retained a psychologist to assess any mitigating factors. The psychologist diagnosed: (1) personality disorder (NOS), mixed with dependent, histrionic, and antisocial features; (2) drug dependency; (3) depressive disorder; and (4) developmental reading disability. He believed there was support for the statutory mitigating factor that the "defendant was under the influence of extreme mental or emotional disturbance." After counsel learned that the defendant had an incestuous relationship with his sister though, counsel never discussed this information with the defense expert and did not present the expert testimony because she feared that this information had been disclosed to a state examiner, who had examined the defendant's sister, and that this harmful information would be revealed to the jury. In sentencing, counsel presented only the testimony of a social worker who described the defendant's family background of chaos, violence, sexual abuse, sexual promiscuity, beatings, excessive drinking, and lack of love and support. Counsels' conduct was deficient because the decision not to call the expert was not based on an adequate investigation because counsel failed to investigate to determine whether the court-appointed examiner was aware of the defendant's incestuous relationship with his sister. They never obtained his report or interviewed him. Counsel also failed to discuss this information with the defense expert, whose opinion would have been strengthened by the incestuous relationship because it demonstrated even greater problems than he had previously realized. Prejudice was found because presentation of the expert testimony in support of the extreme mental or emotional disturbance mitigating factor would have substantially affected the jury's deliberations at the penalty phase. While the additional mitigating evidence had a potential downside, the defense expert's opinion would have been supported by the additional evidence of incest, along with undisclosed evidence of the defendant's abuse of animals and sexual abuse of a child.

Commonwealth v. Moore, 860 A.2d 88 (Pa. 2004) (trial in 1983). Appellate counsel was ineffective in failing to assert trial counsel's ineffectiveness for failure to prepare and present mitigation evidence. Counsel presented no mitigation evidence. He asserted that the defendant declined to testify and he had no other mitigating evidence. Thus, counsel presented no opening and no evidence and only referred generically to possible mitigating circumstances in closing. The jury found two aggravating circumstances and no mitigating circumstances. On appeal, counsel alleged trial counsel's ineffectiveness but failed to specify what mitigating evidence had been available. Thus, the issue of trial counsel's ineffectiveness was denied on appeal. Appellate counsel was ineffective for failing to adequately present the available mitigating evidence, which included testimony from the defendant's mother, sister, and wife of the defendant's traumatic and abusive childhood, including witnessing his father slash his mother's throat. The mother and sister had not been subpoenaed and had not been advised of the need for their testimony in sentencing. Although the ex-wife did appear under subpoena to testify at trial concerning an alibi, she would have testified in sentencing if counsel had explained the nature of the proceeding to her. While these witnesses were "obviously more cooperative in 2000 than in 1983," *id.* at 99, and the defendant was an "uncooperative client," *id.* at 100, counsel's conduct was deficient because counsel was not "relieved of the duty to investigate potential mitigating evidence, particularly where counsel had no other penalty phase strategy," *id.* at 100. Counsel's conduct was not excused by any strategic reason. Prejudice was found because without any mitigating evidence, the defendant's only chance for a life sentence would have been if the jury did not find either of the aggravating circumstances, which was unlikely based on the evidence presented by the state. New sentencing granted.

Commonwealth v. Malloy, 856 A.2d 767 (Pa. 2004) (sentencing in March 2000). Counsel was ineffective for failing to adequately prepare and present mitigation. Counsel's conduct was deficient because counsel met with the defendant only twice, did not apply for co-counsel or an investigator, and conducted no investigation. No evidence was presented in mitigation. Counsel's conduct was not excused by the defendant's failure to inform counsel of possible mitigation evidence and witnesses.

> The onus is not upon a criminal defendant to identify what types of evidence may be relevant and require development and pursuit. Counsel's duty is to discover such evidence through his own efforts, including pointed questioning of his client.

Counsel's conduct was also not excused by the defendant's statement in sentencing that he was satisfied with counsel.

> The fact that appellant was satisfied with counsel at the sentencing hearing colloquy in no way proves that trial counsel's investigation and performance satisfied Sixth Amendment standards. Appellant is not a lawyer, nor was he in a position to know whether his counsel had performed competently. The measure of effectiveness is not whether one's client appeared satisfied at the time. A client is entitled to trust in the fact that his attorney will know what investigation to undertake, what leads to pursue, and what evidence to look for.

Prejudice found because, if counsel had adequately performed, the evidence would have shown that the defendant was physically abused as a child, he lived with his grandmother after his drug-addicted mother abandoned him, and he was institutionalized by age 12 because his grandmother could not control him. Although this evidence is not overwhelming, it was a "close case" and the state presented only one aggravating circumstance. On the other hand, counsel completely failed to "personalize appellant for the jury."

Von Dohlen v. State, 360 S.C. 598, 602 S.E.2d 738 (2004) (trial in May 1991). Counsel was ineffective in capital sentencing for failing to adequately prepare and present mitigation. Counsel presented evidence that the petitioner was a good husband, a good father, and a dependable employee. He grew up in a poor family and had suffered physical and emotional abuse as a child. He had no prior criminal record. His brother was murdered just two weeks before the crimes and petitioner became withdrawn and depressed and began abusing alcohol and Valium. The "violent murder was completely unexpected and out of character for a man who had never displayed violent tendencies." During sentencing, counsel presented testimony from a defense psychiatrist that petitioner suffered an "adjustment reaction with mixed features of emotions and conduct," and pathological intoxication of alcohol and Valium abuse. The psychiatrist testified, however, that petitioner "did not have a chronic mental illness" and the prosecutor capitalized on this in closing arguments. Counsel's conduct was deficient in failing to provide the defense expert with available medical records and testing relating both to the petitioner, as well as his father and brother. Prejudice found because, with the available records, the defense expert would have testified that the petitioner "suffered from severe, chronic depression, a major mental illness," 360 S.C. at 606, 602 S.E.2d at 742, with "psychotic and suicidal tendencies." Counsel's conduct was also deficient in failing to object to the prosecutor's closing argument in sentencing inviting the jurors to put themselves in the "victim's shoes," which was improper under state law and impermissible under *Payne v. Tennessee,* 501 U.S. 808 (1991). Prejudice was not, however, established on this issue.

2003: *State v. Williams,* 794 N.E.2d 27 (Ohio 2003), *modified on reconsideration,* 814 N.E.2d 818 (Ohio 2004) (trial in March 1999). Counsel was ineffective in capital sentencing case for failing to object to improper prosecutorial argument and an improper instruction on mitigation. The court found that the trial court erred in denying counsel's motion to withdraw from representation after the defendant assaulted one of his attorneys in front of the jury following his conviction. After the assault, counsel had very little communication with the defendant because they were frightened of him and they were worried that their fear would be revealed to the jury.

> This is particularly damaging to a defendant during the penalty phase of a capital case when counsel must humanize the defendant for the jury, show his character in the best light available, and bring his good qualities to the fore.

Id. at 50. In closing arguments in sentencing the prosecutor argued that the jury should weigh non-statutory aggravating circumstances that included the final thoughts of the murder victim, the suffering of the victim's mother, and the death of the victim's unborn child. All of these arguments were improper under state law. At the conclusion of sentencing the trial court instructed the jury that mitigating factors are those that are "extenuating or reducing the degree of the defendant's blame or punishment." This instruction was improper because mitigation is not about blame or culpability, but rather about punishment. Despite the prosecutor's improper arguments and the improper instruction, counsel failed to object. The court found that there was no possibility, particularly in light of the prior physical assault of one counsel and the misgivings of both counsel about their ability to continue the representation of the defendant, that the failure to object was a conscious tactical decision. Prejudice was found because there was substantial mitigation in the case and the crime appeared to be a crime of passion. The defendant's family testified that he had a strong close knit family that loved him and was willing to stand beside him. Prejudice was also found because the jury deliberated for six and a half hours before announcing a deadlock and when they were required to continue deliberations they deliberated for an additional eight and half hours before reaching a unanimous decision for death.

2003: *State v. Coney,* 845 So. 2d 120 (Fla. 2003) (sentenced in March 1992). Counsel was ineffective in capital sentencing for failing to adequately prepare and present mitigation evidence. Coney was convicted of killing his jailhouse lover who had spurned him by dousing him with a flammable liquid and setting him on fire when the lover ended their homosexual relationship. In sentencing, counsel presented testimony in general terms concerning the defendant's childhood and upbringing but did not present any mental health evidence. Eleven months prior to trial counsel requested a psychological evaluation, but made no attempt to have the evaluation conducted until just prior to the sentencing hearing. Following the conviction the court-appointed examiner apparently did not evaluate the defendant because of a fee dispute. Counsel did obtain an examination several days prior to sentencing from both a psychiatrist and a neurologist, but neither of these experts was provided with any background information and their testimony and reports made it clear that they were not familiar with the meaning of statutory mitigating factors. The neurologist found no evidence of neurologic disease but did recommend neuropsychological testing, which trial counsel never obtained. Counsel's conduct was deficient, because if counsel had obtained qualified experts and provided them with sufficient background information in time to adequately evaluate the defendant, counsel could have presented testimony both from a neurologist and a neuropsychologist that the defendant suffered from frontal lobe dysfunction and deficits in his right brain functioning that resulted in impulsive behavior and revealed that the defendant was suffering from an extreme mental or emotional impairment at the time of the commission of the offenses. Prejudice was found because the jury recommended imposition of the death penalty only by a seven to five vote, and if only one of the seven jurors had changed his or her vote, the recommendation would have been for a life sentence. In view of the law requiring the presence of compelling evidence to override a jury's recommendation of life, the court would likely have followed a recommendation for a life sentence. The court also found prejudice because, even though the state vigorously challenged the mental health evidence and presented contrary evidence, the court found "it is peculiarly within the province of the jury to sift through evidence, assess the credibility of the witnesses, and determine which evidence is the most persuasive." *Id.* at 132.

Head v. Thomason, 578 S.E.2d 426 (Ga. 2003) (tried in October 1996). Counsel ineffective in capital case for failing to call mental health experts he knew could provide mitigating evidence in sentencing. The defendant "is a burglar who shot and killed the homeowner who came upon him while he was burglarizing the victim's home." Following a bench trial, the defense presented mitigation evidence that showed only the defendants profession of remorse, his lack of violent tendencies, that he is easily influenced, and that he had previously been hospitalized for marijuana use. Counsel was aware of mental health experts who could have testified but did not present their testimony. One of the experts, a clinical psychologist, had testified at the competence hearing that the defendant had an IQ of 77. The expert, a psychiatrist, had interviewed the defendant during a forensic evaluation and informed counsel that there were indications of intellectual impairment, low self esteem, and depression. Counsel possessed the defendant's prior school, medical, and institutional records, but never gave the records to the psychiatrist or presented this evidence in mitigation because counsel testified they did not know how to do it without an expert. Counsel did not have the expert to execute an affidavit stating the need for additional funding, but instead simply requested an additional $25,000 for mental health expert assistance. When the trial court rejected the additional funding trial counsel never contacted the expert again even though the expert testified that he would have worked with counsel without further funding or for an amount significantly less then $25,000. "We conclude, given the importance of mitigating evidence in death penalty cases, that an attorney has not acted reasonably when he fails to call mental health experts he knows have mitigating evidence and explains his failure to present lay mitigating evidence by asserting that he had no experts to call."

2002: ***State v. Lewis***, 838 So. 2d 1102 (Fla. 2002) (sentenced in August 1988). Counsel was ineffective in capital sentencing for failing to adequately prepare for presentation of mitigation evidence in sentencing, which resulted in the defendant's waiver of his right to present mitigation evidence being not a knowing, voluntary, and intelligent waiver. Trial counsel spent a significant amount of time preparing for the guilt or innocence phase of trial, but did not make any attempt to prepare for sentencing until after the conviction. Counsel then attempted to talk with the defendant's mother but "this attempt was hampered because of [the] delay in starting the investigation." The mother was angry that her son had been convicted and blamed the trial attorney. The only other witness interviewed by counsel was the defendant's father, who was also a convicted felon. Counsel never attempted to interview any other potential mitigating witness or obtain any background records, including the defendant's hospitalization records, school records, and foster care information. Counsel did request a mental health expert but did so only two weeks after the defendant had already been convicted. The expert interviewed the defendant but told counsel that he needed documented corroboration before he could render a professional opinion or conclusion. The expert discussed possible theories with defense counsel but did not receive any additional information prior to sentencing. On the day sentencing began, the expert was the only witness willing and able to testify for the defense and the defendant stated that he did not want the expert to testify and waived mitigation. If counsel had adequately investigated the evidence would have revealed that the defendant's mother was an alcohol, he was exposed to violence and severe neglect as a child, he suffered a skull fracture at the age of 2 or 3 that required 2 weeks of hospitalization, and he observed his fathers violence and domestic abuse on a daily basis. After his parents separated, the parents tried to kidnap the children from each other. The defendant was turned over to foster care and shuffled back and forth between numerous homes. He had diminished mental capacity and brain damage. He had a recorded history of serious alcohol and drug abuse and he had consumed a considerable amount of alcohol on the night of the crimes. The trial expert testified that, if he had been provided with the background records and documentation, he would have been able to render a complete diagnoses and testify to substantial mitigation. The court held, "Although a defendant may waive mitigation, he can not do so blindly; counsel must first investigate all avenues and advise the defendant so that the defendant reasonably understands what is being waived and its ramifications and hence is able to make an informed, intelligent decision." Counsel's conduct was both deficient and prejudicial in failing to adequately investigate and prepare for the penalty phase.

Valdez v. State, 46 P.3d 703 (Okla. Crim. App. 2002) (arrest in 1989). In a successor post-conviction action after the denial of clemency, the court held that counsel was ineffective in failing to adequately prepare and present mitigation for Mexican National client. Counsel's conduct was deficient because counsel did not seek funding to conduct the investigation "trial counsel's inexperience in capital litigation caused him to believe such funds were unavailable." Likewise, if counsel had sought assistance from the Mexican Consulate, "the Government of Mexico would have intervened in the case, assisted with Petitioner's defense, and provided resources to ensure that he received a fair trial and sentencing hearing." Investigation of the defendant's background and medical history revealed severe organic brain damage, extreme poverty, limited education, and "a family plagued by alcohol abuse and instability."

In hindsight, and so many years following Petitioner's conviction and direct appeal, it is difficult to assess the effect consular assistance, a thorough background investigation and adequate legal representation would have had. However, this Court cannot have confidence in the jury's sentencing determination and affirm its assessment of a death sentence where the jury was not presented with very significant and important evidence bearing upon Petitioner's mental status and psyche at the time of the crime.

Commonwealth v. Ford, 809 A.2d 325 (Pa. 2002) (sentenced in March 1992). Counsel ineffective in capital case for failing to adequately investigate and present mitigation evidence in sentencing. Appellate counsel was also ineffective for failing to assert trial counsel's ineffectiveness. In sentencing, trial counsel presented the defendant's sister to testify but not prepare her testimony, which amounted to only a plea of mercy. Counsel also presented evidence of the defendant's low IQ and that his educational achievement was at the 2d or 3d grade level. The jury found two aggravating circumstances and no mitigating circumstances. Trial counsel was aware of a competency evaluation that revealed that the defendant had a troubled childhood and learning problems. Counsel did not investigate to obtain prior hospitalizations, mental health records, or school records. He also did not obtain additional information form the defendant's family or have a mental health professional evaluate the defendant with respect to mitigation. Counsel's conduct was deficient because there was no reasonable basis for failing to investigate and present this mitigating evidence. Although counsel did state that he did not present psychiatric records because the prosecution informed him that they contained reports that the defendant was "explosive," this decision was based on very little information and without actually reviewing the supporting documents. If counsel had adequately investigated, the evidence would have revealed schizophrenia, brain impairments including mental retardation, learning disabilities, and post traumatic stress. The defendant showed signed of dementia early in life and had a long history of psychiatric treatment for impaired reality, including hearing voices, and alcohol dependence. The defendant also had an extensive history of abuse and family dysfunction. The available evidence would have supported three statutory mitigating circumstances. The Commonwealth presented rebuttal evidence in post- conviction showing that the defendant had previously been convicted of sexual assault of a 12 year old boy, had been a gang member in his youth, and had threatened to kill his grandparents. The Commonwealth also presented psychiatric evidence of antisocial personality disorder and a clinical psychologist that would have testified that the defendant does not suffer from organic brain damage or learning disabilities. The court still found prejudice because the jury was given no meaningful evidence of mitigation to consider in their weighing process. Moreover, even without any mitigation evidence, the jury was still deadlocked at one point during the penalty phase deliberations.

2001: *Ragsdale v. State*, 798 So. 2d 713 (Fla. 2001) (tried in May 1988). Counsel ineffective in failing to prepare and present mitigation evidence in sentencing. Counsel was a sole practitioner with only his wife assisting. Counsel did not conduct any investigation and relied only on a few calls made by his wife to Ragsdale's family members. Counsel did not even know who his wife contacted or the content of the conversations. Counsel only called one witness to testify that Ragsdale suffered several head injuries as a child without any explanation of how or whether this affected him. If counsel had investigated, the evidence would have established that defendant grew up in an impoverished home with numerous moves and had an abusive father. He observed violence towards his mother, was made to fight with his siblings until they bled, and was sometimes handcuffed to a pole for hours at a time. In addition, Ragsdale's father had shot at him twice with a pistol. It was so bad that Ragsdale began to run away to an aunt's by age eight and quit school and moved out permanently at age 15-16 to live with a cousin. He had extensive alcohol and drug abuse. He also had numerous head injuries, including having an eye shot out accidentally with an arrow, being thrown through a car windshield in an accident, and being hit with a metal pipe. Following these incidents, he would have severe headaches and behavioral changes, including violent snaps. A defense expert found that Ragsdale was psychotic at the time of the offense, and thus the statutory mitigating circumstances of extreme mental or emotional disturbance and inability to conform to the requirements of law applied in the instant case. This doctor also identified a list of nonstatutory mitigating factors including organic brain damage, physical and emotional child abuse, history of alcohol and drug abuse, marginal intelligence, depression, and a developmental learning disability. Prejudice was established because even the state's expert, who disagreed with the conclusion that Ragsdale was psychotic and suffered organic brain damage, expressed no opinion on the statutory mitigators. He did, however, testify to the existence of mitigating evidence which was not presented at the penalty phase, including a severe learning disability and that Ragsdale's IQ score was in the borderline retarded range. He also concluded that Ragsdale's brain was impaired and that Ragsdale had a personality disorder with paranoid features. The court, thus, found it be "inescapable" that there was available evidence from experts which would have supported substantial mitigation had counsel performed adequately. *Id.* at *5.

2000: ***Sanford v. State***, 25 S.W.3d 414 (Ark. 2000) (sentenced in 1996). Counsel ineffective in capital sentencing for failing to investigate and present mitigation evidence concerning defendant's school records showing long- standing mental retardation, age, medical records, family history, and jail records, reflecting commendations he had received. Counsel conceded that he did little to prepare for sentencing, even though he had a social worker available to him, because he was "disappointed" with guilty verdicts and "tired." Counsel called only the 16-year-old defendant's parents, who testified generally that defendant was young, had been a good son, had a mental problem, and his life was worth saving. Counsel did not recall the defense expert from the trial, but did argue additionally based on that expert's testimony that defendant was mentally retarded, which was disputed by state based on one IQ score of 75. If counsel had investigated he would have discovered that the school records showed defendant had been in special education, had been considered mildly mentally retarded during much of his time in school, and had a good record with only one disciplinary incident. His medical history reflects he almost suffocated to death as a child when a load of cotton seed fell on him; and defendant's mother testified he acted a "bit slower" after the cotton-seed incident. Later he suffered a blow to the head with a two-by-four wielded by his sister. Proof also available, but not investigated or presented, showed siblings and other family members to be either slow or retarded. Although the court did not specifically discuss prejudice, the court noted that the jury found three aggravating factors and no mitigating factors and state law prohibited the death penalty if the jury concluded the defendant was mentally retarded at the time of the crimes.

State v. Riechmann, 777 So. 2d 342 (Fla. 2000) (sentenced in August 1988). Counsel ineffective in capital sentencing for failing to prepare and present mitigation. Defendant and his girlfriend had moved to Florida from Germany. Girlfriend was killed. State's theory was that she had been a prostitute for the defendant and, once she stopped prostituting, he killed her for insurance proceeds.

The defense did not investigate or contact any witnesses in Germany and presented no mitigation evidence at all. Available yet unpresented mitigation revealed that defendant had positive personal qualities and good character and at least 15 witnesses were available to testify for him. No real discussion of prejudice. [Court also found error because the prosecutor prepared the trial court's sentencing order after an ex parte discussion and the defense was not provided with the draft order, which found no mitigation.]

People v. Thompkins, 732 N.E.2d 553 (Ill. 2000) (tried in June 1982). Counsel ineffective in capital sentencing for failing to prepare and present mitigation evidence. Counsel never met with defendant's brothers, children, aunt, supervisors, coworkers, friends, or writers of letters on defendant's behalf, nor did he seek records as to defendant's education, employment, military service or prison incarceration. If counsel had prepared, evidence could have been presented to show that, in witnesses' opinions, defendant was a good son, husband, father, friend, and worker, that he may have helped save the life of a youth officer who later became a police chief, and that he was kind to, and protective of, women. Counsel presented only four stipulations concerning the possible origin of bullets used in the murders. Counsel also presented brief testimony from defendant's wife concerning his history. Following the court's *sua sponte* order for a presentence report, counsel presented more than 50 letters in defendant's behalf, including some of the information listed above. Many of the letter writers acknowledged that they hardly knew the defendant though. The court acknowledged reading the letters but found no mitigation. "[B]ecause counsel failed to conduct an investigation and uncover what the possible mitigation witnesses would have to say, he was in no position to make a reasoned decision whether their testimony would have any impact on the judge.
… In conclusion, counsel's rationale for failing to investigate mitigating evidence stemmed not from a reasonable strategy, but from an objectively unreasonable failure to investigate. As such, counsel's performance was constitutionally deficient." *Id.* at 571 (citations omitted). Counsel's conduct was not excused by uncooperativeness of defendant. "The mere fact that a client is uncooperative will not excuse a failure to investigate in a capital case." *Id.* at 572. Counsel's conduct also was not excused by fear of the aggravating evidence that could be introduced in response. This was the finding of the lower court, but there was no evidence to support the finding. Counsel simply failed to investigate and did not know of the available evidence. *Id.* at 573.

1999: *People v. Morgan*, 719 N.E.2d 681 (Ill. 1999) (sentenced in June 1983). Counsel ineffective for failing to prepare and present mitigation evidence. Defendant convicted of several murders and rape by jury and then proceeded to sentence before the judge alone. In opening statement, defense counsel argued statute unconstitutional and made a religious appeal. He told the judge he would hear from the defendant and his family and would here evidence of medical problems. State presented numerous violent convictions and incidents in defendant's past in aggravation. In 10 pages of mitigation, the defense presented the defendant's girlfriend and mother to say they loved him. Mother also testified that the defendant has had seizures since age 8 due to a spot on brain caused by trauma and that he sometimes blanks out. Counsel also cited 1978 presentence report that revealed seizures. In closing prosecutor pointed out that there was no medical testimony as promised and no showing of how the seizures were relevant as mitigation evidence. Defense closing was basically just an irrelevant and nonsensical religious appeal citing "love" as mitigation. In sentencing, the judge found no "rhyme" or "reason" for the "senseless" crimes and found no mitigation. Although the judge expressed distaste for the death penalty, because the statute required a death sentence if no mitigating evidence found, he sentenced the defendant to death. Post-conviction evidence revealed that counsel had been retained the day of arrest and told shortly thereafter by mother of seizure history. Counsel did not talk to other family members or witnesses. If he had investigated, he would have discovered lay witnesses who would testify that the defendant suffered from an illness at age 20 months that likely caused the seizures. He has suffered severe seizures since that time. He was frequently hospitalized as a child. He has fainting and black-outs and engages in violent behavior for no apparent reason. He also has features of paranoia and drug and alcohol problems. Eyewitnesses, including even the rape victim, would have established that he was paranoid and using drugs and alcohol at the time of these offenses. Experts, including neurologist, Dr. Pincus, would have testified that the defendant has severe frontal lobe damage and other diffuse damage. The combination of the brain damage, drugs and alcohol, and paranoia rendered the defendant under extreme mental or emotional disturbance for these offenses and explains prior violent episodes because defendant can not control violence. In addition to this evidence, the evidence would have also established that the defendant was physically abused by his mother during his childhood. Deficient conduct found because defense counsel's recollections that he knew nothing of seizure history and defendant appeared normal to him were not credible. Counsel was clearly, as is apparent from sentencing hearing, that the defendant had a history of seizures. Moreover, even if the defendant appeared normal and neither he or his family mentioned history, counsel's conduct was still deficient for failing to investigate. "We have repeatedly held that the duty to make a reasonable investigation concerning potential mitigation evidence is imposed on counsel and not upon a defendant. Moreover, we have also held that defense counsel's duty to investigate is not limited to matters about which defendant [or his family] has informed defense counsel." *23 (citations omitted). Prejudice found because the available evidence would have mitigated the aggravation evidence of prior violent episodes and would have provided the "rhyme" and "reason" for these offenses found lacking by the sentencing judge.

*Rondon v. State, 711 N.E.2d 506 (Ind. 1999) (tried in 1985). Counsel ineffective in sentencing phase for failing to prepare and present mitigating evidence. Counsel focused primarily on guilt phase and did not prepare at all for sentencing until the night before the penalty phase of trial, except by interviewing a minister. At that point, they arbitrarily agreed to limit their investigation of background to the two years the defendant had lived in the county. They did not even ask the defendant to summarize his experiences prior to 1982. Counsel presented only three witnesses in sentencing who testified about good work habits and friendliness, but counsel waived opening statement and in closing did not even argue that this evidence should be considered as mitigating evidence. A simple interview of client would have revealed, as a competence evaluation following the jury's recommendation of sentence did, that the defendant had a second grade education, had been treated for psychiatric problems in Cuba where he was born and raised, had been given shock treatment for psychiatric problems, and possibly had brain damage from being hit in the head with a machete.

*Washington v. State, 989 P.2d 960 (Okla. Crim. App. 1999) (trial in 1996). Counsel ineffective in capital sentencing because "counsel did little to contest the State's case in second stage." Counsel made no opening statement. Counsel then acquiesced in the admission of the state's only evidence in sentencing: two letters that were termed "impact" or "victim impact" evidence. Under state law, "victim impact evidence should be restricted to the financial, emotional, psychological, and physical effect of the crime itself on survivors and include [only] a few personal characteristics of the victim."

*Capital Case

Here, one of the letters was written by the victim to her parents prior to the murder and, thus, "does not constitute impact evidence … and does not address how [her] murder affected her family." While the letter arguably contained some information about the victim's personal characteristics, "the letter is hearsay for which no exception applies and its admission was error." Likewise, the other letter was a letter written by the victim's father to the prosecutor that "exceeded the bounds of permissible victim impact evidence given the overamplified request for the death penalty and the biblical references," including "eye for eye."

> We have condemned prosecutors who attempt to make the capital sentencing decision somehow easier by implying God is on the side of a death sentence as an intolerable self-serving perversion of Christian faith as well as the criminal law of Oklahoma. We can neither permit such references in victim impact evidence because victim impact evidence is limited to the financial, emotional, psychological, and physical effect of the crime itself on survivors…

Following the state's uncontested victim impact evidence, counsel presented no evidence "either to rebut the alleged aggravating circumstances or to mitigate punishment" and relied only on the defendant's trial testimony to argue that death for the murder of his ex-wife was not warranted because the defendant "served in the military, … did not have a history of criminal acts, … did not resist the police and he was under emotional stress at the time of the shooting." Counsel made a "disjointed and rambling closing argument" in which counsel conceded the murder in this case was (as are all murders) heinous, atrocious, or cruel and failed to challenge the state's case even though the physical evidence did not support the state's "uncontested theory" that the defendant shot the victim "in non-vital areas as she crawled away from him over four minutes before delivering the fatal shot." Finally, counsel "failed to object to the prosecutor's second stage closing argument in which the prosecutor exceeded the bounds of proper argument by invoking societal alarm and improperly arguing the jury had a duty to impose death based on the prosecutor's personal sense of justice." Counsel failed to object even though the argument "contain[ed] remarks strikingly similar to those condemned" by the court in a case decided years before this trial. Cumulative prejudice found based on "the combination of this improper argument, the admission of improper victim impact evidence and the deficient performance of trial counsel." Sentence modified to life without parole.

1998: *In re Gay*, 968 P.2d 476 (Cal. 1998) (tried in June 1983). Counsel ineffective in sentencing phase and the cumulative prejudicial effect of counsels' errors required that death sentence be vacated. Defendant was charged with killing a police officer and numerous armed robberies. The defense counsel tricked the defendant into retaining him with the help of a psychologist/minister and then got himself appointed. Counsel then advised the defendant to confess to the numerous armed robbery charges, based on an alleged deal that the defense did not have, even though the state's evidence was based only on weak circumstantial evidence and accomplice testimony. The confession allowed the state to convict and to portray the defendant as a serial robber, which was devastating in light of the absence of substantial mitigating evidence in sentencing. Counsel then selected and used the psychologist and a psychiatrist based on a fee arrangement. The psychologist would help trick people to get the attorney retained and in turn the attorney would retain these "experts" who worked together. The psychiatrist was unwilling to take the case if extensive work was required, but counsel assured him that death was a foregone conclusion and extensive time was not required. The psychologist, who was not licensed, did only a Bender Gestalt (neuropsychological screening test) and a WISC test, which is a children's intelligence test. The psychiatrist interviewed the defendant and reviewed a single parole report. He did not request and was not provided with any additional information. He testified only that the defendant is sociopathic, but adapts well to structured environments. A few other defense witnesses that counsel spoke to briefly, if at all, prior to their testimony, testified that the defendant has good character. Counsel did virtually no investigation for mitigation and relied only on interviews of the defendant. If counsel had adequately investigated, the evidence would have revealed that the defendant was raised in a deprived, physically and emotionally abusive, and chaotic home. His alcoholic father suffered from substantial mental impairments and subjected defendant to extreme physical abuse. His mother was emotionally neglectful and abusive. The defendant suffered from PTSD and was dissociating at the time of the offense. He had organic impairments, including areas of the temporal and parietal lobes, and had temporal lobe seizures. He had attention deficits, learning disabilities, a mood disorder, characterized by periods of depression and manic activity, and substance abuse disorder, as well, and was using drugs prior to the offenses. His impairments made him susceptible to the aggressive influence of his codefendant. In addition to being mitigating, much of this evidence would have lessened the impact of the state's aggravating evidence by explaining it from a mental health standpoint. Counsel's failure to investigate was not excused by reliance on the defendant or by his preoccupation with the guilt-or-innocence phase. His failure to investigate apparently resulted from his uninformed belief that if the defendant was found guilty, the death penalty was inevitable. In addition to all of these problems, during his representation of the defendant, counsel was being investigated by the same prosecutor for misappropriation of funds, which presented a potential conflict of interest that was undisclosed. Reversed based on cumulative prejudice.

Turpin v. Lipham, 510 S.E.2d 32 (Ga. 1998) (sentenced in February 1987). Counsel ineffective in sentencing for failing to adequately prepare and present mitigation evidence. During sentencing for rape, murder, burglary, and robbery counsel presented 2500 pages of records from the Department of Family and Children Services and the Anneewakee Treatment Center (a home for children with behavioral problems), but did not present any testimony concerning these records other than the brief testimony of the records custodians. The only other mitigation evidence offered was the defendant's wife asking for mercy because of their son. Trial counsel obtained the records but did not have a mental health expert to examine them. Instead, trial counsel asked a friend, who was a family counselor to review the records. The friend reported that the records were both aggravating and mitigating. While they established childhood abuse and neglect, they also chronicled violent, antisocial behavior from an early age and that he was not insane or incompetent. One expert also examined the defendant and found that he was not insane or incompetent. Based on these findings and the two-edged nature of the records, trial counsel decided not to hire a mental health expert. The Court stated, "While trial counsel is afforded tremendous deference over matters of trial strategy, the strategy that is selected must be supported by adequate investigation." *Id. at* . Trial counsel were deficient in relying only on the family counselor's review of the records, because he had no medical or doctorate degree and is not even licensed as a counselor. In addition, the counselor only reviewed the records in his spare time as a favor to a friend, without any anticipation that he might be called to testify, and he did not even see all the records. The records he did see were not reviewed in depth. In addition, the counselor testified that he was only told to look at the records for competence and sanity, not for mitigation evidence. Trial counsels' failure to read these records or hire a mental health expert to examine the records was not reasonable under the circumstances, because trial counsel knew the defendant had been institutionalized in mental hospitals, children's homes, and treatment centers for nine years. The records revealed that he had been subjected to, or diagnosed with, chronic poverty, physical abuse, alcoholic parents, severe neglect, isolation from his family, severe behavioral problems, conduct disorders, anxiety disorders, a possible learning disability, inadequate socialization, and head injuries. Even though counsel made the records the center piece of the mitigation case, they did not hire an expert to review the records and did not contact any of doctors or psychologists identified in the records. If counsel had even had an expert to review the records, they would have been told that the disparity between verbal and performance IQ scores and the results of the Minnesota Multiphasic Personality Inventory suggested organic brain damage and post-traumatic stress disorder. The Court stated that no reasonable lawyer would have given the jury 2500 pages of raw institutional documents and asked them, without any guidance, to read through them for mitigation evidence. In addition to the sheer volume, the records were at times illegible handwriting, difficult to understand because there was wording and abbreviations used by the institutions that were meaningless to outsiders, jurors would not understand medical and psychological terms in the records, and jurors could not understand raw test data and diagnoses "without the proper interpretive expertise." Slip Op. at *9. The Court observed, "It is usually true that evidence of a defendant's troubled childhood will present him in a more sympathetic light to a jury." Slip Op. at *9. Nonetheless, "the average juror is not able, without expert assistance, to understand the effect [the defendant's] troubled youth, emotional instability and mental problems might have had on his culpability for the murder." Slip Op. at *9. Trial counsels' deficient conduct was not excused by the strategy to avoid the two-edged nature of the records, because counsel presented the records in evidence. Thus, the jury could have easily discovered the aggravating aspect of the records. The Court also found prejudice because, even though the crimes were "horrific," presentation of the evidence of the defendant's mental disorders and the abuse, neglect and isolation he experienced as a child may have resulted in a sentence less than death.

Turpin v. Christenson, 497 S.E.2d 216 (Ga. 1998) (sentenced in March 1990). Counsel ineffective in sentencing due to a number of errors in the trial and sentencing and due to counsel's failure to adequately prepare and present mitigation. Counsel knew from the beginning that "there would likely be a conviction and that the crucial phase of the trial would be the penalty phase," but assigned primary responsibility for the penalty phase to the least experienced counsel who had "no experience trying a murder case, let alone a death penalty case." Counsel did virtually nothing to prepare "until the eve of trial." During the opening statement of the trial, counsel asserted that the defense would show that the victim, had been a drug-dealing homosexual who had initiated the events which led to his death by attempting to trade sex for drugs." There was no evidence to support this theory, including no evidence of drug involvement or any credible evidence that the victim was even a homosexual and there was no mention of this "theory" even in the defendant's confessions. Nonetheless, counsel "persisted with this theme on closing argument." No prejudice during trial due to the overwhelming evidence, including the confessions, but these actions added to the prejudice in sentencing "[b]ecause the evidence introduced in the guilt/innocence phase carries over into the penalty phase." Counsel was also deficient in preparing and presenting mitigation. Counsel knew from the beginning that the defendant "seemed aloof and detached" and often uncommunicative without his father's intervention. They were also aware that he had been treated in an in-patient psychiatric facility three years before when he was 15 years old. These files revealed diagnoses of "dysthymic disorder, alcohol abuse, conduct disorder, and under-socialized, non-aggressive, narcissistic personality disorder with features of sociopathy." The files also contained information of: a "genetic disposition toward alcohol abuse" in the family; the defendant's alcohol abuse history, including blackouts; and problems with reality perception. While lengthy treatment was recommended, treatment ended after six weeks because the defendant's parents "reached the limits of their insurance coverage." Counsel asked for a psychiatric evaluation but, because they "believed that this evidence would be more relevant to guilt/innocence issues, such as competency to stand trial or a verdict of guilty but mentally ill," the counsel dealing with the guilt/innocence phase primarily handled this aspect. The court-appointed examiner found the defendant competent and sane but diagnosed "a Personality Disorder Not Otherwise Specified and Psychoactive Substance Abuse Not Otherwise Specified" and also "noted a dramatic 20-point decline in … IQ" in the three years since his hospitalization, which she attributed to drug usage. Despite all of this information, "counsel did no further investigation of his mental health" and did not even ask the court-appointed examiner about "her opinion on mitigation issues or consider using her report." Counsel did seek funding for a private psychiatrist and file a second motion for psychiatric evaluation but "they did not argue specific findings" from the available information "other than the decline in IQ." These motions were denied and counsel "did not seek any other means of obtaining expert assistance," such as seeking "the advice or resources of any criminal defense or capital defense organizations in Georgia, although they admitted at the habeas hearing that they were aware of these organizations. They did not contact any mental health professionals for reduced fee or pro bono support, or for referrals. They completely abandoned the mental health issue and did not use it at trial." If counsel had pursued the issue, the evidence would have revealed "an anxiety disorder characterized by a 'pervasive sense of nervousness or anxiety [even] in a normal, non-threatening environment,' … an obsessive-compulsive disorder and an impulse-control disorder." A "licensed clinical social worker" could have testified in detail about the extensive family history of "alcoholism and mental illness." Counsel were not aware of much of this information because they had not even thoroughly reviewed the prior psychiatric records and relied on the defendant's father, who the prior records revealed was "estranged from his son" for years. Counsel's conduct was not excused by strategy or their belief that "drug usage and 'narcissistic' personality would not go over well in … [the] County," because "before selecting a strategy, counsel must conduct a reasonable investigation into the defendant's background for mitigation evidence to use at sentencing." Here "counsel possessed a wealth of information regarding … psychiatric problems and drug abuse, which they essentially ignored." They failed almost completely to investigate or to even understand this information. "They did not understand the mental health material that they did review and took no steps to further their understanding."

> Although trial counsel acknowledged they believed that the penalty phase would be the crucial phase of the trial, they failed to investigate adequately … possible defenses to a death sentence. The decision to forego a line of defense, without a substantial investigation, must be reasonable under the circumstances. Trial counsel's abandonment of the mental health mitigation issues, after only a cursory investigation of their client's psychological health, was not reasonable under the circumstances.

> A more complete investigation would have only entailed a more careful reading of the materials already in their possession and a few phone calls.

The decision not to investigate further … was also not strategic. Trial counsel ceased any investigation of … mental health after the trial court denied their second request for a psychiatric examination. It is apparent from the record that this failure to proceed may have stemmed in part from the division of labor.

Id. at (citations omitted). In essence, the attorney investigating mental health stopped after learning that competency and sanity were not issues and the other attorney responsible for sentencing and mitigation "failed to pick up where … [he] left off." During sentencing, the state presented only one witness in aggravation in the form of a detective who testified that the defendant told him that he had previously planned to kill another man in a car theft like the one involved in this case. Counsel was aware that the detective had not included this information in his report and only "remembered" this a year later when he issued a supplemental report. In mitigation, the defense "presented 19 witnesses and 27 exhibits" focused on establishing the defendant's "happy and normal childhood." The witnesses testified, most very briefly, that he was a good child until his grandmother died when he was 14 and then he "became withdrawn, his grades dropped and he began to get into trouble due to drugs." Even the school records admitted in evidence by the defense contradicted the mitigation theory because the records "clearly showed that [the defendant's] grades began to plunge two years before the death of his grandmother." Because counsel had failed to prepare the witnesses, the state was able to impeach each witness because most were not aware of the defendant's "extensive juvenile and criminal record" and some had had no contact with him since "he was an adolescent." Counsel was also unaware of the extent of the juvenile record because, even though they were aware that he had been in trouble with the law, counsel "did not seek to obtain a copy of his juvenile record under the mistaken belief that specific juvenile offenses could not be referred to on cross-examination (trial counsel did no research on this point)."

[T]rial counsel's mitigation defense, to 'humanize; their client, was inadequately presented and appears to have been cobbled together at the last minute. Trial counsel did not contact some mitigation witnesses until the trial had already begun. Witnesses were put on the stand who had only limited contact with [the defendant] in the several years before the crime. Witnesses were unprepared for the State's cross-examination about … prior offenses and had to admit that they did not know the extent of his criminal record. Witnesses, after having testified (at trial counsel's urging) about how [the defendant] was a good but troubled kid with a supportive family, were forced on cross-examination to validate the State's theme that [he] had deliberately squandered his opportunities in order to become a criminal. In addition, a key defense exhibit contradicted the testimony of the family witnesses about when and why [he] began to have trouble as an adolescent. [Counsel] could draw no support in his closing argument from the mitigation evidence that trial counsel had presented; he admitted that the defense had *no* explanation for why [the defendant] had committed the crimes or why he should be spared, other than to show his family mercy.

Not surprisingly, the prosecutor "hammered home" that the defendant had squandered his opportunities and chose to become a criminal. Without objection, the prosecutor also argued, contrary to the autopsy report and the medical examiner, who could not determine the order of the shots, that it was the last of five shots that was fatal. The prosecutor also argued lack of remorse based in part on the defendant's "fish-eyed" demeanor during trial, which could have been but was not rebutted with the information from the prior psychiatric records that the defendant's "unresponsive demeanor" was caused by "his mental disorders" and the fact that "he would simply withdraw in stressful situations." Finally, the prosecutor "reminded the jury that … [the] main trial defense had been a vicious, wholly unsupported attack on the dead victim's character." Prejudice was established. The trial argument "that the victim was a drug-dealing homosexual, without any evidence to support this assertion, could only have prejudiced the jury against their client." In addition, counsel failed to challenge the allegation that the defendant had planned to kill someone else and "permitted [the state] to argue, without objection, that [the defendant] had inflicted four non-lethal wounds before deciding to fire the fatal shot. Lastly, in the closing argument, trial counsel specifically declined to ask for mercy for their client and implied that their client did not deserve mercy." In addition:

> The psychiatric evidence, if properly investigated and presented, could have totally changed the evidentiary picture. Psychiatric evidence may have provided the jury with an explanation for [the defendant's] actions; trial counsel admitted to the jury that the mitigation evidence which they had presented provided no explanation for the crime.

Finally, prejudice was clear because there was only one aggravating circumstance (armed robbery), "no torture and the shooting was not execution-style," and "the evidence at trial showed that [the defendant] had not planned to kill the victim during the robbery but had shot the victim during a struggle over the gun."

State v. Johnson, 968 S.W.2d 686 (Mo. 1998) (en banc) (tried in May 1995). Counsel ineffective for failing to present the testimony of a forensic psychiatrist that the defendant suffered from "cocaine intoxication delirium" at the time of the offenses. Counsel never spoke directly to psychiatrist (paralegal spoke to him) prior to trial because of work on another capital case. A motion for continuance was denied a week before trial and counsel never renewed until just before penalty phase arguments. Counsel scheduled a few conference calls with psychiatrist during the trial, but missed for a variety of reasons. Finally, counsel had paralegal to call psychiatrist to drive the 120 miles to testify and the psychiatrist responded that he would not come until he spoke personally to the attorney. Without requesting a continuance, the attorney presented mitigation and rested. The jury heard testimony concerning the defendant's background and expert testimony from a pharmacist about the long term effects of cocaine abuse, but the expert was prohibited from testifying concerning mental state at the time of the offense because he had not examined the defendant and was not a forensic expert. Trial counsel testified that there was no strategic reason for not calling the forensic psychiatrist and that the defense strategy was based on the psychiatrist as a cornerstone. Counsel repeatedly requested instruction on the mitigating circumstance concerning diminished capacity to appreciate criminality of to conform conduct to law but was denied because there was no evidence to support the mitigator. In evaluating prejudice, the court declared: "The evaluation of the aggravating and the mitigating evidence offered during the penalty phase is more complicated than a determination of which side proves the most statutory factors beyond a reasonable doubt," because the jury still has the discretion to sentence to life. 968 S.W.2d at 700. "In analyzing the existence of this reasonable probability [under *Strickland*], we must consider the weight of evidence supporting each statutory aggravating and mitigating factor on which the jurors would have been instructed had they been presented with … [the questioned] testimony. We must also consider the impact of … [the questioned] testimony in the context of all the evidence presented." *Id.* Prejudice found in this case regardless of whether the judge would have instructed on the additional statutory mitigator or not because the jury still could have considered the psychiatrist's testimony in mitigation.

Brimmer v. State, 29 S.W.3d 497 (Tenn. Crim. App. 1998) (sentenced in March 1991). Counsel ineffective in failing to adequately prepare and present mental health evidence in sentencing.

> Here, defense counsel did present all of the then available mitigating evidence during the sentencing phase. The concern is not that defense counsel failed to present the available mitigating evidence. It is that he presented expert testimony in such a deficient manner that it justified the trial court's refusal to instruct on the two available mitigating circumstances. Defense counsel did not establish an adequate foundation for either mitigating circumstance to be charged to the jury.

Counsel had concerns about the defendant's mental condition and obtained a psychological evaluation. This expert diagnosed "borderline personality disorder" and noted "the possibilities associated with Abandoned Child Syndrome and Burned Child Syndrome." He found no issue related to competence or sanity, but informed co-counsel six weeks before trial that there was some evidence of mitigation. Nonetheless, counsel did not talk to the expert about mitigation evidence until "an hour or so" before the penalty phase began and then "defense counsel never specifically asked about the statutory mitigating circumstances." During sentencing, the defense expert testified that the defendant "suffered from borderline personality disorder." He listed a numbed of factors that led to the disorder: abandonment by an alcoholic mother; no contact with his father; transfer from one foster home to another; emotional and physical abuse and neglect; and placement in a home for severely emotionally disturbed children." These factors also led to "'Burned' or Abandoned Child Syndrome," which is where a person who has "repeatedly suffered emotional injuries . . withdraw[s] 'into [a] shell.'" After leaving the home, the defendant was essentially "a drifter." He was hospitalized at one time and diagnosed with "factitious disorder, which occurs when an individual feels so helpless and isolated that he seeks to play the role of patient." Following this testimony, the trial court refused to instruct on two statutory mitigating circumstances: (1) the "murder was committed while the defendant was under the influence of extreme mental or emotional disturbance"; and (2) the "capacity of the defendant to appreciate the wrongfulness of [his] conduct or to conform [his] conduct to the requirements of the law was substantially impaired as a result of mental disease or defect or intoxication which was insufficient to establish a defense to the crime but which substantially affected the defendant's judgment." The court reasoned that the defense had not proved a "connection" between the defendant's background and disorder to the offense. If the expert had been asked, he could have provided testimony supporting both statutory mitigating circumstances. Prejudice established because state law required a death sentence if the "statutory aggravating circumstance[s] … outweigh any mitigating circumstance." Here, it was "inevitable" that the jury would find the aggravating circumstance (murder committed during a felony), but the only instruction they received on mitigating circumstances was "brief and general" and "failed to address the defendant's mental illness or mental condition at the time of the offense." Thus, "the errors by the defense made a sentence of death more likely."

1997: *People v. Ruiz*, 686 N.E.2d 574 (Ill. 1997) (tried in 1980). Counsel ineffective in sentencing where, even though counsel couldn't remember whether he investigated or not, it was apparent from the record that he conducted no investigation, gathered no school records, no criminal records, retained no experts, and talked to no family members. Counsel presented only evidence that defendant was 19 and was not the triggerman. If counsel had adequately prepared and presented the mitigation the evidence would have also revealed that the defendant had been physically abused by his father, his father was involved in organized crime and gave the defendant drugs when he was only 11-14 years old, the defendant's older brother was in gangs, the defendant had no male role model, he was involved in drugs and alcohol by age 11 due to the influence of his brother, and he had a learning disability.

People v. Howery, 687 N.E.2d 836 (Ill. 1997) (sentenced in February 1991). Counsel ineffective for failing to prepare and present mitigation evidence because counsel believed it would be futile. There was extensive evidence available from witnesses who would have testified that the defendant made extensive civic contributions and worked for the betterment of the community, he had no criminal history, was under emotional distress, and had an alcohol problem. No evidence was presented even though some witnesses had contacted counsel and volunteered to testify and the sentencing judge had asked for more information regarding the defendant. The court found that the "sentencing proceedings were a mere post-script to the trial" and added nothing to the guilt-or- innocence trial.

Games v. State, 684 N.E.2d 466, *modified on reh'g*, 690 N.E.2d 211 (Ind. 1997) (tried in February 1984). Trial court PCR granted a new sentencing based on ineffective assistance. The state did not appeal on this issue, so there is no discussion of facts on issue.

State v. Hamilton, 699 So. 2d 29 (La. 1997) (tried in January 1992). Counsel ineffective for failing to investigate and present mitigation. Counsel told the jury in opening statements in the trial that the only issue was sentencing. During trial, two court-appointed examiners testified that the defendant suffers from paranoid schizophrenia or psychotic illness but was legally sane. In sentencing counsel made no opening statement, called no witnesses and presented a two paragraph closing argument in which he failed to discuss mitigating circumstances relevant to defendant's mental impairment. If counsel had adequately investigated, the evidence would have revealed prior hospitalization and a diagnosis of "acute schizophrenic disorder" from the Texas Department of Corrections. Additional out-patient records covering almost a year revealed a diagnosis of "chronic undifferentiated schizophrenia" and continued treatment up until a few months of the crime. Counsel did not present this evidence. In addition, one of the court-appointed examiners "recommended a full neurological examination of defendant. This was never done." Finally, counsel presented no family members to "elaborate on defendant's history of mental problems or to make a plea for a life sentence." Counsel's conduct was not excused by strategy because counsel presented an insanity defense. Prejudice established because the evidence of mental illness "had the potential to totally change the evidentiary picture by altering the causal relationship which can exist between mental illness and homicidal behavior. Psychiatric mitigating evidence not only can act in mitigation, but it also can significantly weaken the aggravating factors." Here, the evidence would have established that the "defendant had suffered [for years] from the same visual and auditory hallucinations that he told authorities about upon his arrest.

1996: *Rose v. State*, 675 So. 2d 567 (Fla. 1996) (sentenced in July 1983). Counsel ineffective in resentencing for failing to prepare and present mitigation evidence. Counsel failed to investigate the defendant's background or obtain school, hospital, prison, and other records. Counsel proceeded with an accidental death theory that even he believed was weak because he was inexperienced, had only 79 days to prepare (during which he got married and honeymooned for 10 days) and another attorney told him that was the best defense. If counsel had investigated available evidence would have included expert and lay testimony to prove poverty, emotional abuse and neglect, slow learner and low IQ, organic brain damage, personality disorder, and chronic alcoholism. Evidence would have supported at least two statutory mitigating circumstances when the trial court had found none.

State v. Van Cleave, 674 N.E.2d 1293 (Ind. 1996), *affirmed on reh'g*, 681 N.E.2d 181 (Ind. 1997) (sentenced in May 1983). Counsel ineffective in sentencing for failing to adequately investigate and present evidence of a difficult childhood, including parents' divorce and racial issues, and a nonverbal learning disorder.

Doleman v. State, 921 P.2d 278 (Nev. 1996) (sentenced in May 1990). Counsel ineffective for failing to adequately investigate and present testimony from family members and employees of resident school. Family members would have testified that mother was a prostitute and drug addict, the defendant was physically abused, and was abandoned to a series of foster homes and reform schools beginning at age 4. Although school records contained some of this information, live testimony "could have effectively humanized Doleman in the eyes of the jury." (281). Moreover, the testimony of school teachers at a resident school would have revealed that the defendant flourished in a structured environment and was able to adhere to and adapt to institutional rules. In addition, the testimony would have supported defense theory that defendant was a follower and had been dominated by his accomplice.

Commonwealth v. Smith, 675 A.2d 1221 (Pa. 1996) (sentenced in September 1991). Counsel ineffective in capital sentencing for failing to prepare and present evidence of the defendant's "mental problems." Counsel was told by a witness that the defendant had mental problems but did not pursue this with investigation or presentation. Prejudice found because the jury found mental state as a mitigating factor (although possibly just a verdict form error) anyway.

Goad v. State, 938 S.W.2d 363 (Tenn. 1996) (sentenced in 1984). Counsel ineffective in sentencing where theory of mitigation was mental illness based on Vietnam experience, but counsel presented only lay testimony and failed to prepare or present the available PTSD testimony of an expert who had examined the defendant at the VA hospital several months prior to trial. Counsel knew the defendant had been examined at the VA hospital and intended to present expert evidence based on this. Counsel did not, however, subpoena the doctor they intended to call or make an adequate proffer of his testimony to preserve the issue when a continuance was denied due to his absence during sentencing and did not investigate to determine that it was a different doctor that actually examined the defendant and, thus, counsel never spoke to him or subpoenaed him either.

1995: *Hildwin v. Dugger*, 654 So. 2d 107 (Fla. 1995) (tried in 1987). Trial counsel ineffective in sentencing phase for failing to investigate and present mitigation evidence. Counsel did present "quite limited" lay testimony that the defendant's mother died before he was three, that his father abandoned him on several occasions, that he had a substance abuse problem, and that he was a pleasant child and is a nice person. Nonetheless, the court held:

> Trial counsel's sentencing investigation was woefully inadequate. As a consequence, trial counsel failed to unearth a large amount of mitigating evidence which could have been presented at sentencing. For example, trial counsel was not even aware of [the defendant's] psychiatric hospitalizations and suicide attempts.

Id. at 109. Available evidence included prior psychiatric hospitalizations and suicide attempts; childhood abuse and neglect; history of substance abuse; organic brain damage; and adaptability to prison. This evidence would have supported two statutory mitigating circumstances when trial court had found none.

Spranger v. State, 650 N.E.2d 1117 (Ind. 1995). Counsel ineffective in capital sentencing for a number of reasons. Counsel changed the defense strategy just days before trial and tried the case on the theory that the co-defendant shot the victim while the two were fighting. Up until just a few weeks before trial, counsel "had pursued a strategy of not denying the crime but attempting to maximize mitigators," but this theory was changed within days of appointment of second counsel. The post-conviction court found counsel ineffective in sentencing because "[t]he eleventh hour change in the defense's guilt phase strategy necessitated a different approach to presentation of mitigation and the development of additional factors to compensate for those eliminated by the new defense." Counsel's conduct was deficient because counsel's did not present available "significant evidence of the defendant's psychological make-up including intelligence, intellectual deficits, learning disability, impulsivity, immaturity, family and social history, academic records, the effect of alcohol and the ability to make appropriate decisions in rapidly changing circumstances." Prejudice established because, "[e]ven without this information, the jury deliberated for seven hours before recommending the death penalty" and the trial court gave this recommendation great weight. The Indiana Supreme Court upheld this decision finding that it was not "clearly erroneous."

State v. Brooks, 661 So. 2d 1333 (La. 1995) (tried in October 1985). Counsel ineffective for failing to prepare and present mitigation evidence. Neither counsel had conducted any investigation or even obtained the defendant's records, even though the defendant had signed a release for them. Lead counsel, who was later disbarred was drinking and using cocaine during the trial. Just prior to sentencing, he told co-counsel to take over for sentencing. He had reviewed the previous transcript and met with the defendant for a half an hour before trial only and presented no evidence and gave only very limited argument. Adequate investigation would have revealed available evidence from psychologists, medical records, and family members to show that the defendant had a history of mental problems, including borderline personality disorder; was taking prescription antidepressants at the time of the offense; and was dominated by his homosexual lover/co-defendant.

1994: *State v. Wright*, 653 A.2d 288 (Del. Supr. Ct. 1994) (sentencing in October 1992). Counsel ineffective in sentencing. Counsel presented testimony only from the defendant's mother and girlfriend about general background information. Counsel failed to present evidence that the defendant had been in special education programs and had failed three grades before quitting school in the eighth grade. In addition, counsel did not obtain a mental health evaluation. Although counsel asserted this was due to lack of funding, this reason was not accurate. Although counsel was retained and the family lacked funds to pay for experts, the court approved payments for the experts. The court also rejected as insufficient counsel's statements that "he did not believe a psychiatric examination would have been helpful because there was no indication that [the defendant] was insane or incompetent to stand trial. The fact that a defendant is not mentally defective or incompetent does not mean that the defendant does not have other potentially mitigating conditions and disorders." Expert evaluation would have supported diagnoses of mixed personality disorder and drug dependence, along with other mitigating information.

> Defense counsel knew that [the defendant] was young, poor, of marginal intelligence, and had dropped out of school at an early age. A reasonable investigation of a client with those characteristics should have included a psychiatric evaluation, an investigation of that client's school records, and an investigation into his prior criminal history. Only upon this proper investigation could defense counsel have known what potential mitigating factors were available for [the] defense. …

> [I]t is acceptable for defense counsel to choose not to use certain information which, in one sense, may be considered mitigation; however, before deciding not to use such information, defense counsel must have adequately investigated the mitigating evidence available and made a strategic choice not to use it. In the case at hand, defense counsel did not investigate the evidence in mitigation sufficiently to support a contention that he made a strategic choice not to use it.

Torres-Arboleda v. Dugger, 636 So. 2d 1321 (Fla. 1994) (tried in 1987). Trial counsel ineffective in sentencing phase for failing to adequately investigate. Counsel made no attempt to investigate the defendant's family history and background, work history, or school record in Colombia and never even applied to the court for funds to investigate in Colombia because he did not think the court would approve such a request. Adequate investigation would have revealed evidence of abject poverty as a child; supported his family after his father's death; and his co-defendant was granted immunity in exchange for testimony. Evidence was also available of good prison behavior in California, no police record, and college attendance, which would have supported the defense psychologist's opinion testimony that the defendant was adaptable to prison.

State v. Sanders, 648 So. 2d 1272 (La. 1994) (sentenced in January 1991). Counsel ineffective where: counsel's opening was little more than apology for being unprepared because he didn't expect a first degree conviction and didn't address mitigation; counsel failed to object to inadmissible hearsay which showed that the defendant was guilty of the unadjudicated crime of being a felon in possession of firearms in violation of probation and allowed prosecutor to argue "shocking array" of weapons; counsel did not present any mitigation evidence other than testimony of defendant and wife which caused more damage than good because of grilling cross-examination; and counsel did not make a closing argument at all.

State v. Haight, 649 N.E.2d 294 (Ohio Ct. App. 1994). Counsel ineffective for inadequately advising the defendant prior to his waiver of the right to jury trial and for essentially abandoning their role as adversaries. Counsel urged the defendant "to waive his right to a trial by jury" because "an agreement had been reached between the prosecution and the defense that if [he] waived his right to a trial by jury and minimized objections to certain evidence in the prosecution's case, the prosecution would inform the three-judge panel during the mitigation phase of the trial that the prosecution and the next of kin were not in favor of the death penalty being imposed." Counsel spent minimal time, at most around 40 hours, working on the case prior to trial. Counsel waived opening statement in the trial; stipulated to allow the prosecution to present almost 100 photographs, 40 other exhibits through testimony of people with a lack of personal knowledge, and the defendant's prior conviction of aggravated burglary. Indeed, counsel "objected to none of the state's exhibits." The only defense witness (in support of the Not Guilty By Reason of Insanity plea) was a psychiatrist. He testified that the defendant had been raised in poverty; had been in special education classes because he was "a slow learner with attention deficit disorder; was treated with Ritalin starting at an early age; began abusing substances at approximately age eight, with the substance abuse increasing until his incarceration; was hospitalized at age eleven for taking an overdose of Valium in what may have been a suicide attempt, and suffered from complex partial seizures. Prior prison records showed that the defendant "had been medicated with Thorazine … . to assist with his hyperactivity." He was also medicated at various times with Haldol, Stelazine, Lithium, and Visteril. The records also revealed that the defendant "had been observed making peculiar, unexplained moves and had been found hiding under a table" and that the defendant reported a history of hallucinations. The psychiatrist testified that the defendant denied guilt to him and "attributed the fingerprints and other evidence indicating his responsibility to a conspiracy to frame him," although he acknowledged prior blackouts in which he might have committed offenses. The psychiatrist diagnosed organic personality disorder, alcohol dependency, cannabis dependency, and mixed substance dependency. He testified that the defendant was "unable to appreciate the wrongfulness of the acts he committed or, in [his] mind, may have committed." Two experts testified for the prosecution as rebuttal witnesses. One, a psychiatrist, testified that the defendant had been "dysfunctional practically all his life," and diagnosed mixed substance abuse, antisocial personality disorder, and organic personality disorder based on his view that the defendant "is mentally retarded," but he disagreed with the defense expert about other symptoms and signs of the disorder. The other state expert, a psychologist, found the defendant's "performance I.Q. to be in the low forties and his verbal I.Q. to be in the lower seventies." She diagnosed "the borderline range of intellectual functioning," however, but also testified about his "serious learning disabilities, probably based on minimal brain dysfunction," based on evidence of brain injury from psychological tests administered. Both state experts rejected the insanity defense. Counsel then gave a closing argument "which consumes less than forty lines of transcript." In sentencing, the defense expert testified again that the defendant denied guilt and could be suffering from "posttraumatic stress disorder and from amnesia secondary to repression." He testified that the defendant was not "competent to proceed with the mitigation hearing because of his inability to recall the occurrences surrounding the death of [the victim]." The inability of recall foreclosed the availability of certain potential mitigating factors." The psychologist that had testified for the state during the trial as a rebuttal witness also testified in mitigation, based on additional records and information provided by the defense, "that she felt the mitigating factors outweighed the aggravating circumstances." Counsel's conduct was deficient.

> Because death is unique as a penalty, more is and should be expected of attorneys who undertake the responsibility to represent individuals who face the prospect of being executed. … The work is personally demanding, because counsel in death penalty cases are expected to develop a personal relationship with the accused so that the accused can feel he or she is

represented by someone who cares whether he or she lives or dies.

Even if a higher standard were not expected of counsel here, their performance as counsel was deficient.

Counsel had only "a minimum of consultation with the client"; filed only two pretrial motions, but did not challenge the "constitutionality of the death penalty as a penalty for someone who suffers from the mental deficiencies and defects from which [the defendant] suffers" or that he was arrested and/or seized without benefit of a warrant and without probable cause, both of which had arguable merit; did not retain an investigator or otherwise conduct "significant investigation"; "talked their client into signing a jury waiver form," even though "the vote of a single juror could spare [the defendant] the death penalty." Prejudice found because the court found "it hard to conceive of all twelve jurors agreeing with a death penalty sentence." Counsel's alleged strategy was rejected as reasonable. "Counsel apparently relied upon a theory that if, after all the evidence had been presented, the prosecution told the court that it was not asking for the death penalty and that the widow of the victim was not requesting the death penalty, then the three-judge panel would not order the death penalty." Counsel did not, however, inform the court of this strategy, did not offer the stipulated testimony of the widow in mitigation so it was not in evidence, and "the statement of the prosecution was no more evidence than if given in a closing argument."

> The concealing of the defense agreement with the prosecutor from the trial court at the time that a waiver of jury was being discussed in open court robbed the court of the ability to assess accurately whether the waiver of jury was knowing, intelligent and voluntary, and deprived counsel of the opportunity to be advised whether the agreement had any meaning whatsoever to the three-judge panel.

After this, counsel's "strategy" resulted in counsel "pretty much abandon[ing] their role as adversaries." They did not object to the presence of a judge on the panel "who had held a responsible position in the prosecutor's office while the office was prosecuting" the case. During trial, in addition to waiving opening, counsel "engaged in minimal cross-examination," stipulated the testimony of a state forensic expert "[w]hen the prosecution ran into difficulty in presenting the testimony," and gave a closing that "consumes only one and one-half pages of transcript." The sentencing hearing was "only marginally better" with no opening statement, the defense expert's brief direct examination that covered "less than seven full pages," the state psychologist's direct examination "runs approximately four and one-half pages" and the closing argument "was minimal, and is recorded on less than four full pages of transcript." Prejudice found, especially as to sentencing. The court also found reversible error because the record did not support a finding that the defendant made "a knowing, intelligent and voluntary waiver of his right to a trial by jury."

Commonwealth v. Perry, 644 A.2d 705 (Pa. 1994) (tried in March 1990). Counsel ineffective for completely failing to interview eyewitnesses or defense character witnesses or prepare at all for capital sentence hearing because counsel did not even realize until four days prior to trial that it was a capital case.

Adkins v. State, 911 S.W.2d 334 (Tenn. Crim. App. 1994) (sentenced in June 1985). Counsel ineffective in capital sentencing for failing to adequately investigate and present mitigation evidence. Counsel "spoke extensively" with some family members and friends, as well as a jail official, and learned about the petitioner's alcoholic and abusive father. Counsel sought a mental examination to determine competence and sanity "but did not request a psychiatric background and personal history evaluation which might have been used as mitigating evidence or as a means to gather such evidence." In sentencing, counsel presented no evidence. Counsel was concerned that presentation of mitigation would open the door to rebuttal aggravation evidence. Counsel did not, however, file a motion to limit questionable state proof" and "made no attempt to determine the validity of possible mitigation testimony." "Counsel's decision not to introduce mitigating evidence without taking adequate steps to determine the existence of mitigation testimony was … likely based on inexperience rather than a sound strategic choice." Prejudice established because "the jury heard no evidence whatsoever about the petitioner's social background, psychiatric or psychological condition, or post-incarceration behavior." If counsel had adequately investigated and presented the evidence, the jury would have heard from an inmate counselor and a records custodian that the petitioner had not had any disciplinary problems while in prison between 1979 and 1985. A psychiatrist could also have testified about the effects of the petitioner's father's alcoholism and "the extreme nature of the physical abuse that [the petitioner] apparently encountered as a child without reason." In essence, "the petitioner's violent nature was due to his social background," but his "chances of rehabilitation" were "good."

1993: *Deaton v. Dugger*, 635 So. 2d 4 (Fla. 1993) (direct appeal in 1985). Counsel ineffective in failing to adequately investigate, such that "the defendant was not given the opportunity to knowingly and intelligently make the decision as to whether or not to testify or to call these witnesses" prior to waiving the presentation of mitigation. Because substantial mitigation evidence, including mental health testimony, was available, the trial court's findings were affirmed.

Heiney v. State, 620 So. 2d 171 (Fla. 1993) (tried in 1978). Trial counsel ineffective in sentencing phase. Counsel did not conduct or arrange for an investigation into the defendant's background. Adequate investigation would have revealed evidence of chronic substance abuse and use of drugs and alcohol at time of the offenses; borderline personality disorder; chronic physical and emotional abuse as child; and possible organic brain damage.

Averhart v. State, 614 N.E.2d 924 (Ind. 1993) (tried in 1982). Counsel ineffective for failing to prepare and present mitigation evidence. Counsel conducted no investigation and spoke only with the defendant and his mother and he did not even discuss their testimony with them. In their testimony, he simply asked if they had anything to say and gave no guidance or direction. If counsel had adequately investigated the evidence would have established a disadvantaged background, education, and good character.

Woodward v. State, 635 So. 2d 805 (Miss. 1993) (tried in April 1987). Counsel ineffective for failing to present available mitigation, i.e. counsel allowed expert witness to testify only about test results and did not offer detailed history of mental illness because of mistaken belief that it would open the door to unlimited character evidence. Counsel also told jury in sentencing argument that he could not ask the jury to spare the defendant's life.

1992: **In re Marquez*, 822 P.2d 435 (Cal. 1992) (tried in March 1984). Trial counsel ineffective for failing to investigate and present mitigation evidence. Counsel and his investigator only spent two days in the El Pilon area of Mexico investigating the defendant's birth records and interviewing the defendant's family and doctor. They spent a total of 20 to 25 minutes at the defendant's home in El Pilon and interviewed petitioner's parents at a nearby hotel for only an hour or two. There was no other follow-up contact or investigation. Counsel's purported strategy for the failure to investigate further was because of his fear that an investigation would turn up only aggravating evidence after a police officer and an uncle alleged prior uncharged criminal acts. Available mitigation included testimony from family members who supported the defendant and were willing to travel from Mexico to testify in his behalf that the defendant was a good son and brother who worked hard and had positive, good character traits.

*Phillips v. State, 608 So. 2d 778 (Fla. 1992) (tried in 1983). Trial counsel ineffective in sentencing for failing to prepare and present evidence. Counsel conducted no background investigation and spoke only to the defendant's mother. Adequate investigation would have revealed deficits in adaptive functioning; schizoid personality; borderline intelligence; and impoverished, physically abusive childhood. This evidence would have supported two statutory mitigating circumstances and also provided rebuttal to aggravation evidence because the defendant lacked capacity to calculate or premeditate.

*Bates v. Dugger, 604 So. 2d 457 (Fla. 1992). Counsel ineffective in failing to adequately investigate and present mitigation. Trial court's findings affirmed.

*Mitchell v. State, 595 So. 2d 938 (Fla. 1992) (crimes in 1986 and direct appeal in 1988). Counsel ineffective in capital sentencing because counsel "presented no evidence" at the penalty phase. Counsel thought the defendant would be acquitted and had not prepared for sentencing. While the defendant had been examined by two mental health experts, counsel had not made arrangements for them to testify. The available but unpresented evidence would have supported statutory and non-statutory factors, including a history of child abuse, a history of substance abuse, and brain damage.

*People v. Perez, 592 N.E.2d 984 (Ill. 1992) (tried in June 1983). Counsel ineffective for failing to adequately investigate and present evidence. Counsel reviewed the defendant's prison records and possessed his school records and attempted to interview the defendant through an interpreter several times about his background without success. Although the prison records and school records contained evidence of a low IQ and some other mitigating evidence, along with addresses for the defendant's family in Chicago, counsel did not attempt any further investigation until after conviction when the defendant did provide some background information and signed an affidavit because he did not want to testify. The affidavit was not admitted and no other mitigation was available or offered other than the report and testimony of a prison psychiatrist that was more damaging than mitigating. If counsel had adequately investigated, the evidence would have shown the defendant's mental deficiency, substance abuse, an abusive father, and abandonment.

*State v. Sullivan, 596 So. 2d 177 (La. 1992), *rev'd on other grounds*, 508 U.S. 275 (1993) (tried in May 1982). Counsel ineffective for failing to investigate mitigation because of belief that jury would return a conviction for 2d degree murder only. "[A]ny time a defendant is charged with first degree

murder, defense counsel must prepare for the eventuality that a guilty verdict may be returned." *Id.* at 191. A reasonable investigation would have uncovered evidence of severe abuse as a child, paranoid schizophrenia, and family would have testified.

Cooper v. State, 847 S.W.2d 521 (Tenn. Crim. App. 1992) (tried in February 1985). Counsel ineffective in capital sentencing for failing to interview court-appointed mental health experts prior to trial or to present expert mental health testimony in sentencing. Considering the ABA Standards for Criminal Justice, counsel's conduct was deficient because counsel received reports on competence and sanity issues from two court-appointed examiners but did not talk to them about sentencing issues or provide them with any background information. He talked only with the defendant's sister, who was the only brief mitigation witness called in sentencing. He was aware from her that the defendant had been in special education classes in school, suffered from depression, and had a number of suicide attempts. Counsel spoke to no one else and did not obtain any of the defendant's prior records, including hospital records of prior drug overdose suicide attempts. Just 90 days prior to killing his estranged wife, the defendant's sister had taken him to a mental health facility for an emergency evaluation. He was diagnosed with dysthymic disorder and the doctor recommended in-patient treatment, which the defendant refused. On the day of the crimes, the defendant's sister had obtained an involuntary commitment order. In short, the defendant was suffering from recurrent major depression and expert testimony would have established that he was under the influence of extreme mental and emotional disturbance and acting under extreme duress at the time of the crimes. Counsel was focused only on "mental condition [that] was guilt phase related." Counsel also expressed concern that testimony by the court-appointed examiners in sentencing would have opened the door to evidence of a ten-year old conviction for assaulting a former girl-friend. Despite this, counsel had failed to object to cross-examination of the defendant during trial about a prior violent assault and counsel's last question to the defendant's sister in sentencing elicited information about the defendant's violent temper. "When the record shows a substantial deficiency in investigation, the normal deference afforded trial counsel's strategies is particularly inappropriate." *Id.* at 530. Here, "the trial attorney stated that he wanted to invoke sympathy for the petitioner, but he did not investigate the readily available evidence which would have bolstered his position." *Id.* at 531. If counsel had adequately performed, "he would have obtained substantial information, both expert and lay, which would have explained the violence as a result of his mental problems." Prejudice was clear because counsel did not elicit even much of the information the defendant's sister possesses and the state "strongly argued" in sentencing that there was no credible evidence or documentation that the defendant "suffered from real emotional problems," when "substantial evidence corroborating the petitioner's problems was readily available to be used." *Id.* at 532. The evidence would have established several statutory mitigating circumstances and non-statutory mitigating circumstances.

1991: *State v. Lara*, 581 So. 2d 1288 (Fla. 1991) (tried in 1982). Trial counsel ineffective in sentencing because counsel "virtually ignored the penalty phase of trial" and did not investigate in any detail the defendant's background and did not properly utilize expert witnesses regarding defendant's psychological state. If counsel had adequately investigated, the evidence would have shown: defendant's father was brutally abusive (had to eat dirt because dad wouldn't feed; tied and hung upside down over well; left in cane fields alone for days); began drinking at age 8; heard voice of devil; beat head against wall at school; prior hospitalization for mental illness. This evidence would have supported two statutory mitigating circumstances.

State v. Twenter, 818 S.W.2d 628 (Mo. 1991) (crimes in May 1988). Counsel ineffective in murder case for killing parents for failing to investigate and present mitigation where friends, relatives, and coworkers would have testified that the defendant was a loving mother and had been beaten as a child.

1990: *Burris v. State*, 558 N.E.2d 1067 (Ind. 1990) (sentenced in December 1980). Counsel ineffective in penalty phase for failing to investigate for sentencing; arguing in guilt phase closing that defendant is a "street person" and counsel didn't even like him; and arguing intoxication as a mitigator when the only evidence presented was that defendant had one sip of gin. Available evidence would have shown that defendant was abandoned by parents and raised by a man with a long criminal record which included running a whorehouse and manslaughter. Witnesses would have testified that the defendant worked in the whorehouse as a child and his job was to let whores know when time was up. He wasn't allowed to go to school until all chores were finished. He was declared neglected and became a ward of the county at age 12. He didn't know who he was or even his birthday. Witnesses would have also testified to his good character, good employment record, and adaptability to prison.

State v. Tokman, 564 So. 2d 1339 (Miss. 1990) (sentenced in September 1981). Counsel ineffective for failing to conduct any mitigation investigation. Counsel had intended to present only testimony from the defendant but then presented nothing when the defendant indicated that he would ask for death. Adequate investigate would have revealed good character evidence and evidence of domination by accomplice.

1989: *Stevens v. State*, 552 So. 2d 1082 (Fla. 1989) (sentenced in August 1979). Counsel was ineffective in sentencing phase for failing to adequately investigate and present mitigating evidence. Counsel spoke with the defendant and his aunt but never even asked them about the defendant's background. Counsel also made no attempt to contact other background witnesses in Kentucky, even though the defendant had been in Florida for only one year at the time of his arrest. Adequate investigate would have revealed a history of poverty and neglect; abusive childhood including being shot by father; serious drinking problem which worsened just before offenses; and defendant's responsible adulthood. Counsel also made misrepresentations about defendant's background and criminal history including statements that defendant had been dishonorably discharged from military (actually honorably discharged) and had served time in jail in Kentucky (when he hadn't). Counsel also failed to provide trial court with an answer brief in response to State's brief urging the imposition of the death penalty; and failed to correct errors in State's brief including argument concerning two aggravating factors never presented to jury.

Bassett v. State, 541 So. 2d 596 (Fla. 1989) (sentenced in January 1980). Trial counsel ineffective in sentencing phase for failing to investigate and present evidence that 18 year old defendant was acting under the domination of the 29 year old co-defendant. Available evidence included evidence that: defendant was raised in economically depressed and violent family environment with abusive father figures; defendant was a follower who frequently attempted to gain attention in negative ways; defendant was a "punching bag" for other boys in school and was not accepted in peer groups.

Wilson v. State, 771 P.2d 583 (Nev. 1989) (sentenced in 1979). Counsel for one defendant in joint trial was ineffective in failing to present a wealth of available mitigation evidence and making a number of damaging remarks to the three-judge panel in sentencing. Counsel presented only the defendant's parents to testify. "Although their testimony was relevant, it would naturally appear somewhat biased." Counsel also did not elicit their testimony of the defendant's difficult childhood following their divorce and his father's remarriage to an emotionally unstable woman, his dyslexia, or that he saved his cousin's life as a child. He also did not elicit information that the 18-year-old defendant called both parents two days before the crimes asking for permission to return home, but was rejected by both parents. Counsel believed "it would be a waste of time to present that type of background" evidence. Counsel also did not employ investigators allowed by statute, even after the defendant's father personally offered to hire an investigator. Counsel also rejected the defendant's sister's assistance when she provided the names of approximately 20 people willing to testify in sentencing. Counsel also did not produce "the hundred some-odd letters" he had received attesting that the defendant was "a good kid; he's not violent." Counsel also did not present the father's testimony that he had been present during the defendant's confession, but the detectives turned off the tape when the defendant became emotional and expressed remorse for his crime and sympathy for the victim's family. Counsel also did not present the testimony of a Mormon bishop who visited the defendant in jail and would have testified about the defendant's sorrow, remorse and repentance. Finally, "[i]n both his opening statement and closing argument, [counsel] alternated between comments intended to spare his client from the death penalty, and remarks that were more appropriate for the district attorney," including downplaying the defendant's remorse, distancing himself from the defendant ("I have a job as an attorney. I took an oath to do a job."), and stressing "the horror of the crime and his status as an appointed representative. Reminding the sentencer that the undertaking is not by choice represents a breach of counsel's duty of loyalty to his client."

1988: *State v. Michael, 530 So. 2d 929 (Fla. 1988) (direct appeal in 1983). Counsel was ineffective in sentencing in failing to obtain expert opinions on the applicability of statutory mental mitigating factors, even though counsel was on notice of the defendant's "disturbed condition." The trial court's findings upheld on appeal.

*State ex rel. Busby v. Butler, 538 So. 2d 164 (La. 1988) (tried in February 1984). Counsel ineffective for failing to make an opening statement, not asking that client's life be spared, not contesting elements of the state's case, and failing to prepare and present mitigation despite the fact that counsel was aware that the defendant had been in and out of mental institutions since he was 12. Adequate investigation would have revealed severe mental and emotional problems including anti-social personality disorder. Family would have also testified if asked.

1987: *People v. Bloyd, 729 P.2d 802 (Cal. 1987) (arrested in 1981). Reversal required due to counsel's failure to present any mitigating evidence or argument in penalty phase even though it was available because client did not want to present mitigation evidence.

1986: *People v. Burgener, 714 P.2d 1251 (Cal. 1986) (tried in 1981). Reversal required due to counsel's failure to present any mitigating evidence or argument in penalty phase even though it was available because of client's belief and statement that he deserved to die and did not want to present mitigation evidence.

> ***State v. Johnson**, 494 N.E.2d 1061 (Ohio 1986) (tried in October 1983). Counsel ineffective for failing to prepare and present mitigation evidence and presented only an unsworn statement of the defendant and counsel's argument which damaged defendant by berating jury for guilty verdict. Counsel did not investigate and did not even speak with the defendant about mitigation until after the guilty verdict. Available mitigation evidence included supportive family, no emotional or mental problems, high school graduate who held same job seven years and owned his own home, wife and child, conquered his own drug abuse problem, lost eye at age 10 and spent several months in hospital, mother died of cancer one year prior to trial, and defendant voluntarily turned himself in when he learned of arrest warrant. Counsel was also ineffective for failing to object to submission of non-statutory aggravating circumstance that the defendant had a firearm in his possession which is not a circumstance that is permitted in aggravated murder indictment or as statutory aggravating circumstance in sentencing.

1985: ***People v. Deere**, 710 P.2d 925 (Cal. 1985) (sentenced in October 1982). Trial counsel ineffective for failing to present any mitigating evidence in penalty phase because of his client's belief and statement to the judge that he deserved to die and where counsel told the judge that mitigation evidence was available but would not be presented because of counsel's belief that he had no right to present mitigation where the defendant was asking for a death sentence.

1984: ***Mazzan v. State**, 675 P.2d 409 (Nev. 1984) (crimes in December 1978). Counsel ineffective in capital sentencing for "harshly berat[ing] the jury for returning its guilty verdict during the prior phase," failing to present any evidence in mitigation, and "virtually invit[ing] the jurors to condemn his client to death" in argument that "covers only four pages." In short, the defendant's "cause would have been far better served without benefit of his counsel's representation during the penalty phase."

1983: ***State v. Smith**, 665 P.2d 995 (Ariz. 1983) (tried in March 1982). Counsel ineffective in sentencing for advising the defendant not to discuss the facts of the crimes with the presentence investigator and not to present any mitigation evidence in sentencing. Counsel's gave "bad legal advice" because of concern that any cooperation with the presentence report would be admissible in a new trial. Under state law, however, a defendant's statements made in connection with the preparation of the presentence report are not admissible at any new trial. "We do not believe that advising a client incorrectly about the black letter Rules of Criminal Procedure, especially in a matter of life and death, can be called minimally competent representation."

> ***Holmes v. State**, 429 So. 2d 297 (Fla. 1983) (sentenced in November 1975). Counsel ineffective in sentencing.

> > Instead of arguing that the crime was not heinous, atrocious, or cruel, defense counsel conceded the existence of this questionable aggravating circumstance. Furthermore he made no reference to the reports of the two court-appointed psychiatrists who suggested that [the defendant] may have been in some kind of disturbed psychological state at the time of the murder. Although these reports were delivered after the sentencing hearing was held, counsel made no attempt to reopen the proceeding for the purpose of presenting the reports or testimony of the psychiatrists. As a result, the court imposed sentence without the benefit of available expert opinion pertaining to [the defendant's] mental and emotional condition. …

Defense counsel also avowed that it did not occur to him to request a presentence investigation even though appellant's lack of a criminal record would have rendered the report, at least in part, a favorable one for mitigation.

***Zant v. Hamilton**, 307 S.E.2d 667 (Ga. 1983) (direct appeal in 1979). Counsel ineffective in sentencing for failing to adequately prepare and present mitigation. Trial court's findings affirmed.

1982: ***State v. Carriger**, 645 P.2d 816 (Ariz. 1982) (direct appeal in 1979). Counsel ineffective in sentencing for failing to present or argue mitigation because of counsel's assertion that presentation of mitigation would be an admission of guilt when the defendant was innocent.

> At the punishment or sentencing stage, the duty of the attorney is clearer and easier to evaluate. At a minimum, defendant's attorney had the obligation to challenge the admission of aggravating evidence where reasonably possible and to present available pertinent mitigating evidence.

Here, however, "the attorney's conduct approached that of a neutral observer."

1981: ***Neal v. Arkansas**, 623 S.W.2d 191 (Ark. 1981). Counsel ineffective in sentencing. Evidence of counsel's diminished capacity was presented during trial, but counsel did not pursue mental health issues in sentencing. "Because Appellant's diminished mental capacity did not render him insane does not mean that Appellant has sufficient mental capacity to be able to conform his conduct to the requirements of law." "[T]rial counsel did little to impress the jury with the significance of this evidence as mitigating against a sentence of death." Counsel also failed to introduce available expert testimony "that Appellant could have been influenced by others to commit the criminal acts with which he was charged, but this testimony was never introduced."

1979: ***State v. Myles**, 389 So. 2d 12 (La. 1979) (sentenced in May 1978). Counsel ineffective in sentencing for failing to present any evidence in mitigation and failing to expressly ask the jury to spare the defendant's life. In short, "[t]he advocacy for [the defendant's] life was tepid and virtually nonexistent."

> In his closing argument the defense counsel did little more than acknowledge the existence of an aggravating circumstance, state that the confession may be regarded as a mitigating circumstance, and submit the matter to the jury. He did not ask the jury to spare the defendant's life. He did not remind the jury that [the defendant] is a human being or urge the jurors to be mindful of their awesome responsibility in deliberately choosing whether he should live or die. Nor did he emphasize to the jurors any of their legal obligations designed to prevent the arbitrary or capricious imposition of the death penalty, e. g., the requirement that they base their findings upon a beyond a reasonable doubt certainty; their duty to weigh any aggravating circumstance found against any and all mitigating circumstances; the duty of each individual juror to hold fast to his honest convictions and to vote to prevent a unanimous verdict in the event he is convinced that the death penalty is inappropriate. Moreover, the defense attorney's lack-luster argument followed his submission of the case for his client's life without evidence.

Id. at 30. Evidence was available to establish the defendant's severely deprived childhood resulting from the death of his mother at the hand of his father.

Capital Case

II.   ONE DEFICIENCY

A.   STATE AGGRAVATION EVIDENCE OR ARGUMENT

1.   U.S. Court of Appeals Cases

1999: **Parker v. Bowersox*, 188 F.3d 923 (8th Cir. 1999). Counsel ineffective in sentencing phase for failing to present evidence to rebut the only two aggravating circumstances (both involving murder of a potential witness). The defendant had been arrested for assaulting his girlfriend. He was charged with assault and with probation violation because he was then on probation. His attorney notified him two weeks prior to the murder that she had worked out a plea agreement. He would admit the probation violation and the assault charge would be dismissed. The murder occurred the night before the scheduled probation hearing, but because the state was unaware of the murder, the deal went through. The defendant admitted the probation violation and got 90 days. The assault charge was dismissed that day. The only aggravating circumstances presented by the state was that the victim was killed because she was a witness to the probation violation and the assault. The prosecutor testified about the pending charges and the resolution, but defense counsel failed to present the testimony of the previous defense counsel who would have testified that the defendant knew two weeks before the murder that the victim was no longer a witness against him. Deficient conduct easily found because the previous counsel had called new counsel when she saw publicity saying that the state was alleging that the murder was committed because the victim was a potential witness. State's arguments of no prejudice rejected. No one revealed any damaging information that would have been revealed due to waiver of attorney-client privilege and any possible danger was outweighed by the value of the testimony. Likewise, the testimony would not have been cumulative. While the prosecutor testified to the ultimate outcome, the defense counsel could have testified that the defendant was aware that the victim was no longer a witness against him. Prejudice found because the jury rejected the aggravator that she was killed because a witness in the probation violation where the defendant entered a guilty plea. If the jury had heard defense counsel's testimony that the defendant knew that the assault charge was going to be dropped and that the victim would not be a witness against him, the jury may also have rejected that aggravating circumstance and the defendant would not have been eligible for a death sentence.

1986: **Summit v. Blackburn*, 795 F.2d 1237 (5th Cir. 1986). Trial counsel ineffective for failing to object to or argue the lack of corroborating evidence of the sole aggravating factor (attempted armed robbery) when state law holds that a defendant cannot be convicted based solely on uncorroborated confession and the only evidence of aggravating factor was defendant's confession.

2.   U.S. District Court Cases

2015: **Roybal v. Davis*,   F. Supp. 3d   , 2015 WL 7961358 (S.D. Cal. Dec. 2, 2015). Under AEDPA, the death sentence was vacated due to counsel's failure to object to the prosecution's improper closing arguments in sentencing based on "biblical law," which diminished the jury's sense of responsibility for sentencing under Caldwell v. Mississippi, 472 U.S. 320 (1985). The state court held that the arguments were improper but found no prejudice because the bulk of the state's closing was focused primarily on the brutal circumstances of the crime" and the biblical references were brief and "amounted to little more than commonplaces, to emphasize his point that the jurors should … judge defendant primarily by his acts." The district court rejected this finding as objectively unreasonable because "[t]he circumstances of this case strongly suggest the prosecutor's remarks were anything but harmless." The prosecutor "clearly and improperly advocated that religious authority supported a death verdict" and included "direct biblical quotations demanding a sentence of death." In finding that this argument could not have diminished the jury's responsibility, the state court's holding was objectively unreasonable because it focused only on the remainder of the prosecutor's closing argument rather than reviewing the prejudice in the context of the entire trial. Considering that context, the district court noted that the state's case on guilt was entirely circumstantial and the death verdict was "obviously close and difficult" because: (1) the jury heard substantial mitigation evidence "replete with physical and emotional abuse and neglect, substance abuse that started before age ten, and significant brain dysfunction and damage"; (2) the jury deliberated for portions of six court days, after hearing sentencing evidence for nine days, before reaching a verdict; (3) the jury requested to rehear the testimony of the defendant's "alcoholic and neglectful mother"; (4) the jury requested to rehear the testimony of two mental health experts who testified at length about the defendant's "brain dysfunction, long-standing substance abuse, personality disorders, and the possibility that he suffered from fetal alcohol effects from his mother's alcohol use when pregnant") and (5) the jury twice sent out notes "expressing their inability to reach a verdict." "By any measure, this was an extremely close penalty phase trial where the prosecution sought to impermissibly minimize the jury's sense of personal decision-making in violation of the Eighth Amendment." The trial court's general instructions that arguments of counsel were not evidence and that the jury must base the verdict on the evidence and the law were "insufficient to cure the misconduct or blunt the impact of this highly improper argument." Counsel's conduct in failing to object was deficient and not based on any strategy. If counsel had raised a timely objection to the prosecutor's initial biblical argument, "he could have at the very least curtailed the remainder of the argument and requested a curative instruction neutralizing the condemnable misconduct." Prejudice was clear.

3.   State Cases

2013: *Miller v. State*, 313 P.3d 934 (Okla. Crim. App. 2013). Counsel was ineffective in capital sentencing for failing to object to the prosecutor's improper and misleading arguments that a life sentence would be a "freebie" since the defendant was already serving a federal life sentence. Prejudice was determined in a cumulative error analysis due to multiple other issues.

2010: *Vasquez v. State*, 388 S.C. 447, 698 S.E.2d 561 (2010) (sentenced in October 2003). Counsel was ineffective in capital sentencing for failing to object to the prosecution's arguments referring to the Muslim defendant as a "domestic terrorist" and referencing the events of 9/11/01 during this trial, which occurred on the second anniversary of 9/11. The defendant was charged with murdering several restaurant employees after he had been fired from the restaurant. He wore "traditional Muslim headgear" during the trial. Jurors were questioned in *voir dire* about prejudice against Muslims. The "domestic terrorist" arguments began in the first sentence of the state's opening statement in the trial. Both aggravation and mitigation witnesses, including an imam, testified in sentencing. Then in closing, the state continued the "domestic terrorist" argument and made the 9/11 references. Counsel's conduct was deficient in failing to object because there was no evidentiary support for characterizing the defendant's acts as "terrorism," as his acts did not constitute "'terrorism' by the legal sense of the word." The prosecutor was intentionally using inflammatory references that "improperly evoked religious prejudice and, thus, served only to inflame the passions and prejudice of the jury." Prejudice was also established as the defendant's "Muslim faith was a key theme throughout the trial proceedings which coincided with the second anniversary of September 11th."

2009: *Gill v. State*, 300 S.W.3d 225 (Mo. 2009). Counsel ineffective in capital sentencing for failing to discover child pornography, bestiality content, and sexually explicit instant message conversations on victim's computer that could have been used to limit or rebut the state's evidence of the victim's good character. The victim's computer was in the defendant's car at the time of his arrest and an investigator's report included a list of instant message accounts and a list of the users with whom the accounts exchanged messages. Defense counsel reviewed the report but did not notice anything unusual even though the users the victim was communicating with had user names such as "a_slutty18girl_w38c," "daddoesme15," and "sweet_tasting_slute." Counsel's conduct was deficient as these entries "should have alerted them to the presence of pornography on the computer." Counsel also failed to interview the investigator, who became aware a few days after preparation of the report that there was pornography and sexually explicit instant message conversations referencing sex with underage girls, including a sexually explicit discussion about the victim's daughter, on the computer. Prejudice established in light of the co-defendant's ability to have the state limit the victim impact testimony to avoid opening the door to this rebuttal evidence with "good character" evidence, which resulted in the co-defendant being sentence to life rather than death.

2007: *Malone v. State*, 168 P.3d 185 (Okla. Crim. App. 2007). Counsel was ineffective in failing to object to improper victim impact testimony. Specifically, counsel failed to object when the state trooper victim's widow read from a prepared statement saying that her husband had been shown no mercy when he begged for his life and the defendant should be shown no mercy. She also cited the Bible as giving citizens duties and obligations to enforce the law. She also "beseech[ed]" and "beg[ged]" the jury to impose death. Counsel's conduct was deficient (and the trial court committed plain error) because "[t]his invocation of religious belief and obligation in the context of a capital sentencing recommendation is totally inappropriate." *Id.* at 210. Counsel also failed to object to the improper reading of cards the victim sent to other family members. Counsel's conduct was deficient (and the trial court committed plain error) in failing to object that the victim impact testimony was too long and overly emotional. The testimony covered 36 transcript pages, 28 of which was uninterrupted narrative.

> While this Court declines to adopt specific rules governing the length of such testimony, we note that we have previously held that such statements should not be "lengthy" and that they should contain only a "quick glimpse" of the life that has been extinguished. Victim impact statements were never intended to be–and should not be allowed to become–eulogies, which summarize the life history of the victim and describe all of his or her best qualities.

Id. at 210. Here the victim impact evidence was "'too much'–both too long and too emotional." The court also failed to give an instruction on how the jury was to evaluate and consider the victim impact evidence, within the context of its overall sentencing decision even though a uniform instruction is generally given. Prejudice established even though the defense conceded the three aggravating factors as part of a reasonable strategy. The court emphasized, however, "that although a defendant's crime may make him eligible to receive the death penalty, a jury is never obligated to sentence a defendant to death, and that a single juror has the power to prevent a death sentence in a given case." *Id.* at 214-15. Here, the prejudice was enhanced by the prosecution's reliance on the improper victim impact testimony in the closing argument that asserted a sentence other than death would be "a travesty." *Id.* at 215. The court's "confidence in the jury's sentencing verdict" was also undermined by counsel's failure to prepare and present mitigation evidence from former co-workers, who could provide "powerful, varied, unbiased, and potentially result-altering mitigating evidence." The evidence would have established the defendant had been a good and caring person as a fireman and EMT, had saved a number of lives, and was a good father prior to his descent into drugs culminating in this methamphetamine-related murder. His descent was fueled, in part, by his ex- wife's very public affair with his supervisor in the fire department and then his mother's death. The court did not reverse on this basis, however. It noted that the defendant would be entitled to an evidentiary hearing on this claim, but the issue was mooted because of the victim impact ruling.

2005: *State v. Fudge*, 206 S.W.3d 850 (Ark. 2005). In split decisions for varying reasons, the court affirmed the trial court's ruling finding counsel to be ineffective in capital sentencing for failing to object to evidence of a prior conviction the defendant did not have that was used to support an aggravating circumstance. The aggravating circumstance was that the defendant had been convicted of prior felonies "an element of which was the use of threat or violence to another person or the creation of a substantial risk of death or serious physical injury to another person." The state submitted three exhibits in support of this factor, which were read but not given to the jury. The exhibits included prior convictions of: (1) battery in the first degree; (2) two counts of terroristic threatening; and (3) an additional two counts of terroristic threatening. The issue involved only the battery in the first degree because the lower court found that the defendant had actually only been convicted of "robbery, a less violent offense." Three judges found no deficient conduct (based on the defendant's statements to counsel) and no prejudice (due to the other evidence supporting the aggravating circumstance). Two judges declined to review the issue of deficient conduct because the State had not raised the issue on appeal and affirmed on the prejudice prong on the basis that the lower court's ruling was not clearly erroneous. A third judge voted to affirm without a separate opinion stating the reason. Yet another judge voted to remand for additional fact-finding because the actual exhibit showed a conviction for battery in the first degree, but the state conceded in briefing that it was only a robbery conviction.

2004: *Hall v. Catoe*, 360 S.C. 353, 601 S.E.2d 335 (2004). Counsel was ineffective in capital sentencing for failing to object to the prosecutor's closing argument that asked the jury to compare the defendant's worth and the victims' worth in an emotionally inflammatory fashion unrelated to the circumstances of the crime and traditional victim impact evidence.

2001: *Evans v. State*, 28 P.3d 498 (Nev. 2001). Both trial and appellate counsel were ineffective in capital sentencing for failing to object to (1) the state's improper rebuttal argument in which the prosecutor challenged the jurors to have the "intestinal fortitude" to sentence the defendant to death and (2) improper argument that the jury should consider evidence of the defendant's "other crimes" before deciding death eligibility. The first argument was improper because the United States Supreme Court has said it is improper "to exhort the jury to 'do its job'; that kind of pressure ... has no place in the administration of criminal justice." *United States v. Young,* 470 U.S. 1, 18 (1985). The second argument was improper because, under state law, "other crimes" evidence can only be considered after finding the defendant death-eligible, i.e., after a statutory aggravator is found and each juror has found that the mitigation does not outweigh the aggravation. Prejudice found due to the tremendous risk that character evidence would mislead the jury.

1996: ***Commonwealth v. McNeil***, 679 A.2d 1253 (Pa. 1996) (superseded by statute). Counsel ineffective for failing to object to victim impact testimony that "the victim was gracious, kind and generous and that he had concern for the underdog and the elderly." Prejudice found because there was only one aggravating circumstance and one mitigating circumstance found and "the jury may have improperly relied upon [this] testimony to tilt the balance of evidence in favor of the death penalty."

1995: ****State v. Storey***, 901 S.W.2d 886 (Mo. 1995). Counsel ineffective for failing to object to state's improper closing argument which argued facts outside the record (most brutal slaying in history of county); injected personal opinion (what victim accomplished in life and difficulty of getting out of abusive relationship); personalized to jury(put yourself in victim's place); argued death sentence was justified (because victim's husband would have been justified to kill in self-defense); and argued relative worth of victim and defendant. Prejudice was found due to the four "egregious errors, each compounding the other." *Id.* at 902.

*Commonwealth v. Lacava, 666 A.2d 221 (Pa. 1995). Counsel ineffective for failing to object to prosecutor's sentencing phase closing argument which improperly invited the jury to sentence appellant to die because he was a drug dealer. The focus was shifted from the one aggravating circumstance of killing a police officer to retribution for society's victimization by drug dealers.

Capital Case

B. INSTRUCTIONS

1. U.S. Court of Appeals Cases

2006: ***Lankford v. Arave***, 468 F.3d 578 (9th Cir. 2006). Under pre-AEDPA law, counsel ineffective in capital trial for requesting a jury instruction that eliminated Idaho's requirement that an accomplice's testimony must be corroborated by other evidence in order to convict a defendant. Petitioner and his brother were arrested based on fingerprints in the victim's van and other evidence. The petitioner's brother testified against him in exchange for a life sentence and the state's theory that petitioner was the actual killer depended heavily on his uncorroborated eyewitness testimony about the events. Counsel's conduct was deficient. He had conducted research at a law school library and took the instruction from a collection of federal instructions because there were no model instructions for Idaho at the time. While the instruction was correct under federal law, it was clearly incorrect under Idaho law, which expressly forbids" conviction on the basis of uncorroborated accomplice testimony. "It was a young lawyer's mistake, akin to failing to check the pocket part, but it was a mistake, plainly enough," *id.* at 585, based on "a misunderstanding of the law," *id.* at 584 (quoting *United States v. Span*, 75 F.3d 1383, 1390 (9th Cir.1996)).

2002: ***Carpenter v. Vaughn***, 296 F.3d 138 (3d Cir. 2002). Under pre-AEDPA analysis, counsel was ineffective in capital sentencing for failure to object to trial court's misleading response to jury's question about availability of parole if the defendant received a life sentence. The defendant was convicted for murder and the state presented evidence of only one aggravating circumstance that defendant had a significant history of felony convictions involving the use or threat of violence. Under Pennsylvania law the defendant could be sentenced to death or life imprisonment without parole. The only mechanism for parole under state law would be that the sentence was first commuted by the governor to a term of years. During sentencing deliberations the jury sent out a note asking "can we recommend life imprisonment with a guarantee of no parole." The court responded, "the answer is that simply no absolutely not." The court went on to instruct the jury that its decision would be the sentence and not a recommendation and that the question of parole was irrelevant. Counsel's failure to object or to ask for more clarification was deficient under state law because the court's response that the jury could not give such a sentence was a misstatement of state law since a person serving a life sentence would not be eligible for parole. The court also found prejudice because the jury was aware that the defendant had previously been convicted of murder and assault and had been released on parole. The jury deliberated for less then nine minutes after the court's improper response to its question. The court made it clear that this decision was not based on Simmons or any federal constitution right, but was simply a finding of ineffectiveness of counsel for failing to object based on state law.

1994: ***Starr v. Lockhart***, 23 F.3d 1280 (8th Cir. 1994). Trial counsel ineffective for failing to object to "heinous, atrocious, or cruel" aggravating circumstance because of previous Supreme Court decisions finding this circumstance unconstitutionally vague.

1986: ***Woodard v. Sargent***, 806 F.2d 153 (8th Cir. 1986). Trial counsel ineffective in penalty phase of capital trial for failing to request a jury instruction on lack of a prior history of significant criminal activity when record supported such an instruction. (No evidence either way so its doubtful same conclusion would be reached now in light of *Delo v. Lashley*.)

2.   U.S. District Court Cases

2009: ***Judge v. Beard***, 611 F. Supp. 2d 415 (E.D. Pa. 2009) (sentenced in April 1987). Trial and appellate counsel ineffective for failing to assert *Mills* error based on the trial court's instructions that "erroneously led the jury to believe that it could not return a verdict at the penalty phase of the trial without agreeing unanimously both as to individual mitigating circumstances and the ultimate penalty." Counsel's conduct was deficient, even though the case was tried before the Supreme Court granted cert. or issued the opinion in *Mills v. Maryland,* 486 U.S. 367 (1988). The case was pending on direct appeal at the time of the decision. Although the Supreme Court determined in *Beard v. Banks*, 542 U.S. 406 (2004) that *Mills* announced a new rule that could not be retroactively applied to cases on collateral, Third Circuit cases prior to *Beard* concluded that *Mills* was simply an extension of *Lockett v. Ohio,* 438 U.S. 586 (1978) and *Eddings v. Oklahoma,* 455 U.S. 104 (1982). Thus, the court held that "reasonably competent defense counsel would or should have been aware of the ongoing developments in the state of capital law in April, 1987, and subsequent thereto." There was also no conceivable strategy for failing to object, "as the worst that could have happened would have been its denial."

3.   State Cases

2004: ***Thomas v. State***, 83 P.3d 818 (Nev. 2004). Counsel ineffective in capital sentencing for failing to object to the trial court's erroneous instruction that informed the jury that the Board of Pardons could, under certain circumstances, modify a life without parole sentence. While the Nevada Supreme Court had approved this instruction in 1985, the state statute was amended in 1995. The amendments provide that the Pardons Board cannot commute a prison term of life without possibility of parole to a sentence allowing parole. Because the Defendant's crimes were committed in 1996, there was no circumstance or condition under which the Pardons Board could modify a life without parole sentence. Counsel's conduct was deficient in failing to object to the erroneous instruction to the jury. Prejudice found because the jury could have reasonably believed that a death sentence was necessary to prevent the possibility that the defendant could eventually receive parole if they returned a sentence of life without possibility of parole. Prejudice was exacerbated by the prosecutor's future dangerousness arguments. Trial and appellate counsel's conduct was also deficient in failing to object to the prosecutor's improper arguments in the closing argument of the penalty phase. First, the prosecutor asserted, "This is not a rehabilitation hearing. There is no program that we know of that rehabilitates killers." This argument was based on facts and inferences not supported by the record. Second, the prosecutor argued: "The defendant is deserving of the same sympathy and compassion and mercy that he extended" to the victims. This argument was improper because it "implored [the] jury to make a death penalty determination in the cruel and malevolent manner shown" by the defendant and was calculated to incite passion rather than a reasoned moral response to the evidence. While this argument has been approved by the Nevada Supreme Court when the argument is made in response to defense counsel raising the issue of mercy, defense counsel in this case did not invoke "mercy" or "sympathy" or "compassion" in closing argument. While trial and appellate counsel's conduct was deficient in failing to object to these arguments, the court declined to address prejudice since a new penalty hearing was already required.

2002: ***Deck v. State***, 68 S.W.3d 418 (Mo. 2002). Counsel ineffective in capital sentencing in failing to request two pattern mitigation instructions during the penalty phase. Due to a printer or operator error two paragraphs were excluded from the standard jury instructions. The excluded paragraphs included the instruction that the jury should consider non-statutory mitigation ("any (other) facts or circumstances which you find from the evidence in mitigation of punishment") and that unanimity was not required on mitigation. Counsel's conduct was deficient. "Although counsel's actions should be judged by her overall performance, the right to effective assistance of counsel 'may in a particular case be violated by even an isolated error of counsel if that error is sufficiently egregious and prejudicial.'" *Id.* at (quoting *Murray v. Carrier*, 477 U.S. 478, 496 (1986)). Prejudice established because "the jury is never required to impose the death penalty, no matter how egregious the crime." Here, the defense relied heavily on mitigation and presented substantial evidence concerning the defendant's abuse, neglect, poverty, multiple foster home placements, and eventual return to his mother despite a loving family's desire to adopt him. "The missing paragraphs of the instruction told the jury about the need to balance this mitigating evidence with the aggravating circumstances focused on by the State, and what evidence the jury could consider in deciding mitigation." In addition, counsel did not explain "the concept of mitigation during *voir dire*," which made "the jurors more dependent on the instructions." "Most tellingly, the jurors themselves indicated that they were confused about the very issue of mitigation" in their questions during deliberations." Finally, reversal was required even though the court had reviewed this issue for plain error on direct appeal and affirmed. The failure to find plain error on direct appeal was not a rejection of a prejudice finding under *Strickland*.

> More specifically, while, under Missouri law, plain error can serve as the basis for granting a new trial on direct appeal only if the error was outcome determinative, *Strickland* clearly and explicitly holds that an outcome-determinative test cannot be applied in a post-conviction setting. Therefore, the two tests are not equivalents.

Id. at (citations and footnote omitted).

1994: ***Commonwealth v. DeHart***, 650 A.2d 38 (Pa. 1994). Counsel ineffective in sentencing for failing to object to use of verdict slip that stated: "We the jury have found unanimously one aggravating circumstance which outweighs any mitigating *circumstance*" rather than "mitigating circumstances" after jury was presented with one aggravating circumstance and two separate mitigating circumstances to consider. Prejudice established because the jury could have weighed the sole aggravating circumstance against each mitigating circumstance individually rather than collectively and improper weighing process could have resulted in sentence of death even though mitigating circumstances, when taken as whole, would have outweighed aggravating circumstances. The mitigating circumstances were: (1) the age of the defendant at the time of the crime and (2) any other evidence of mitigation concerning the character and record of the defendant and the circumstances of his offense.

C.   MISCELLANEOUS

1.   U.S. Court of Appeals Cases

2008: **Duncan v. Ornoski*, 528 F.3d 1222 (9th Cir. 2008) (sentenced in March 1986). Under pre-AEDPA standards, counsel ineffective in capital sentencing for failing to investigate and present evidence that the blood samples from the crime scene that did not belong to the victim, who was stabbed to death in a struggle, and also did not belong to the defendant, which supported an inference that the defendant had an accomplice and that the accomplice killed the victim. There was no prejudice during trial, but prejudice was established with respect to the special circumstance findings that required an intentional killing or an intent to kill. The state's serologist was given no blood to compare to samples other than the victim's and could state only what did not match the victim. The defense argued in closing that the state should have tested the defendant's blood, but the prosecutor responded that if inconsistent blood evidence had been present, the defense would have presented this evidence.

> Although it may not be necessary in every instance to consult with or present the testimony of an expert, when the prosecutor's expert witness testifies about pivotal evidence or directly contradicts the defense theory, defense counsel's failure to present expert testimony on that matter may constitute deficient performance.

Here, the defense argued that the defendant was not the killer, but "did not advance any plausible alternative theory or present any specific evidence that he was not the murderer." Counsel had the serology report and understood the significance but opposed the state's motion for blood testing of the defendant and did not consult a serologist or have the defendant's blood tested.

> It is especially important for counsel to seek the advice of an expert when he has no knowledge or expertise about the field. ... Additionally, the central role that the potentially exculpatory blood evidence could have played in [the] defense increased [the] duty to seek the assistance of an expert.

Counsel did not have a valid strategy not to incriminate the defendant further because the defendant admitted presence and his fingerprints and palmprints were present at the scene. In addition, state law allowed "confidential testing by defense experts," which the prosecutor even pointed out to the jury in closing in arguing the unfavorable inferences. Even if defense counsel was concerned about maintaining confidentiality, counsel could have obtained a small sample of the defendant's saliva in a vial or cloth and used that to determine his blood type without notifying the court or the State so there was "nothing to *lose* by testing [the defendant's] blood, but he stood to *gain* crucial evidence by doing so." Prejudice found

> especially considering that the blood evidence was the only physical evidence that had not been linked to [the defendant] at the time of the trial. The evidence that [counsel] failed to present would have been highly significant because it would have suggested that [the defendant] had an accomplice and that the accomplice was likely the actual killer. Under the State's own theory, the small money room likely would have accommodated only one killer. Given the blood found at the crime scene that did not belong to the victim or to [the

defendant] and that was likely shed in the course of the attack, it appears probable that [the defendant] was not in the money room during the murder.

Id. at .

Lawhorn v. Allen, 519 F.3d 1272 (11th Cir. 2008) (trial in April 1989). Counsel was ineffective in capital sentencing under AEDPA for waiving his closing argument in sentencing. Counsel's conduct was deficient and was not based on a reasonable strategy because counsel's decision was based on "a gross misunderstanding" of state law. While counsel believed that by waiving his closing, the state would be prohibited from making a closing, this was incorrect under state law and counsel had failed to adequately research the issue in preparation for trial. "Such preparation includes an understanding of the legal procedures and the legal significance of tactical decisions within these proceedings." The court reviewed *Bell v. Cone* but found this case factually distinguishable. The state court's decision was unreasonable because the court found that counsel had researched the issue and found a state case in support of his "strategy," which was not supported by the evidence. Prejudice was also found because counsel forfeited the opportunity to remind the jury of important mitigation evidence presented during the trial that indicated substantial domination of the defendant by his aunt, who requested that he kill the victim because she was afraid of him. Here, the jury recommended death by a vote of 11-1. Under state law, at least a 10-2 vote was required for a verdict of death, so the defendant needed only to convince two more jurors.

2005: ***Canaan v. McBride***, 395 F.3d 376 (7th Cir. 2005). Counsel was ineffective in sentencing for failing to advise the defendant of his right to testify. The court was not constrained in this case by the AEDPA standards because the state courts failed to address this issue even though it was "squarely presented" in state court. Thus, the issue was not "adjudicated on the merits" for purposes of 28 U.S.C. § 2254(d), just as the Supreme Court's review was "not circumscribed by a state court conclusion with respect to prejudice [in *Wiggins*], as neither of the state courts below reached this prong of the *Strickland* analysis." (quoting *Wiggins v. Smith*, 123 S. Ct. 2527, 2537 (2003)). The court noted, however, that the result would be the same under the AEDPA. The court declined deference to the state court finding that counsel advised the defendant of his right to testify in sentencing because this finding was "flatly contradicted" by counsel's testimony. In determining whether counsel's conduct was deficient, the court "look[ed] first to the ABA Standards for Criminal Justice and the ABA Guidelines for the Appointment and Performance of Defense Counsel in Death Penalty Cases." The court noted that the 2003 ABA Guidelines for death penalty cases provide that "[c]ounsel should consider, *and discuss with the client*, the possible consequences of having the client testify … ." In failing to advise the defendant of his right to testify, "counsel also defaulted on their 'duties to consult with the defendant on important decisions and to keep the defendant informed of important developments in the course of the prosecution." (quoting *Strickland v. Washington*, 466 U.S. 668, 688 (1984)). Although counsel's advice "might go either way, … [t]he point here is that the final choice must be the client's…" The defendant was prejudiced because no mitigating evidence was presented. State law requires that the jury weigh aggravating and mitigating circumstances. "With nothing to put on the mitigating side of the scale, the jury was almost certain to choose a death sentence." If counsel had performed adequately, the defendant's testimony would have revealed "a deeply troubled history" of the kind found to be relevant in *Wiggins*. *Id.* at 386. He suffered physical and emotional abuse and struggled with drugs and alcohol.

2002: **Roche v. Davis*, 291 F.3d 473 (7th Cir. 2002). Counsel ineffective in capital sentencing for the failure to object to the petitioner's shackling and the failure to ensure that the jury could not see the shackles. The state court decision was unreasonable because the court only considered counsel's efforts to reveal the shackles during his testimony but not when seated at the defense table when the record revealed the shackles were visible to the jurors. No prejudice during the trial due to the overwhelming evidence of guilt. Prejudice found in sentencing – even though the "final determination about the appropriate sentence" rested with the trial judge – because there was considerable mitigation available and the jury deliberated for eight hours and was unable to recommend the death penalty.

2000: **Skaggs v. Parker*, 235 F.3d 261 (6th Cir. 2000). Counsel ineffective in capital sentencing for calling appointed expert witness after having observed the "expert's" testimony during the trial. During trial, appointed clinical and forensic psychologist's testimony in support of insanity defense was "rambling, confusing, and, at times, incoherent to the point of being comical." *Id.* at 879. Jury convicted. Counsel did not call expert in sentencing, but jury hung and mistrial was declared. Four months later in new sentencing, defense called "expert," who again testified that defendant was of average intelligence but had insanity defense at time of crimes based on depressive disorder and a paranoid personality disorder. Counsel's decision to call expert in sentencing was deficient because the knew the testimony could be more harmful than helpful, but they did not ask for a different expert because counsel simply did not believe the court would grant the motion. On appeal, defense discovered that court-appointed defense "expert" was not actually a licensed clinical or forensic psychologist, and had no academic degrees or training as a psychologist whatsoever. His diagnosis of the defendant, who was actually mentally retarded, was also incorrect. Prejudice found, not based on lack of competent expert but on lack of competent counsel, because counsel's actions denied defendant his only real mitigation, which was evidence of mental retardation and abnormal neuropsychological tests indicating brain damage. Counsel also presented no other real mitigation evidence.

1995: **Thomas-Bey v. Nuth*, 67 F.3d 296 (4th Cir. 1995) (*affirming Thomas-Bey v. Smith*, 869 F. Supp. 1214 (D. Md. 1994)). Counsel ineffective for consenting to a post-conviction interview of the defendant by a psychiatrist retained by the state for sentencing and the psychiatrist testified that defendant had no mitigating mental impairments and was a serious risk of future dangerousness to society and prison population.

1994: **Foster v. Delo*, 11 F.3d 1451 (8th Cir. 1994). Counsel ineffective in capital sentencing for failing to inform the defendant of his right to testify in sentencing and failing to inform him that his own plea for mercy was necessary. During trial, counsel relied on an alibi defense but the defendant did not testify because of counsel's concerns that his prior convictions would be used to impeach him. During sentencing, counsel believed a plea for mercy would be inconsistent with the alibi, but counsel failed to advise the defendant of his right to testify, which is a fundamental constitutional guarantee that can only be waived by the defendant himself. The defendant's knowledge of his right to testify during trial did not justify a finding that he knew he could testify in sentencing. Likewise, counsel's reason for advising him not to testify during trial was gone as his prior convictions were admissible in sentencing regardless of whether he testified. Prejudice established because "[h]is only chance to escape the death penalty required a plea for his own life, asking the jury for mercy, portraying himself as a human being." *Id.* at 1458.

2.   U.S. District Court Cases

2016: ***McLaughlin v. Steele***,   F. Supp. 3d   , 2016 WL 1106884 (E.D. Mo. Mar. 22, 2016) (tried and sentenced in 2006). Under AEDPA, counsel ineffective in capital sentencing for failing to investigate, retain, and present the testimony of a qualified psychiatrist. Without independent investigation of the expert's credentials, counsel retained a psychiatrist based on the recommendation of his mitigation specialist, who had seen the psychiatrist speak at a capital defense seminar. After examining the defendant for at least seven hours, the psychiatrist opined, among other things, that the defendant was under the influence of extreme mental or emotional distress at the time of the murder and that his capacity to appreciate the criminality of his conduct or to conform his conduct to the requirements of the law were substantially impaired at the time of the murder. While the jury was out deliberating on guilt-or-innocence, the retained psychiatrist disclosed to defense counsel that he had engaged in professional misconduct during medical school that might subject him to serious impeachment. The next day in opening statements in the sentencing phase, defense counsel told the jury that it would hear from the psychiatrist and summarized in detail his expected testimony, but then counsel decided not to call him to testify because of the likely impeachment. Prior to closing arguments in sentencing, counsel informed the trial court that he did so because after the opening he had done an internet search of the retained psychiatrist's name and quickly found information about the expert's prior misconduct. He then met with co-counsel and their bosses in the public defender office and decided not to call the expert because the potential for impeachment might seriously harm the defendant's case. Instead, in sentencing, counsel presented two mental health experts, who had evaluated the defendant at age 9; the testimony of a psychologist (Mark Cunningham, Ph.D.), who had reviewed the defendant's records and interviewed family members but who had not interviewed the defendant; and a mental health expert who treat the defendant months before the murder. Because this issue had not been raised until the appeal of the denial of state post-conviction relief, the issue was procedurally defaulted. Thus, the court first considered whether "cause" and "prejudice," based on post-conviction counsel's ineffectiveness, excused the default under *Martinez*. This standard was met because the court found the underlying claim of ineffective assistance of trial counsel to be "substantial." Likewise, the court found that post- conviction counsel's conduct was deficient in that counsel was aware of the issue simply from reading the trial transcripts, as trial counsel had expressed concern to the trial court that he may have been ineffective. In addition, post-conviction counsel intended to raise the issue, but unintentionally omitted the issue. Thus, there was no tactical decision for the omission. The prejudice analysis was intertwined with the sentencing prejudice discussed below. On the issue of trial counsel's ineffectiveness for failing to present the testimony of a psychiatrist, which had been raised, the state court held that counsel's decision not to present testimony from the retained psychiatrist was reasonable trial strategy. The state court also found no prejudice because the psychiatrist's testimony would have been largely cumulative to Dr. Cunningham's testimony. The District Court held that counsel's "ultimate decision" not to call the retained psychiatrist to testify was reasonable.

> But counsel's representation during trial is not the extent of his constitutional duty to his client. Counsel should never have been in the situation of deciding, at the last minute, between calling an expert with a serious truthfulness problem and calling no expert at all.

It is, of course, common practice for capital defense attorneys to rely on mitigation specialists to *propose* potential experts, whom they may eventually call to testify in mitigation. But in making the decision whether to retain a potential expert, counsel must do something beyond reviewing what the expert says about himself on his resume.

Id. at (citations omitted.) Here, counsel did nothing more than review the resume and, as such, "had not done the groundwork reasonably necessary to make a strategic decision" about whether to hire the expert. This is not a case about failing to engage in expert-shopping. It is instead, a case where counsel failed "to investigate the expert he *did* hire and to reasonably develop the strategy he *had* settled on." Counsel's conduct was deficient in failing to conduct "*some* investigation" of the expert prior to his retainer. He could have easily done an internet search, spoken to other lawyers who had previously hired the expert, or even asked the expert about potential impeachment. "But he did none of these things." This was not strategy, as "[n]othing in the record suggests any strategic rationale, no matter how farfetched, for failing to conduct this investigation." Counsel's conduct was also established as "there was no built-in redundancy to counsel's penalty-phase strategy. . . . None of the other experts that were presented by the defense presented opinions based on current evaluations of the Petitioner or his mental state at the time of the crime." Moreover, the State "emphasized this gap repeatedly in its closing argument." Thus, the jury heard no testimony about two statutory mitigating factors that were present. The deficiency in counsel's conduct was heightened because, "even *after*" counsel became aware of the problem, "counsel went on to make an opening statement wherein he described [the psychiatrist's] anticipated testimony in detail, mentioning him by name six times." Even if there was not constitutional error before, the "decision to plow forward with an unedited opening statement would have magnified the error into one of constitutional proportion." Prejudice was also established. A competent, qualified psychiatrist could have opined that the defendant suffered from borderline personality disorder with narcissistic features and intermittent explosive disorder and that two statutory mitigating factors were present. This "would have comprised the only evidence from a mental-health expert bearing on Petitioner's psychological state at the time of the murder. The defense also would not have broken its promise to the jury about what it would hear as mitigation evidence." This likely would have made a difference in what the jury "obviously found . . . to be a close case," as the jury "rejected three statutory aggravators and ultimately deadlocked" sending the decision to the trial court, which imposed a death sentence.

3.   **State Cases**

2008: ***Green v. State***, 975 So. 2d 1090 (Fla. 2008) (crimes in 1989 and direct appeal in 1994). Counsel ineffective in capital sentencing for failing to investigate a prior New York robbery case used by the state in support of a prior violent felony conviction aggravating factor. Counsel challenged admissibility unsuccessfully on the basis of remoteness and the failure to offer a certified copy of the judgment. Counsel's conduct was deficient because counsel failed to obtain the file from New York even though it was readily available. Counsel's conduct was not excused even though the defendant admitted to the robbery. Prejudice established because the file revealed that the defendant had pled guilty to a simple robbery when he was 18 rather than an "armed robbery" as the state's witnesses testified. The New York court then vacated the robbery conviction and entered a youthful offender finding and sentence. In short, under New York law, a youthful offender adjudication is not a "conviction" and, therefore, does not satisfy the prior violent felony conviction aggravator under Florida's death penalty statute. In addition to the prejudice of this aggravating factor, the defendant was prejudiced by the characterization of the prior as an "armed robbery" rather than a simple robbery because the capital murder was committed during the course of an armed robbery.

2006: ***Commonwealth v. May***, 898 A.2d 559 (Pa. 2006). Trial counsel ineffective in failing to assert as error the trial court's ruling in capital sentencing that the defendant's proffered mitigation evidence was irrelevant and inadmissible. Specifically, the defendant sought to present evidence, under the "catchall" mitigator, that his father physically and sexually abused him and forced him to watch the physical and sexual abuse of his sisters and mother. Prejudice was clear because, with an aggravating circumstance established and no mitigating circumstances, state law required the jury to impose a sentence of death.

2005: ***Salazar v. State***, 126 P.3d 625 (Okla. Crim. App. 2005). Counsel ineffective in jury trial determination of whether the defendant was mentally retarded due to counsel's failure to investigate with respect to the testing conducted by the state's expert. Although the defendant's IQ score fell in the mentally retarded range on his testing, the state's expert testified that, based on two tests, the defendant was malingering.

> [The state's expert] effectively discredited Petitioner's experts by claiming they used improper testing procedures, by using tests not "normed" for a person like Petitioner, and by not properly reporting the results. Had [he] not done the exact same things, there would be no problem.

Counsel did not cross-examine him, however, with respect to the malingering tests he conducted or other investigate to determine the nature of that testing. "One test counsel recognized as the TOMM test and the other he did not recognize but it did not occur to him to inquire into the origins of that test." Counsel did not cross-examine the state's expert concerning the malingering tests for strategy reasons but "it was a strategy based upon counsel's admitted failure to recognize the significance of and determine the origins of [the expert's] testing and raw data."

> We cannot fathom, in a case which boiled down to a battle of experts, why Petitioner's counsel failed to research the tests [the state's expert] performed on Petitioner to confirm the origins of and the scientific validity of those tests before Petitioner's mental retardation hearing. The raw data was provided to counsel prior to the mental retardation jury trial. The evidence was discoverable with due diligence–that is clear from another attorney's discovery of the information in a separate and unrelated proceeding.

If counsel had adequately investigated, he would have discovered that one of the malingering tests given by the state's expert was a non-standardized test the expert "made up and ... it was not administered pursuant to accepted scientific norms." "No reasonable trial strategy would have supported a decision not to utilize this important impeachment evidence." Prejudice found because counsel could have discredited the state's expert in the exact same way that he had discredited Petitioner's experts. Prejudice was also clear because "three juror surveys" revealed that the state's expert testimony was the most credible to the jury. Because the court was "bothered that this State's witness seemingly, intentionally, misled the trial court and the parties about the reliability of his own tests to strengthen the State of Oklahoma's case," the court modified the sentence to life without parole rather than remanding for a new hearing.

Morrisette v. Warden of Sussex I State Prison, 613 S.E.2d 551 (Va. 2005). Counsel ineffective in capital sentencing for failing to object to verdict form that did not provide "expressly for the imposition of a sentence of imprisonment for life and a fine of not more than $100,000 when the jury finds that one or both of the aggravating factors have been proven beyond a reasonable doubt." Counsel's conduct was deficient because the court ruled this language must be included in a case decided two months prior to this trial. Prejudice found because "a jury is likely to be confused when there is a conflict between the sentencing instructions and the verdict form" and the instructions included this language while the verdict form did not.

2004: *In re Davis*, 101 P.3d 1 (Wash. 2004). Counsel was ineffective in sentencing for failing to object to the shackling of the defendant. Counsel objected to the shackling on the first day of jury selection but was overruled. A mistrial was subsequently granted due to the trial court's poor health and an order was entered that continued all prior rulings unless modified by the new judge. Counsel did not object to the shackling during the second trial, which resulted in the defendant's conviction and death sentence. "Assuming that the failure to object was deficient performance," *id.* at 30, there was prejudice during the trial even though one juror saw the leg restraints on two occasions because there was overwhelming evidence of guilt. Prejudice was found during sentencing, however, because "placing the [D]efendant in restraints indicates to the jury that the Defendant is viewed as a 'dangerous' and 'unmanageable' person, in the opinion of the court, who cannot be controlled, even in the presence of courtroom security." *Id.* at 32. Thus, even though no juror saw the shackles in sentencing, the court could not "be assured that any negative inference as to Petitioner's character was cured" from the juror's viewing of the shackles during trial. *Id.* In so finding, the court declined to consider juror testimony of no impact because of "the remoteness in time of the reference hearing from the actual verdict." *Id.* at 24.

2001: *Warner v. State*, 29 P.3d 569 (Okla. Crim. App. 2001). Counsel ineffective in capital case for failing to properly request one day continuance with written motion supported by an affidavit. During sentence on a Friday, defense counsel orally requested a continuance until Monday because the defendant's mother was supposed to testify but could not arrive until Monday due to transportation and health problems. Counsel did not, however, follow the proper procedures for request. The result was that the defense presented no mitigation at all. Court blurs this issue with trial court error by saying that regardless of the defense counsel's failure the court should have granted the one day continuance, especially since the court had allowed the jury to consider whether they wanted to delay instructions. Also not necessary for court to discuss this issue at all since the case was reversed due to trial court errors in jury selection anyway.

1997: *Clark v. State*, 690 So. 2d 1280 (Fla. 1997). Counsel ineffective in sentencing phase because closing argument virtually encouraged giving the death penalty by telling jury, inter alia, that counsel had no choice, it was the worst case he had seen, and that the defendant was from the "underbelly of society."

Miscellaneous

1993: ***Garcia v. State***, 622 So. 2d 1325 (Fla. 1993). Trial Counsel ineffective in sentencing phase for failing to seek admission of statement made by co-defendant to cellmate which corroborated defendant's statement that he was not the triggerman in shootings during robbery.

   People v. Pugh, 623 N.E.2d 255 (Ill. 1993). Counsel ineffective for stipulating to defendant's eligibility for death penalty based on counsel's mistaken belief that defendant was eligible solely because of felony murder conviction. Counsel unaware that to be death eligible defendant must have intended to kill the victim. Defendant continuously maintained that shooting was accidental.

1985: ***People v. Frierson***, 705 P.2d 396 (Cal. 1985). Counsel ineffective for waiting to sentencing phase to present diminished capacity defense when the defendant demanded on the record that it be presented at the special circumstances phase.

NON-CAPITAL SENTENCING ERRORS

I.   U.S. Court of Appeals Cases

2016: *United States v. Abney*, 812 F.3d 1079 (D.C. Cir. 2016). Counsel ineffective in crack cocaine case for failing to seek a continuance of the defendant's sentencing until after the Fair Sentencing Act (FSA), which lowered the mandatory minimum sentences for crack cocaine offenses, became effective. The act was passed by Congress five days before sentencing. Counsel's conduct was deficient in failing to seek a continuance as Presidential approval was virtually assured. In addition, it was "reasonably probable – if not more likely still – that courts would interpret the FSA's new mandatory minimums to apply to defendants sentenced after its effective date." "Any competent criminal defense attorney familiar with federal sentencing principles would have understood that" and the defense bar was universally seeking continuances in sentencing until after the FSA took effect. In short, counsel's conduct was deficient. "The FSA's impending enactment was so important and widely publicized – and the reasonable likelihood of it's retroactive effect so apparent – that objectively reasonable counsel would have known about it and the open retroactivity question, irrespective of what Abney's counsel subjectively knew." Prejudice was also established in that application of the FSA cut the mandatory minimum sentence from ten years to five years.

2013: *Gonzalez v. United States*, 722 F.3d 118 (2nd Cir. 2013). Counsel ineffective in sentencing for failing to advocate on the defendant's behalf at all. The defendant pled guilty in narcotics and bribery case. In essence, the defendant and others were conspiring to use drugs and cash to bribe an allegedly corrupt Immigration and Naturalization (INS) official to provide certain aliens with "green cards" establishing Permanent Resident Alien status. While there were plea negotiations in which the defendant sought a sentencing reduction in exchange for cooperating with evidence against a codefendant, the final agreement simply dismissed some charges in exchange for the plea. The agreement said nothing about sentencing, although the prosecutor noted during the plea hearing that the guidelines range was 262 to 327 months. Following the plea hearing, for the 10 months until sentencing, counsel had no contact with the defendant. Counsel did not attend post-plea debriefing sessions with the government, did not attend the defendant's interview by the probation department, did not communicate with the defendant about the pre-sentence report (PSR), did not file a sentencing memorandum or respond to the government's sentencing memorandum, and did not even point out orally the feasible grounds for a departure from the Guidelines range. While the District Court, who had been the trial and sentencing judge, found deficient conduct, it found no prejudice in that the defendant was sentenced to 210 months, which was on the low end of the Guidelines range. The District Court erred, however, in simply finding "no adverse affect" due to counsel's deficient conduct. This is the wrong standard for prejudice under *Strickland* in that it is "a standard at least as demanding as more-likely-than-not." The District Court also erred in considering the sentence the defendant actually received in determining whether there was prejudice from counsel's complete failure to act as an advocate in sentencing. Indeed, counsel "did little more than simply attend" the sentencing hearing. The arguments for departure from the Guidelines advanced by 2255 counsel, some of which the District Court referred to as potentially "effective," was sufficient to establish prejudice.

2012: *United States v. Rodriguez*, 676 F.3d 183 (C.A.D.C. 2012). Counsel ineffective in non-capital sentencing for distribution of 500 grams or more of cocaine for failing to assert the "safety valve provision," which permits the court to impose a sentence below the statutory minimum if certain conditions are met when the PSR recommended a guidelines range below the statutory mandatory minimum sentence. While counsel initially asserted this provision, counsel did not do so after the defendant belatedly met all five elements required for the safety-valve provision. Prejudice found because the provision is "mandatory" and the guidelines range would have been reduced from 78-97 months to 63-78 months. Even though the actual sentence was 72 months, there is a reasonable probability that he would have received a lower sentence if counsel had performed adequately.

2010: ***United States v. Tucker***, 603 F.3d 260 (4th Cir. 2010). Counsel ineffective in felon in possession of weapon sentencing for failing to object to the use of a prior misdemeanor conviction as a predicate violent felony conviction for purposes of designating him as an armed career criminal in sentencing. To be a felony, the crime must be punishable by imprisonment exceeding one year. Nonetheless, without objection, the prosecution relied on a common law assault and battery conviction in state magistrate court which had jurisdiction to impose punishment not to exceed 30 days in confinement. Counsel's conduct was deficient. It was also prejudicial. The government had relied on four prior convictions and had to prove three that "arose out of a separate and distinct criminal episode" to prove the enhancement. Two of the remaining three convictions were burglaries of storage units with an accomplice on the same night. Because the evidence was insufficient to establish these offenses occurred sequentially on separate occasions rather that simultaneously with the aid of the accomplice, these two burglaries had to be considered as one offense. Thus, without consideration of the improper misdemeanor conviction, the defendant could not be punished as an armed career criminal.

Theus v. United States, 611 F.3d 441 (8th Cir. 2010). Counsel ineffective in failing to object either in the trial court or on appeal to the district court's error in imposing a ten-year mandatory minimum sentence for a quantity of cocaine that required only a five-year minimum sentence. The defendant was charged with five co-defendants to conspiracy to distribute or possess with intent to distribute five kilograms or more of cocaine. The evidence at trial established, and the district court held post-trial, that the defendant was not a member of the conspiracy charged, but he was a member of a different conspiracy with two individuals not charged in the indictment. The presentence investigation report (PSR) attributed only 1.02 kilograms of cocaine to the defendant and explicitly concluded "there is not enough evidence to support that the defendant was involved with 5 kilograms of cocaine." The guidelines range for the defendant (at 1.02 kilograms) was 70-87 months, but the PSR inexplicably concluded that the 10 year mandatory minimum (at 5 kg) had to be applied rather than the 5 year mandatory minimum (at 1.02 kg). The district court rejected the government's argument that the guidelines range should be based on 5 kg, but still imposed the mandatory minimum sentence based on that amount, despite announcing that the court would like to impose a sentence in the 70 - 87 month range. Counsel's conduct was deficient and prejudicial under these circumstances.

United States v. Washington, 619 F.3d 1252 (10th Cir. 2010). Counsel ineffective in drug distribution case failing to understand the impact of "relevant conduct" under the sentencing guidelines and, as a result, failing to adequately advise the defendant of the consequences. The defendant was convicted of distributing 61.98 grams of cocaine base. Another four kilograms was attributed to him by a confidential government informant. During his interview by a probation officer for his presentence report, the defendant admitted an additional 2.5 kilograms attributable to him.

Thus, a total of 6.5 kilograms was considered in sentencing. Counsel's conduct was deficient.

> The instant case is not one of misinformation by counsel; rather, the record reflects that [the defendant] was never *in any way* informed about the applicability or impact of relevant conduct because his counsel did not understand its significance in the sentencing scheme. As a panel of this court has pointed out, "failing to predict a sentence correctly is not the same as failing to understand the mechanics of the sentencing guidelines. ..."

Id. at 1259. Here, "counsel failed to understand the basic structure and mechanics of the sentencing guidelines and was therefore incapable of helping the defendant to make reasonably informed decisions throughout the criminal process." *Id.* at 1260. Prejudice established. The defendant's admissions ultimately resulted in his loss of a downward adjustment in sentence under the 2007 Crack Cocaine Amendments. The two level reduction of these amendments could not be applied if the offense involved 4.5 kilograms or more. The defendant's admissions moved his drug quantity from 4 kilograms to 6.5. If the amendments could be applied, the defendant's sentencing range would be 324-405 months rather than being even above the statutory maximum sentence of 40 years.

2009: ***United States v. Polk***, 577 F.3d 515 (3rd Cir. 2009). Counsel ineffective in sentencing for possession of a weapon by prison inmate for failing to object to the court's characterization of the offense as a "crime of violence" in calculating the Guidelines range of 37-46 months. Without the enhancement, the range would have been 27-33 months.

2007: ***United States v. Otero***, 502 F.3d 331 (3rd Cir. 2007). Counsel ineffective for failing to object to improper sentencing enhancement for a prior crime of violence. The defendant's prior was a simple assault in Pennsylvania, which does not require the "the use of force." Counsel's conduct was deficient just based on the statutory language but there was also available case law that should have alerted counsel to the issue. "[C]ounsel does have a duty to make reasonable investigations of the law," including citing "favorable decisions from other courts of appeals." Prejudice established because, absent the enhancement, the guideline range would have been only 18 to 24 months but the defendant was sentenced to 60 months.

Miller v. Martin, 481 F.3d 468 (7th Cir. 2007). Counsel in securities violations and frauds case deprived the defendant of representation by standing silent during sentencing and prejudice was presumed. The petitioner was convicted following trial *in absentia*. He retained new counsel for sentencing. Due to counsel's belief that the convictions would be reversed due to the *absentia* trial, counsel advised him to remain silent because he was concerned the court would learn that the defendant had been noticed with the trial date. Counsel also remained silent other than to inform the court that they would not participate. The state court applied *Strickland* and found that while counsel's choice to stand mute was "unorthodox" it was a "purely strategic decision" that was not unreasonable and not prejudicial. The court held that the state court ruling was contrary to Supreme Court precedent because the issue should have been addressed under *Cronic*. Even assuming that *Strickland* was the appropriate standard, the court held that the state court findings were unreasonable under AEDPA. Counsel's "advocacy" at sentencing was "non-existent" by his own admission. While counsel explained a "strategy" for the petitioner to remain silent during sentencing, he "never explained his own silence." Even if he had been concerned that the court would question him about his client's knowledge, he could have declined to discuss this issue. Likewise, even if he were concerned that a presentation at sentencing could have somehow prejudiced the appeal, "which is not the reason he gave the sentencing court for his decision," he was wrong and had not conducted any research or consulted the court about his concerns. The state court decision of "strategy" was unreasonable. Prejudice was presumed under *Cronic*. Prejudice was found under *Strickland* in the alternative. Counsel's silence allowed the sentencing court to rely on errors in the petitioner's criminal record, the state's aggravating factors to go unchallenged, and offered no mitigation, even though the petitioner had already paid restitution to some victims. Counsel said nothing even though the court was clearly considering imposing maximum punishments and running some of the sentences consecutively.

2003: ***United States v. Conley***, 349 F.3d 837 (5th Cir. 2003). Trial and appellate counsel were ineffective in conspiracy and mail fraud case for failing to object to the defendant's sentence, which was greater than the maximum set for the crime for which he was convicted. The defendant was initially charged in a 15-count indictment with conspiracy, mail fraud, and money laundering. he was convicted of one count of conspiracy and four counts of mail fraud, but acquitted on the 10 counts of money laundering. The conspiracy indictment and verdict was ambiguous but "a sentence imposed for a conviction on a count charging violations of multiple statutes or provisions of statutes may not exceed the lowest of the potentially applicable maximums." Nonetheless, the judge sentenced the defendant for conspiracy with respect to the money laundering allegation to 121 months. The maximum sentence for conspiracy with respect to mail fraud though was only 60 months. Because the error "was obvious" and greatly increased the defendant's sentence, trial and appellate counsel were ineffective in failing to assert this meritorious issue.

Alaniz v. United States, 351 F.3d 365 (8th Cir. 2003). Trial and appellate counsel were ineffective for failing to object to the trial court's error in adding a second uncharged drug type to the charged drug type in order to trigger a higher quantity-based statutory penalty range. The defendant was convicted of conspiring to possess marijuana with intent to distribute and distributing marijuana. In determining the penalty range for the conspiracy count, however, the trial court applied the penalty range applicable to a person with a prior felony drug conviction involving 1000 kg or more of marijuana for which the sentence was 20 years to life. The court held that the defendant had a total of almost 1150 kg of marijuana by aggregating two different drug types. The judge added the approximately 800 kg of marijuana involved in the conspiracy with 12 ounces of methamphetamine the defendant sold during the conspiracy period, which the court converted to its equivalent of approximately 340 kg. If the court had not added the methamphetamine, the defendant's statutory penalty range would have been 2 years to life as opposed to 20 years to life. Under the sentencing guidelines, there was a difference of 210 to 262 months versus 240 to 262 months. While the Eighth Circuit had not previously addressed the aggravation issue, the court noted that every circuit that has addressed the issue has concluded that a second uncharged drug type cannot be added to the charged drug type in order to trigger a higher statutory penalty range. The court, therefore, found that counsel's conduct was deficient in failing to raise this issue in sentencing or on appeal. The court found prejudice because, under *Glover*, an error increasing a defendant's sentence by as little as six months can be prejudicial within the meaning of *Strickland*. If counsel had objected and the appropriate guideline range had been used, the district court would have been authorized to impose a sentence up to 30 months shorter than the one the defendant actually received. The court remanded to the district court to determine what sentence it would have imposed if it had used the appropriate guideline range and, if the sentence would have been less than the original sentence, the district court was instructed to re-sentence the defendant.

2002: ***Johnson v. United States***, 313 F.3d 815 (2d Cir. 2002). Counsel was ineffective in possession with intent to distribute crack cocaine case because counsel failed to object to the erroneous calculation of the defendant's base offense level in sentencing. The drugs the defendant sold was less that fifty grams but the government alleged that the defendant had agreed to sell more that fifty grams. The pre-sentence report recommended that the base offense level be set based on over fifty grams. Counsel did not object. At sentencing, the court noted that the defendant showed a lot of promise and a lot of capability and sentenced him to the minimum allowed of 151 months. Counsel's conduct was deficient because the notes in the sentencing guidelines provide that, if a sale is completed, the amount delivered should be used to establish the defendant's base level. The defendant was prejudiced because the district courts favorable comments revealed that if the proper offense level of 121 to 151 months had been used it is unlikely that the district court would have sentenced the defendant to the maximum of 151 months.

2000: ***Coss v. Lackawanna County Dist. Atty.***, 204 F.3d 453 (3d Cir. 2000). Counsel ineffective in aggravated assault case for failing to challenge prior conviction used to enhance sentence. Defendant had been convicted of assault in 1986 and completed sentence, but federal court had jurisdiction to review the underlying conviction since the offense was used to enhance the present sentence. Counsel were ineffective during the 1986 representation because counsel met with defendant only twice prior to trial and was given names of witnesses present at the high school party where the assault on a police officer allegedly occurred. Counsel did not subpoena these witnesses and gave the defendant only one hour of notice prior to trial so the defendant had time only to pick up his brother and show up. During trial, police testified to assault and the defendant and his brother denied that there was a party, denied that they were drinking, and denied the assault. Prejudice found even though the other witnesses contradicted the defense testimony at trial that there was no party and no drinking because they were consistent in the major point that the defendant was not guilty of assault and because the defendant and his brother may not have testified or would have testified differently if these witnesses had been available. Court gave the state the option of resentencing on the present conviction or new trial on the prior conviction.

United States v. Franks, 230 F.3d 811 (5th Cir. 2000). Counsel ineffective in sentencing for armed bank robbery and using a firearm in connection with a crime of violence for failing to object to enhancement for an express threat of death where, under sentencing guidelines, offense level enhancement for an express threat of death may not be applied where defendant is also convicted on charge of using firearm in connection with the crime, if the threat of death is related to the possession, use, or discharge of the firearm. Defendant was sentenced to 74 months on armed robbery charge, which was three months more than that actually allowed. Thus, prejudice found because there was a specific, demonstrable increase in sentence.

1999: ***Prou v. United States***, 199 F.3d 37 (1st Cir. 1999). Counsel ineffective in drug case for failing to challenge the enhancement of sentence based on a prior drug conviction because the government's notice was untimely. At the time, the government was required to give notice prior to trial, which included jury selection. Notice was given in this case 19 days after the jury was empanelled. Counsel challenged the enhancement on other grounds but not on timeliness. The issue was not raised on direct appeal. Petitioner raised in a pro se motion under § 2255. Cause and prejudice found for the default because the same counsel represented the defendant on appeal. Counsel's conduct was deficient because there was no plausible reason for failing to challenge enhancement based on untimeliness. Prejudice found because the sentence given exceeded the authority of the court, due to the untimely enhancement which was jurisdictional, and surpassed the proper guideline by almost two years. Sentence vacated and resentencing ordered.

1997: *United States v. Soto*, 132 F.3d 56 (D.C. Cir. 1997). Trial counsel was ineffective in drug case for failing to specifically request a downward departure from the sentencing guidelines based on minimal or minor participation despite fact that facts appear to warrant such a departure.

Patrasso v. Nelson, 121 F.3d 297 (7th Cir. 1997). Counsel ineffective in sentencing of attempted murder and aggravated battery case because counsel by his own admission did absolutely nothing in preparation for or during the sentencing. It was so bad that the defendant personally had to object to prosecutor's misstatement of a prior conviction and defense counsel only argued a couple of sentences because the judge told him he should. Court used *Cronic* standard of complete denial of counsel and presumed prejudice.

1996: *United States v. Breckenridge*, 93 F.3d 132 (4th Cir. 1996). Remanded for evidentiary hearing to determine whether prior offenses were related, but declared that if they are trial counsel was ineffective for failing to raise this issue to prevent defendant from being sentenced as a career criminal. Ordered district court to vacate sentence if prior offenses related.

1994: *United States v. Castro*, 26 F.3d 557 (5th Cir. 1994). Trial counsel ineffective for failing to seek judicial recommendation against deportation even though it could not be said with certainty that the sentencing court would have granted relief.

1993: *Prichard v. Lockhart*, 990 F.2d 352 (8th Cir. 1993). Defendant denied effective assistance of counsel when counsel failed to object to court's use of a prior out of state marijuana conviction for enhancement of sentence in violation of a statute prohibiting the use of such priors.

1992: *Tucker v. Day*, 969 F.2d 155 (5th Cir. 1992). At resentencing hearing, court appointed counsel failed to provide any assistance to defendant at all and the sentencing judge based the resentencing entirely on his familiarity with the original sentencing hearing. Per se violation despite inability to show prejudice.

1991: *United States v. Headley*, 923 F.2d 1079 (3d Cir. 1991). Trial counsel ineffective for failing to argue that defendant was entitled to downward adjustment in base-offense level under Sentencing Guidelines on basis that she was a minimal or minor participant in criminal activity.

1989: *United States v. Ford*, 918 F.2d 1343 (8th Cir. 1989). Counsel ineffective for not objecting to base offense level at sentencing hearing on ground of defendant's acceptance of responsibility which could have lowered the sentence by over three years.

Harrison v. Jones, 880 F.2d 1279 (11th Cir. 1989). Counsel was ineffective during the sentencing phase of defendant's trial by failing to object to the use of one prior conviction resulting from a plea of *nolo contendre* and another prior conviction for an offense that relied on the *nolo contendre* conviction. Under state law, admission of *nolo contendre* conviction was improper. As a result, inmate received enhanced punishment under the state Habitual Felony Offender Act.

1987: *Cook v. Lynaugh*, 821 F.2d 1072 (5th Cir. 1987). Trial counsel ineffective for failing to investigate whether prior conviction used to enhance defendant's sentence was assisted by counsel because facts of case would have alerted reasonably competent attorney to issue. If counsel had investigated and raised issue, there would have been no conviction usable to enhance defendant's sentence.

Burley v. Cabana, 818 F.2d 414 (5th Cir. 1987). Trial counsel ineffective for failing to inform judge of sentencing alternative under state youthful offender act when judge mistakenly believed that life imprisonment was only sentence available and stated his opinion that sentence was too harsh.

II.   U.S. District Court Cases

2015: *Petrillo v. United States*,   F. Supp. 3d   , 2015 WL 7574744 (D. Conn. Nov. 25, 2015). Counsel ineffective in sentencing of bank robbery plea case for failing to object to sentencing as a career offender, even though the plea agreement explicitly left this question open for argument. The government argued the defendant was a career offender because his two prior convictions qualified as "crimes of violence" under the statute. One of those convictions was a 1996 Connecticut conviction for attempted assault on a police officer. Under that statute, the Second Circuit had held that the actual causing of physical injury to an officer qualified as a crime of violence but no determination had been made concerning other crimes under the statute, which included throwing paint or dye or similar substances on an officer. Because it was unclear which subsection the defendant had been convicted of, counsel's failure to challenge the career offender designation was deficient conduct. Prejudice established because the career offender designation raised the sentencing range from 151-188 months to 188-235 months.

Bowers v. McFadden,   F. Supp. 3d , 2015 WL 9294981 (D.S.C. Dec. 21, 2015). Under AEDPA, counsel ineffective in failing to challenge imposition of mandatory life sentence under "two strikes" statute. The defendant was convicted of common law assault with intent to ravish in 1976. In 2004, he was convicted of armed robbery. In sentencing, the state asserted that the "two strikes" statute was applicable. Under the statute, only a "most serious offense" qualifies as a strike. Qualifying offenses, not including common law assault with intent to ravish, are listed in the statute, but some other criminal sexual conduct offenses (CSC) are. The CSC rubric was established by statute in 1977 and includes varying degrees of offense. First and second degree CSC offenses do qualify as a "most serious offense" under the two strikes law. Other CSC offenses do not. Trial counsel's conduct was deficient because counsel failed to conduct any research which would have revealed that common law assault with intent to ravish included only two elements: (1) an assault by a male on a female, (2) with the intent to rape. No aggravated circumstance, such as force or coercion, was required. *State v. Lindsay*, 355 S.C. 15, 583 S.E.2d 740 (2003), which was decided just a year before trial, was all the research counsel would have needed. Nonetheless, in sentencing trial counsel conceded that assault with intent to ravish was "the same basically" as CSC 1st or 2nd and the mandatory life sentence was imposed. Prejudice was clear. Post-conviction counsel failed to raise the issue of trial counsel's ineffectiveness until the appeal to the Court of Appeals from the denial of post-conviction. The state court recognized that assault with intent to ravish may not be a "most serious offense" for purposes of the "two strikes" statute but declined to reach the merits because of the procedural default. After reviewing the elements of the offenses, the federal court also rejected the state's argument that the underlying facts of the assault with intent to ravish qualified as a "most serious offense." The indictment did not contain sufficient information to reach this conclusion and the court held that it would be improper to rely on an affidavit from an arresting officer. South Carolina courts had never relied on this type of information and federal courts would not do so in the analogous circumstance of the Armed Career Criminal Act (ACCA) where only "conclusive judicial record[s]" could be considered. Finally, under *Martinez v. Ryan*, 132 S. Ct. 1309 (2012), the federal court held that it could reach the merits of the trial ineffectiveness claim, despite the state court procedural default, because the claim "is a substantial one that state PCR counsel was ineffective in failing to raise the issue and such failure was obviously prejudicial."

United States v. Jones, F. Supp. 3d , 2015 WL 4256822 (D.S.C. Jul. 14, 2015). Counsel ineffective in sentencing following guilty plea to felon in possession of a firearm under the Armed Career Criminal Act ("ACCA") for failing to object that five of the defendant's prior convictions did not qualify as predicate offenses under ACCA. A Pre-Sentence Report ("PSR") found that four prior convictions of South Carolina burglary third degree, as well as convictions for assault on a correctional officer and taking of hostage by inmate, all qualified as "violent felonies" under ACCA. Thus, the PSR concluded that Jones faced a minimum term of 15 years to life under ACCA, which is applicable if the accused has three or more prior felonies "violent" felonies. Counsel's conduct was deficient in failing to object to the use of the third degree burglary convictions as "violent" felonies because the Supreme Court's holding in *Shepard v. United States*, 544 U.S. 13 (2005), and subsequent Fourth Circuit cases made clear prior to sentencing that these convictions did not qualify as predicate offenses under ACCA. Counsel's conduct was also deficient in failing to object to use of assault on a correctional officer as a predicate offense because the Supreme Court's holding in *Johnson v. United States*, 559 U.S. 133 (2010), and subsequent Fourth Circuit cases made clear prior to sentencing that this offense, which "requires no contact between the victim and the perpetrator," did not qualify as a violent offense under the "force clause" of ACCA. Prejudice established as the maximum sentence was only 10 year's imprisonment rather than the minimum 15 years to life under ACCA.

2014: ***Mann v. United States***, 66 F. Supp. 3d 728 (E.D. Va. 2014). Counsel ineffective in sentencing for conspiracy to distribute oxycodone case for failing to object to the calculation of the drug quantity attributable to the defendant. The drug quantity was calculated, based solely on patient prescription records, at an offense level of 34 with a sentencing range of 151 to 188 months. Counsel's conduct was deficient in failing to move for a reduction based on the quantity of pills consumed for personal use pursuant to valid prescriptions. Prejudice established, as the offense level likely would have been reduced to 32 or a sentencing range of 121 to 151 months.

2013: ***Rogers v. United States***, 949 F. Supp. 2d 879 (N. D. Iowa 2013). Counsel ineffective in sentencing for bank fraud via a check cashing scheme for withdrawing his objection to a two-level sentencing enhancement for use of an "access device" and failing to present mental health evidence in mitigation. Counsel initially objected to both a two-level enhancement and a three-level enhancement, but then argued that a two-level enhancement was proper. At the time of sentencing, the Eighth Circuit had not addressed whether or not this enhancement would apply to a bank fraud scheme that originated solely from the use of fraudulent paper checks, as the scheme in this case did, but the Fifth Circuit and Tenth Circuit had ruled that the term "access device" would not apply to a fraudulent check cashing scheme. Trial counsel asserted that he withdrew the objection because he was aware that three co-defendants had made the objection unsuccessfully and that he made a strategic decision to focus his arguments on more important issues. None of the co-defendants had made this argument in the District Court. One of the co-defendants raised this specific issue, for the first time, on appeal and the prosecution conceded error. The alleged strategy, made without knowledge of the favorable rulings in the other circuits, was not "a decision based on diligent preparation and investigation." Prejudice found. Counsel was also ineffective in failing to present evidence that the defendant had been diagnosed with intermittent explosive disorder in 2007, which causes him to engage in violent outbursts that are "disproportionate to the situation at hand." Prejudice was clear as the District Court varied upward from the guidelines sentence, by a significant amount, based solely on the defendant's history of violent behavior. Counsel alleged strategy not to present this evidence without even obtaining and reviewing the prior mental health records. Thus, "trial counsel did not have a sufficient record upon which to make this allegedly strategic decision."

Carnesi v. United States, 933 F. Supp. 2d 388 (E.D.N.Y. 2013). Counsel ineffective in conspiracy to commit money laundering case for failing to challenge the restitution order due to procedural defects under the Mandatory Victims Restitution Act (MVRA). The defendant was a former attorney and president of business consulting firms. His sentence included restitution to the victims of his fraudulent schemes in the amount of $5,422,000. Counsel's conduct was deficient in failing to object to the court's failure to identify the victims and the actual amount of loss, which was required under the MVRA.

2012: ***Krecht v. United States***, 846 F. Supp. 2d 1268 (S.D. Fla. 2012). Counsel ineffective in sentencing for failing to pursue safety valve relief. The defendant, a pharmacist with no prior criminal record, was sentenced to 210 months, which was at the bottom of guidelines range, for drug conspiracy that involved filling fake prescriptions. The defendant pled guilty pursuant to a plea agreement in which he agreed not to seek a downward departure from the guidelines range. In the PSI, the government calculated a total offense level of 37, which gave a guidelines range (considering the maximum statutory penalty) of 210-240 months. Trial counsel filed objections asserting that the defendant was entitled to a safety valve reduction, which would have reduced the total offense level by two points. The reduction was based on the defendant's first time offender status and cooperation with the government. Counsel withdrew the objection at sentencing. Counsel's conduct was deficient because application of the safety valve reduction is mandatory for narcotics crimes and "is an offense characteristic and not a downward departure." Prejudice found and court ordered resentencing at a total offense level of 35.

2010: ***Carter v. United States***, 731 F.Supp.2d 262 (D. Conn. 2010). Counsel was ineffective in robbery and other offense case sentencing for failing to challenge enhancements under career offender sentencing guidelines and the Armed Career Criminal Act (ACCA). The defendant had five prior convictions in state court: (1) 1985 robbery; (2) 1988 risk of injury to minor; (3) 1992 sale of narcotics; (4) 1992 possession of narcotics; and (5) 1994 sale of narcotics. To apply the career offender sentencing guidelines, the government had to prove two prior felony convictions involving either a "crime of violence" or a "controlled substance offense." The 1985 robbery did not qualify as a "crime of violence" because the government did not count it in the PSR in the criminal history. The 1988 conviction did not qualify as the state statute included conduct outside the guideline range. Specifically, the defendant could be convicted in state court for "psychological harm" only, when the guideline required physical force or harm. The government had not attempted to prove that the defendant's specific facts met the standard. Of the defendant's three drug offenses, only one qualified as a "controlled substance offense" under the guideline because again the state statute was broader and included "any form of delivery which includes barter, exchange or gift" rather than just "selling" and the like. The government had included sufficient information in the PSR to establish that the 1994 conviction qualified, but had not attempted to prove the facts of the other two. To apply ACCA, the government was required to prove three felony convictions that were either a "violent felony" or a "serious drug offense." While the 1985 robbery qualified and the 1994 sale of narcotics qualified, the other three did not for basically the same reasons that the did not qualify under the career offender sentencing guidelines.

Parks v. United States, 687 F. Supp. 2d 564 (W.D.N.C. 2010). Counsel ineffective in sentencing following guilty plea in drug case for failing to understand the importance of the fact that the indictment did not set forth a specific drug amount. Counsel objected to a drug quantity in sentencing but withdrew the objection without explanation. This conduct was deficient as "no matter what evidence the Government might have presented at the sentencing hearing, the fact would remain that such evidence had not been found by a jury beyond a reasonable doubt." There could be no reasonable strategy for withdrawing the objection because, in doing so, "counsel automatically increased Petitioner's sentence 120 months beyond that to which he was otherwise exposed." In short, the defendant was prejudiced because the court sentenced him to 360 months when the maximum statutory sentence based on the indictment was 20 years. Sentence vacated.

2009: ***Baxter v. United States***, 634 F. Supp. 2d 897 (N.D. Ill. 2009). Counsel ineffective in sentencing of criminal tax case for failing to retain and consult with tax expert and stipulating to the tax loss compilation included in the presentence investigation report by the U.S. Probation Office. Counsel's conduct was deficient because counsel failed to independently examine the loss and simply accepted the government's position. While "[d]efense counsel in criminal tax cases need not always retain a tax expert to assist, … [t]he tax-loss question as it relates to [the defendant] was sufficiently complicated so as to require expert assistance." Reasonable counsel would have obtained expert assistance prior to entering a plea bargain in the case, especially in light of the fact that the defendant, a CPA, believed at the time she prepared the questioned tax documents for her clients that the tax returns were lawful. When she discovered they were not, she attempted to correct the error by cooperating with the IRS, which resulted in the clients paying all of the back taxes, etc., and not being criminally charged. The defendant was "duped … into believing it was legal." Prejudice established. The government asserted that the defendant was responsible for more than 5 million tax-loss. The court rejected this, finding that the government had not proven that the defendant was accountable for that loss. The more than $500,000 tax-loss the defense stipulated to was in the amount already rejected by the court but the court was not aware of that fact. Both government and defense experts in 2255 agreed the actual tax-loss related to the defendant's actions was only about $22,000. Sentence vacated.

Robinson v. United States, 638 F. Supp. 2d 764 (E.D. Mich. 2009). Counsel ineffective in drug conspiracy case for failing to file motion for new trial, even though the defendant filed a post-trial motion for judgment of acquittal, and failing to challenge the sufficiency of the evidence of the drug quantity attributable to the defendant. The defendant, who was from Indiana, was charged with his brother and others of growing a large crop of marijuana in between rows of corn on a rural farm. The government's only evidence connecting the defendant to the farm was in January of February, which, of course, was not in the growing season. The only other evidence connected the defendant to the operation was the testimony of the defendant's ex-sister-in-law, whose testimony was not credible in the court's view. Another woman had also testified that the sister-in-law bragged that she lied at trial to get even with the brothers. Despite a month long trial, the jury deliberated less than four hours before convicting all six defendants. During the trial, the defendant had moved a judgment of acquittal under Federal Rule of Criminal Procedure 29, which the Court took under advisement. After trial, counsel filed a brief in support of this motion but did not file a motion for new trial under Rule 33. Counsel's conduct was deficient because, under Rule 29, the court must consider the evidence in the light most favorable to the government. Under Rule 33, the court can consider the credibility of witnesses. Counsel's conduct was not strategy because he was unaware of Rule 33 or its standards. "A decision based on a misunderstanding of the law is not a strategic decision." Here, "counsel's failure to file the motion was not a strategic choice; it was based on ignorance of the law." Prejudice found because "the present case represents one [of] those extraordinary matters in which a motion for a new trial would have been appropriately considered and granted." Likewise, counsel's conduct was deficient in failing to challenge the sufficiency of the evidence of the drug quantity attributable to the defendant. "Again, it does not appear that it could have been a strategic decision to challenge guilt but not the amount for which the [defendant] was to be held accountable." Prejudice established because "the statutory mandatory minimum sentence in this case was tied directly to the amount of drugs charged." A successful challenged could have reduced the sentence exposure by half.

United States v. Frost, 612 F. Supp. 2d 903 (N.D. Ohio 2009). Counsel ineffective following plea to drug distribution for failing to object to a career offender sentence enhancement. The government sought the enhancement based on two prior convictions, one of which was for a 1996 Attempted Drug Trafficking offense under Ohio state law. Defense counsel conceded that this offense met the requirement for consideration but argued for a downward departure because the career offender designation substantially overstated the defendant's criminal record. The Court found a guideline range of 168-210 months, but granted the downward departure to 135 months. Under the guideline, a prior controlled substance offense had to involve distribution or an intent to distribute to qualify as a predicate offense for career offender status. Under the statutory definition, the defendant's state conviction involved only simple possession. There were conflicting unpublished decisions in the circuit at the time of defendant's trial as to whether the determination would be made only on statutory language or whether the court would look through to the facts of the defendant's offense. There was a case pending in the Sixth Circuit addressing this issue. That case (*Montanez*), decided one month after sentencing, held that the determination would be made solely on the statutory definition. Counsel's conduct "was deficient in light of the conflicting Sixth Circuit caselaw and the pending *Montanez* litigation. … Simply put, caselaw in the Sixth Circuit at the time of … sentencing was conflicted and none was controlling" and there was one case squarely in the defendant's favor. Counsel's conduct was not excused by strategy because "there was nothing to lose, regardless how *Montanez* came out." Even if the defendant would not have succeeded in sentencing the record would have been preserved for appeal. Prejudice was thus established.

2008: ***Sasonov v. United States***, 575 F. Supp. 2d 626 (D.N.J. 2008). Counsel in bribery of public official case ineffective for several reasons. First, counsel affirmatively misrepresented the immigration consequences of a guilty plea. Counsel's conduct was deficient because counsel informed the defendant that, as a resident alien with a green card, he would not be subject to deportation following his plea. Prejudice established because "it is likely that Petitioner would have taken his chances at trial because he faced only six to twelve months more than the sentence he received," due to his guilty plea. Second, counsel failed to conduct discovery and, thus, failed to argue petitioner's minor role in the crimes and failed to establish that the value of the benefit received from the bribe was less than $10,000, which would have prevented a four-point enhancement of the offense level. Prejudice established because the court might otherwise have reduced the sentence to less than one year or at least allowed the defendant "to negotiate a more favorable plea agreement with the Government."

Potts v. United States, 566 F. Supp. 2d 525 (N.D. Tex. 2008). Counsel ineffective in child pornography case for failing to object to the district court's impermissible double counting of sentencing enhancements. Specifically, the court enhanced his offense level by two for possession of ten or more items of pornography under one section and by four for possession of more than three hundred images under another section. Guideline amendments effective in November 2004 should have alerted counsel to this problem. Prejudice established. "When the Court imposes a sentence at the bottom of an erroneously calculated sentencing range, that sentence demonstrates prejudice even when the imposed sentence also falls within the accurately calculated guideline range." Here, the court had imposed a sentencing "at the very bottom of the erroneously calculated range."

2007: ***Abraham v. United States***, 477 F. Supp. 2d 1232 (S.D. Fla. 2007). Counsel ineffective in sentencing on conspiracy, kidnapping a postal employee, and other charges for failure to assert that a prior escape conviction was a non-qualifying offense under the affirmative defense provision of the federal three strikes law. Counsel argued that the escape was not a serious violent felony, under 28 U.S.C. § 3559©, because it did not involve weapons or violence. The court found it was and that the court was, therefore, required to impose the mandatory life sentence. Counsel's conduct was deficient in failing to make the additional argument, under § 3599(c)(3)(A), of an affirmative defense, which allowed the defendant the opportunity to establish that the conviction was a non-qualifying conviction by showing by clear and convincing evidence that no weapons or guns were used or threatened to be used, and no injuries or death occurred in the commission of his escape. Counsel's conduct was deficient because counsel "failed to simply turn the page of the statute and continue the analysis under § 3599." Prejudice found because the sentencing record made clear that the court believed it had no alternative other than to impose a mandatory life sentence. Likewise, although the court found the movant's trial testimony to be less than truthful, it had accepted as true the proffer on this issue, which was proven by clear and convincing evidence with the supporting state court record in this proceeding. Sentence vacated and resentencing ordered.

Veal v. United States, 486 F. Supp. 2d 564 (N.D. W. Va. 2007). Counsel ineffective in sentencing following guilty plea to drug offenses for failing to review the presentence report prior to sentencing. He also did not prepare objections or even review the objections submitted by the defendant *pro se*.

2006: ***United States v. Gentry***, 429 F. Supp. 2d 806 (W.D. La. 2006). Counsel ineffective following guilty plea to bank robbery for failing to file any objections to the loss calculation in the presentence report (PSR). The loss calculation included not only the robbery proceeds but worker's compensation indemnity and medical expenses associated with a police officer's wounds incurred during pursuit of the defendant and co-defendants when he was shot by a co-defendant and certain home repairs that were necessary due to a co-defendant's actions in breaking into a home during the pursuit. Counsel's conduct was deficient because his notes indicated that he was aware of a potential issue, but he failed to object and could not articulate any strategy or rationale for the failure. Although there was no existing case authority supporting the objection at the time, the plain language of the guidelines excluded consideration of the worker's compensation payments and medical payments associated with the injuries to the police officer. Moreover, the fact that the sentencing court rejected the objections raised by co-defendants did not excuse the omission. "[R]easonably effective criminal defense counsel do not shy from confrontation and must zealously present their client's arguments." *Id. at* . Prejudice found because the defendant received a sentence that was 16 months over the guidelines maximum. If counsel had objected and appealed, as two co-defendants did, the Fifth Circuit would have held that the worker's compensation indemnity benefits and medical expenses associated with the officer's wounds were not properly included in the computation. New sentencing ordered.

2005: *United States v. Holland*, 380 F. Supp. 2d 1264 (N.D. Ala. 2005). Counsel ineffective in sentencing and on appeal in bank robbery case where the defendant and his co-defendant separately plead guilty and received an order of restitution payment under the Victim and Witness Protection Act (VWPA) as part of their sentence. The amount of restitution was not addressed by a jury and was based solely on hearsay in the probation officer's report. Counsel's conduct was deficient in failing to object because "[e]verybody in the courtroom knew that this court considered the federal restitution scheme constitutionally flawed" and the court ended up imposing "an ambiguous and impossible restitution obligation" on the defendant that was also inconsistent with the terms placed on the co-defendant, even though restitution was to be "paid jointly and severally." To make matters worse, the BOP informed the defendant on numerous occasions while he was in confinement that his restitution had been paid and then 9 years later informed him that he owed the full amount without even accounting for the $999 paid by the co-defendant. While the government challenged jurisdiction, the court held that the defendant "is not barred from access to this court to right a wrong that is partly the fault of this court." The court found that the disparity in treatment between the defendant and his co-defendant "is a travesty that calls for correction," especially since the VWPA "limited the collectibility of restitution to 'five years from the date of the sentence.'" The court thus allowed equitable tolling in these 2255 proceedings. Although this case preceded *Booker*, *Ring*, *Apprendi*, and *Jones* (decided a month after this sentencing), the court found that counsel was ineffective in failing to test the constitutionality of the restitution award procedure since restitution was not charged in the indictment, not found by a jury, and the amount ordered to be paid was based on a standard other than proof by the Government beyond a reasonable doubt. Counsel "was required to recognize the potential constitutional claim" that came later in court rulings because "[t]he law has long recognized that defense counsel, both trial and appellate, is required to raise potential constitutional claims in view of developing law." Here, "this court was on record as doubting the constitutionality of the VWPA, and counsel in other cases had raised the issue in this court."

2004: *Banyard v. Duncan*, 342 F. Supp. 2d 865 (C.D. Cal. 2004). Trial counsel was ineffective in failing to investigate and object to the use of a prior assault conviction as a "serious felony" in sentencing the defendant to 25 years to life under the "Three Strikes Law" following a conviction for possession of a controlled substance. Appellate counsel was also ineffective for failing to assert trial counsel's ineffectiveness. Counsel's conduct was deficient because counsel advised the defendant to admit to two prior serious felony convictions even though the defendant's second strike was not a "serious felony," as required by state law. The second strike was for an assault conviction, "which arose from a domestic dispute and is the only arguably violent behavior in [the defendant's] record." The court found that the record on this offense revealed that, although the defendant was initially charged with a serious felony, he ultimately plead no contest only to assault, which was not a serious felony, and was sentenced to time served and probation. The court found that the state court erred in its judgment in finding that the defendant entered a no contest plea to a serious felony when the plea transcript revealed otherwise. Even if the alleged victim of the assault was believed, the "minor nature" of the defendant's "assault conviction show that it was outside the heartland of what would normally constitute assault." In addition, the "sentence of probation is not consistent with a desire to punish [the] crime as a serious felony." Without any real analysis, the court held, under the AEDPA, that the state court's decision was an unreasonable application of clearly established federal law."

Garcia v. United States, 301 F. Supp. 2d 1275 (D.N.M. 2004). Counsel ineffective in sentencing for drug conspiracy for failing to object to the pre-sentence report, which improperly calculated points based on the erroneous finding that the instant offense occurred while the defendant was a probation for a DWI offense. The defendant was investigated by the DEA for a conspiracy to sell marijuana. Several co-defendants were arrested long before him with the last being on February 19, 1999. Following these arrests, but prior to his own arrest, the defendant was arrested and plead guilty to DWI. He was ordered to serve one-year of probation on March 8, 1999. He was indicted for these offenses in June 1999. He plead guilty pursuant to a plea agreement in which the state would recommend the lowest penalty available under the sentencing guidelines as long as the defendant participated in a "debriefing." Counsel at sentencing had not represented the defendant in the plea negotiations. During sentencing, although the petitioner asserted he was entitled to "the safety valve" downward departure, counsel asserted that he was ineligible without having a full understanding of the underlying facts. Because of the confusion, the court continued sentencing to allow counsel to investigate. Nonetheless, because the court had stated earlier that he would not give the "safety valve," counsel convinced the defendant that he was ineligible and the case proceeded to sentencing the same day. Because the court's statement of ineligibility was based on counsel's inaccurate summation of the facts, the court rejected the government's argument that the court had already exercised its discretion to reject the "safety valve." The court found a guideline range of 168 to 210 months and sentenced the defendant to 168 months. Counsel's conduct was deficient in convincing the court and the defendant that the safety valve did not apply because there was no evidence and the government never argued that the defendant was involved in any distribution after February 1999. Indeed, the pre-sentence report attributed no drug activity to the defendant after July 1998. Thus, any activity alleged preceded the defendant's DWI arrest. Thus, the defendant was entitled to application of the "safety valve," so long as the defendant participated in the agreed upon debriefing, which counsel never scheduled because of the erroneous belief that the defendant was not eligible for the "safety valve." Counsel's failure to object to the pre-sentence report was deficient because it "was based entirely on his lack of understanding of the underlying facts." Prejudice was found because absent counsel's error, under the appropriate sentencing guidelines and the government's agreement to recommend the low end, the defendant would have been given a sentence 53 months shorter than the one he actually received. The court ordered the government to afford the defendant an opportunity to comply with the debriefing requirements prior to resentencing.

Blount v. United States, 330 F. Supp. 2d 493 (E.D. Pa. 2004). Counsel was ineffective in sentencing on drug charges for failing to request a downward departure for time the defendant had already served in state and county custody on unrelated charges.

2003: ***Somerville v. Conway***, 281 F. Supp. 2d 515 (E.D.N.Y. 2003). Counsel was ineffective in sentencing in a burglary and assault case where he failed to challenge the legality of the defendant's sentence as a second violent felony offender. The defendant's status as a second violent offender was predicated on a previous conviction in Maryland for robbery with a deadly weapon. Under New York law, however, the Maryland offense could not be used as a first offense if the Maryland offense was not equivalent to any New York felony. In state court, the prosecution conceded that if trial counsel had raised the issue that the Maryland prior offense should not have been used. Nonetheless, the state court affirmed the sentence stating that the defendant received meaningful assistance from his trial counsel. In federal court, the state no longer conceded that the crime for which the defendant was convicted in Maryland could not be used as a predicate for the second violent felony offender status. The court found that the prior conviction from Maryland could not be used under New York law because the defendant in Maryland could be convicted of armed robbery if he used force without an intent to take property and afterwards stole from the victim. While this would be felony robbery in Maryland, it would not in New York under the statute. The court found prejudice because if counsel had raised this issue, the defendant would not have been adjudicated a second violent felony offender and would have been eligible for, although not guaranteed, a sentence far below what he was given. Even if the trial court had sentenced the defendant to the exact same sentence without finding a second violent felony offender status, the defendant was nonetheless prejudiced by being adjudicated as a second violent offender because "[i]n the event he commits another felony at some point in the future, he will be exposed to a mandatory maximum prison term of life in prison." The court also found deficient conduct because "[e]ffective counsel must be familiar with the sentencing law governing a defendant's case." Here, the New York law was manifested both in statute and in case law, and the Maryland law was clear from its case law.

> Given that the only legal question open at petitioner's sentencing was his status as a second violent felony offender and that resolution of the court's adjudication of that status might have significant effects on both petitioner's current sentence and on any sentence he might receive if he were to commit a subsequent felony, defense counsel was obliged to be familiar with this law.

The court also found that counsel's failure could not have been motivated by any strategic rationale. Analyzing the case under the AEDPA, the court found that the state court's decision was an unreasonable application of clearly established Supreme Court precedent as set forth in *Strickland*.

2000: *Hill v. United States*, 118 F. Supp. 2d 910 (E.D. Wis. 2000). Counsel ineffective in sentencing in possession of firearm case because counsel failed to contest a sentence enhancement for armed career criminal status when circumstantial evidence revealed that defendant had received discharge certificates from previous felonies that contained no firearm restrictions. Prejudice found because without the improper enhancement the maximum sentence would have been 10 years rather than 15 years.

1995: *Cabello v. United States*, 884 F. Supp. 298 (N.D. Ind. 1995). Trial counsel ineffective in sentencing for not objecting to the erroneous application of the career offender provision of the Sentencing Guidelines to petitioner's case which resulted in sentence that was too long. Habeas relief granted despite procedural default of not raising on appeal because trial counsel was also appellate counsel.

1994: *Wogan v. United States*, 846 F. Supp. 135 (D. Me. 1994). Trial counsel ineffective for failing to advise defendant that government could appeal downward departure of sentence and obtain resentencing based on 750 grams of heroin. Based on counsel's advice that he would get the same sentence as his co-conspirator, defendant waived his right to testify to challenge the finding of 750 grams even though defendant's testimony could have reduced it to only 50 grams.

1991: ***Butler v. Sumner***, 783 F. Supp. 519 (D. Nev. 1991). Trial counsel ineffective during sentencing for complete failure to present argument or evidence in mitigation. Defendant had been convicted of numerous sexual assaults on a young boy and was sentenced to maximum possible (21 consecutive life sentences) even though state didn't ask for maximum.

1988: ***Gardiner v. United States***, 679 F. Supp. 1143 (D. Me. 1988). Trial counsel ineffective in cocaine distribution case where counsel completely failed to speak on the defendant's behalf in sentencing or present any evidence in mitigation. Prejudice presumed.

1987: ***Janvier v. United States***, 659 F. Supp. 827 (N.D.N.Y. 1987). Counsel ineffective for failing to petition the sentencing court to issue a recommendation against deportation because counsel was ignorant of the deportation consequence.

III.   State Cases

2016: ***Richardson v. Belleque***, P.3d , 2016 WL 1579300 (Ore. Ct. App. Apr. 20, 2016). Counsel ineffective in manslaughter for failing in sentencing to consult with or call an expert witness to testify in rebuttal to the state's expert who diagnosed antisocial personality disorder. While counsel cross-examined the state's expert, in an attempt to show that the diagnosis was improper, the jury found that the defendant qualified as a dangerous offender. Counsel's conduct was deficient in failing to investigate to determine what evidence was available. Prejudice was also established. A defense expert with all the available evidence would have opined that the defendant's juvenile records reflected an adjustment disorder due to his mother's abuse rather than a conduct disorder. If the jury had accepted this and not found the dangerous offender status, the defendant would not have been facing a maximum punishment of 30 years and the sentence imposed could have been much reduced.

2015: ***Davis v. Commissioner of Correction***, 126 A.3d 538 (Conn. 2015). Counsel in manslaughter plea case ineffective in sentencing for agreeing with the prosecutor's recommendation of the maximum sentence allowed under the plea agreement even though the agreement contained a provision entitling defense counsel to advocate for a lesser sentence. The Court of Appeals denied relief by applying the prejudice test of *Strickland*. This was error, however, because there was a complete breakdown in the adversarial process, such that prejudice was presumed under *Cronic*. The defendant had been charged with murder. Believing that the defendant only had a few prior drug convictions, counsel negotiated the plea agreement to manslaughter with a range of 20-25 years punishment and each party free to argue within that range. Counsel learned from the presentence investigation report (PSI) recommending a 25-year sentence that the defendant had a much more extensive criminal record than he thought. Because counsel believed, based on this information, that 25 years was appropriate, counsel did not argue on the defendant's behalf in sentencing and, instead, affirmatively agreed with the prosecutor's recommendation of the maximum 25-year sentence. It was this affirmative agreement that distinguished this case from *Bell v. Cone*, 535 U.S. 685 (2002), and revealed the lack of any strategic decision. "The petitioner's sentence was already capped at twenty-five years pursuant to the plea agreement and, thus, assenting to that sentence did nothing to advance the petitioner's interests." Under *Cronic*, prejudice was presumed.

Lampkin v. State, 470 S.W.3d 876 (Tex. Ct. App. 2015). Counsel ineffective in sentencing of driving while intoxicated case for failing to adequately investigate and present mental health mitigation evidence. Counsels' conduct was deficient because counsel had concerns about the defendant's mental health prior to trial, including concern about whether the defendant was competent to stand trial. While counsel's conduct was not deficient in failing to challenge trial competence, counsel was deficient in failing to discovery and present the same evidence as mitigating evidence in sentencing. Counsel did not retain an investigator or speak to family members or even inquire of any jail personnel about whether the defendant was receiving or had received mental health treatment, despite counsels' concerns. This conduct was not reasonable and was not based on strategy. Prejudice was established because the jury was precluded from considering the defendant's mental health history in mitigation where the defendant was facing up to 99 years' confinement for the non-violent offense of driving while intoxicated where no one was injured. The information that the defendant "had been homeless and impoverished, had diminished capacity, suffered from psychotic delusions and major depressive disorders, had attempted suicide, and had a long history of drug abuse" might well have influenced the jury, especially in "cast[ing] a better light" on the defendant's prior convictions.

Director of the Dept. of Corrections v. Kozich, 779 S.E.2d 555 (Va. 2015). Counsel was ineffective in grand larceny and obtaining money by false pretenses case for failing to timely file a motion to reconsider the sentence, which had been invited by the sentencing judge. In sentencing, counsel submitted some evidence and argued that the defendant's crimes, including his extensive prior criminal record, were a direct result of his drug addictions and, therefore, he should be sentenced to a drug treatment program rather than prison. The judge sentenced the defendant to three consecutive two year terms but added that she would grant leave to file a motion to reconsider if counsel wanted to submit a specific recommendation for an appropriate treatment program. The final sentencing order was issued two and a half weeks later with no mention of leave to file a motion for reconsideration. Counsel did not file the motion to reconsider until more than three months later when the defendant had already been moved to a state penitentiary, which, under state law, deprived the sentencing court of jurisdiction. While there is no right to the effective assistance of counsel to file a post-trial motion to reconsider the sentence after a final sentencing order has been issued, there was a right in this case during the time between the sentencing and issuance of the written order two and a half weeks later. While there may not be a "categorical" right, there was in this case because the motion to reconsider was "expressly invited" by the court during sentencing. Thus, the defendant "remained in a critical stage of his criminal prosecution even after the conclusion of the sentencing hearing." Counsel's conduct was deficient in failing to pursue the matter by filing a motion to reconsider and by simultaneously making efforts to ensure that the motion would be heard before entry of the final sentencing order. This could have been accomplished by delayed entry of the sentencing order or by including language in the sentencing order that leave to file a motion to reconsider had been granted and that the matter would be held in abeyance until further order of the court. Prejudice was also established even though it likely would not have been with a different post-conviction judge and just an objective record. Here, however, the post-conviction court was the sentencing court and the judge relied on her own recollections that she had intended to order drug treatment, if the motion to reconsider had been filed, and that she would have reduced the defendant's sentences and ordered his confinement in a drug treatment program, as she did in issuing the writ. While the court questioned "the propriety of a habeas court's reliance on subjective intentions of this kind for purposes of establishing prejudice," the court "accept[ed] the judge at her word" in this case because the state failed to object in post-conviction or to raise the issue on appeal.

Hillman v. Johnson, S.E.2d , 2015 WL 3936971 (Ga. Jun. 29, 2015). Counsel in armed robbery, felon in possession of a firearm, and other offenses case was ineffective in failing to challenge the trial court's imposition of the maximum punishment on the felon in possession charge under the mistaken belief that it was required under state law. While a state statute requires courts to sentence defendants with a prior felony conviction to the maximum time authorized for any subsequent conviction, this statute does not apply to the offense of felon in possession for which the statute authorized a range of one to five years imprisonment. While there was no error and no ineffective assistance of counsel in the trial court's mandatory imposition of the maximum punishments on the other offenses, counsel's conduct was deficient in failing to challenge trial court's belief that the maximum sentence was also required for the felon in possession charge. Prejudice was established given the trial court's denial of the state's request for consecutive sentences and the trial court's criticism of the mandatory sentences during the sentencing hearing. Thus, there was a reasonable probability that the trial court would have sentenced the defendant to less than the maximum five years on the felon in possession conviction.

Lopez v. State, 462 S.W.3d 180 (Tex. Ct. App. 2015). Retained counsel was ineffective in aggravated robbery plea sentencing for failing to adequately investigate and present mitigation evidence. The defendant pled guilty without a recommendation of sentence and was sentenced to 30 years' confinement. Counsel's conduct was deficient. The state had offered a plea deal that included a 15-year sentence, which was the minimum available sentence. On the day of trial, counsel moved to withdraw asserting an inability to communicate with the defendant and that his legal fees had not been paid. Counsel also sought a continuance indicating a need for additional time to prepare and that the defendant had retained new counsel. The record contains no rulings on these motions before the defendant pleaded guilty without a sentencing recommendation. The court ordered a presentence investigation and scheduled sentencing for two months later. Counsel sent the client a letter telling him to collect "good guy" letters to give to the person who interviewed him for the presentence investigation and to meet with counsel 15 minutes before sentencing, along with the people who "support you." Counsel also asked that he "get current" on his fee payments. The defendant gave the investigator one letter from his girlfriend proclaiming his innocence. On the day of sentencing, counsel did not appear and it was rescheduled. Again, counsel did not appear. Without counsel, the defendant asked to withdraw his plea, his bond was revoked, and he was taken into custody to await sentencing. When the next hearing was held with counsel finally in attendance, the plea was not changed and the defendant was sentenced. No mitigation evidence was presented and counsel gave a two sentence statement informing the court that the defendant wanted the minimum sentence and believed that he could be a good "role model." After sentencing, counsel withdrew and new counsel was appointed and filed a motion for new trial alleging ineffective assistance for failure to investigate and present evidence of the defendant's mental health issues. Counsel's conduct was deficient. Trial counsel admitted that he was unaware of this information as counsel conducted no investigation. Instead, as indicated by his letter, counsel tasked the defendant with preparing his own mitigation "without any assistance of counsel." Likewise, counsel received the pre-sentence report 10 days prior to sentencing. The report indicated the defendant "had a below-normal IQ and mental-health diagnoses," but still counsel did not investigate. Even if the defendant had rounded up witnesses, counsel could not have adequately interviewed and prepared these witnesses in 15 minutes just prior to sentencing. Prejudice was also established. New sentencing ordered.

2014: ***People v. Speight***, 174 Cal. Rptr. 3d 454 (Cal. Ct. App. 2014). Counsel was ineffective in murder case sentencing for failing to raise an Eighth Amendment objection to the length of the defendant's 69 years to life sentence because the murder was committed when the defendant was 17-years-old. Under state law, the sentencing court was required to consider mitigating circumstances for juvenile offender's and would have been required to consider the lack of any prior criminal history and remorse if counsel had objected on the basis of cruel and unusual punishment.

State v. Mills, 137 So. 3d 8 (La. 2014). Counsel ineffective in sentencing for possession of cocaine and possession of drug paraphernalia in that counsel encouraged the court to take into consideration improper factors, which likely enhanced the sentence. In essence, the defendant was facing a 10-year maximum sentence. The defendant desired to avoid the Orleans Parish Prison and be housed in a facility operated by the Department of Corrections. Based on counsel's argument to this effect, the trial court imposed the maximum punishment for the expressed purpose of effectuating the defendant's desires. Prejudice established because without this improper consideration, there is a reasonable probability that the defendant would have received a sentence that was significantly less harsh.

Ex parte Howard, 425 S.W.3d 323 (Tex. Crim. App. 2014). Counsel was ineffective in sentencing for failing to obtain mental-health experts and present testimony in sentencing concerning the defendant's voluntary intoxication-induced psychosis during his attack of his adult son at the son's home. While the trial court initially found ineffectiveness related to the guilt-phase, the appellate court found no prejudice and remanded for a determination of whether there was prejudice in sentencing. The record supported the trial court's finding of prejudice in sentencing.

In re Williams, 101 A.3d 151 (Vt. 2014). Counsel ineffective in sentencing following guilty plea to four counts of involuntary manslaughter for failure to provide more than just perfunctory assistance. The defendant, who was 19 years old, was initially charged with four counts of murder and arson after he intentionally set fire to paper in his waste basket in his bedroom. The fire spread and killed occupants of the apartment above, a woman and her three grandchildren. The parties entered a plea agreement amending the original charges to four counts of involuntary manslaughter with a maximum sentence of 50-60 years, but the agreement allowed the defense to argue for a sentence from 20-60 years. A pre-sentence investigation (PSI) report by a probation officer recommended a sentence of 40-60 years, which was imposed by the trial court after hearing a number of "bereaved" victims' family members express their desire for maximum punishment. The PSI had identified mitigation evidence, including petitioner's lack of a criminal record, no drug or alcohol abuse, graduation from high school as a foster child, remorse, efforts to get people out of the burning building, and descriptions by people who knew him as a good, hard-working person. Counsel's conduct was deficient and not based on strategy because counsel called no witnesses and did not even submit a sentencing memorandum in advance of the hearing "to present his arguments for the minimum sentence in a less hostile and emotionally-charged atmosphere. Instead, he offered a few remarks about petitioner's childhood, essentially repeating the information in the PSI." Attorney experts testified for both the defense and state. The defense attorney expert testified that counsel's conduct was a "gross deviation from the standard of care." Remanded for new sentencing before a different trial judge.

2013: ***In re Brown***, 160 Cal. Rptr. 3d 822 (Cal. Ct. App. 2013). Counsel was ineffective in vandalism case for failing to investigate the legitimacy of a prior strike before advising the defendant in sentencing to admit to the prior strike based on a juvenile adjudication for robbery. The defendant's juvenile adjudication was actually for grand theft, which did not qualify as strike. As a result of the defendant's admission of the strike, however, the trial court doubled the defendant's prison term (four years rather than two). While the state conceded that the defendant's prior did not qualify as a strike and that the defendant was prejudiced by the error, the state, nonetheless, argued that counsel was not ineffective because his investigation was objectively reasonable under prevailing professional norms. This was rejected in light of *Lewis v. Lane*, 832 F.2d 1446, 1458 (7th Cir.1987) (defense counsel's conduct in stipulating in capital sentencing to four prior felony convictions based solely on information contained in an 'FBI rap sheet'" and the defendant's statements that it was accurate was "shockingly inferior"). Here, counsel allegedly relied on a packet of materials from the state, but neither counsel nor the state had identified the documents or produced them. "Defense counsel has a duty to investigate allegations made against his client, not merely assume their truth." It was not reasonable for counsel "to assume that his non-lawyer client had the specialized knowledge to understand the specific crime or section of the Penal Code in his prior adjudication as a juvenile. Nor was it reasonable for trial counsel to assume his client could accurately recall exactly what offense or section of the Penal Code was sustained against him in a proceeding that occurred five years prior, when the defendant was only 16–years old." In addition, even if trial counsel had a reasonable basis for believing the defendant could accurately recall the specific offense underlying his prior adjudication, "counsel had a duty to ensure that the prosecution possessed evidence that would be sufficient to prove the prior strike allegation."

Johnson v. State, 120 So.3d 629 (Fla. Dist. Ct. App. 2013). Counsel ineffective murder case for failing to object to the trial court's consideration of improper factors in sentencing in violation of due process. The trial court imposed the maximum sentence of life in prison with a minimum mandatory of twenty-five years based on the discharge of a firearm. He explained that he was doing so because the defendant, who denied guilt, had shown no remorse. "A sentencing judge may not consider a defendant's claims of innocence or refusal to admit guilt when imposing sentence." Counsel's conduct was deficient and prejudicial. "We are unable to envision any tactical reason that trial counsel would have had for standing mute when the trial judge imposed the harshest sentence available based on improper sentencing factors."

State v. Phillips, 130 So.3d 146 (La. Ct App. 2013). Counsel in sentencing for armed robbery was ineffective in failing to object to the state's failure to meet its burden of proof at the habitual offender hearing. Specifically, the state relied on an out-of-state guilty plea but did not prove, as required under state law, that the defendant was represented by counsel during the plea.

State v. Guillory, 120 So. 3d 764 (La. Ct. App. 2013). Counsel ineffective in possession of firearm by felon case for failing to move to quash the additional habitual offender bill under the fourth offender section. The defendant had three prior offenses but under state law the prior offense used as a basis for the convicted felon offense (possession with intent to distribute) could not also be used as a predicate for the fourth habitual offender status. The state conceded deficient conduct. Prejudice was also clear as the defendant was sentenced to mandatory life under the fourth offender section when he was only a third offender with a sentencing range of 13-40 years rather than a mandatory life sentence.

Levering v. State, 315 P.3d 392 (Okla. Crim. App. 2013). Trial counsel ineffective in sentencing of kidnapping and second-degree rape by instrumentation case for failing to object to admission of prior transactional felony convictions for enhancement purposes. During trial, propensity evidence of sexual assault was admitted, which had resulted in three convictions. These prior convictions were committed on the same day against a single victim. During sentencing these three prior convictions, as well as four additional prior convictions were admitted to enhance the sentence. "In the absence of any instruction explaining the jury's consideration of propensity evidence in relation to transactional prior convictions, we find that counsel's deficient performance, combined with the improper admission of all six prior sexual assault convictions, prejudiced Appellant and warrants remand for resentencing." The jury should have been instructed that the sexual propensity evidence admitted during trial should be considered as a single conviction in sentencing and that the state was required to prove the prior convictions beyond a reasonable doubt.

State v. Phuong, 299 P.3d 37 (Wash. Ct. App. 2013). Counsel ineffective in unlawful imprisonment and attempted rape case for failing to argue that these offenses covered the same criminal conduct for purposes of sentencing. The Cambodian defendant and his wife were involved in divorce proceedings when he grabbed her outside his home, drug her inside, and attempted to rape her. During the incident, their children ran to a neighbor's home for help. The defendant stopped only when the neighbor knocked on the door. Under state sentencing laws, these offenses should not have been considered separately because the defendant's "objective criminal purpose" for each offense was the same, i.e., his purpose for both offenses was rape.

2012: ***Radmer v. State***, 362 S.W.3d 52 (Mo. Ct. App. 2012). Counsel ineffective in statutory sodomy sentencing for failing to present evidence of the defendant's impaired intellectual functioning. The defendant was initially charged with statutory rape in 2003. Counsel retained a psychologist to evaluate whether the defendant had the intellectual capacity to knowingly waive his *Miranda* rights before confessing. The expert diagnosed adjustment disorder with depressed mood and borderline intellectual functioning. The motion to suppress the statements on this basis was denied, but the charges were dismissed anyway because the alleged victim refused to testify. Four years later, when these charges arose, the same counsel again represented the defendant. In sentencing before the jury, the state presented evidence and argument that the defendant was a pedophile. In response, counsel presented two family members and an employer to testify, but presented no evidence about the defendant's "impaired intellectual functioning." Before the judge, prior to imposition of the 90 year sentences, counsel argued that the pre-sentence report might be inaccurate because is was based on the defendant's statements. He noted specifically that the defendant had a low IQ and may not have understood the questions asked of him. He also asked the judge to "remember" that the defendant has "mental deficits." If counsel had called the psychologist that examined the defendant previously, he would have testified that the defendant has an IQ of 75 and "his functioning age was ten years old." He also testified that "a person with borderline intellectual functioning who behaves sexually inappropriately is different than a pedophile" and would be amenable to treatment.

Ex parte Rogers, 369 S.W.3d 858 (Tex. Crim. App. 2012). Counsel ineffective in jury sentencing for attempted aggravated sexual assault for failing to object to prior bad acts evidence from a former rape victim. The crime charged was essentially hiding in the women's room of an office building and assaulting a woman who came in by pinning her against the wall with a knife to her throat. She escaped and the defendant was arrested. He possessed at the time nylon rope, duct tape, handcuffs, and gloves. During sentencing, the jury heard evidence of a similar crime in a different office building bathroom 11 years before. The jury also heard, however, about an extraneous offense where a woman was raped in her apartment after a man broke through the glass of her window from a balcony. Her arms, legs, and eyes were duct taped and she was raped twice and cleaned afterwards with bleach or a similar cleaning substance. The defendant was matched to this crime because of his possession of duct tape when arrested in the current case. He was put in a lineup and identified by the prior rape victim. At the time of sentencing in this case, the defendant had been indicted for the prior rape, but those charges were dismissed after this trial because the actual rapist in the prior case was identified through "CODIS (the FBI's combined DNA index system)." That person pled guilty to the prior rape. Counsel's conduct was ineffective in failing to investigate and object to this prior rape evidence in sentencing. If counsel had investigated, counsel would have learned that the defendant was wearing an electronic monitor from a deferred adjudication at the time of the prior rape. The monitoring records established that the defendant was at home five miles away at the time of the apartment rape. Prejudice established as this "emotional testimony" was "likely particularly inflammatory to the jury."

2011: *People v. Roberts*, 125 Cal. Rptr. 3d 810 (Cal. Ct. App. 2011). Counsel ineffective in assault on officer case for failing to object to statements from the underlying proceeding in the sentencing findings under the Three Strikes Law. The State enhanced punishment with a prior felony conviction for second degree assault from Washington. Counsel's conduct was deficient in failing to object to transcripts of unsworn statements following the defendant's Washington plea. Enhancement required showing that the defendant had personally inflicted "great bodily harm." When the record does not disclose the underlying facts, the court presumes the prior conviction was for the least offense punishable under the foreign law. The elements of the prior conviction in Washington were most similar to California crimes that did not qualify as a strike under the Three Strike Law. The documents showing conviction in Washington did not provide details of the underlying offense and alleged only infliction of "substantial bodily harm." Washington law distinguishes between "substantial bodily harm" and "great bodily harm." Even if they were the same, Washington law allows conviction for second degree assault without the defendant having personally inflicted the harm. The state thus had to rely on the specific underlying facts. Under state law, the court could consider "otherwise admissible evidence from the entire record of the conviction." Here, the defendant's statements, his counsel's statements, and the alleged victim's statements made after the court had accepted the *Alford* plea and were not "part of the record of conviction" and should not have been relied on to establish a strike. While counsel objected to this evidence as hearsay, he did not object of this basis even though state law had been established on this point almost three years prior to trial. As counsel *did* object, albeit on the wrong ground, there clearly was no tactical reason for failing to make this meritorious objection to the same evidence. Prejudice established as the evidence supporting the enhancement was clearly insufficient without this evidence.

Velazquez v. State, 70 So. 3d 741 (Fla. Dist. Ct. App. 2011). Counsel ineffective in sentencing for violation of probation for failing to object when the trial court announced a sentence greater than that intended. Counsel's conduct was deficient because the trial court said several times on the record that the court intended to impose a six-year sentence with credit for three years time served. In announcing three consecutive five-year sentences with credit for three years on each, the court actually required the defendant to serve six years instead of the intended three, but counsel failed to recognize this fact and object. The prejudice was "patent."

Fegley v. Commonwealth, 337 S.W.3d 657 (Ky. Ct. App. 2011). Counsel ineffective in sentencing on six counts of complicity to first-degree robbery for failing to object to erroneous testimony of a probation and parole officer that the maximum possible sentence was 120 years when it was actually "only 70 years." The state asked for a sentence "in the middle" of 60 years, which was returned by the jury.

State v. Hess, 23 A.3d 373 (N.J. 2011). Counsel ineffective in sentencing for aggravated manslaughter in failing to present relevant Battered Women's Syndrome mitigation evidence and failing to object to lengthy, unduly prejudicial victim-impact video. The defendant shot and killed her husband, a police officer, in his bed. "The only issue was, why." After going to work, the defendant called authorities. In her initial statement she described a history of domestic violence, psychological belittlement, and victimization leading up to the killing. She said that she had only intended to scare the victim by pointing a gun at his head, as he had done to her the evening before, but it went off accidentally. The day after her arrest, the defendant was admitted to a psychiatric hospital for four days due to suicidal ideations. A defense investigator interviewed nine friends and co-workers who corroborated the victim's physical abuse, threats, and attempts to dominate and control the defendant. Nonetheless, a year and a half later, counsel allowed the prosecutor and a detective to take a second statement from the defendant in counsel's absence. In this one, with prompting and leading by the prosecutor, the defendant "downplayed the level of abuse" and said that she had decided to kill the victim the night before. The defendant entered a negotiated plea agreement that included: (1) a 30-year sentence, subject to service of 25; (2) defendant's concession that aggravating factors outweighed the mitigating factors; and (3) defendant's agreement that neither she nor her attorney would seek a lesser term of imprisonment. After hearing a "tour-de-force presentation" by the state and no evidence or argument by the defense, the court imposed the agreed upon sentence. Counsel was ineffective in failing to present the substantial mitigation evidence the investigator had developed. Nothing in the plea agreement prohibited counsel from presenting the evidence or arguing that the defendant was "a physically and psychologically battered woman to explain her motivations." In addition to the Battered Women's Syndrome evidence, there were four other mitigating factors, including provocation by the victim, that the evidence would have supported. To the extent counsel believed he was "handcuffed by the restrictive plea agreement," the agreement itself was improper and the court had expressly prohibited "this type of gag provision" less than a year after this plea. This type of agreement deprives the court of necessary information in order to impose an appropriate sentence. Counsel was also ineffective in failing to object to the victim-impact video. "The music [religious and pop] and the photographs of the victim's childhood and of his tombstone, and the television segment about his funeral do not project anything meaningful about the victim's life as it related to his family and others at the time of his death." While the court would not have found prejudice only with respect to the video, the court discussed this in order to resolve the issue on remand. The restrictions on defense counsel in the plea agreement was stricken. The State was free to hold a new sentencing without the restrictions or to vacate the plea.

State v. Rowe, 965 N.E.2d 1047 (Ohio Ct. App. 2011). Counsel ineffective in vehicular homicide case for failing to move the sentencing court to waive the imposition of court costs based upon the defendant's indigence.

Branch v. State, 335 S.W.3d 893 (Tex. Ct. App. 2011). Counsel ineffective in sentencing for possession of cocaine with intent to deliver case for failing to object to the prosecutor's improper statements about the way in which parole law would affect the sentence during closing arguments. While the jury was instructed and the prosecutor could properly generally address parole law, the State here commented specifically on how the parole law and good-conduct time would affect this particular defendant. Instead of addressing when he would be *eligible* for parole, the State affirmatively argued in language of certainty that he would be *released* by a certain time. These comments were an inaccurate statement of the law, inappropriate, and prejudicial. Two trial counsel was ineffective for failing to object. The first testified that he recognized objectionable but did not object because second counsel was handling sentencing. The second counsel stated objectionable and that he had simply missed the argument when it was made and had no trial strategy not to object. Even if there was an alleged strategy, "[t]here can be no reasonable trial strategy in failing to correct a misstatement of law that is detrimental to the client." Prejudice established as jury was misled into believing that a life sentence would result in the defendant serving only seven to twenty years.

2010: ***Gonzalez v. Commissioner of Correction***, 1 A.3d 705 (Conn. Ct. App. 2010). Counsel ineffective in threat and violation of protective order case due to counsel's failure to take adequate steps to ensure that the defendant received sentencing credit for all time served in pretrial confinement. The defendant was initially arrested on a threat charge, but was released the same day on a $500 nonsurety bond. A month later he was arrested on a breach of peace and violation of protective order charge. Bond was set at $35,000 and he remained in confinement for several weeks until the court reduced his bond to a promise to appear. Six months later the defendant was arrested for the third time on violation of protective order and harassment charges. Bond was set at $65,000 and the defendant remained in confinement thereafter. After 73 days had passed since his third arrest, counsel moved successfully to increase the defendant's first two bonds so the defendant could get presentence confinement credit for those arrests. When the defendant entered guilty pleas on charges involved in the first two arrests and received some confinement time, counsel did not request presentence confinement credit for the 73 days counsel had waited in filing the motion to increase the bond. Counsel's conduct was deficient because, under state law, the defendant could get presentence confinement credit only if inability to obtain bail or the denial of bail was the reason the defendant remained in confinement. Thus, "a reasonably competent attorney not only would have known to ask for an increase in bond, but also would have asked for bond to be increased during the ... third arraignment, not two and one-half months later." Prejudice established as the defendant was entitled to credit for the 73 days.

Hernandez v. State, 30 So. 3d 610 (Fla. Dist. Ct. App. 2010). Counsel ineffective in aggravated battery case for failing to object to the trial court's reclassification of the conviction from a second-degree felony to a first-degree felony. The trial court's instructions and the jury verdict form failed to distinguish between aggravated battery causing great bodily harm and aggravated battery using a deadly weapon. Either would be a 2d degree felony, except the court can reclassify to a 1st degree felony when a firearm is used, except where the firearm is already an essential element of the crime. Here, the record was unclear and the court's reclassification resulted in an illegal sentence. Remanded for resentencing as 2d degree felony.

Patterson v. State, 926 N.E.2d 90 (Ind. Ct. App. 2010). Counsel in drug case was ineffective in failing to move to recuse the sentencing judge, who had previously signed the information and participated in the probable cause hearing ten years before as a prosecutor. The delay was caused by the defendant's failure to appear for sentencing following his guilty plea. Counsel's conduct was deficient and prejudicial, as the judge should have recused himself. Likewise, even though the 10 year sentence imposed was within the maximum of 10 years agreed to in the plea agreement, the denial of the right to an impartial judge only established prejudice.

Vaca v. State, 314 S.W.3d 331 (Mo. 2010). Counsel ineffective in robbery and assault sentencing for failing to consider whether to call a psychiatrist as a witness to present evidence of the defendant's low intelligence and mental health issues. By the time of counsel's appointment, the jail psychiatrist had already seen the defendant and prescribed medications for him because he suspected mental illness. Aware of this, counsel retained a psychologist to evaluate competence to stand trial and diminished capacity. The defendant had an IQ of 73, which was confirmed by his school records. Testing suggested the presence of schizophrenia and Social Security Administration records revealed that the defendant was on disability due in part to schizophrenia. Medical records revealed prior head traumas. Counsel knew from the beginning that the state's evidence was "substantial" and that the case "would probably be going to the sentencing phase." "Because defense counsel conceded that conviction was probable, he knew that strategy during the sentencing phase was vital to the representation of his client." Prior to the defense case, the state moved successfully to preclude any mental condition evidence due to counsel's failure to provide notice to the state. Counsel's theory during trial was complete innocence due to misidentification by key witnesses. He attempted to elicit testimony from the defendant's brother about his mental condition, however, but was prevented from doing so. Counsel never attempted to call his psychologist or present his report. During deliberations, the jury sent out four questions asking about the defendant's housing since arrest, psychological testing, and medications. These questions went unanswered. In sentencing, counsel again did not call the psychologist or submit his report. Counsel simply failed to consider whether to call the expert. "This omission, in front of *this particular jury*, undermines … confidence in the sentencing phase's outcome." In short, "the holding of this case is not that counsel was ineffective for not calling [the expert]. Rather, this case rests on the fact that the question of whether to call [the expert] was never considered."

Boan v. State, 388 S.C. 272, 695 S.E.2d 850 (2010). Counsel ineffective in criminal sexual conduct and lewd acts case for failing to move for clarification of the sentence when the trial court announced a twenty year sentence on the most serious charge but signed a sentencing order increasing the sentence to thirty years. Prejudice was clear as, ruling on this issue of first impression, the oral pronouncement controls.

DeLeon v. State, 322 S.W.3d 375 (Tex. Ct. App. 2010). Trial counsel ineffective in sentencing of indecency with a child by sexual contact case for calling as an expert witness a probation officer who gave highly inflammatory testimony about risks posed by sex offenders on probation. Counsel was pleading for probation and presented the officer to testify about treatment for sex offenders on probation and the protections in place in the community. On cross-examination, however, he testified that a sex offender will always have the sex offender impulses and "[i]f you want to protect the public, then you put them in a situation where they can't have access to children." Counsel's conduct was deficient in calling this witness in the first place and in failing to object to this highly inflammatory testimony. Prejudice established, given the nature of this testimony, the emphasis placed upon it (with more than half of the sentencing transcript covered by this testimony), and that this witness was the only expert in sentencing.

Ex parte Harrington, 310 S.W.3d 452 (Tex. Crim. App. 2010). Counsel ineffectiveness in felony driving while intoxicated (DWI) plea case, due to counsel's failure to investigate a prior DWI conviction used to enhance the defendant's misdemeanor DWI to a felony charge. The indictment listed prior DWI convictions in 1986 and 2003 for purposed of enhancement. The defendant informed counsel that the 1986 conviction was not his. A man who had stolen his driver's license used it when he was arrested and was convicted using his name. Nonetheless, counsel failed to investigate and the defendant pled guilty. Subsequently, a police department fingerprint analysis confirmed that the defendant was not person attached to the 1986 conviction. There was a reasonable probability that the defendant would not have entered a plea to the felony charge if counsel had performed adequately.

State v. Ott, 247 P.3d 344 (Utah Ct. App. 2010). Counsel ineffective in non-capital murder case for failing to object to inadmissible victim-impact evidence in jury sentencing where the defendant could be sentenced to life with or without the possibility of parole. Specifically, counsel failed to object to a six-minute videotape of pictures of the victim set to "moving music," and testimony of family members about the impact on them and their opinions of the defendant's character and the appropriate sentence. The opinions of the defendant's character (i.e. that he could not be rehabilitated) and opinions on the appropriate sentence were "at odds with United States Supreme Court precedent" in *Payne* and *Booth*. Thus, counsel's conduct was deficient. Prejudice also established.

2009: ***People v. Heinz***, 910 N.E.2d 610 (Ill. App. Ct. 2009). Counsel ineffective in burglary and theft case for failing to object to restitution order in sentencing. The defendant was ordered to pay $7,000 in restitution following convictions from breaking into and stealing from a bowling alley. Counsel's conduct was deficient and not based on strategy because the State's restitution request "was cursory at best" and the supporting evidence was inconsistent, ambiguous, vague, or completely absent. Counsel's conduct was deficient in "remaining silent under these circumstances." Prejudice found because if counsel had objected, the trial court would have held a hearing to determine the actual amount of damages.

Farris v. State, 907 N.E.2d 985 (Ind. 2009). Counsel ineffective for failing to challenge consecutive habitual offender sentence. Defendant was initially charged with robbery and while pending trial was charged with murder committed by someone he hired and who was attempting to kill his robbery co-defendant who was cooperating with the state. The defendant was convicted first of the robbery and his sentence was enhanced by 30 years as a habitual offender. Following his murder conviction, his sentence in that case was also enhanced by 30 years and ordered to run consecutive to sentence in robbery case. Counsel's conduct was deficient and prejudicial because state case law from at least seven years before the defendant's offenses or trial prohibited the state from seeking multiple enhancements by bringing successive prosecutions for charges that could have been consolidated for trial. These charges could have been consolidated because they were based on a "series of acts connected together" as required by statute.

In re A.E., 922 N.E.2d 1017 (Ohio Ct. App. 2009). Counsel ineffective in juvenile sex offender case for failing to advise the juvenile and the court of the proper classification procedures related to the statutory duty to register as a sex offender for the rest of the juvenile's life and failing to advocate on the defendant's behalf. The defendant was 15 and had no prior sex offense adjudications. Under state law, registrations requirements for a 14-15 year old with no prior sex offense adjudications was discretionary. Nonetheless, defense counsel sat silently in court when the court stated incorrectly that registration for the juvenile would be mandatory. Even assuming that counsel and the court understood the discretionary nature of the determination, counsel made no argument that the court should decline registration requirements or that the court should consider the mandatory factors listed in the state statute.

Gordon v. Hall, 221 P.3d 763 (Ore. Ct. App. 2009). Counsel ineffective in sentencing of first degree sexual abuse case where the defendant was given an enhanced sentence of life imprisonment without the possibility of parole (LWOP). Under state law, the presumptive sentence for a felony sex crime was LWOP if the defendant had been "sentenced" for two prior felony sex crimes. The state presented evidence of two prior sex "convictions" and counsel did not challenge this evidence, despite informing the court that the defendant did not believe he had a second conviction. Counsel's conduct was deficient in failing to investigate the defendant's prior criminal record and in failing to challenge the imposition of the enhanced sentence. First, the plain text of the statute required two prior "sentences" for the enhancement. Second, while counsel discussed prior "convictions" with the defendant, he did not discuss prior "sentences" with him and "failed to look beyond the face of the documents offered by the prosecutor to determine whether they had actually involved the imposition of sentences." Third, counsel failed to object to the enhanced sentence on the basis that the state had failed to prove two prior "sentences." The defendant was prejudiced because one of his prior convictions did not result in the imposition of a sentence because his sentence was suspended and he was placed on probation in California. At the completion of the probation, the court sentence aside the guilty plea, entered a not guilty plea, and dismissed the complaint. Thus, no prison sentence was ever imposed. Under the applicable law at the time in both California and Oregon, "probation was not a sentence." Thus, the defendant did not have two prior sentences for felony sex offenses and the presumptive LWOP sentence did not apply to him.

Ex parte Lane, 303 S.W.3d 702 (Tex. Crim. App. 2009). Counsel ineffective in methamphetamine sentencing for failing to object to improper testimony during the trial and sentencing about "the methamphetamine problem." During trial, counsel's conduct was deficient in failing to object to an officer's testimony "that there is a methamphetamine epidemic in Texas." Counsel's conduct was also deficient in failing to object to the prosecutor's closing argument, which was not supported by evidence, asserting that the defendant was bringing methamphetamine into the county to poison the children and turn them into addicts and that children were in fact shooting up and smoking methamphetamine. The defendant suffered no prejudice during trial, but counsel's deficient conduct continued in sentencing. Counsel failed to object to testimony by a DEA agent about the societal problems caused by methamphetamine. Counsel also failed to request pre-trial notice of the State's experts, including the DEA agent, to properly object to his testimony about addiction and that 45,000 people could get high from the amount of methamphetamine possessed by the defendant, and to call an expert in rebuttal. The DEA agent was not qualified to testify about the addictive nature of the drug or about the number of people who could get high on the amount possessed by the defendant. Prejudice was established as the state asked for and obtained a life sentence, relying heavily on the objectionable testimony and argument in both phases of the trial.

Ramirez v. State, 301 S.W.3d 410 (Tex. App. 2009). Counsel ineffective in intoxication manslaughter sentencing for failing to elect jury sentencing based on counsel's misunderstanding of the law. The state alleged use of a vehicle as a "deadly weapon," which, if found by the jury, meant that only the jury (and not the judge) could assess a punishment of probation in sentencing. In order for the jury to be eligible to assess probation, defense counsel was required to file a sworn motion prior to *voir dire* that the defendant had not previously been convicted of a felony. Here, counsel filed the sworn statement, but failed to elect jury sentencing prior to *voir dire*, which meant under state law that the jury could assess punishment only if the prosecutor consented. Counsel did this because she believed the defendant could get probation if he had judge sentencing and she advised the defendant that he would have a better chance of getting probation before the judge. When counsel learned of her error, she met with the prosecutor in an attempt to resolve the problem. The state did consent to jury sentencing, but only on the condition the defendant waive his right to appeal on the basis that the jury had not been asked any questions relating to punishment in *voir dire*. Defense counsel believed she could not do this, but failed to even consult with the defendant about it. The prosecutor, who had offered a probationary sentence in pre-trial and post-guilty verdict negotiations, then agreed to a 10 year probationary sentence, but the trial court refused to accept this agreement and sentenced the defendant to 18 years' confinement. Counsel's conduct was admittedly deficient as it was "based on her misunderstanding of the law" and precluded a probationary sentence even though counsel argued that the defendant was "a good candidate for probation." Prejudice was also clear in that the jury may well have assessed probation as evidenced by the prosecutor's actions in the case in attempting to negotiate for a probationary sentence even after the guilty verdict. The prosecutor also testified in post-conviction that the victim's family agreed that probation was an appropriate punishment.

State v. Bounhiza, 294 S.W.3d 780 (Tex. App. 2009). Trial court did not err in granting a motion for mistrial in sexual assault case based on ineffective assistance of counsel. Prior to trial, the defendant filed an application for probation. After conviction, however, the parties realized that the trial court was statutorily prohibited from considering probation as a sentence. The punishment range was 2-20 years. Counsel conceded his error and that he had incorrectly advised the defendant to choose the court rather than the jury for sentencing based on this error.

State v. Adamy, 213 P.3d 627 (Wash. Ct. App. 2009). Counsel ineffective in child rape and assault case for failing to advise the court that it could consider a special sex offender sentencing alternative (SSOSA) under state law, despite a federal immigration hold. The defendant's parents were U.S. citizens and he always believed he was also, but learned shortly before the charges were filed that he had been born during a visit to Mexico and his mother had never filled out the required paperwork for citizenship. The defendant pled guilty and the state agreed he could seek a SSOSA if he was, in fact, a citizen and eligible. The court denied the SSOSA believing it could not grant a SSOSA because the defendant was subject to a deportation order. Under state law, however, the court could have sentenced under SSOSA regardless of the defendant's citizenship or immigration status. Counsel's conduct "was deficient for failing to recognize and cite the appropriate case law ... to the sentencing court." Prejudice shown.

In re Personal Restraint Petition of Crawford, 209 P.3d 507 (Wash. Ct. App. 2009). Counsel ineffective in sentencing following robbery and assault convictions for failing to challenge the use of an out-of-state conviction in designating the defendant as a persistent offender, which resulted in a sentence of life without parole. The prior conviction was for sex abuse in Kentucky. State law required the court to classify this according to the comparable offense in Washington law, based on the elements of the offense (legal comparability) or based on the defendant's conduct as evidenced by the indictment or information (factual comparability). Here, the Washington statute included several elements that the Kentucky statute did not and, although the defendant's conduct almost certainly violated the Washington statute, the necessary information to establish the elements was not contained in the Kentucky documents. Thus, counsel's conduct was deficient and the defendant was prejudiced because the Kentucky offense was improperly counted as a strike under the persistent offender statute.

2008: ***Thompson v. State***, 990 So. 2d 482 (Fla. 2008). Counsel ineffective in burglary, false imprisonment, and sexual battery case for failing to timely move to disqualify the presiding judge from sentencing. Prior to trial, counsel moved to withdrew stating the defendant had threatened to kill him, his family, and anyone associated with the case following conviction. The defendant denied the allegations and the motion was denied based on the court's finding that he would likely be sentenced to life and unable to carry out his threat if he was convicted. Counsel filed a motion to disqualify the court 14 days later, which was denied as untimely under state rules requiring that a motion for disqualification be made within 10 days after the discovery of the facts constituting the grounds for disqualification. Following conviction, the court sentenced the defendant to concurrent life sentences. Counsel's conduct was deficient and not based on strategy. Prejudice found because "the statements made by the judge ... sufficiently evince judicial bias and predisposition so as to undermine confidence in the eventual sentence imposed."

Robinson v. State, 380 S.C. 201, 669 S.E.2d 588 (2008). Counsel ineffective following plea to drug trafficking offense for failing to challenge the use of a prior uncounseled magistrate court conviction to enhance the sentence, which resulted in a 20 year sentence. Prejudice found even though the sentence imposed was less than the maximum allowable punishment for a first trafficking offense. No sentencing ordered.

Lair v. State, 265 S.W.3d 580 (Tex. App. 2008). Counsel ineffective in sentencing in possession of ecstasy case. Counsel presented only the defendant's sister-in-law to testify, despite the availability and willingness of over twenty witnesses, including the defendant's mother, relatives, and neighbors, who would have given good character type evidence. Counsel's conduct was deficient because he "did not even interview these witnesses, let alone present their testimony at the punishment hearing. This fact ... necessarily defeats counsel's subsequent representation that the testimony of these additional witnesses would have been merely cumulative since, without conducting any sort of investigation into their testimony, he could not know whether the testimony was cumulative or not." Counsel's alleged concern about the state cross-examining these witnesses with the defendant's prior 50-year sentence also did not explain the failure because the jurors were already aware of the prior sentence. Prejudice found because the evidence the jury heard "was brief and lacking in the detail and information that the additional witnesses would have offered." In addition, the jury sentenced the defendant to 70 years when the State had requested only a 50 year sentence.

2007: ***Pettis v. State***, 212 S.W.3d 189 (Mo. Ct. App. 2007). Counsel ineffective in sentencing following guilty plea to possession of a controlled substance within a correctional institution for affirmatively misstating the parole consequences of a consecutive sentence to the court. The defendant was serving a life sentence and had been approved for parole prior to these charges. Following these charges, his parole was cancelled and a new parole hearing was scheduled. The defendant entered a plea in this case pursuant to an agreement wherein the state agreed to maximum of five years but left to the court the determination of whether the sentence should be concurrent or consecutive to the life sentence. During the sentencing, the court inquired about the impact on parole and clearly wanted to impose a sentence with some deterrent effect but also to show some leniency to the defendant. In response to the court's inquiries, counsel stated that his "release date is to going to be pushed backward" and urged the court not to impose a consecutive sentence. The court gave the defendant a sentence of four years consecutive. Counsel's conduct was deficient because counsel affirmatively misstated the real consequence, which was that a consecutive sentence of any length effectively converted the life sentence to one of life without parole. Prejudice was clear because the court had no inkling the defendant's parole eligibility would be extinguished by a consecutive sentence when the court clearly wanted to show some leniency in sentencing the defendant to four years rather than the five recommended by the state.

State v. Thiefault, 158 P.3d 580 (Wash. 2007). Counsel ineffective in sentencing following indecent liberties and attempted rape convictions for failing to object to the sentencing court's comparability analysis regarding the defendant's prior Montana conviction for attempted robbery, which led to the sentencing court counting that offense as a strike under the Persistent Offender Accountability Act (allowing a life without parole sentence based on three prior convictions or "strikes) and sentencing the defendant to life without parole. Counsel's conduct was deficient because the Montana offense was broader than its Washington counterpart because the Montana statute required a lesser *mens rea*. There was also insufficient evidence in the record for the court to factually compare the offense to make a proper comparability determination. Prejudice found because counting the Montana offense as a strike allowed the court to sentence the defendant to life without parole.

2006: *People v. Thimmes*, 41 Cal. Rptr. 3d 925 (Cal. Ct. App. 2006). Counsel ineffective in sentencing for felony drug case for failing to advise the court that the defendant had been warned of the consequences of his prior conviction and the Three Strikes Law prior to the defendant's no contest plea in exchange for a sentence of 32 months. The strike offense admitted was a 1999 criminal threat for which the defendant was sentenced to probation. Counsel's conduct was deficient because the trial court assumed that the defendant had been advised that the 1999 conviction would count under the Three Strikes Law even though criminal threat was not included for purposes of that provision until 2000. Prejudice found because the trial court was permitted to decline to apply the Three Strikes Law and had stated that the case was "a pitiful one," but applied the law based on the assumption that the defendant had previously been advised of the consequences.

People v. Le, 39 Cal. Rptr. 3d 146 (Cal. Ct. App. 2006). Counsel ineffective in robbery and burglary case for failing to object based on double jeopardy to consideration of both offenses in calculating the restitution fine. Counsel's conduct was deficient and prejudicial because state law precluded multiple punishment for a single act or omission and the defendant's sole intent was to steal from a drugstore. Thus, the defendant should have been sentenced solely on the robbery conviction but the burglary conviction was included, which essentially doubled the restitution fine.

Estrada v. State, 149 P.3d 833 (Idaho 2006). Counsel ineffective in plea to rape case for failing to advise the defendant of his right to refuse to cooperate with a court-ordered psychosexual evaluation for purposes of sentencing. After accepting the plea, the trial court ordered a psychosexual evaluation of the defendant, which counsel informed the defendant must be completed, even though the defendant initially refused to participate. Counsel's conduct was deficient in failing to advise the defendant that he still retained his right against self-incrimination following his plea and he was not required to participate in the psychosexual evaluation. Prejudice found because the sentencing judge's specific, repeated references to the psychosexual evaluation suggest that it played an important role in the sentencing and the evaluation report included a number of unfavorable and derogatory comments, including references to the defendant's potential for future violent actions.

2005: *Matthews v. State*, 868 A.2d 895 (Md. Ct. App. 2005). Counsel ineffective and prejudice presumed in probation violation case for failing to file a motion for modification of sentence when requested to do so by the defendant. Defendant entitled to filed a belated motion for modification of sentence.

Shanklin v. State, 190 S.W.3d 154 (Tex. Crim. App. 2005). Counsel ineffective in punishment phase of non-capital murder case for failing to investigate or present evidence from at least 20 available witnesses and instead called only the defendant to testify that he was sorry. The prosecutor requested a sentence of 25 to 35 years but the jury imposed a sentence twice that length. The available witnesses would have testified that the defendant was an excellent father, helped his friends and relatives, and worked hard.

Freeman v. State, 167 S.W.3d 114 (Tex. App. 2005). Counsel ineffective in sentencing on aggravated sexual assault charge for failing to adequately investigate and present evidence of the defendant's history of mental illness. While counsel was aware that the defendant had previously been hospitalized on a couple of occasions (and the defendant testified about this during trial), counsel presented only testimony from the defendant's mother in sentencing asking the jury to take his illness into account. If counsel had adequately investigated, the evidence would have shown that the defendant had another prior hospitalization following an attempted suicide and had been receiving regular outpatient treatment for more than a year prior to the crime. He had last been seen three weeks before the crime. Counsel's conduct was deficient under *Wiggins* because counsel failed to investigate and there was no strategy for this failure. Prejudice was found because counsel only presented lay testimony from the defendant and his mother on this issue. Although "it is sheer speculation" that the jury would have given a lighter sentence if additional evidence had been presented, the court found a reasonable probability of a different outcome.

Andrews v. State, 159 S.W.3d 98 (Tex. Crim. App. 2005). Counsel ineffective in sentencing for indecency and sexual assault of child case for failing to object to the prosecutor's argument that the defendant's sentences could not be made consecutive, which was a misstatement of law and contrary to the state's pretrial motion asking to make the sentences consecutive or cumulative. Counsel's conduct was deficient (and could not be explained by trial strategy) because "counsel has a duty to correct misstatements of law that are detrimental to his client." Prejudice was found because the argument left the jury with the false impression that the maximum the defendant would serve was 20 years when the maximum sentence was actually 80 years.

2004: *Bargeron v. State*, 895 So. 2d 385 (Ala. Crim. App. 2004). Counsel ineffective in theft case for failing to appear at the restitution hearing, which was "a component of the criminal-sentencing proceeding." Remanded for new restitution hearing.

McCarty v. State, 802 N.E.2d 959 (Ind. Ct. App. 2004). Counsel was ineffective in failing to prepare and present mitigating evidence in sentencing following the defendant's plea to child molestation.

Counsel's conduct was deficient because he met with the defendant only once, conducted no investigation, and did not retain an investigator or mental health expert. Prejudice was found because adequate investigation and presentation would have revealed that the defendant was mentally retarded, he had been molested himself as a child, there was a likelihood that he could be successfully rehabilitated, and his confession admitted acts beyond what the victims had reported. Because of the trial court's reluctance to find prejudice and grant relief, the court exercised its state constitutional authority to revise the defendant's sentence and reduced his sentence by 10 years to the presumptive term of 30 years.

Storr v. State, 126 S.W.3d 647 (Tex. Crim. App. 2004). Counsel was ineffective in sentencing in aggravated kidnapping case for failing to obtain an instruction on voluntary release of kidnapping victim in a safe place. The defendant was charged with aggravated kidnapping, which is a felony in the first degree. Under state law, however, if the defendant raises the issue of voluntary release of the victim at the punishment stage and proves that by a preponderance of the evidence, the offense is a felony in the second degree. The first degree felony is punishable by imprisonment of 5 to 99 year. The second degree felony is punishable by a term of 2 to 20 years. Counsel's conduct was deficient in failing to request the instruction because the evidence conclusively established that the appellant voluntarily released the victim in a safe place. The victim was left in his car at a post office which is exactly the point were he had been abducted to start with. The court found that it was inconceivable that counsel had some trial strategy for not requesting an instruction on safe release given the significant difference in punishment. Prejudice found because the defendant was sentenced to 35 years which is 15 years more then the maximum imprisonment allowed for the second degree felony.

State v. Saunders, 86 P.3d 232 (Wash. Ct. App. 2004). Trial counsel was ineffective in sentencing in murder, rape, and kidnapping case for failing to argue that rape and kidnapping constituted the "same criminal conduct" for purposes of calculating offender score. "Same criminal conduct" refers to the situation where there are two or more crimes that (1) require the same criminal intent, (2) are committed at the same time and place, and (3) involve the same victim. Here, the primary motivation for sexually assaulting the victim by inserting a television antenna in her anus was to dominate her and to cause her pain and humiliation. Because this intent arguably was similar to the motivation for the kidnap, defense counsel was deficient for failing to make this argument. Prejudice was found because the case law provides strong support for this argument. New sentencing granted.

2003: *Carswell v. State*, 589 S.E.2d 605 (Ga. Ct. App. 2003). Counsel's performance was deficient in an aggravated assault case for failing to object to two prior convictions used by the state in aggravation of sentence because those guilty pleas may not have been entered into voluntarily. Because the court found that reversal was required on the substantive issue, the court found that the question of prejudice with respect to the ineffectiveness of counsel was moot.

Turner v. State, 578 S.E.2d 570 (Ga. Ct. App. 2003). Counsel was ineffective in drug distribution case for failing to object to the use of a prior conviction in sentencing when the defendant had received no notice it would be used. The defendant pled guilty and the prosecutor recommended a sentence of 15 years with four or five to serve, but the trial court had been provided with a probation report that revealed two prior convictions for selling drugs. Based on this, the judge rejected the prosecutor's recommendation and sentenced the defendant to 20 years with 10 years to serve. State law provides that only such evidence in aggravation as the state has made known to the defendant prior to trial shall be admissible. The court has interpreted this statutory provision to prohibit use of an undisclosed probation report showing prior convictions in sentencing. Counsel's conduct was deficient in failing to object to the state's use of the undisclosed probation report in sentencing. The defendant was prejudiced "because the length of his sentence was fixed based in part on the improper evidence."

State v. Washington, 68 P.3d 134 (Kan. 2003). Counsel was ineffective in sentencing hearing for premeditated murder. Following the trial, initial counsel was suspended from the practice of law and relieved by the trial court. New counsel was appointed and requested a copy of the trial transcript, but that was denied. She attempted several times to meet with the prior counsel but he did not meet with her. She did nothing more to prepare for sentencing even though she had four months to do so. Although ineffectiveness was not raised on appeal (just a general unfairness of the sentencing proceedings argument, the court addressed the issue *sua sponte*. Counsel's conduct was deficient because counsel apparently did not read the court file or talk to defense witnesses that had testified in the trial to learn of the defendant's PTSD. She also was aware even of the statutory provisions that required a 50 year sentence without parole. She presented no evidence and made no argument in sentencing. Prejudice found because "counsel simply abdicated her position with the excuse that she had not been given a trial transcript." *Id.* at 159.

2000: ***West v. Waters***, 533 S.E.2d 88 (Ga. 2000). Counsel ineffective in sentencing in sale of cocaine case for failing to object to a prior conviction presented in aggravation of sentence without timely notice, since statute requires "clear notice" prior to the jury being sworn for trial. Prejudice found even when defense counsel was aware of conviction. [This opinion reverses prior Georgia cases to the contrary.]

State v. Jones, 769 So.2d 28 (La. Ct. App. 2000). Counsel ineffective in sentencing in drug case for failing to object that deferred adjudication probation, which was not a valid conviction under state law, should not have been used as predicate conviction for sentence enhancement under Habitual Offender Law.

Gary v. State, 760 So. 2d 743 (Miss. 2000). Counsel ineffective in armed robbery case for failing to argue for sentencing under Youth Court Act. Defendant was 17 years old with no priors and did not possess gun during robbery (as he codefendant did). State law did not require the court to sentence under the youth act but did require the court to consider it. Counsel's conduct in failing to request youth sentencing was deficient and prejudice was found because the defendant was sentenced to 45 years when he could have gotten only a year under the Youth Act if the court had accepted the argument.

Milburn v. State, 15 S.W.3d 267 (Tex. App. 2000). Counsel ineffective in drug case for failing to prepare and present mitigation evidence. Counsel conducted no investigation. Numerous witnesses were available to testify that defendant was a good father to his daughter who had severe medical problems and that he was a good employee. Counsel presented no evidence and made only a benign argument responding to the state's argument that the defendant was previously on probation, that he had not been rehabilitated, and that he should be given 30 years and a $50,000 fine. Jury gave 40 years and $75,000 fine. Court found that this was a close call of constructive denial of counsel because essentially no different that if trial court had prohibited the defense from presenting mitigation in light of strong state case. Prejudice found "even though it is sheer speculation that character witnesses in mitigation would have in fact favorably influenced the jury's assessment of punishment," *Id.* at 271, because any mitigation better than none and the jury gave even harsher sentence than state asked for.

1999: ***Kellett v. State***, 716 N.E.2d 975 (Ind. Ct. App. 1999). Counsel ineffective in DUI causing serious injury case for failing to object to the admission of a ledger in sentencing or to adequately cross- examine the witness concerning facial errors in the ledger. The injured victim's mother prepared the ledger to show uncompensated medical bills and testified that the total was approximately $140,000. State allowed the trial court to order restitution of the actual costs and the court did so based solely on the mother's testimony and the ledger. Review of the ledger, however, would have revealed that several charges for over $30,000 and $10,000 were duplicated and that there were mathematical errors in the document. While the court did not find deficient conduct solely related to admission of the ledger or solely related to failure to cross-examine the witness, the court found that counsel's conduct was deficient in failing to do one or the other and the defendant was prejudiced.

State v. Robinson, 744 So. 2d 119 (La. Ct. App. 1999). Counsel ineffective in armed robbery case for failing to properly move to reconsider the sentence on the basis of excessiveness following the trial. Defendant was convicted of armed robbery for stealing tennis shoes and was sentenced to 30 years (without parole) out of a possible 5 to 99 years. Under state law, counsel can raise excessive sentence issue in motion to reconsider either orally at the time of sentencing or in written motion following sentencing. Counsel made no oral motion and filed a form motion afterwards but did not check the block on excessive sentence. He instead checked the block for statute being unconstitutional with respect to maximum or minimum punishment, which appellate counsel conceded was frivolous in this case. Failure to raise excessiveness of sentence in the motion to reconsider waives the issue for appeal. Thus, excessiveness issue procedurally barred. Nonetheless, the court vacated the sentence on the basis of ineffective assistance of counsel. The trial court stated no basis for sentencing the defendant to 30 years, other than guilt and that he lied on the witness stand. Likewise, the facts did not support such a harsh sentence. The defendant was 19 years old and had no prior convictions or arrests. Counsel should have moved to reconsider because the sentence was excessive on this record.

Davis v. State, 336 S.C. 329, 520 S.E.2d 801 (1999). Counsel ineffective for failing to object to trial court's consideration of exercise of right to trial in sentencing the defendant to ten years for distribution of crack. Following sentence, counsel moved to reconsider on the basis that several similarly situated defendants got lesser sentences. The court said that the other sentences were lower because the other defendants plead guilty. Because it is an abuse of discretion for the trial court to consider the defendant's exercise of his right to trial as an aggravating factor, counsel was ineffective for failing to object.

Scott v. State, 334 S.C. 248, 513 S.E.2d 100 (1999). Counsel ineffective in drug trafficking case for failing to object to the court considering a 1987 misdemeanor conviction for simple possession and sentencing the defendant as a second offender under the statute. The 1987 charge was actually a bond forfeiture for failure to appear and not a "conviction" for purposes of sentencing under the drug statute. A bond forfeiture may be considered a "conviction" only when the legislature specifically provides that the two are equivalent. Because the legislature has done so in other contexts, the court infers the legislature did not intend for a bond forfeiture to be the equivalent of a conviction in this context. The defendant was prejudiced because the maximum sentence for a first offense is 10 years and for a second offense 30 years. The defendant was sentenced to 30 years.

1998: ***Trinh v. State***, 974 S.W.2d 872 (Tex. App. 1998).[5] Counsel ineffective in possession of weapon case because counsel filed a motion for probation and to have the jury assess punishment which she intended to amend after conviction to elect that the trial court assess punishment because Trinh would have been ineligible for probation from a jury due to a previous felony offense. Counsel was unaware, however, that the sentencing election could not be withdrawn after the verdict without the State's consent. Thus, the defendant was denied any possibility of probation.

State v. Anderson, 588 N.W.2d 75 (Wis. Ct. App. 1998). Counsel ineffective in child sexual assault case for failing to seek an adjournment of the sentencing hearing to permit him to finish reviewing the presentence investigation report with the defendant. Counsel received the report only 30 minutes prior to the hearing and notified the court that the defendant objected to the report because the victims' had recanted some of the information included, and that some of the allegations of sexual abuse in the report had not been substantiated. The trial court offered to allow the defendant to withdraw his pleas or to adjourn the hearing in order to allow the defense more time to prepare. The defense declined both offers. Counsel only noted that the defendants pleas were only two fondling two children as opposed to the more aggravated allegations of sexual abuse in the PSI. The appellate court held that counsel was ineffective in failing to seek the adjournment in order to prepare to refute the inaccurate information and to argue the defendant's theory that much of the sexual abuse was done by others. The court found prejudice because it was clear from the trial court's statements that the court relied on much of the disputed information in sentencing the defendant to 80 years out of a possible 100 year sentence.

1997: ***State v. Jones***, 700 So. 2d 1034 (La. Ct. App. 1997). Counsel ineffective in a case where the state sought habitual offender status because counsel did not file the required written response denying the allegations which would have placed burden on state to prove. Likewise, counsel did not object to the state's documentary evidence which failed to prove a required element that the defendant had been advised of his privilege against self-incrimination prior to pleading guilty to the prior offenses.

Oliva v. State, 942 S.W.2d 727 (Tex. App. 1997). Counsel ineffective in sentencing because counsel failed to object to the prosecutor's closing argument which referred to defendant's lack of remorse and failure to testify in the sentencing despite the fact that defendant testified in the guilt-or-innocence phase.

1996: ***People v. Siedlinski***, 666 N.E.2d 42 (Ill. App. Ct. 1996). Counsel ineffective for failing to request sentencing credit against fine where statute allowed credit of $5/day for each day of pretrial confinement.

Glivens v. State, 918 S.W.2d 30 (Tex. App. 1996). Counsel ineffective in sentencing of aggravated

[5]Prior to *Hernandez v. State*, 988 S.W.2d 770 (Tex. Crim. App. 1999) (en banc), Texas did not apply the *Strickland* standard in non-capital sentencing hearings. Texas previously applied a state law standard of "reasonablyeffective assistance," *Ex parte Duffy*, 607 S.W.2d 507 (Tex. Crim. App. 1980), in non-capital sentencing hearings.

robbery case where extraneous unadjudicated prior robbery admitted during guilt phase for limited purpose of establishing identity, motive, etc., but counsel did not object to consideration of the extraneous offense in sentencing and the record does not reflect that judge did not consider. Law changed in 1993, however, and under current law not applicable here extraneous unadjudicated offenses could be considered in sentencing.

People v. Brasseaux, 660 N.E.2d 1321 (Ill. App. Ct. 1996). Counsel ineffective where defendant was seeking to attack sentences and filed pro se motion to reconsider sentences but counsel did not contact defendant or conduct any investigation prior to the hearing at which the defendant was not present.

1995: *Kucel v. State*, 907 S.W.2d 890 (Tex. App. 1995). Counsel ineffective in sentencing for aggravated sexual assault on child for arguing that defendant would not be eligible for parole for at least two years when it was actually fifteen years. Counsel also ineffective for failing to correct error or object to erroneous jury charge even after prosecutor pointed out error.

Thomas v. State, 923 S.W.2d 611 (Tex. App. 1995). Counsel ineffective in sentencing for organized crime activity for failing to object to evidence concerning extraneous unadjudicated crimes of threatening police officers, stalking police officers and the prosecutor, and soliciting the murder of police officers. [Statute has since been amended effective 9/1/93 to allow evidence of extraneous unadjudicated crimes in sentencing.]

Durst v. State, 900 S.W.2d 134 (Tex. App. 1995). Counsel ineffective in sentencing after guilty plea for possession of marijuana for eliciting during direct examination of defendant testimony concerning six other unadjudicated extraneous marijuana hauling trips which would have been inadmissible otherwise under the state law at the time of this trial.

1994: *Ware v. State*, 875 S.W.2d 432 (Tex. App. 1994). Trial counsel ineffective for failing to offer evidence in jury sentencing to prove that the defendant had no prior felony convictions (or ask the defendant that question during his testimony) and was thus eligible for probation where counsel sought probation and jury asked for information on probation eligibility and unsuccessfully attempted to probate portion of sentence.

1993: *Craig v. State*, 847 S.W.2d 434 (Tex. App. 1993). Counsel ineffective in murder case for jury sentencing purposes where counsel: did not object to state argument in guilt phase that jurors now understand why prosecutors ask for certain verdicts in drug cases in order to avoid these tragedies; elicited damaging information about defendant; argued in guilt phase that defendant and "bandito" friends not looking for victim when there was no evidence of "bandito" friends; argued in sentencing that the verdict would not have any deterrent effect on any participants including defendant; elicited testimony that defendant bragged about killing; suggested in argument that there was no favorable evidence for defense and that's why defense called no witnesses; misquoted witness who said defendant said victim was dead and told jury that defendant said "I killed or I shot him"; and during guilt argument summarized evidence in a state-oriented fashion.

1992: *Commonwealth v. Batterson*, 601 A.2d 335 (Pa. Super. Ct. 1992). Counsel ineffective for failing to move for reconsideration of sentence applying deadly weapon enhancement because a motor vehicle is not a "weapon."

1991: ***Jenkins v. State***, 591 So. 2d 149 (Ala. Crim. App. 1991). Trial counsel ineffective for failing to investigate and object to admission of prior Florida convictions which were all based on *nolo contendre* pleas and were thus improperly admitted under Alabama law for purpose of sentence enhancement under habitual offender act.

Weaver v. Warden, 822 P.2d 112 (Nev. 1991). Counsel ineffective in robbery case for failing to present evidence that defendant had PTSD from Vietnam service.

Chubb v. State, 303 S.C. 395, 401 S.E.2d 159 (1991). Trial counsel ineffective in burglary case, where a burglary conviction mandated a life sentence unless the jury recommended mercy, for failing to present mitigation evidence or argue for mercy during the guilt phase because of her erroneous expectation that a separate sentencing proceeding would be held.

Ex parte Canedo, 818 S.W.2d 814 (Tex. Crim. App. 1991). Counsel ineffective for advising defendant in aggravated sexual assault on child case to request judge alone sentencing based on belief that defendant was eligible for shock probation when in fact judge could not give shock probation but jury could have assessed probation.

Ex parte Felton, 815 S.W.2d 733 (Tex. Crim. App. 1991). Trial counsel ineffective for failing to determine that a prior conviction used to enhance punishment from 5 to 15 years was invalid under state law. The prior was robbery by firearm in 1961 which was a capital offense. State law prior to 1965 provided that the court could not accept a guilty plea to a capital offense unless the state affirmatively waived the capital element which they didn't in this case.

Schofield v. West Virginia Department of Corrections, 406 S.E.2d 425 (W. Va. 1991). Trial counsel ineffective in murder case for failing to present mitigation evidence concerning defendant's limited mental ability, her history of social and emotional problems, and her family background, and argue for mercy recommendation where without recommendation there was a mandatory life without parole sentence. Counsel did not argue mercy because defendant insisted she was guilty only of manslaughter and counsel feared that to argue for mercy recommendation would be considered by jury as a concession of guilt to murder.

1990: ***Ex parte Walker***, 794 S.W.2d 36 (Tex. Crim. App. 1990). Trial counsel ineffective for failing to file in timely manner the defendant's motion electing to have the jury assess punishment.

1989: ***People v. Barocio***, 264 Cal. Rptr. 573 (Cal. Ct. App. 1989). Trial counsel ineffective for failing to inform the defendant of his right to request a recommendation against deportation at his sentencing hearing because counsel was unaware of the recommendation possibility.

Commonwealth v. Lykus, 546 N.E.2d 159 (Mass. 1989). Counsel ineffective in murder, extortion, and kidnapping case for failing: to argue defendant's employment history, charitable activities, and civic contributions; to call witnesses on defendant's behalf; and to argue for concurrent sentences.

Commonwealth v. Kozarian, 566 A.2d 304 (Pa. Super. Ct. 1989). Counsel ineffective for failing to preserve claim that sentencing guidelines were improperly applied to enhance punishment.

Commonwealth v. Albert, 561 A.2d 736 (Pa. 1989). Counsel ineffective for filing brief in support of petition for post-conviction adjustment of sentence which was "completely lacking in substance."

Commonwealth v. Arthur, 559 A.2d 936 (Pa. Super. Ct. 1989). Counsel ineffective for failing to raise and preserve issue of legality of sentence which ordered uncompensated confiscation and destruction of defendant's firearms collection as it had never been claimed that the firearms were used in any illegal act.

Ex parte Walker, 777 S.W.2d 427 (Tex. Crim. App. 1989). Trial counsel ineffective for not objecting during sentencing to otherwise inadmissible evidence of the defendant's prior aggravated robbery conviction and defendant's involvement in three other aggravated robberies.

Cooper v. State, 769 S.W.2d 301 (Tex. App. 1989). Counsel ineffective for failing to object to void conviction used for enhancement, allowing defendant to testify about it which opened door to 14 prior convictions from other jurisdictions which would not have been presented otherwise, and failing to object to inadmissible portion of penitentiary packet regarding another conviction.

1988: *State v. Brown*, 525 So. 2d 454 (Fla. Dist. Ct. App. 1988). Trial counsel ineffective per se for failure to advise defendant that he could elect to be sentenced under sentencing guidelines after guilty pleas.

People v. Sagstetter, 532 N.E.2d 1029 (Ill. App. Ct. 1988). Counsel ineffective for failing to assert therapist-recipient privilege with regard to statements made by defendant at suggestion of therapist which were admitted in sentencing hearing.

Gallegos v. State, 756 S.W.2d 45 (Tex. App. 1988). Trial counsel ineffective for failing to inform the defendant that under state law the jury but not the trial court could grant probation prior to defendant electing judge sentencing.

Turner v. State, 755 S.W.2d 207 (Tex. App. 1988). Trial counsel ineffective for failing to inform the defendant that under state law the jury but not the trial court could grant probation prior to defendant electing judge sentencing.

Stone v. State, 751 S.W.2d 579 (Tex. App. 1988). Trial counsel ineffective for advising the defendant that trial court could grant probation when only jury could prior to defendant electing judge sentencing.

1987: *People v. Plager*, 242 Cal. Rptr. 624 (Cal. Ct. App. 1987). Trial counsel ineffective for failing to advise the defendant that the state could not have established that the alleged prior felony convictions were residential burglaries as required to be adjudicated serious felony for enhancement purposes, and counsel even stipulated to the factual basis for the alleged priors.

Medeiros v. State, 733 S.W.2d 605 (Tex. App. 1987). Trial counsel ineffective for failing to inform the defendant that under state law the jury but not the trial court could grant probation prior to defendant electing judge sentencing.

1986: *Steffans v. Keeney*, 728 P.2d 948 (Or. Ct. App. 1986). Counsel ineffective for failing to object to orders for restitution and costs when sentenced to long term confinement and failing to object to order in present case to pay restitution previously ordered in three earlier cases as a condition of probation.

1985: *State v. Stacey*, 482 So. 2d 1350 (Fla. 1985). Trial and appellate counsel ineffective for failing to research and recognize that trial court's retention of jurisdiction over first one third of 99 year sentence was a violation of ex post facto clause because robbery occurred before effective date of statute which allowed retention of jurisdiction.

***State v. Davidson*,** 335 S.E.2d 518 (N.C. Ct. App. 1985). Trial counsel ineffective in kidnapping and armed robbery case for failing to argue in the defendant's favor, stressing counsel's status as appointed counsel, and making arguments that were almost exclusively negative to the defendant.

***Watson v. State*,** 287 S.C. 356, 338 S.E.2d 636 (1985). Trial counsel ineffective in burglary case, where a burglary conviction mandated a life sentence unless the jury recommended mercy, for failing to advise defendant who pled guilty that he had the right to have a jury impaneled following the guilty plea to consider a recommendation a mercy.

***Snow v. State*,** 697 S.W.2d 663 (Tex. App. 1985). Trial counsel ineffective for failing to request a sentencing instruction on probation and asking for prison sentence based on erroneous belief that defendant was not entitled to probation.

Made in the USA
Las Vegas, NV
06 January 2025

15924689R00125